OTHER BOOKS BY LAWRENCE FERLINGHETTI

Blasts Cries Laughter
Time of Useful Consciousness
Poetry as Insurgent Art
Americus
How to Paint Sunlight
Routines
A Far Rockaway of the Heart
These Are My Rivers
European Poems and Transitions
Wild Dreams of a New Beginning
Over All the Obscene Boundaries
Back Roads to Far Places
The Secret Meaning of Things
Her
A Coney Island of the Mind
Starting from San Francisco

Writing Acros.

TRAVEL JOURNAL

LIVERIGHT PUBLISHING CORPORATION

A DIVISION OF W. W. NORTON & COMPANY   NEW YORK · LONDON

Writing Across the Landscape

he Landscape

960-2010

LAWRENCE
FERLINGHETTI

EDITED BY GIADA DIANO AND MATTHEW GLEESON

For information about permission to reproduce selections from this book, write to Permissions,
Liveright Publishing Corporation, a division of W. W. Norton & Company, Inc.,
500 Fifth Avenue, New York, NY 10110

For information about special discounts for bulk purchases, please contact
W. W. Norton Special Sales at specialsales@wwnorton.com or 800-233-4830

Manufacturing by RR Donnelley Westford
Book design by JAM Design
Production manager: Anna Oler

ISBN 978-1-63149-001-9

Liveright Publishing Corporation
500 Fifth Avenue, New York, N.Y. 10110
www.wwnorton.com

W. W. Norton & Company Ltd.
Castle House, 75/76 Wells Street, London W1T 3QT

1 2 3 4 5 6 7 8 9 0

To my mother, Clemence Albertine Monsanto,
and my brothers, all now in some heaven.

Every journal is a confessional. If it's in the first person, it cannot help but be. Unless the author of it lies to himself—and that makes it even more of a confessional. I am trying to draw the rake of my journal over the landscape. Perhaps I will uncover something.

...figures wh...
...ng through a Samuel Beckett wastel...
waiting for Godot, ▮or a final th...
of fate lays us all out ▮▮▮
in Pompei, only this time the r...
is neutronic, as billions gesticul...
wildly at the ▮▮▮▮ sky. I can...
cannot fly through it. Nor can I
son.

CONTENTS

V. THE NINETIES

VI. 2000-2010

July 89 - Puerto Escondi

enzo saved an Americ

man from drowning to d

was out at the veranda fa

when the woman's husba

running across the beach

hotel shouting "Help! 2 nove

PREVIOUSLY PUBLISHED WORKS

"Normandy Invasion": published in a newspaper, October 1994

"Picturesque Haiti": *Journal for the Protection of All Beings* #1, 1961

"Poet's Notes on Cuba": *Liberation*, March 1961

"Berlin Blue Rider": *Earthquake*, 1967

Beginning of "Russian Winter Journal" (first entry)

"Santa Rita Journal": *Ramparts*, March 1968

"Paris: May 1968": originally published in slightly different form as "An American in Paris," *Art-Story Magazine*, Fall 2006

"The Mexican Night": New Directions, 1970

"Ferlinghetti—Ginsberg Australian Trip": excerpts were published in a letterpress chapbook

"Mule Mountain Dreams" section of "Bisbee Poetry Festival": chapbook

"Ristorante Vittoria" section of "Milan": published in poem form in *European Poems & Transitions*, New Directions, 1981

"Seven Days in Nicaragua Libre": City Lights, 1984

"Naples Notebook" section of "Rome—Napoli—Sicily": *Il Mattino*, September 1984 (September 13), only in Italian

"Journal Notes, New York": originally published as poem in *How to Paint Sunlight*, New Directions, 2001

"Italy—France" (2006–2007): the excerpt "Après-midi—chez Whitman" was published in a slightly different form in a newspaper after George Whitman died

PUBLISHED POEMS

Untitled poem on Pound at Spoleto: *Open Eye, Open Heart* (New Directions)

"Recipe for Happiness in Khabarovsk or Any Place"

"Moscow in the Wilderness, Segovia in the Snow": *The Secret Meaning of Things*, New Directions

Lord's Prayer Parody

"High Noon, Oaxaca," published in Mexican paper, 2004, only in Spanish

"Dirty Tongue": *How to Paint Sunlight*, New Directions, 2001

"O long-silent Sybil" (poem in "Greece—Italy") was incorporated in a longer poem and published as "To the Oracle at Delphi," *How to Paint Sunlight*, New Directions, 2001

"At Sea," Meridian Press

AUTHOR'S NOTE

I see this book in the tradition of D. H. Lawrence's travels in Italy or Goethe's Italian journeys. . . . It is as if much of my life were a continuation of my youthful *wanderjahr*, my walkabout in the world.

I wrote these peripatetic pages for myself, never thinking to publish them. I never reread them until Giada Diano and Matt Gleeson brought me photocopies of the original notebooks that had been slumbering away in the Bancroft Library, U.C. Berkeley.

Seeing myself years later through the wrong end of the telescope, a wandering figure in momentous times. . . . I was part of that "Greatest Generation" (so dubbed by a newsman) that came of age at the beginning of the Second World War. . . . As I worked in San Francisco and traveled, days and years fell away into the great maw of time. . . . The war ends, decades whir by, there is a rumble in the wings, the scene darkens, and Camelot lost!

America went through a sea change after that. San Francisco, which had been a small provincial capital, grew up. So did I, and I started voyaging. I was usually traveling to some literary or political event or tracking down some author for an undiscovered masterpiece to publish at City Lights Books.

Europe of course was a "going back," finding roots. Since my earliest days in France with my French Aunt Emilie, I had always thought of France as my second home. When my ship was able to dock in Cherbourg after the Normandy invasion,

I felt like kissing the ground. Three years later as a student at the Sorbonne in Paris, I still felt that way.

I came late to my father's Italy, first as a student of Italian, *la bella lingua*, and later to track down my father's birthplace. So much came from that!

I didn't keep journals consistently, so that some literary capers went unrecorded, as when I visited Paul Bowles in Tangier to pry from him his Moroccan tales in *Hundred Camels in the Courtyard*. This was agreed to, and then we sat dully in his high-rise apartment near the American embassy. And when Jane Bowles suggested we turn-on, Paul said he didn't have any hash. I was clean-shaven in a white suit, and I imagine he thought I was a narc. Paranoia, the doper's constant companion!

What else can I say about these interior monologues, except that some may pass as news stories filed by a reporter from Outer Space, to cover the strange doings of these "humans" down here, sent by a Managing Editor with a low tolerance for bullshit.

—LAWRENCE FERLINGHETTI
10/23/14
S.F.

EDITORS' INTRODUCTION

The journals in this book are the fruits of over five decades of travel. A few have been previously published, but most were typed from handwritten notebooks in the Bancroft Library at the University of California, Berkeley, or in Ferlinghetti's own possession. They were selected and edited in close collaboration with the author. A generous offering from Ferlinghetti's wealth of drawings has been chosen too. Together, these records of observations and experiences show that the poet's journeys around the world form one of his most crucial and rich sources of creative inspiration. Although Ferlinghetti is famously associated with San Francisco, in fact he was molded by many formative years abroad. And though he is often identified with the writers of the Beat Generation because he published them through City Lights, Lawrence has never considered himself a Beat. These notebooks testify to his connections to a wide international field of avant-garde literary ferment and poetry of dissent. They are also full of some of his most striking prose, poems and drawings.

Ferlinghetti's life was international from the start; in fact, as a child he assumed he was French. He was born in New York, the fifth son of Carlo Ferlinghetti and Clemence Mendes-Monsanto, and grew up as Lawrence Ferling, the surname having been anglicized. His father died before he was born, and Lawrence ended up being entrusted to his Aunt Emilie, who brought him to live in France when he was two. Eventually they returned to New York, where Tante Emilie worked as a governess for the daughter of Presley and Anna Bisland at Plashbourne, an estate in

Bronxville. When at a certain point Emilie mysteriously disappeared, Lawrence was kept by the Bislands. Only gradually, over the course of his life, would he discover that his father had migrated to America from Lombardy around 1900, and that he was Sephardic on his mother's side.

These journals begin in 1960, but Ferlinghetti had already spent much time abroad before that. As captain of a U.S. Navy submarine chaser during World War II, he saw action in the Normandy invasion, and he visited Nagasaki soon after the atomic bomb had obliterated the city. After the war, he spent some four years in Paris, getting his doctorate in literature at the Sorbonne on the G.I. Bill. When he first arrived in Paris, he met his lifelong friend George Whitman, the future owner of Shakespeare and Company, the Left Bank bookstore to which Ferlinghetti's own City Lights would become the "sister store." These early years, though not directly recorded, resurface frequently in the journals here.

By the time these journals begin, Ferlinghetti had come into his own as a poet and publisher. Living in San Francisco with his wife, Selden Kirby-Smith (known as Kirby, she was the granddaughter of Confederate general Edmund Kirby-Smith), Ferlinghetti opened the City Lights Pocket Bookshop in 1953 with Peter D. Martin. Two years after that, he began publishing the Pocket Poets Series, starting with his own first book, *Pictures of the Gone World.* In 1956 he published Allen Ginsberg's *Howl*, for which he was arrested and charged with publishing obscene material, a case he won with the help of the ACLU. In 1958, New Directions published his seminal book of poetry, *A Coney Island of the Mind.*

And so by the 1960s Lawrence was giving readings across the United States and attending poetry festivals around the world. The journals of the sixties open with Lawrence attending his first international literary conference, the Primer Encuentro de Escritores Americanos in Concepción, Chile. Both Ferlinghetti and Allen Ginsberg were invited, the first U.S. countercultural poets to attend such an international affair. From this starting point, decade after decade, Lawrence would attend events such as the Festival of Two Worlds in Spoleto, Italy, in 1965, various wild Happenings organized by the radical French artist Jean-Jacques Lebel, the One World Poetry Festivals organized in 1980 and 1981 in Amsterdam by Dutch countercultural impresario and communard Benn Posset, the 1984 International Festival of Poetry in Morelia (actually moved to Mexico City at the last minute), and the 2001 festival at Delphi, Greece, sponsored by UNESCO. Meanwhile, his work as a publisher brought him to British Columbia to acquire Malcolm Lowry's poems, to

Morocco to get *Hundred Camels in the Courtyard* from Paul Bowles, and to London to get *The Yage Letters* from William S. Burroughs. In early 1967, after attending the Literarische Colloquium Berlin, Lawrence visited the Soviet Union, his access to literary circles behind the Iron Curtain during the Cold War having been smoothed by his association with the famous Soviet poets Andrei Voznesensky and Yevgeny Yevtushenko. Ferlinghetti's brief memoirs of spending time with both of them in San Francisco in 1966 also belong here.

But official literary events tend to be the jumping-off point and not the focus in these journals. In many cases, the readings and gatherings themselves are not described at all—it is other details, experiences, and impressionistic visions, as well as the landscape itself, that are most essential to the poet's eye. After his visit to Berlin and Moscow in 1967, Lawrence took the Trans-Siberian Railway, crossing the continent to its eastern shore and meeting with obstacles and adventures recounted in his "Russian Winter Journal." The lush, dream-soaked 1972 journal describing his travels with his son, Lorenzo, through Fiji, Australia and Tahiti was kept during a trip to read at the Adelaide Festival of the Arts along with Allen Ginsberg and Andrei Voznesensky, but the festival itself is hardly mentioned. Later, his description of the exhilarating 1981 One World Festival leads into one of the most hilarious satirical pieces in the book, a sojourn through touristic Germany recounted in the "Rhine Journal." Eccentric characters, broken-down hotels, joyous wordplay, the vitality of human connection, and the presence of the sea are ultimately more important here than depictions of the literary life.

In times of political turmoil across the globe, Ferlinghetti's involvement in Leftist politics forms another important theme in the travel journals. After the Cuban Revolution overthrew the Batista regime, he became involved with the Fair Play for Cuba Committee, and in late 1960 he visited Cuba to see what the euphoric promise of revolution might bring; he vividly recounts his experiences there in "Poet's Notes on Cuba." His acquaintance with Jean-Jacques Lebel led to his being in Paris for the worker-student uprising in May 1968, and he reported it with a poet's eye; the aborted revolution of May '68 reappears throughout the book. Ferlinghetti was also active in protests against the Vietnam War, and his "Santa Rita Journal" records his time in jail for picketing the Oakland Army Induction Center. Even when the purpose of a trip isn't political, he casts a sharp eye on the political landscape. Thus his "Nerja Journals," which record three months in Franco's Spain, are filled with comment on the repressive dictatorship. And pieces like the "Salton Sea Notes" are humorous caustic portrayals of the "outback" of America. The "Boulder Notes" record the 1984 conference celebrating the twenty-fifth anniversary of Jack Kerouac's *On the Road* at the Naropa Institute.

As the decades go on, Ferlinghetti's journals grow sparser—this is particularly true of the 1970s. In general this was not because Lawrence traveled less or wrote less, but because his style of responding in writing to the places he passed through shifted—many of the notebooks he kept during these voyages consist mainly of drafts of poems that he would later publish, rather than prose travel journals. Many of his books of poetry are grounded in his travels, and the genesis of poems in books such as *Starting from San Francisco, Over All the Obscene Boundaries: European Poems and Transitions,* and *Wild Dreams of a New Beginning* can be found in the experiences in this book.

Two of the sets of journals here have been previously published as books. In 1970, *The Mexican Night* was published by New Directions; the back cover text announced that it was the first in a series of Ferlinghetti travelogs to be entitled "Writing Across the Landscape." In fact, it was the only one until now, and has been out of print for years. *The Mexican Night* collects more than a decade of Ferlinghetti's writing in Mexico, which he visited more than any other foreign country. It was an important locale for several of his touchstone writers—D. H. Lawrence and Malcolm Lowry, as well as Antonin Artaud, the visionary French playwright, poet, and theater director whose life and work skirted the realm of madness. Their voices echo throughout *The Mexican Night*, but Ferlinghetti's vision of Mexico is very much his own. Keeping this set of travel notes and oneiric prose poems together in this volume is the only departure from straightforward chronology.

In 1984, City Lights published *Seven Days in Nicaragua Libre*, also out of print. During the Reagan years, Ferlinghetti continued to excoriate predatory capitalism and militarism, and to explore radical Leftist politics. In 1979, the Sandinista Revolution had ousted the U.S.-backed dictator Anastasio Somoza in Nicaragua. In 1983 City Lights published a collection of radical Central American poetry entitled *Volcán*, and when Ferlinghetti was invited to Nicaragua by his friend poet Ernesto Cardenal (then the Sandinista minister of culture) he took the opportunity as a self-described "tourist of revolution" to write the journalistic and personal reportage included here.

As this volume moves into the 1990s, Europe becomes the most frequent destination in Lawrence's travels. By this point the poet had become something of a
father figure for the counterculture, an inspiration to a new generation of literary
radicals. This is evident in his visits to two Italian literary centers, Calusca City
Lights and City Lights Italia, both named in honor of his iconic San Francisco bookstore. And during a 1998 trip to Prague almost ten years after the Velvet Revolution, Ferlinghetti finds a marathon day-and-night reading of his poetry going on in
a great church on the Old Town Square—a reminder that his *A Coney Island of the
Mind* had been circulated for years in samizdat editions throughout Eastern Europe
behind the Iron Curtain. Back at home, 1998 was the year that Lawrence was
appointed San Francisco's first poet laureate. The hopes and humor often expressed
in this decade's journals alternate with gloomier, apocalyptic moods considering the
possibility of ecological or nuclear catastrophe. Meanwhile, his painting and visual
art had become recognized internationally. In Italy, he was embraced by the Fluxus
group through the art collector Francesco Conz in Verona, and many journals here
describe his further travels in Europe for shows and exhibitions.

In the 2000s, there is a sense of Lawrence coming full circle, of meeting his
early years again. His fullest portrait of his old friend George Whitman is found
here. Meanwhile, Lawrence's search for his roots naturally concentrated on Italy.
Thoughts of his father's voyage from Old World to New and of his brothers in
America often surface in these journals. As he traveled, Ferlinghetti learned that
his father was from somewhere in the north of the country, based on his surname.
Finally, in 2004, through the help of Riccardo and Fausta Ferlinghetti from Chiari,
he located his father's birth certificate in the archives of the town of Brescia, and
went to find the house where his father had been born. The absurd incident that
ensued, and its emotional underpinnings, later inspired the molten flow of "Running Thoughts." Finally, the lyrical poem "At Sea," written in Belize in 2010, is
the true culmination of this poet's wanderings in the world, but also the poet's final
testament, the *ars poetica* of his life.

—GIADA DIANO. MATTHEW GLEESON
11/10/14
S.F.

Writing Across the Landscape

Darkness, Dying + Death
the image of crowded stree[t]
and mud people - Everyw[here]
I walked + looked the sam[e]
Enough to drive any Voyeur
back home.....Later, fou[nd]
the tourist part of town
and the American border :
big sign over it saying
UNITED STATES.
Showed my California Driv[er]

FIRST TIME ABROAD

In a small back bedroom in South Yonkers, N.Y., my brother Harry heard my first cry.

But my earliest memory was abroad. Strasbourg in the early 1920s. Someone was holding me on a balcony. One of those fifth-floor running balconies on French apartment buildings. Perhaps I am a year or two old. There is a parade passing by on the boulevard down below. Someone is holding me, perhaps my dear *Tante* Emilie. And waving my hand at the parade. I remember white mountains in the far distance, beyond the city. The white mountains of Alsace, the Vosges, no doubt. Whose parade is it and what army is parading, I have no idea. I am waving my hand. The scene fades, and that is all I remember of Alsace, of France back then.

NORMANDY INVASION

June 6, 1944

We were so young, but didn't know it, and we were running a ship. That is, Executive Officer Lt. Eugene Feinblatt, USNR, age twenty-four or -five, was running it, doing all the dirty work that keeps a ship running, provisioning it, training the crew, etc. As skipper (same age as Gene) of the USS *SC-1308*, all I had to do was "steer"—that is, command the ship. It was a great sea-boat and could go through anything. And did.

It was before dawn, June 6, 1944, and we were blacked out as part of a convoy escort antisubmarine screen. Out of Plymouth, England, we were steaming in formation, east northeast in the English Channel, toward the beaches of Normandy. We were thirty-three men and three officers on a 110-foot diesel-powered wooden-hulled subchaser, the USS *SC-1308*. The night before loading at Plymouth, the deep country lanes between hedgerows were clogged with transport and troops, loaded weapons carriers, thousands and thousands of soldiers in battle gear, all blacked out and silent. And in the whispering fields all around, great encampments, whole armies bivouacked in tents, with small hooded cooking fires. And it was the night before Agincourt, the King visiting his men around campfires in the muffled dark. Now it was 4 or 5 a.m. on the blacked-out bridge of our little ship, the first light just cracking the black eastern horizon, the whole crew on deck at battle stations, Gene and myself and the quartermaster-signalman on the bridge, Doug Crane the third officer engineer down below. And in the very first light on

the western horizon behind us we were just beginning to see a forest of masts rising up from below the horizon, first just the tops of the masts and then the hulls—
a huge armada of thousands of great ships and troop transports and escort vessels
steaming together from separate ports, converging with the first light off the Normandy coast. We could hear waves of Allied bombers going high over toward
Utah and Omaha Beaches still shrouded in darkness, and then the distant explosions on the coast becoming a roar in the darkness, as we stood at our stations,
Gene in his helmet, red hair showing, binoculars trained on the French coast just
coming into range in the dawn light, the armada steaming full speed for the
beaches now, dead ahead.

And fair stood the wind for France!

I've been around

San Francisco—R...
SEPT 1984

Ferlinghetti

ets

0

71723 40250

We fly from San Francisco to Santiago, my wife, Kirby, and I, meeting Allen (Ginsberg) and changing planes in Panama, in the middle of the night, seeing nothing but bus-station-type Panama airport. My body transited this Canal some fifteen years ago on a U.S. Navy troop transport headed for the Occupation of Japan. . . . As navigator, went ashore to Navy Hydrographic Office to get charts, hit swinging door bars on way back to ship, barely made it aboard before ship left Canal. . . . Now we sit in dim waiting room while they juice up the plane. . . . Allen and I cram into a phone-booth-size "photomat" and take pictures of ourselves, mugging it up. . . .

It's our first trip abroad as poets—an international literary conference, arranged by Fernando Alegría, Chilean poet and professor at U.C. Berkeley. It's to be the first big comprehensive meeting of writers from all Latin American countries. And it turns out half of the writers—the most important in their countries—cannot enter the U.S. for political reasons. Let's not have any of them dirty foreign influences. While we're keeping things homogenous (like Borden's milk), Latin America is striving to homogenize itself enough to communicate across its own continent, exchange ideas, books, etc. . . . It will be the 21st century before they're at all ready for a United States of Latin America.

The conference is at the University of Concepción. First night, Allen makes great wild speech in Spanish—reads Whalen, Lamantia, Snyder, with translations by Luis Oyarzún. There is a sense of literary excitement in the cross-fertilizations going on.

Zendejas[1] interrupts solemn speech to demand one minute of silence for the death of Alfonso Reyes. Granted. All stand in silence. Five minutes later rises and interrupts again—now demands *two* minutes of silence. Five minutes later, he demands *three*.

One day at the conference, the local Communist Party organizes a tour of writers to go to the minehead at Lota, an undersea coal mine. We arrive just as the miners are coming up from their twelve-hour shifts. They come to the surface in little elevator cages, like animal cages in a zoo. The miners' faces are illegible in the coal dust which coats their bodies, white eyes staring out of black masks. The pay is said to be a dollar a day. They walk undersea for a mile or so to get to the minehead. . . . Naturally the press has been invited by the CP to get our reactions. They thrust mikes in our faces and demand what we think of it. Back at the university they give us a questionnaire. The questions are like such: What do you consider the most important literature of South America? (My answer: The faces of the miners at Lota.) What do you see as the future of South America? (The faces of the miners at Lota.) Whom do you consider the greatest poets in Chile? (The faces of the miners at Lota.) There were twenty questions like that. Same answer for all—published in a big paper in Santiago.

The impression I have is that a great fat omnivorous crab named United States of America is sitting on top of the Pan-American hemisphere, sucking the marrow from its soft underside. The Coca-Colonization of the world. . . .

La Paz, Bolivia, January 27

Native Indian woman in the crumbled Church of San Francisco—kneeling, with baby on back in sling, praying out loud to the white images of god at the altar— but it was not just a prayer, it was a loud plaint, a wail in a high girl's voice, a child's voice wailing her Let me out! Save me from this! Help me to escape from this incomprehensible black mute helpless desperate situation of life! God, god, god! What am I doing here?

LA PAZ—Miserable, mud-covered dung-hole of humanity at the top of the world, with one fine tree-lined Prado cut through the sinkhole city of decaying Indian beggars, con men, and German fascists. . . .

Bolivia—4 million inhabitants, of which 3½ million are a slave population— Indians ruled over by 500,000 whites of European extraction. The Indian women wear soft brown derbies with high crowns uncreased; the men wear felt hats and shoes made of old rubber tires.

The Indians may be converted by the Methodist & Catholic missionaries but they really still worship the Earth God. I saw the old god of the earth in the profile of a hillside—buried in the crater/mountain of La Paz, he was face-up—a huge flat outcropping of rock for a nose, green grass on his cheeks and chin, his eye a grim tree.

January 30—Ship & train ride La Paz–Cuzco: riding on electric train thru the Andes.

After dark—Inca raindrops hit the train window shaped like balsa boats, glowed silver against the outside night, and the window became a cloth of silver, a silver mesh.

Three Jesuit padres on the train, all very young, just ordained, in brand-new uniforms—new shoes, new cassocks, new linen—two played cards, drank whiskey poured from wood flask statue of Inca idol, smoked American cigarettes—third one did not smoke, play or drink. They were on their way to study for six months at Cuzco—had just been at Arequipa where great earthquake just devastated city. How came they to be looking so elegant coming from Arequipa? A copy of a manual of *Christian Perfection* one of them carried was not opened during the trip. They read the *Reader's Digest* Spanish edition. From Lake Titicaca to Cuzco through a great wild valley, becoming more & more fertile as we descended from 12,000 feet, streams becoming rivers, mud huts becoming adobe houses with red tile roofs inside of adobe walls, the towns growing into bigger towns, all adobe, all tiled. . . . So into Cuzco as night fell, and in the dark roaring of the train a sudden jolting as we ran into great rocks fallen from hillsides onto the tracks. All stopped. The tracks cleared finally, and we went on again, rocking.

Someone had bought a baby fox from an Indian at one of the stops, and he got loose in the car, and no one could get him from under a seat. He bit all hands extended. Finally he was pulled out in a towel.

January 30

In Cuzco the cathedral bells sound like a great forge at six in the morning. Two separate kinds of infernal clanking, shaking the city awake. . . . The Spaniards put so many churches in Cuzco in order to baffle the Incas into servitude.

I don't stay in the best hotels but I'm a faithful user of their men's rooms. Swastika on men's room wall in best hotel in Cuzco. . . .

The cocks crow all night. It must be the end of the world.

A SHORT RIDE TO MACHU PICCHU

Cuzco, ancient Inca capital in the Andes, to Machu Picchu, lost Inca city the Spaniards never found. It took a certain Hiram Bingham from Yale University to discover it around 1915 (and he absconded with a booty of artifacts).

Now in a one-car electric train bus, zigzag up the heights above Cuzco, shut-tling backward and forward on forked tracks without turning, Cuzco down below made of tile roofs and adobe and mud, filling the plain, with cemeteries like great blooming ruined gardens. . . . Wind away north over the highlands, turning and turning between small hills and ridges at 12,000 feet. . . . Thirty passengers, mostly Americans and German Argentinians. . . . High up, in a great green pasture with sheep and llamas, a shepherd Indian running . . . what's his hurry, up here by himself with his mute animals and eternity. . . . One American with camera and sportcoat says to wife, "They have more than two hundred varieties of potatoes up here." Adobe farms, mud roads, Inca ruins on hillsides, caves with crosses in them, mud fields trampled by mud-colored cows, herds of sheep on stony hills farther on, the shepherd boys same color as sheep, clay brown. . . . "Very scenic," says American tea-lady in bird's-nest hat. . . . Fields of maize, streams filling little winding valleys snaking over horizons. . . . Indians in *sarapes* at one-room stations do not wave back at tourist traincar. . . . Trucks with Indians jammed into open back, standing, climbing the dirt roads in the gray mist morning . . . springtime here, February, thatched huts in patches of yellow flower, cows eating trampled red flowers. . . . Rows of poplar and eucalyptus, moss under them by the tracks. . . . Now we zoom through a eucalyptus forest, and on, through another settlement, where brown man with boy at station waves stick, black dog barks, springs away between trees, chases train barking, little boy peeing in rutted trainside road, as we hurtle on. . . . "Lots of potatoes 'round here," American says. . . . Stop now at country station, with Indi-ans clustered with bundles, baskets, bags of straw, *sarapes* wound around, babies hung on backs, men in Western felt hats, women in huge high-crowned white panamas with five-inch-wide black ribbons, long black braids hanging down behind. . . . ACCIÓN POPULAR painted in white on adobe wall. . . . Pigs in street puddles, burros with milkcans tied on them, driven down mud streambeds. . . . Now a great *alta*-plain of maize with higher Andes peaks ringing it, tops hid in cotton clouds. . . . "Lots of animals 'round here," says American. . . . The plain fill-ing up with grazing cows, horses, shoats, burros, forlorn bedraggled chickens. "Must be a chicken farm 'round here." Inca terraces on lost far mountainsides. . . . Dogs keep chasing the train. . . . We pass a field full of Indians working. German girl in tweed suit in seat behind says the towns here all organized along lines of ancient Inca socialist system, with new chiefs and magistrates, etc., elected every January by farmers' conclaves. Also says anyone who wants to get married here must live with each other for one year before marriage. Has her arm around younger girl she's traveling with. Now winding through narrow precipitous valley, like the Feather River Canyon, Northern California, following roaring mountain stream. . . . Words in cut in red earth of high hillside: "*VIVA* ———" (the last part obliterated). . . . Great cliffs hang out over train, 1000 feet above it, in narrow passes, with tracks and stream squeezed in between. The stream's become a rushing torrent, the Urubamba River, plunging toward the Amazon. . . . Woman with silvergray hair and hat with flowers in seat ahead reveals herself as being from Berkeley. . . . At mountain station stop everybody gets out and walks around adobe station, Berkeley woman exclaiming, "Oh, this train is only one car!" But another "train" now pulls up behind—an old bus with regular wheels replaced by train wheels, filled with a whole tribe of Indians in red *sarapes* and guitars being transported to Machu Picchu for a festival to be put on for the President of Mexico who's coming tomorrow. . . . The mayor of Urubamba is along, to make a welcome speech in Quechua. Also a regular freight car groans up on the tracks behind, loaded with llamas. . . . Whistle snorts, and we're off again through widening gorges, by sacred river of the Incas. . . . We overtake handcar on tracks, being pushed by seven Indians, all grinds to a stop while handcar is lifted off, then on again, below Inca farm terraces, steppes climbing higher and higher, and an old Inca fort at a riverbend, an abandoned Inca suspension bridge between high cliffs beyond it, broken ropes hanging from it, a Bridge of San Luis Rey with no paths leading to it. The river now grown dark brown, roaring, growing larger all the time, falling into monster rapids, fed by churning streams the color of green tea, rushing out of every ravine. . . . Now another mountain stop, all out again, by ruined Inca fort, and a band of Mongolian-looking Indians all in identical red *sarapes*, the men in round black felt plate-like fringed hats, carrying very long bamboo flutes, the women in the same red color, with shawls and baskets of yellow pears, all waiting together at the tracks in a still group, with llamas hobbled in the background and dogs barking, and practically everyone from the tour car taking their pictures with German cameras, the Indians standing very still for it, except for one wild one in the back playing his long flute, wailing, an Inca Beat poet. . . . Several Americans throw coins at him, and at the whole group, so that they'll stand for more pictures. . . . The tour guide, a fat moustached cat in Western suit and safari-type pith helmet, explaining the whole scene in pig-English. . . . "Don't eat them pears without washing them," Texas voice says. All board car again, we rush on, along the chocolate-colored river. Man in back asks someone, "Ever been in the States?". . . River boils higher, washing over tracks ahead. "It'll be hot water by the time it gits where it's goin'," same voice says. Says another: "We're going to have a meeting every Monday, Wednesday, Friday, from now on, everybody in the Agricultural Products Division—we got offices in São Paulo, Rio, Lima, Mexico City. It's a big organization. My wife and me were born in Sacramento but now everybody lives in Los Angeles. Dow International undergone tremendous development down here in last year. Some think it's too big, they'll get lost in it, but people I know very happy. . . ." Train passes cave with smiling face made of painted rock staring out of it. . . . Later, there's picture writing on rocks, like weird Morris Graves symbols. . . . "You seen the Madison," Texas voice says, "where it comes out of Yellowstone, well, it ain't as wild as this. Señor and I were planning a canoe trip out here but we've given it up." . . . "This is trip of a lifetime," old lady says, other old lady nodding yes. . . . Through rock tunnel now and out into field of blue cypress. The river still rising. Straw hut with one side open has three white forms on crosses hung in it, human ghosts in a grotto. "Did I hear you say you was in the aviation business?" Answer is lost in screeching to another stop. "I got to wash my fruit somewhere," Texas says. We're stopped in a great gorge, with monster cliffs hung over. I get out and walk along the track, looking up. Man of Distinction with silver hair and camera walking along behind me says, "Pretty wild here, isn't it?" German girl comes along in a minute, tells me, "Here they sell a medicine for sadness. I told man there please I want some. He says he not want to give me any. He says 'You would not be cured because you do not believe.'" I go over and see. Bent beat Indian smiles in my eyes, hands me some. It's not *yagé*. The old bus on train wheels pulls up behind us again, with more Indians jammed into it and hanging on all over the outside, and one of them inside is playing an old broken tune on a tin-sounding guitar. . . . We plunge on again now, the high precipices swaying in sky over the train, the wild river now plunging into deep jungle, with huge matted banana trees and jungle vines, monkeys among the big leaves, the river rushing faster and faster through it, the train whistling and howling as it bowls along, rushing water washing its wheels. "You kin almost see the cannibals," man in front says. A cross on a rock where someone must have drowned floats by. . . . Fog on lost peaks 2000 feet above us, the train still blowing and rocking onward, stops screeching again now, to let another handcar with Indians get off track. I see small gray butterfly with one great white perfectly round spot on each wing, flying alone across the river. . . . Now we come to a hydroelectric plant and a big mine with derricks. . . . We zoom on through its clearing and on through jungle, the river flooding over the tracks, waves crashing thirty feet high over boulders, whole islands inundated, trees floating in it, roots thrown up like wild tousled heads. . . . An enormous waterfall looms up, leaps down toward us as we zoom under. A great boulder the size of a house is falling through it. I look up through the dome skylight, see it falling, straight down. Berkeley woman in seat ahead in the act of adjusting her hat as I raise camera and with a click arrest boulder in air, just as it is about to hit.

We careen to the stop for Machu Picchu, and tumble into big old bus with wooden seats and a driver in a cowboy hat, with several crucifixes swinging from the rearview mirror, as if he needed them for guidance, and we start up steep grade, up and up, then winding around and around for hours, and everybody silent, hanging on. Finally we lurch to a stop where it seems there's nowhere to go but into the sky, and we're here, Machu Picchu laid out in the late sun, and all in a strange silence. There's no inn or other sign of tourist development, though a government hotel is rumored. "Civilization" hasn't reached here yet.

I think of Neruda's "On the Heights of Machu Picchu." Here and now, nothing but the great tumbled ruins stretched out before us, with one huge jagged peak towering over it all, smaller ragged peaks ranged around, and we stand like dumb wanderers looking down at the spent ruins. We creep among the roofless temples and homes, doorways agape, gullies that once were streets, warehouses fallen flat. Whole fallen city laid out, silent in late sun. . . . Hidden door of the Andes at 13,000 feet, seacoast far below. . . . The sunset reddens. . . .

Some Indians go by dancing, playing their flutes and beating drums.

AMERICA! AMERICA!
March–November 1960

Train to Burlington, Vermont—Wednesday morning, March 30—forty-one yrs old and in my right wrong mind. . . . And the Boston & Maine with conductors that look like Calvin Coolidge. Springfield, Northampton, Greenfield, East Northfield, and on, into Vermont. White River Junction & a hundred Dartmouth students get off. On, through the wet snowhills & melting rivers, spring coming, through the long dark afternoon, the whole white landscape melting into black. Dusk descending over Vermont mountains, and night upon us as the diesel twocar train rocks silent into Essex Junction. . . .

My poetry reading here at the Vermont Conference, and my topic "Love and Death." What do I know of the mystery of either? The conference also addressed by a spokesman for Dr. Teller, an atomic physicist—Mr. Christofilos[2] (Christ & filosopher), who spoke the opposite of what Christ would have said—a militarist. . . . Boom boom.

Question by serious student before huge crowd at University of Vermont conference: "Sir, how do you stand as to fornication?"

Answer: "As for fornication, I very seldom stand; I lie down."

Second question: "Do you really think Christ is dead?"

Answer: "The way the world acts today, you would think so. He's not here tonight, is he? I don't see him."

Voice from back of auditorium: "Here I am."

New York, N.Y., April 1

With Jack Kerouac at midnight we stumble down East 2nd Street, and suddenly out from a broken tenement front rushes a whole living room upside down with dark Puerto Ricans carrying sofas tables and armchairs on their heads upside down, growling at us as they run past and around the corner.

And what am I doing with him here anyway, sometime in eternity? Yeah, well, it's a long story, as everything is. I am not my brother's keeper but I do feel a kind of older brother empathy with him. . . . Well, Jack has nothing to do with Beat or beatnik except in the minds of thousands who read *On the Road* thinking he's some sort of crazy wild rebel whereas really he's just a "home boy" from little ol' Lowell and certainly no rebel. And I keep telling him to stop wandering around the planet and go back home to Lowell Mass. and stay there, even though it would probably not work out, with him staggering around bars and not finding any "home" . . . and old friends all changed, etc. . . . All the while remembering Thomas Wolfe's *Look Homeward, Angel*, one of our favorite books.

Spent night with him, ending up at his girl's house in the West Seventies. Woke at ten a.m. Sunny and warm. I leave with ms. of Kerouac's *Book of Dreams* for City Lights to publish, and that alone worth the trip . . . a clutch of wild beautiful dreams uncensored and not for Freudians to dissect. . . .

April 7

Left N.Y. under a cloud—still hungover— Had vision of evil on the half shell—in flight jet to Chicago.

Train—Zephyr—Chicago to San Francisco, April 8

West from Chicago, contemplating the landscape. Yellow barns, yellow houses, purple hills, lavender trees, gold cornfields in late sunlight, windmills, silos, mows, white houses with green roofs, telephone lines, brown banks of earth, creosoted railroad ties, all the animals already put away for the night, dusk falling, white fences, more corn, more trees, white bones of trees by a river, filigree against the sky, standing in water up to their knees, branches like bones of arms reflected, gray sky now, brick houses, brown leaves, gray unpainted barns, day going now, now one lone bird, blown away. . . . Red ball of sun thrown down.

Crossed the Mississippi at Burlington, Iowa— Last light still in sky—glints in far windows, neons coming on, fillingstations lighted, dingdong red train light suspended & swinging at crossing . . . in center of wooded city. . . . The sad unalterable loneliness of houses on hillsides lost among trees, lights white in them. . . . Cemeteries going by, lonely too . . . somehow not so lonely as the living. . . . Black trees now, on small hills . . . night, night. Dark ponds and pools.

Later, nothing but night, under the Vista Dome, alone, peering out. . . . Nothing but moon, stars, night flashing by—gooking with suitcases along Charles Sheeler platforms—no sound through the glass—walking, sacks and satchels in hand, lost in night of America. . . . Thomas Wolfe's, Whitman's, Kerouac's, yours, Ferlinghetti's America. . . . Indian land I hitchhiked through a long time ago. . . . The whole of the ancient Indian continent now occupied by "Americans."

April 28

Heard Thelonious Monk at Blackhawk in San Francisco last night. He played nonobjective funeral dirges. Later, at intermission, saw him walking very fast down a dark street and around a corner, as if he had to get somewhere fast to make a connection, and get back to the Hawk for the next set— Reminded me of how I escaped from funeral of foster father in mourning clothes and went flying away on a bicycle, down free spring lanes. . . .

*　　*　　*　　*　　*

November 10—Southern Pacific Coach

White dawn bursts across plains, islands of land in the distance, mesas, tablelands, all flat, all laid away, great glory sun; wood bridge over water. In still light we rock onward. ONWARD?

Back and forth across the continent, bang bang, by any wheel, by rail, by car, by buggy, by stagecoach, walking, riding the Great Plains, prairie schooners into the night. Forever. All that day, rolling thru Wyoming, snow on steppes and plains, mining towns, once roaring, now shrunk to the railhead, streetlights drunk with loneliness. Huge spaces of indomitable still new land—horizons of mesas—like Don Quixote country, with sharp eroded towers of bluffs like windmills, abandoned and propellerless. Great long rectangular stone islands sticking up on far plains like forts, like immense empty cargo ships, becalmed and rudderless, stranded. . . . Finally one small half-ass town followed by solitary pumping stations, each with a tank, a car, a hut, a dog, no people anywhere. Must be a cowboy someplace. Lone church sticks up, "out of Nowhere." This must be Interzone between Heaven and Brooklyn. Do they have a classified section like in phone books in the back of the Bibles here?— Otherwise they'd never find anything. . . . Try Instant Zen.

Later again, wagon-lits, bed wagons, human bodies nested in them, inscrutable, hurtling horizontal thru night. . . .

Huge snow fields, on and on and on, still no one anywhere. . . . Indians all gone to Florida. Or Cuba! Birds flap from fences, trestles. . . . Sunset and strange clouds like udders, rayed, from below, with light. Some God's hand sticks through. Black trees stand out. The world is a winter farm. . . . Much later, one brakeman's face in night, in high peaked cloth cap, gray-striped; swings a railroad lantern, as our window whizzes past, his figure flashed upon it, slanted, very tall, muezzin-like, in darkness, disappearing. . . . Who killed America?

November 12

The only people that ride the cross-country trains now are old women & babies & defunct men and servicemen—and ugly girls—carloads of them. . . . And Gad those vast empty expanses of northern Wyoming, and toward the Great Divide—and the sad monstrosities they erected and still call "towns"— To be condemned to live here forever would be murder—the Siberia of America. . . .

Nebraska, Iowa—the woods are more poetic here—more intimate, closer in, smaller and nearer than in Wyoming, where they stood away on horizons at enormous distances, tenantless. Here the farms are smaller, people can be seen in the houses—more "poetic" because more human. The Pathetic Fallacy again. . . .

But these fall woods—bare trees—swamps full of leaves—long brown grasses—fields of yellow-brown cornstubble—are Eastern—it's the nostalgia of what I once knew—

Chicago finally, at noon, I stroll out into it, with raincoat, small satchel, books, carrying my pencils with me. Later, at night, street lamps lit with leftover sun they drank too much of during the day. . . . Walked across town from Union Station, north on Dearborn from the Loop, past Gate of Horn where I'll read poetry tomorrow afternoon, on toward Paul Carroll's[3] where I'll stay the night, probably. Came to beautiful park in front of a stone church & Newberry Library in middle afternoon, sat down, wrote this. . . . Pigeons, of course, fall leaves on the ground, of course. Pigeons make soft crowing, mooning sound. The trees bare, of course, black branches against black-gray stone of library, old men in felt hats sitting about on wood benches, of course. Blue-white sky, other birds in it, they wheel, make squeaky songs, circular small stone center fountain, dry, of course, has pigeons perched on it all facing inward, a stone merrygoround that will never turn, of course. A squirrel comes down from a big tree that still has leaves, disappears while I look down to write this.

November 13

Arrive in Greensboro, North Carolina—what a bring-down, from great time in Chi—gooky Carolina in the night—Southern jitney to town & King Cotton Hotel. In the middle of the night I hear a sudden howling way below in the street—sounds like a man is dying down there—I go to the window and look down— It's midnight & there's a car stalled in the middle of the street in front of the hotel—with the door on the driver's side wide open. The man must have run off up another street, howling as he went—flipped in the Southern Night. Ten minutes later, a police car arrives. The cops don't get out but question someone standing there—No one seems to know what happened.

November 14

Next morning, awakened by sound of electric drill-hammers tearing up a street below, eternal machine chewing up world's street everywhere. . . . But it's clear & bright outside! I see the land for the first time—autumn trees—rust red everywhere (whereas all was black & white, uninteresting in night, now all's color). Sweet, peaceful fall comes in Southern Window. . . .

Noon: The twin birds of faucets above the hotel bathtub take on a curious aspect—their shadows flying off together, while they remain apart, self-contained. One whispers—"Let's Turn On—I'm Hot." But the other is Cold to the idea. . . .

November 16
Enormous live audience at N.C. State Raleigh. Really turned it on.

November 17
Return to Chapel Hill, my old alma mater,[4] after fifteen years, the same trees, the same streets, the same buildings among them, same main street, same people (but more "cosmopolitan" now, and shops more cosmopolitan-looking), and the air the same, the same slow sweet air. All forgotten, not out of memory, but forgotten, stoned in time.

Had another huge mob at Chapel Hill reading. . . .

ST. THOMAS—PUERTO RICO

November 1960

T ook off at 5 p.m. for San Juan, Puerto Rico—13,000 feet above the snowfields of clouds, at sunset, red horizon above white plains, a little like Arizona—only this a land that never existed and that does not exist—imaginary
plains, plateaus, uplands, sierras, ridges, ravines, palisades, and peaks . . . world
above world, bays of air below, pockets of pockets, voids in the void, ahead all is
dark, night creeps up. Still, above this plain of cloud is another real sky, with its
own clouds still higher up, with stars in it, and a moon. I recognize it as the moon.

November 22

Inside, the plane is still. Hardly any passengers, lights on, dozens of little white
pillows stacked up over empty seats. . . .

> Parrots hanging upside down in Puerto Rico
> The way I look at the round world. . . .

November 24 (Thanksgiving Day)

Sailed to St. Thomas, Virgin Islands, aboard SS *Potomac*. In the lounge are hung
photos of FDR and Eleanor Roosevelt, who sailed in this ship. . . . The portrait of
FDR, in boat-cloak, looks alive, seems to criticize me as an American, looking
down at me critically. The false clouds in the background of the picture look wet

under the frame glass, the whole picture moves on the bulkhead as the ship rolls—it's a flat-bottomed boat! A rough crossing, from Puerto Rico. FDR must have had an iron stomach.

Came out on deck to see St. Thomas looking like Palma de Mallorca. . . . Late afternoon . . . many sailing vessels . . . quays . . . a very few cars in sight . . . sand piles . . . old LST hull, couple small tankers, big low white modern building on high hill, mountains like Marin & Tamalpais . . . American flag . . . red roofs, white houses. . . .

Why we came to St. Thomas, wife Kirby and I, is a long story indeed. My mother's name was Clemence Albertine Mendes-Monsanto, descended from Sephardic Jews in Portugal, and her ancestors fled to the New World to escape the Spanish Inquisition. For years I thought they had landed in Puerto Rico, and I found out they had come to St. Thomas, through a bookseller named Tram Combs who moved his bookshop from San Francisco to St. Thomas sometime in the early 1950s. Since I had mentioned to him that my mother's family came from the Caribbean, he began looking up the Monsantos in St. Thomas. He found my Aunt Gladys Woods and her brother Désir Mendes-Monsanto who were related to my mother by marriage, and Gladys remembered that my Aunt Emilie took care of me when I was a baby, my father having died just before I was born and my mother too distraught to take care of me.

St. Thomas was originally a Danish crown colony, and the Monsantos had intermarried with Danes and Dutch and later English. And in the 19th century they became quite prosperous—Aunt Gladys pointed to a great New Orleans–type mansion with wide verandas and filigree balustrades on a hillside that had been the family estate, and she showed me faded daguerreotype photos in oval frames of Monsantos in panama hats and black string ties—but then in a great depression in the 1890s with a great drop in sugar prices, they had lost it all!

And Aunt Gladys took me to see William Smith who is a Monsanto but I can't remember exactly what his relationship is—perhaps Gladys's father—or older brother—in straw hat, glasses, one eye totally blind, spoke as a seaman—a fisherman all his life—strong hands—shook mine. . . . He eighty-one now—his wife died six months before—he said she came back to him in sleep last night—came tapping with her stick and lay down beside him and slept with him all night long.

But to me when I shook his hand he was like some mythical lost father or Ulysses on the beach beside the fishnets where the boats knocked. He lives in a Gauguin shack with tin roof—inside walls plastered with newspapers, posters, cardboards—two beds—made up neat—a seaman's pad, at wind's end. He'd lived all his life on beaches, in shacks like this one—on island off St. Thomas for a long time—till he got too old to make the trip back & forth— This was on Thatch Quay. Now he'd been in St. Thomas beach shack for fifteen or more years—and developer was coming to build a big hotel & move him forever and away. . . .

November 27

Woke to hear the soft slow bells ring—early Sunday church—a low bell coming in the window as if the church itself were coming in—sprung up and went to it—turned into street by hotel and there was the church— There in the street lay a tiny round holy medal—silver—I picked it up. That church fell in the window, knocked me out of bed.

Sunday still— Went out to Thatch Quay island, mainly owned by Aunt Gladys's family, by boat—and met another Viking—uncle or brother or son of the other Smith. This one Allyn Smith—looked like a Great Dane—tall, well over six feet, tanned, heavy but not fat, solid brown man with Viking face, great prow of a nose—bright dark eyes—high brows. An old man he was, maybe seventy—strong, with two drunk sons or nephews, that spoke as he did—only wildly, drunkenly, &

their speech sounding Danish and/or Dutch—inflections definitely Scandinavian, only with English words curiously twisted and diphthonged—Vikings out of the Sea—blue-black eyes out of it. . . . The family once knighted by the King of Denmark—I saw the decree in Danish, at Uncle Désir Monsanto's house, conferring the title of "Kamaraad."

And Uncle Désir fished out old daguerreotypes of my grandfather Herman and his brother Jacob looking like Spanish lotharios. Here he was—not a great gray man—but young (thirty-year-old) lover-boy—who later left his French wife (my grandmother), returned from N.Y. to the Islands, and philandered into various other women, then got involved in Guatemalan revolution, contracted yellow fever or something, and returned to St. Thomas and died at age thirty-eight. . . .

November 28—Back in San Juan, Puerto Rico

Near the great fort, between the battlements and the ocean, is a great encampment of the poorest Democráticos, in jumbled huts & shacks, all of them with bright Puerto Rican flags and the Pan-Tierra-Libertad flag flying over them, like an encampment before Agincourt. . . . All behind barbed wire; an enclave the government would like to get rid of, but can't . . . political squatters?

PICTURESQUE HAITI

November–December 1960

P ORT-AU-PRINCE—There was this girl with the pure sex look who sold people on a rack. She was tall, mulatto, stood beside her rack with its people hung on it, on hangers, like so many pants and dresses swaying, each person with a string attached, somewhere, which the Girl with the Pure Sex Look pulled, to make that person act the way she wanted that Person to act. She jiggled the long string (which was so long it gave the illusion of real Freedom, Equality and Fraternity), causing different looks to come on the faces and on the bodies of those dark inhabitants to which strings were attached. Everyone in the world had some string attached. The Girl with the Pure Sex Look had no visible string attached to herself. She squatted behind her rack and pissed. A string of water attached. . . . HER RACK was the great Iron Market of Port-au-Prince, casbah of the Caribbean, this Iron Market an enormous native *mercado* (as in Guadalajara, La Paz, Cuzco, any Indian town)—a whole city block of death and dung and pissing desperation, an Exposition of it, everyone on their own hunger-hanger. Some Desolation Photographer should come and do a real Death Magazine job on this Market of Iron, huge hive aswarm with obsidian natives, all hawking, puling, pulling at you, running after you with wares, shouting, crying, laughing, eating and smoking strange leaves. Take picturesque postcard photos of stringbean children with rubbertire shards tied to feet, the Iron Market building itself open on all sides, arcades choked with gypsy encampments of vendors and families, babies and hags squatted among burlap bundles, like voyagers at some end-of-the-world station or Third Avenue Elevated terminal fallen into jungle, a Meccano Erector set, all girders and iron plates bolted together and hung on castiron columns with twin Victorian Gothic iron towers over all like clanking sentry stations on iron prisons . . . the iron death . . . weird Reaper with a scythe on those battlements above (Let none escape!): if He had any flesh on him here, would it be White or Black? Those who are starving, some Consul said, still have the strength to dig their own graves.

II.

But it's a beautiful tropical island, really. There's the *Champ de Mars*—huge empty park with concrete shell bandstand with loudspeakers blaring government speeches and martial music all day. From a distance you'd think a great celebration were in progress, great crowds gathered there—only, upon approaching you find no one at all in the great park—at least this season. It's now forbidden to congregate there, last night people were shot walking across it, martial law's in effect, schools have closed, students on strike against the government, the legislature suspended, the Catholic bishop thrown out of the country, the U.S. ambassador temporarily "on leave" in the States. The coins all read Liberté, Égalité, Fraternité. These noble savages are all absolutely equal, except for the 6 percent that owns everything not owned by foreigners. If money's the blood of the poor, in the Port of the Prince the blood has black corpuscles. The Prince has long since washed his hands of it . . . Ah but—our guidebook tells us—"Tourists beset by beggars, fresh children, arrogant young men and petty thieves in Port-au-Prince will do well to remember that the first and last belong to the declassed riffraff found in any large city, and the others are insecure members of a rising and still-unaccepted middle-class." Our guidebook is written by a noted American poet. It goes on to say that the average cash income of the Haitian is under seventy-five dollars a year. But we can skip this part, our guidebook tells us: "The reader who comes to Haiti to enjoy himself . . . can be grateful that everything related to the 'dismal science' of economics has been relegated to one chapter—where he is at liberty to skip it."

Happiness Waits for You in
HAITI
Unique in the Caribbean
and All the World

So reads the Tourist Card of Identity issued by the Republic of Haiti, costing two dollars and good for two consecutive years. (But am *I* good for two years of *it?*) A real tropical paradise (even better than Bolivia where the population still craps in the streets). Here we have truly unique living conditions, unique childlike native women still available for only sixty cents (American money), colorful happy natives dancing innocent voodoo dances. Voodoo versus the Catholic Church: as a primitive form of Christianity, voodoo serves its purpose here, its gods made to dance on strings. . . .

III.

They are shooting in the *Champ de Mars* this morning. In front of the Presidential Palace some "gaily-uniformed" troops are parading, with fixed bayonets. Out in the *Champ de Mars* from time to time you can hear the dull *whack-whack* of bullets hitting the pavement. Then all is quiet, as if nothing had ever happened, the soldiers disappeared, the great white tropical sun burns toward noon. Bands of black kids are out in the park now, after all, sun and bullets don't stop them, they're indomitable, there's always more where they came from, yaws in their feet ("a historic disease of Haiti, contagious as syphilis and having many analogies with it"). Here comes a whole horde of them across the park, chasing a tall, ragged scarecrow of a figure—a mardi gras carnival figure—they're ragging him but they're scared to death of him and they scatter—it's *Baron Samedi*, Voodoo god, always dressed in black, always *hungry*, here He comes, Baron Saturday, carrying a cross, a huge black iron cross he carries askew, dressed in black with a black mask, very tall, smoking a black cigar and wearing dark glasses, through the park at high noon, tilted forward in a lurching walk, as if dragged from above by marionette strings, a death rattle in his throat. He's the Voodoo hunger and death, the yawfeet flee before him, and the herd of flapping feet lead through the *Museum of Primitives* (where its director mumbles in passing, "A revolution won't help them!") and the herd of feet bleats onward and into the Episcopal Cathedral, famous for its murals by Catholic and Protestant primitive painters, and the floor of the cathedral suddenly filled with ulcerous children's feet running from Baron Hunger, more crowding in all the time, the tide of bare yawfeet rising up the walls and over the murals of the Virgin and the Assumption and the flying angels on the ceiling, the flesh of all the figures in the murals turned into knots of bare feet, Christ a black skeleton picked clean, dangling on his Cross like a marionette.

IV.

Pétionville by *camionette* (a jitney, a group taxi) late in the hot afternoon. The half hour ride above the main casbah city costs ten cents. A shaded steep paved road winds up. You catch views between tropic trees, looking back and down, of masts and sails and cracked *quais* of the port. In this town you'll find some pretty fine clubs, for foreigners and the Haitian elite. In this town there's a fine *Club Arabe* on the Place, below low hills where nestle modernist private mansions. There's a funeral just coming up to the Church (of course there's a church on the square)—a black hearse followed by a long black shadow of mourners on foot. "Must be some-one important," I say to a little black girl who just happens to be standing around. She answers: "Oui, tous les morts sont importants pour quelques instants, chaque a son petit moment d'importance—" ("Yes, all the dead are important for a few moments, each has his little moment of importance—") It's a curious, grave voice issuing from such a little girl, no more than four feet tall, no more than fourteen. She almost curtsies picturesquely, introduces herself. Her name is Marie, her eyes as grave as her voice. The whites of her eyes are not white but pinkish-brown. Her black hair is wound tight around her head in braids, with little pigtails sticking out. She's got good shoes, too big for her, with enormous rubber soles. She's got a nice skirt and white blouse—a proper Little Person, also with string attached— It turns out it's not just by chance she happens to be hanging around the Place when the *camionette* arrives— It's part of her work at the Sunshine Home to go to the square everyday and pick up tourists and lead them to her orphanage. She leads the way, with a peculiar springy step, down dirt streets with ruts two feet deep. The Sunshine Home is a concrete block house, about the size of a one-family tract home in the States, set beside a mud road in a mud field. There's maybe six rooms altogether, stacked with iron bedsteads to the ceiling—no mattresses—several dozen mostly naked babies and infants of all sizes wandering around—no furniture but the bedsteads—no stove or icebox in the kitchen—there's a wood fire on the cement floor, with kids poking things into it—no grownups in sight—ten-year-old girls nursing one-year-old babies, with pacifiers—the babies have swollen stomachs—smell of sweat and flies and ?— "Mother" is Mrs. Doris Burke, old gaunt Negro woman from Jamaica—they've got photo of her in bird's nest hat— She's out at the moment but Marie gets all the kids posed together on cement front porch, standing skinny and sad, to sing a *bon voyage* song for the American visitor who's sure to send shoes. During the singing, an old man resembling Gandhi stumps by in the dusk of the road, carrying his father on his back. . . .

V.

Still, in a place like this, one should disbelieve about 85 percent of what one sees or hears, and check the spelling of the other 15 percent. That's a good foreign correspondent. Things really couldn't be as picturesque as all that. . . . Let us return to our hotel. The Park Hotel, even at the height of the tourist season, is a very non-tourist hotel. (It happens there aren't any tourists at the height of this season—all scared away by the political situation, across the Windward Passage from Cuba—someone's going to break wind very soon. And it'll blow through this island in an hour, including the Dominican Republic.) The Hotel du Parc, on the upper edge of the *Champ de Mars*, is a *pension*. The *pensionnaires* are either cast-up French colonialists (like the *patron* and his bulbous wife-with-concierge-tongue, and the old fat Balzac couples whose tables are in the same corner of the dining room as the *patron*'s) or black Haitian civil servants and mulatto *fonctionnaires* (like the head of the Haitian-American Institute, who looks like some U.N. delegate from India) or American residents (a "businessman" from Miami, an English teacher, a soil engineer with hookworm face, a geologist on a project to find drinking water in the hills).

. . . In the night of the winter of 1960–61, after the usual five-course family dinner, this strange cargo sits rocking in separate chairs on the front veranda, looking out into the dense cricket vegetation of the courtyard through which still filters martial music from the now totally black *Champ de Mars*. I am advised not to venture out there at this hour. The speaker is Leo the Lip. Leo the Lip is several saints in one act, if you take him at face value. Leo the Lip has a face from a very common coinage. It is only the eyes that stamp that face with value. It is a high-domed Jew-face, such as you may see walking through the Clothing District or on Miami's beach any day. Leo the Lip claims to be a millionaire. Leo the Lip's mother, a Polish immigrant, "battled her way out of the ghetto" (he tells me). Leo the Lip did the same, out of Jersey City. Now, totally bald, fat with meat lips, forty-eight years old, he's rich after buying Miami land at a few dollars an acre, said land now being nothing but the Miami Airport. Now he runs horses at various tracks, speculates in overseas crops (strawberries in Haiti), reads geopolitics, conceptual philosophy, visionary poetry. Been married "many times" (he tells me), now doesn't know where to go, what to do with himself anymore, feels himself too old to make a home anywhere again, though he has two plush houses, one in Miami, one in Santa Barbara. When he talks his great, longing eyes are a long way from the meat lips, raising his long white bullface out of the Life of Eat and Shit—his gaze is somewhere out over the bougainvillea in the Haitian dark. He's on the side of the Haitians, loaded with all kinds of fascinating, weird info on everyone on the island, a kind of walking, farting U.S. Information Service in reverse. Leo the Lip is heated up, at the moment, about Ugly American from World Bank who's just been down here "insulting the natives"—addressing Haitian agricultural experts and economists as if they were illiterate children, talking down to a commission of them, speaking neither of their languages (French, Creole), understanding nothing but Pure American—Leo the Lip's telling me all this on the dark porch of this life—everyone hung there together in the night, rocking and nodding— A loud wind that came up, clacking the palm branches, has suddenly died down—Leo the Lip stops short, aware of everyone listening. I'm composing a poem in my head, which I hope will turn out Revolutionary. After a long time rocking (rapidly, as if a string were attached) Leo the Lip says to me: "The residue of time is compassion." He looks around at the other cast-up earth-passengers, still rocking, not about to leave this ark in the dangerous night, prisoners of history. . . . *Loose leaves and aeroplanes blow away on the wind, in what they call Freedom.*

REVOLUTIONARIO SIN BARBA
Cuba

POET'S NOTES ON CUBA

December 1960

Havana—Plane lands, doors open, we sit trembling in seatbelts, waiting for Rebel guards to come and carry us away. Are we not to believe our own free press that publishes all the news that's print to fit? Unless Our Leaders and our newspapers have been deceiving us and spreading great monstrous evil lies about Cuba—unless the United Press International and the Associated Press and Time, Inc., and the CIA and all the radio commentators and all the big newspapers from the *New York Times* to the *San Francisco Examiner* are wrong—unless even most "liberal" writers in the United States are wrong in condemning Castro or in failing to back him—unless they along with most everyone else in the United States have been "brainwashed by news blackout" and, worse still, don't even know it or won't admit it—then I'm a naïve fool and a creep, then I'm out of my head to be landing here just when the United States is about to break off diplomatic relations with this Moscow baby. . . . Sweet Southern Delta voice asks everybody please to disembark, including those in transit for the United States (this plane having come from other Carib islands). First thing you see upon alighting is red lettering on airport:

TERRITORIO LIBRE DE AMÉRICA

PATRIA O MUERTE

[Free Territory of America—Our Country or Death]

In Immigration Office, Police State is represented by health officer in white and one citizen in leatherjacket who might be a militiaman if he has a gun someplace. I'm ready with fine Spanish phrases to explain "purpose of visit"—no one asks anything. Little band of strolling guitarists in sombreros strikes up, tourist guide smiles and beckons, tourist photographer dressed like an Arab snaps picture. (I consider for an insane moment whether he's Cuban agent—or even under-the-rug member of CIA—such are the untaxable wages of fear.) Free rum drinks are spread at bar—maybe it's a trap. . . . In three minutes everybody's through the wicket, and there go the rest of our countrymen back to the plane (one of them whispering to another in fierce voice: "Let's get out of here"). . . . It's ten or fifteen miles into Havana, with old beatup driver full of enormous enthusiasm pointing out window all the way at new housing projects, other new buildings with banners on them:

REVOLUCIÓN ES CONSTRUIR
[Revolution Is to Build]

and

VENCEREMOS
[We Will Win]

It's late Saturday afternoon in city . . . great empty waterfront, spray crashing over endless seawall, Morro fort at one far end. . . . Am keeping sharp eye out for roving bands of armed Rebel soldiers with orders to shoot on sight anyone looking suspicious, as reported by United Press International two days ago. There's two young soldiers with rifles slung on backs, looking quite dangerous, directing traffic. Two more pass us in new-looking jeep, no arms visible, wearing new black boots that look like they were made in Russia. They pull up at house with sign:

DEATH TO ILLITERACY
Sign Up Here to Learn How to Write

Probably lots of guns in there, things beginning to look really ominous. . . . We wheel into old Paseo del Prado, stop at small hotel. First off, I meet Greek in lobby who says he's from Jersey City, has been here a month, and "everybody's happy and like brothers." Windows of closet-like hotel room hang over great trees on center island of Paseo, alive with starlings, filling the dusk with their cries. Taxis toot, birds drown them out, four militiamen in berets go by, whistling. . . . Later, down on Paseo, shoeshine boy has sign on shoebox:

GRACIAS FIDEL
YA SOMOS PROPRIETARIOS
[Thanks Fidel—We're Owners Now]

Dignified Paseo, with its glaucous streetlights among the laurels, gives illusion of Old World city, one of the great autumn capitals, another seaside Madrid, like Lima. Rest of Havana blasts said illusion. Whole population seems "turned on," a kind of euphoria in the air. . . . (May be my imagination: "One sees what one comes to see." . . .) In bar on adjoining Plaza Central is small sign:

AVISO
SE PROHIBE TERMINANTEMENTE: LA INGESTIÓN DE BEBIDAS
ALCOHÓLICAS POR MIEMBRAS DE LAS FUERZAS ARMADAS
REVOLUCIONARIAS
SERÁN EXPULSADOS DE LAS FUERZAS REVOLUCIONARIAS

[Absolutely Prohibited: Consumption of Alcoholic Drinks
by Members of the Revolutionary Armed Forces—They Will Be
Expelled from the Revolutionary Forces]

Across the plaza, on the grounds of the Capitol building, a Cow Fair is going on, sponsored by INRA, with booths full of canned farm products from INRA cooperatives, displays of model farm projects, shooting galleries, sideshows, booths with pamphlets for sale on the New Cuba, including speeches by Fidel in Spanish and English. . . . Plenty of soldiers wandering around here, some with rifles on backs, some with musical instruments going up to big bandstand where concert's about to start, a big crowd gathering, now about a hundred Rebel soldiers on stand, about to blow, waiting while man in civilian suit with little pistol in holster rigs up mikes on stage, two or three thousand people on wooden chairs in front of bandstand in the balmy night, lots of babies and kids with mothers, a few big black beards (they *look* "way out"), hardly anybody dressed like upper middle class. Looks more like some factory has just let out, plus a lot of cowtown wrastlers come in from the country. Over one farm display, a sign: The Earth Is Our Factory. Big floodlight turned on blowup of Cow's Head behind bandstand—INRA has set up Cow as Great Dictator. (Fidel is said not to allow large blownup pictures of himself.) . . . Something that sounded like a big bomb just went off a mile away. Couple of musicians on stage look up, otherwise nobody pays any attention. (Later I learn this was regular nine o'clock salute from Morro Castle.) Band stands and starts blasting what must be Revolutionary Anthems since everyone else stands, some at attention. Everyone claps and sits down, and concert starts—Souza strained through a sombrero. . . . Later, across the square in an open-air bar, two middle-aged colored guys playing guitars and singing at one table look like they might fit into cool group at Five Spot, except when music comes out it's old Spanish Moan. . . . At movie house on corner there's *El Salario del Miedo* (*The Wages of Fear*). . . . Back at hotel at midnight, night clerk is like belligerent CCNY student, reads *New York Times* aloud to me—"Eisenhower allots one million for resettlement of refugees from Reds." Reading this, he interjects "*What* Reds?" The money, he informs me, is for "resettlement" of Cuban counterrevolutionaries *in* Cuba. . . .

SUNDAY—The starlings start up at dawn, trees full of them in the early dawn. Big black church bells toll once somewhere, starlings suddenly stop, all at once. . . . At eight a.m. when I come out under the trees, they're silent still. I sit on huge stone bench, writing this— Statue of José Martí in the great plaza, illuminated last night, now still stands white under palm trees, arms upraised. . . . Toward noon, I take busride out to Miramar, through Vedado district—along the route there are no Christmas displays of any kind in stores or houses, though stores are loaded with clothes, food, household goods. (Lots of shoestores, thousands of shoes in windows waiting for feet, more shoes than people here now; maybe they'll wade across Windward Passage to Haiti—shoes very special sign of status anywhere down here—if you got shoes in Haiti, beggars follow you, you're somebody—there must be some beggars still in Havana but I've not seen one—these shoes will go where bare feet are. . . .) I also pass windowful of naked manikins huddled together—what weird novelist-of-the-soul stripped them down and left them standing there on a Sunday corner, waiting for celestial streetcar? . . . Out past Vedado, toward the beaches, bus rolls through rich suburban streets, past big deserted mansions, beach clubs. Farther out it's more and more like Miami, Batista-land. (Current Batista joke repeated with amused scorn by Fidelistas: What's the largest country in the world today? Cuba—its capital is in Havana, its government is in Moscow, and its population is in Miami.) . . . Later, back in center of city again, I walk around government buildings, each guarded by one militiawoman sitting on campchair with rifle over knees, looking like she's about to knit. Banner over bank says:

ESTE BANCO PERTENECE AL PPUEBLO
VENCEREMOS!
[This Bank Belongs to the People—We Will Win!]

Over nationalized department store:

APOYAMOS LA REFORMA AGRÍCOLA
[Support the Agricultural Reform]

Dada time goofs by, here as anywhere else—it's night again before I know it, and toward midnight, crossing the plaza again, I come upon big groups of *campesinos* from the Cow Fair, standing around arguing in country accents. There's about fifty of them, and there are two men in sharp business suits doing most of the talking. The whole thing looks like a scene from *Salt of the Earth*, with these two Organizers haranguing the men, most of whom stand there looking very dubious about the whole thing, now and then making critical remarks. Floodlights are still on all around the square and more and more people stop to listen or get in on the bullsession, no soldiers or gendarmes in sight. At one a.m. they're still at it, at two they're still at it. Still later, I look out from hotel room and see the crowd still there, the Revolution being argued out in the night, in what looks like Free Speech. . . . Or is some movie director, or hidden director of propaganda, deceiving everybody?

MONDAY—Morning again, begins with the birds again. . . . As day proceeds it becomes less lyric. . . . The sitters in the great plaza know the side streets exist. . . . Buses roar along them, loaded. Everybody's out, rushing along, sidewalk coffee-stands are full. . . . Where's the Iron Heel of the Dictator crushing the People today? Must be out in the country somewhere. . . . In big bookstore, La Poética Moderna, is sign at cash register:

EL CLIENTE SIEMPRE TIENE LA RAZÓN
MENOS CUANDO ATACA A LA REVOLUCIÓN
[The Customer Is Always Right Except When He
Attacks the Revolution]

There's plenty of school supplies, and Spanish books published in other Spanish-speaking countries. There are also three series of books published this year in Cuba as part of literacy campaign, six or eight books in each series sold together for three dollars. Next year is to be proclaimed Literacy Year. . . . United States papers for sale in center of Havana include the anti-Castro *Miami News* and *Miami Herald* and the *New York Times*. No *Time* or *Life International* in Spanish, no *Havana Times* in English. . . . Address of Associated Press listed in phone book turns out to be *Havana Times* building in rundown waterfront section—no one there except one militiaman in little dark lobby—where is AP gone? All those sinister dispatches coming out of this hole in the wall? . . . Early in evening I go out to Plaza Cívica to one of streamlined buildings that house newspaper *Revolución*. Plaza Cívica is huge empty space, maybe a mile across (filled with million people when Castro makes speech here) with great modernist buildings sticking up far apart. I walk across it in silent dark,

no one anywhere, like some Kafkaesque no-man's-land. No one shoots me and I reach entrance to *Revolución*. It's guarded by woman with rifle (who, they tell me later, is leading abstract painter). Sign over entrance says *Prensa Libre*—this is name of other paper in building. In lobby is bust of José Martí with inscription:

No Hay Monarca Como un Periodista Honrado
[No Monarch Like an Honest Journalist]

Carlos Franqui, editor of *Revolución*, has just returned from Russia, as has Guillermo Cabrera Infante, editor of literary supplement *Lunes*. They're not in now but I meet other writers in one editorial room upstairs, none of them over thirty. They all tell me they are not Communists and that this newspaper is not Communist (Masthead says: "Organ of the 26th of July Movement"). They tell me they met C. Wright Mills and that he seemed "pretty naïve" but that he'd "gone everywhere and talked to everyone"—his book *Listen, Yankee* hadn't reached Havana yet. On desk are books recently published by Revolución Press: *Sartre Visita a Cuba* (Sartre's essays resulting from his visit here); *Cuba: Zona de Desarrollo Agrario* by Lisandro Otero—it's a cross-country reportage on rural Cuba during first year of Agricultural Reform; *Así en la Paz Como en la Guerra*, short stories by Guillermo Cabrera Infante (b. 1929), these stories being pictures of the "Cuban world under the Dictatorship," showing prostitution, bourgeois neuroses, and the "hedonistic and sadistic life of the aristocracy" (quotes from jacket-blurb). There's also one book of poems: *Poesía: Revolución del Ser* by José A. Baragaño (b. 1932), this book also growing out of *los años del terror* leading up to Revolution. . . . We go out to restaurant—expensive-looking joint in Vedado district. Looks like it should be counterrevolutionary to eat in such a place, but it's been nationalized, complete dinner costs $1.50. . . . I see big guy with beard wearing fatigues and smoking cigar come out of restaurant kitchen: it's Fidel, no one acts surprised, no one jumps up. He passes out street-door, nodding at us with shy look as he goes by. By the time I get up, he's already out on sidewalk. I say Come On to one writer at table, hoping he'll come out with me as intermediary but he hangs in background as I rush outside, Fidel has one lone soldier with him who smiles goofily as I come up and shake Fidel's hand and tell him I am *poeta norteamericano*—he's speechless—my news really astonishes him—he shifts gun he's carrying under arm, takes out cigar and gives me big smile, shakes my hand again—I mutter some other insanity in taxi-cab Spanish including word *gracias* just as some old woman rushes up and embraces him and he is carried off, having said not a syllable—Fidel was gentle, had soft handshake, calm direct look in eyes. I return to table inside, thinking it curious at least one of three Cuban writers with me did not come out. Seems there's considerable distance between them—they've actually never met him, don't consider him exactly an "intellectual." Most of their thirty-year-old generation grew up in exile, in New York, Mexico, France. Very few of them fought with Castro in mountains, the present editor of *Revolución* one of the few who did. Most returned to Cuba after the Insurrection was over, around November '59. And they tell me there aren't any young Cuban poets who've published what could really be called Revolutionary (or Apocalyptic) poetry. . . . Whenever poetry has a revolution, it too returns at least briefly to the Apocalyptic. . . .

TUESDAY—I go to Casa de las Américas in afternoon and meet subdirector Alberto Robaina, who shows me new issue of literary quarterly published by this "cultural institution dedicated to serve all peoples in their fight for liberty." (Masthead quote.) This issue includes Nicolás Guillén, Leo Huberman, Paul Sweezy, and article by Harold Cruse on Cuba and the North American Negro. They promise to send me books in the States, ask me to send them U.S. writers' manuscripts. . . . I wander around city by myself rest of day, get lost at night in desolate outskirts, riding beatup buses with madcap drivers—Latin America loaded with secondhand city buses from Bronx America, old Thirdavenue El coaches careening as streetcars through Lima—I end up at waste land bus terminal among blocks knocked down for new housing—no soldiers or policewomen anywhere, no bombs going off out here either. . . . Perhaps it's at the AP offices they're going off. . . .

WEDNESDAY—Meet Pablo Armando Fernández, poet and assistant editor of *Lunes*—lived in New York a large part of his early life—now thirty—came back after the Insurrection. At his apartment in modern Medical Security building he shows me huge choral poem of his which was performed before thousands at 26th of July Celebration in Sierra Maestra last summer—parts of it have Fidel speech set in typography of poetry—he says Fidel is a great natural poet. Talking about American Beat writers, he says he read a lot of Kerouac and others and dug their weird dissent but has lately gotten disillusioned with them since they won't come far enough out of their private lives and commit themselves (like Revolutionary writers, for instance). (Before I left States, Kerouac told me on phone from Long Island: "I got my own Revolution out here—the American Revolution.") I ask Pablo Armando what was Hemingway doing in Cuba all during Batista regime—fishing? And had he noticed any of the older American poets or novelists or other "avant-garde" writers (many of whose reputations were built on "liberal" or "radical" bases)—had he noticed many of them raising their voices for Fidel? They're all just plain scared, he tells me. . . . Late in afternoon we go over to offices of *Lunes* and meet editor Guillermo Cabrera Infante—he's very serious, sharp, phones Pablo

Neruda (who's just arrived by ship from Chile—a new book of his poetry just about to be published here) and arranges for me to meet him. *Lunes* offices very new and empty, workmen still putting up partitions, etc. They show me recent issues on "Poets and the Atomic Bomb," on Beat Generation, on American Negro, and on "USA vs. USA." (This includes Truman Capote, Faulkner, Henry Miller, Hemingway, John O'Hara, Kerouac, Ginsberg, Langston Hughes, Carl Sandburg, Edgar Lee Masters, John Steinbeck.) I note Neruda's *Canto General* on table, also Hart Crane in English. Fellow in corner is working on article while another (Negro editor) reads to him out of pamphlet in French, from Indochina, translating it into Spanish as he reads. On same desk is mass of overturned books including pamphlet in English published by Italian Communist Party—Fidel a great *pragmatist*, they tell me, *Fidelismo* his own blend of past and future. . . . U.S. policy of relentless hostility *forcing the radicalization* of his Revolution. . . . It's a *praxis*, says Sartre in his Cuba book. . . . Guillermo Infante and wife (in cocktail dress) drive me in British sportscar over to Miami-type Riviera Hotel where Neruda is staying and leave me at entrance. . . . Neruda sitting in plush suite with open spiral notebooks, gets up smiling, shakes hand heartily—bald with eagly eyes in round face, grave ship's-prow eyes—dressed to go out someplace, has only a few minutes but tells me he's delighted I called since he'd followed news of Ginsberg and myself in Chile last winter—asks if Ginsberg is still up to his "antics." . . . I ask him if he thinks Apocalyptic stage of Revolution is about over. He says No, it'll go on for years, and the most dangerous period is just ahead because counterrevolutionaries first thought the Revolution would fall of its own accord, but now they see it will not fall by itself and they will have to act to bring about its downfall. . . . It's time for Neruda to leave for public appearance at Capitol where Chief of Rebel Army is to make speech commemorating death of Antonio Maceo, Revolutionary martyr. Neruda says why don't I come along. Down we go with his beautiful wife and get in limousine from Casa de la Amistad, new international "friendship house" set up by Fidel. En route I tell him I'm staying in hotel near Capitol where there are the biggest bedbugs I ever saw. He laughs and says when he first came to Santiago de Chile from the country as a boy there were bedbugs but he didn't know what they were until they bit. Then he had Battle of Bedbugs all night, burning them up with a candle. I say I'm a pacifist and am against killing anything—he commiserates, says he still has candle back at hotel, in case I should change my mind during night. . . . We stop at Casa de la Amistad and pick up lady director, and then, going on, he suggests to lady director that I send her list of poets and writers and editors (including conservatives) who might make for some Understanding if invited to Cuba to see for themselves. She agrees, we arrive at Capitol, inch through great crowd gathering outside—limousine we're in is very out of place—people's poet Neruda separated from people, etc. . . . The crowd's controlled not by armed Rebel troops but by girls' militia stretching daisy chain of arms to keep paths clear. . . . Crazy crowd pouring in—we go in back entrance, I leave Neruda behind stage, since he's to sit on it, and I go round to main floor of big senate chamber which is already full—Wow, what a Turn-On—the People have really taken over the joint—all the red leather armchairs and elegant desks where once the senators sat (there ain't no more senators, baby, and old Batista judges are fleeing in row-boats) now occupied by young Revolutionaries of all colors, in fatigues and work clothes, a few with guns, a very few still wearing beards—the galleries now full to the roof with *campesinos* and students. In seat next to me at back is big black militiaman with gun in holster on desk, very friendly, his name Cortez, from Peru via Venezuela, has been here several years, very enthusiastic about what Revolution has done for People, eager to convince you. Everybody stands and starts clapping, and Cortez tells me it's for delegates from Russia and China just coming in— Chinese delegates look like young genius University of California Ph.D. students, very slim with studious faces and glasses—they raise both arms to galleries, looking up, turning from waist like hero wrestlers about to perform in a colosseum. . . . Slim colored cat in Rebel uniform, looking like member of Modern Jazz Quartet with chin beard, gets up and starts speaking—I figure this is intro for Chief of Army Juan Almeida—but no, it's himself— He reads dull speech, audience gets restless after about fifteen minutes, students in balconies start clapping and shouting, hubbub up there keeps growing until finally Almeida stops and just stands there looking up without irritation—he knows what's up—it's Fidel at back of balcony with students—everybody in hall catches on and starts clapping in unison and chanting louder and louder FIDEL FIDEL FIDEL FIDEL until finally after about five minutes of this he comes forward to edge of balcony, immediately sits down and motions for everyone please to be quiet and listen to speech—he uses kind of benign gesture with one hand, almost a benediction, and gesticulates at Almeida to forgive him. And then when the speech is over in a minute the place starts rocking again with chants of FIDEL! FIDEL! but Fidel disappears with a wave, and the whole scene falls apart. . . .

THURSDAY—Flying out of it today. . . . No hassle or inspection at airport—in minutes we're 18,000 feet up and going away. . . . Camus's Rebel down there, Havana far gone, way below, standing white in sunlight. . . . We wheel above white disk of it, turn and turn away from it, forever, it spun down, hull down into great ocean, our harpoon in it, white whale sunk. . . .

NEW ORLEANS

December 8, 1960

Landed New Orleans, 6 p.m., back in Woolworth's Civilization— Wow, the lights really are on in America—Christmas trees!— Two hours by plane from Fidel and one of the strangest biggest phenomena of the 20th century, Revolutionary Cuba—a few hours from that wide-awake hotbed, here's New Orleans, three-quarters asleep and one-quarter dead and still segregated, its citizens sound asleep standing up, girl at Western Union, man at newsstand (whom I asked street directions) in their own little dream worlds. . . . Cuckoo existence made of pure Woolworth, all wool, all yours, take it home, "your correct weight free if you guess it. . . ."

BIG SUR JOURNAL

September 1961

Above Bixby Canyon,[5] September 12

I am up here in the golden fields at the top of Big Sur, on one of the highest hills, over the ocean, the long wheat grass is gold-yellow up here, its tares blow in the wind, I sit cross-legged, naked under the hot sun.

Homer the Dog has made himself some shade under a bush, he is full of tares and burrs, and the flies bother him, he's panting. . . . It's early afternoon—a high noon—way down below, westward, the blue-gray sea fading into a vague horizon of clouds; a car creeps like an ant on the highway. I think I could wander this way the rest of my life—a small knapsack, sneakers, an old Navy CPO shirt, khaki pants, a small knife, a bottle opener, a nail clipper, a pencil & pad, a book, all I have. . . . So to India one day.

The wind blows thru me, over the hills.

September 14

I sit in the lotus position, naked, and contemplate one stalk of long gold grass. It has maybe two dozen barbed tares on it, all pointing & leaning in the same direction, from the direction of the wind they grew in. Yet when I turn it against the wind, the tares turn with it, now point into the wind: the habit of a lifetime is easily broken, once the thing it stems from is forgotten, once one is freed from it. *Revolt and you shall live?*

September 16

. . . stars out tonight, enormous, myriad traceries! Webs! Sad mute histories! Wheeling by. All these suns gone down already, at midnight, the universe itself not there anymore, nothing up there, out there anymore, all burned up millions of light-years ago, nothing left but the light of it now reaching me, in sleeping bag, staring up— at Nothing. I like small constellations best, like the Pleiades and Delphinus—they wheel by, hours apart but in the same plane, both passing thru the same frame of the open overhang of my lean-to. And I dream I am making a book cover for a book of the story of my life, and dream the square open frame of stars as the cover, first with Delphinus in it, then the Pleiades, then a still more distant, and colder, smaller & stiller constellation I don't recognize. But, bang, now comes great Orion over the dark trees, waving his great spangled belt— Flashing lightbulbs in it!

I see dark things rushing across the country.

September 17

Alone with myself climbing by Pico Blanco, found no mescal on Mescal Ridge, walking over the high open mesas, high meadowlands, the sun beating down, no shade anywhere on the high ridges, then descending into little canyons full of scrub oak, manzanita, willows, small firs, the dirt road full of deer tracks & horseshoe prints, Homer the Dog chasing deer up the steep banks barking, always frustrated. . . . Coveys of quail flush out thru the trees, a hawk sails high over. Farther on, in a dark redwood gulch, a bad blue jay scolds, a sign by a rancher's gate says: No Trespassing—SURVIVORS WILL BE PROSECUTED. It's the sixties.

While I was walking from Bixby Canyon to Point Sur, a plane flew from New York to San Francisco, a satellite circled the Soviet Union, another with a man in it shot into the cosmos and circled the earth and came back to report there was no God up there, as we had suspected.

SALTON SEA NOTES
October 1961

TIRED OF THE FOG AND COLD? COME TO CALIFORNIA'S RIVIERA—
Sailing, Water Skiing, Swimming, Seaside Dining—
A DESERT PARADISE AT THE GREAT SALTON SEA
—promotional brochure

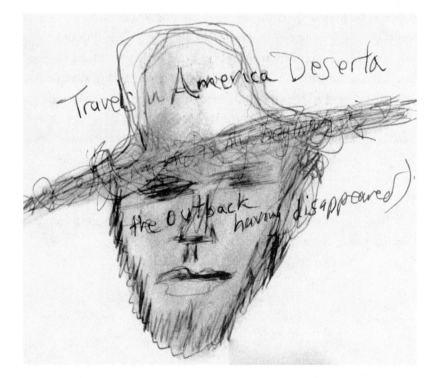

October 28

Henry Miller was right. "Some other breed of man has won out." Some strange breed has taken over America. I sit in a soda-fountain on the main street of El Centro, California—inexplicably I have ordered & have eaten a Mexican Combination Plate—tacos, enchiladas, and all that. Outside, at the curb, sits the junk of American civilization—cars, cars, cars. On the jukebox inside, a Mexican crooner with a tear in his voice. . . . An hour north of here lies the Salton Sea. I have not figured out what "El Centro" could be the center of. Not the universe. The Salton Sea may offer a clue. The Salton Sea is in America. In California, in fact. Very strange. I still have to get there.

I have two hours before the bus to that Sea. I go to the public library. It's Saturday afternoon, and it's closed. Naturally. People that work during the week naturally have no time to go to the library on their day off. I must think of something else. I go to a barber's, that should take at least half an hour, maybe more if I divert the barber with witticisms or dirty jokes. No luck. He whips me thru in a little over ten minutes, including a swipe at my eyebrows and sideburns, which I duck. He drops the comb on the greasy floor several times and wipes it off on his pants and continues. In the meantime I listen to him haranguing the other barber (who looks like a local football player) about how to skin a buck & how to remove its horns & how much you can count a full-grown buck coming to in *net weight* after it's skinned. The other barber keeps saying "Yeah—yeah" like a little halfhearted football cheer. I have a feeling that if I had got this young football barber instead of the old geezer and had a hunting license to show him, he would have cut my hair for free. As it is, I have to pay for my scalping. (The old geezer keeps nicking me every time he gets to a good part of the description of how to skin a buck.) When I am down to "net weight" he steps back with a sour grin, as if to say it's a pretty sad carcass.

The last hour in El Centro is pure Nowhere. In the bus station there is not even a place to sit down. Everyone must be itching to get out of El Centro. I spend the last twenty-five minutes contemplating a rotary ventilator that's going round on a building next door. That's a long time to contemplate a ventilator, turning about as slowly as the earth itself. I should have said the last twenty-two minutes. Three minutes before the bus is announced the ventilator inexplicably stops. This is not allowed. The air-conditioning must work. What are we to do now? On the station newsstand is a paper that says the U.S. will have men on the moon within a year. And on the lunch counter in the bus station is an "Answer Box." It says:

Ask Me Any Yes or No Question—Deposit Penny—
Hold Lever Down to Read
ANSWER HERE

I am wary of knowing the answer to the most important Yes or No Questions. We'd rather *not* know the answers to some, such as Will I Die? Yet we know the answer ahead of time, so how can we ask it as a question? How can we, that is, without such a wondrous philosophy machine as this, which allows us to pose the possibility of more than one answer. I put the penny in, but do not hold the lever down. I run off to the bus. Suppose the machine lied to me—what then of El Centro?

Should I approach the Salton Sea as if it were the Holy Land? I see at the upper end, on the map, there's a place called Mortmar (Dead Sea). The map also says the Sea is 235 feet below sea level. Desert & sagebrush all around. . . .

Bus driver says, This Is the Place. I get down. Bus disappears & here I am in desert . . . miles beyond Death Valley. There's some modern shacks & three motels down by a big puddle, a dozen palm trees around, about a mile from the highway. I walk over there, with my musette bag, thinking I must look pretty

forlorn. Everyone here has *CARS*! Roads run off straight into desert in all directions, like a Florida development gone under in the '30s, sidewalks lost in sand.
So this is the famous resort. It's the final Dead Sea Level of America. I find a
variety store-bar called the Sans-Souci. Inside is a drunk loudmouth of about fifty
and a platinum blonde who looks like she's been thru all the mills and talks
tough. The drunk is saying: Well, if you waz ever in a war, you'd see something.
She says: I ain't gettin near no war! I'm not thinkin of wars, I'm thinkin of *PRIS-
ONS*! What makes you think of Prisons, he says. *NEVER MIND*, she says. . . .
Sans souci, like I say. . . .

All night the wind blows sand across the Sea against the "beach house" I'm in.
There is no beach but there are "beach houses." The water in the sea has shrunk
toward the center of it. On the other side is a mountainous crenellated desert. And
Christ walked on that water? Anything to get away. . . .

Every journal is a confessional. If it's in the first person, it cannot help but be.
Unless the author of it lies to himself—and that makes it even more of a confessional. For some reason, travel brings out confessions one would never make at
home. I am trying to draw the rake of my journal over the landscape. Perhaps I will
uncover something.

To tell the truth, to tell the truth! Well—this is the most depressing journey I have
ever been on— Imagine having to spend one's life condemned to passing from one
motel to another, one hotel room to another, all of them alike, first class, the same
spotless sheets, the same glasses in sanitary wax paper, the same little soap bars
individually wrapped, Gideon Bible in the drawer, no one to speak with but hotel
clerks, wives running motels in forlorn corners, bus drivers. Loneliness of millions
living like this, between cocktails, between filling stations, between buses, trains,
towns, restaurants, movies, highways leading over horizons to another Rest Stop.
Sad the bundles in bus station waiting rooms, sad the frizzled women sitting next
to them, the old couples on benches talking in old languages, the wetbacks with
satchels they repack in men's rooms. Sad hope of all their journeys to Nowhere and
back in dark Eternity. . . . *In the middle of the Journey of my Life, I came to myself in a
dark wood.*

A vision of America, yes— *Everything seems to be at a complete standstill.* People,
movies, the arts, politics, the land itself, everything marking time, halted, asleep or
dead or—what is going on, anyway? Is anything going on? What will be the next

development? Boom boom, is that it? Is that what everyone's waiting for, that why everything seems suspended, demoralized? I'll take another bus and let you know the answer. . . .

By the Salton Sea, in the night, the rest of America does not exist, *out* there, nothing left but this undersea place, where they don't even know when the buses are scheduled to go by on the highway. Maybe there aren't any more buses, perhaps the one I took was the last bus in America, and it rushed off over the last Frontier. On the map it says there's an Indian reservation to the west of the Sea. I see nothing but desert & barren treeless mountains. . . . Whole tribes of Indians shook hopeless feather lances & disappeared over the horizon, to reappear centuries later at the corner of Hollywood & Vine, feet up and smoking wild cigars like Saroyan Armenians. . . . At the Salton Sea, nothing took their place—*NOTHING*. And San Francisco, USA, doesn't exist, my family, wife, dog, baby, home, bookstore, buddies, friends & lovers don't exist, at the Dead Sea Level of things. . . . This whole episode is an American nightmare. Yes, I will have to admit it, I am carrying Henry Miller's *Air-Conditioned Nightmare* in my pocket, in the pocket Avon edition, published by the Hearst Corporation, which is the most ludicrous irony of all. The Hearst Corporation, up to now the symbol of all the worst features of America which Miller castigates in his *Nightmare*. I wonder if Henry had any control over this reprint, or if they've even sent him a copy, and what he thinks of this. He may have to write a sequel as of 1961. (Or perhaps Kerouac will do it? It happens Miller *digs* Kerouac and has told him so, enthusiastically.) Anyway, everything Miller said about America in his *Nightmare* twenty years ago, has come true—and more he never imagined.

Even at the Salton Sea, the face of death has its smile. In the morning the wind is still blowing but the sun is bright, and life is stirring. Even at the bottom of a well, there's life. A little vignette, a tableau presents itself at the resort Coffee Shop & Bar. The bar part is locked but there's already a man in a new cowboy hat at the door, banging on it, yelling "When Do the Bars Open Up Around Here?" It is 8 a.m. & the bartender comes out & says "God Not Already—I Just Closed Up!"— The man in hat has his cowboy Cadillac out front—a convertible with a dog in it— He plunges into bar, bolts a drink, plugs "South Pacific" on the jukebox, starts whooping for a second drink, his dog hears it outside, barks, jumps out of car, pees on palm tree trunk. In the meantime a good-looking little blonde drives up in other beatup Cadillac & leads her blind fat mother into the coffee shop for breakfast. . . .

"When Do the Gas Stations Open Up Around Here?" I hear the cowboy shouting. . . . That's life in the American West, 1961. Let me out, I'm way down here at the bottom of the well, below the Sea. . . . I'm the cowboy and I paid eight dollars for this fancy resort beach house and I want some action along with it, even some Beauty, I want my money's worth, I'll take a lot of showers, use up all the soap and towels, drink out of both sterilized water glasses, turn on the air-conditioning, the refrigeration, the heater, flush the toilet a lot. I'll go swimming in the Pool even if I freeze to death doing it. ("Please do not urinate in the Pool," the sign says.) I'll spit on the floor as I leave, leave the lights on, forget to leave the key, and then mail it back from another state, postage-due. "Just drop in any mailbox," it says on the tag, "Postage Guaranteed." I will. I leave notes in the empty drawers in my room: "Abandon All Hope, Ye Who Enter Here" and "This Is The End of the World." What better way to enliven life at the Dead Sea?

I have to go back to El Centro to get to San Diego. I arrive back at the bus station there with a half hour in which to get something to eat before the San Diego bus leaves. I sit down at the same place at the lunch counter. There's the Answer Box staring me in the face again, right where I left, same instructions:

Ask Me Any Yes or No Question—Deposit Penny—
Hold Lever Down to Read
ANSWER HERE

THE PICKWICK HOTEL, SAN DIEGO

October 30

The Pickwick Hotel is the grim prototype of the most desolate second- or third-class hotels in the land. It exists because America exists, and even a great country needs drainpipes. The Pickwick Hotel is at the bottom of the drain. It's not that it's the cheapest joint in existence and it's probably not the worst. If only these walls could speak—what true and tragic tales they could tell of life in the Land of Freedom and

Justice for All. The lobby is stocked with live cadavers of one sort or another, the worst of these being the manager himself and his avaricious assistants, the desk clerks (nylon women in their early forties) and the bellhops with gray faces, looking like they hadn't meant to work there at all but just got trapped passing by on a bus years ago. The other fixtures in the lobby are a race of octogenarian residents—the "steadies" of the establishment—old cronies with canes and old old old women with crutches and goiters and hearing aids who spend their evenings sitting in the plastic easy chairs staring ahead of them, wordless, or looking with blank stares at the three caged parakeets the hotel has trapped behind some wire mesh at one end of the horribly "modernized" lobby. Passing through is a transient floating population of bus drivers and passengers, Mexican farmworkers, commercial travelers, sailors, and Okies, plus a continuous flow of broken-down Grant Wood couples on vacation. That's only the street level of this charming oasis graced with Dickens's famous name. The real glories of this Travelers' Rest lie above. (Getting topside in the first place requires my paying for the room in advance, the harpy at the Desk not considering my knapsack to be "baggage.") Entering the elevator, I am drawn upward by an old woman who has no feet and resembles an owl in captivity. This wretched creature sits strapped to a little platform on castors and seems to have her hand tied to the elevator door. Behind her, on the floor, is a conglomeration of paper bags and baskets in which can be seen various articles necessary for her functioning—from toothbrushes to a shoehorn. As we groan upward, toward the fourth floor, I look over her shoulder and see she is reading a clipping titled "Fifty Years Ago Today.". . .

Now we come to the Room itself, a real little piece of a great American vacuum, this empty room. Walk right in, don't be afraid. (The bellhop, who insisted on carrying my knapsack, raises the shades, opens a window on nowhere. *Is There Anything Else, Sir?* No! He departs.) I look around. Beautiful. What else could the bellhop possibly have provided? Forlorn bed with hole in pink comforter! (Comforter?) Old-fashioned easy chair recovered in pink-brown plastic! All night, below the window, the Greyhound buses roar & warm up, shift gears, roar off, roll in, while loudspeakers bellow. Four floors up I am launched every ten minutes in a new direction—Dallas, New Orleans, Tijuana, Los Angeles (pronounced Loss-Angle-less), New York. All night I'm changing from Chicago, Mexico City, San Francisco. All night I am being paged by somebody's mother who misplaced me in another depot.

In the morning I am not there any longer. My nature abhors a vacuum.

A WALK TO LA JOLLA

I am now walking along the beach from San Diego to La Jolla, a distance of some ten to fifteen miles or so. I don't suppose anyone has walked this whole route in a long time. It is almost impossible to *walk* in Southern California. Everyone has a car, and *you are not supposed to walk.* Try it around the San Diego outskirts or in Loss-Angle-less, for instance, you'll find out. Once you get off the downtown streets, there just aren't many sidewalks. Naturally you are not allowed to walk on the freeways which connect everything. *Nothing else connects anything.* And don't carry anything like a knapsack, you'll look suspicious. . . . As I was saying, I was walking along the beach. Even on the beach you can't walk far. Whenever I get tired I stop off in one of the public beach restrooms along the way and sit down on the john and read another chapter of *The Air-Conditioned Nightmare.* Twenty years & America hasn't changed a bit. Except everything is different. Russia has just dropped its fifty-megaton bomb in the Arctic and the face of America is changed, even before the fallout gets here, already it wears a different expression.

EMPTY BOOTH

New Hungerford Hotel, dark winter nighttime downtown Seattle, sunken coffee shop, ten steps down from lobby, seen thru plate glass window like an aquarium, wall-eyed waitresses swimming in it, back and forth, fat guppy lady at Cashier wicket far off by glass street door, puffy mouth opening and closing, anchored—emits bubbles. . . . Whiteface woman sits alone in wooden booth just below plate glass window. Feeding. Soundless. But music on TV in hotel lobby behind me, TV showing forest fire pictures, dramatic newsreel-type music accompanying firefighters' heroics. Underwater Whiteface Woman eating huge white salad, black olives on toothpicks standing up in it like channel buoys or markers on pilings, potatoes, tomatoes sliced—she spears one as music surges. Head down, under gray leather hat, white plastic raincover with tie-strings hanging down, steel rim glasses, puffy nose, big white gauze patch over left eye under eyeglass—white uniform of some kind—nurse maybe—maybe sixty. Eats rapidly, works fast, head down, spearing more tomatoes to unheard heroic music—hill of coleslaw, half cup of milk coffee, spoon aside with drop in it, crushed paper napkin next to it. Coat on seat under her, squirrel collar. Also two large paper shopping bags upright on seat in corner, bright cotton print showing in one. Big leather handbag, folded newspaper. . . . Five minutes later: still eating fast, head down, lots of coleslaw left, half of puffy white roll left, resembling puffy nose. Grasped in forefingers, puffy roll approaches puffy

nose, is engulfed in mouth-hole below it, jaw moving rapidly without pause, like soft piston, white piece of coleslaw stuck to lower lip. No rings on pudge fingers, no earrings on polyp ears, smooth skin, doublechin, no wrinkles elsewhere. Still lots of cold coleslaw. . . . Holds last olive up, on stick, examines it. Gulp. Drops piece of cole slaw in lap to unheard martial music, retrieves coleslaw, music surging as recaptured coleslaw's drawn to whirlpool mouth, sucked down, vanished. . . . Five minutes later: two toothpicks & three olive pits on white plate alone, other toothpick in mouth crevice. Pushes plate away as TV music rises to crescendo. Electric wall clock in coffee shop registers twenty to eight. Music stops dead. Nothing but huge silence as she pushes eye patch up on forehead, spreads newspaper on table, inspects it, picking teeth, wipes face all over with paper napkin, crumples it in coffee cup, lowers eye patch, gets up, struggles with coat, buttons, grapples handles of shopping bags, takes purse out of big handbag, takes out two dollar bills, lays them on pink slip which reads $1.80 in pencil, picks up all, waddles to cashier, pays, waddles out thru plate glass street doors, sucked out by draft on thick white rubber soles, disappears into our civilization, this solitary human being— I mourn for her and all the lost & lonely people of the world. . . . Table already cleared by waitress, wiped clean. Green plastic tabletop gleams, green plastic seat gleams. No sign, no trace. Empty booth, sixteen minutes of eight, February 1962. . . .

February 6

Seattle: Up at 6:45 to catch ferries for Victoria, B.C. Whisked thru Empress Hotel, great gaunt plush Victorian pile of masonry. *It*, not the city of Victoria, is the "provincial capital" of B.C. Prototype of such British piles all over world, including Hotel Gramatan, Bronxville, N.Y. Same scene exactly. Potted palms, dowagers among them (sample of overheard conversation: "South Africa? Oh, the Negroes are still savages! Same in the South. Their fathers were aborigines, . . ." etc., etc.) . . . Whisking thru lobby, I filch fancy crested Empress stationery. Go in Olde English Men's Room, and . . .

February 7

Woke to the cry of a gull far off over the harbor of Victoria. Fog, and the ferry loading— The street lamps on Government Street still on— Deep ship's whistle sounds somewhere— Then a buoy-bell. . . .

Later—the fog lifts—and a great gull comes sailing—alights on my window ledge, four flights up, turns around and regards me, not quite three feet away, thru the closed window. He's gray & white & enormous—about two feet from tail to bill—and the bill itself brown-yellow, with small red smear near end. Looks me in the eye without any fear—probably looking for a handout. In a moment he turns and is off again—glided away to a piling. . . . In spite of all his plebeian ways & visits in the high air, that bird no doubt has a British accent.

I find dandy big pub in backstreet Victoria, with all kinds of British-type Irish-type seamen cabdrivers old men with beards stumblebums beery stares-out-into-space. With sign dividing the place: Positively No Admittance to Ladies Beer Parlor. Fellow at next table is reading paper—aloud: "Ain't that the limit—they've found a way to keep you looking natural two years after you're dead— Guaranteed to keep you looking *natural* for two whole years." Fellow across the table, old German-inn type, says, "Dey have to freeze you to do dat." First fellow say—"Now who wants to visit anybody in an icehouse?" Continues after a while, staring into space—"They did it to Joe Stalin, didn't they? Kept him looking good for four or five years?" Other feller: "What dey do that for?" . . . Leather seats, stag's heads on the walls. . . .

Vancouver, B.C., February 8

Took bus & ferry from Victoria in the middle of the afternoon. . . . A bus driver that looked like Jean-Paul Sartre, with a wall-eye everywhere but on the road. Me in the back. No Exit.

Ferry thru dark Adirondack-type islands. . . . A blue sunset at landing. . . . Then bus again thru flat country, the blue sun flashed in puddles, ditches, just after rain, blueing water and windows, low flights of waterbirds over far poplars. . . .

Arrived at bus station downtown Vancouver in the damp dusk. . . .

Three or four days passed somewhere in here.

Is Vancouver the Dublin of Canada? Seem to be quite a few Gulley Jimsons, or Joyce Carys, around, as well as one or two homegrown Oscar Wildes, James Joyces, etc. . . . Next to San Francisco this is best most turned-on place on West Coast. Great mountains ringing port. . . . Smoked some pot with North Vancouver poets. . . . Was on TV. . . . Had 1500 at University of B.C. reading, all tuned in. . . .

So this is Canada—"whose heart is England and whose soul is Labrador."

—MALCOLM LOWRY

FRANCE—NORTH AFRICA

May-July 1963

Paris, May 30

After my student years in Paris on the G.I. Bill, 1947–51, I come back now, thirteen years later . . . and see myself back then, a stripling wandering poet, and remember Paris as it was after the war when I was hanging out at the Sorbonne and writing my doctoral thesis in the back of cafés. . . . Now I realize it was my *wanderjahr.* . . . I strode through the night streets, high on life, euphoric and pensive, and I was Apollinaire, I was Rimbaud, I was Joyce's Stephen Dedalus setting forth to forge "the uncreated conscience" of his race. So I wandered in that old Paris of thirteen years ago. . . .

Already I'm getting used to this new brighter, louder Paris, with new traffic lights and new cars flooding the old avenues. Still it is "eternal," the eternal city of light, always the city of youth, the old buildings still beautiful, the grand boulevards still grand, the backstreets of the Quartier Latin still full of mystery, and that special Paris light still so luminous. . . . Dark times gone . . . struck into light. *Et je suis voyeur toujours (et je vois).* . . . What happens when one calls up a mistress of thirteen years ago (not that I had one)? Would she find it easier to recognize the face or the voice? Do the eyes grow older?

Supper at Restaurant des Beaux Arts, Rue Bonaparte. Un vieux pensionnaire entre et s'assoit à côté de moi. Il tousse beaucoup. Après un grand silence, je dis: "C'est pas beaucoup changé ici depuis treize ans." Il me regarde, et dit, enfin:

"C'est vrai." . . . Pendant que je mange ma salade de fleurs vertes, des jeunes filles en fleur entrent, en riant. . . .[6]

It really is all an illusion. The city itself doesn't exist. It's a dream I once had. It's a dark place, lost in memory. . . . I've been walking the streets for two days, all those changed places, the map of Paris still stamped upon my brainpan. . . . Everybody's Paris exists in everybody's brain. On top of which a flood of cars has descended. Tranquillity is gone from this town. . . . And such a city of loneliness . . . does strange things to people. . . .

Juin 1

Bright sun . . . warm air . . . the statues must be turning in the Tuileries gardens . . . the leaves laughing. . . . Impossible that everyone in Paris could be as lonesome as I always am when I'm here! . . . Walked another day and night thru the circular streets . . . shades of Dr. Matthew O'Connor gone for good, not even the echo or smell or mood of *Nightwood* anywhere. . . . Watchman, what of the night!

Walked into the dark courtyard of 89 Rue de Vaugirard, where I had my two-room cave those years, saw the shuttered window of my room on the courtyard, felt the new front door. Not a sound anywhere, not a light in any of the flats, dark buildings all around. . . . Walked out thru the black cobblestoned yard, past the shuttered concierge's lodge. Out in the street, directly in front, is a huge plastic yellow sports car which I hadn't even seen upon entering. I persist in believing it wasn't there two minutes before though there's a black canvas hood fastened down all around the driver's plastic cockpit bubble & it's obvious it hasn't moved in a long time; a dream auto washed up, phantom chariot. . . . Even the Rue de Vaugirard itself I hardly recognize anymore; the buildings seeming much taller and more "businesslike," though it's obvious they are the same old buildings. Ghost feet of a hundred schoolchildren next door still sound like mice. As I hear the early morning cry of the walking window-repairer, with the tools of his trade on his back—*Vitrier! Vee-tree-eh!*

During the night it rained and very late at night or early in the morning, the people in the room next door came in and started having a party (just as the night before). The plumbing is so constructed that every noise of running water sounds as if it's in my basin, and every voice comes up thru the drain of my basin as thru a little speaker-tube on board ship so that in half-sleep I hear the laughing low voice of a woman who I am convinced is Egyptian, although I am also convinced I am in "Tunisie." Sometime around dawn, the shadow of Albert Camus drifted by. . . .

I lit a candle to my dead mother in the Church of St. Germain des Près. . . . I continue to walk the city, night and night, day and day. . . . Take the metro and a suburban bus out to Champigny-sur-Marne and walk along the riverbank past terraced villas & restaurants to the next town—Sunday afternoon *fêtes*—picnics in the grass, lovers fondling, boats & rowers on the calm river with islands full of lush trees, the sun lost in willows, tits go by, laughter in a bush, far cries of boys swimming & splashing. Back to town on another bus, thru the spring trees and cured poplars, Clignancourt, Nation, Voltaire . . . get off and look up at my old window five flights up where the continuous balcony is, 2 Place Voltaire, the names on the door changed. See myself on the balcony, with sheaf of copy paper, pale blue or green, now in cardboard carton attic San Francisco . . . thought I was the American Proust in love with Thomas Wolfe, fucking Europe's Great Woman. The owner of the apartment, Monsieur Edgar Letellier, a classical musician looking like Einstein, aged with buxom younger wife & two daughters, too young for me, barely out of childhood, not exactly *jeunes filles en fleur*. I walk on down Rue de la Roquette, same old whores . . . Café du Tambour, Place de la Bastille. . . . Sit for at least two hours on its terrace watching the fantastic faces, real *Enfants du Paradis* street scene, or out of another century. Humanity, Daumier Goya faces, a street fair going on to one side, widget cars, shooting booths, merry-go-round music, burlesque wrestlers on mats on sidewalk. . . . No one, not a face I've ever seen before. One needs other people, perhaps especially women, to construct one's own special illusion of life. . . .

Juin 5

La Coupole the only "scene" left in Paris. In the back enormous room of the Coupole, there they are, the painters from the forties in Paris, the old sculptors (Giacometti looking like Jean Cocteau), the young just come with *their* beards, the old with *their* beards, the beautiful young chicks from the Midwest, the writers who never made it, etc., etc. Sat till 2 a.m. watching the faces. . . . Flush me a caravan, my ears are pinned to the transom, socks wash themselves, and halves of people speak to each other, interchangeable backwaters of conversation flooding back and forth in the café booths, as existence chalks up another calligraph on its endless toilet paper roll. . . .

Left Paris by train for the Dordogne. So passed thru dull Limoges and made it to Périgueux by midnight. Found bad hotel, slept lightly, woke at 5 a.m., and then walked around the town in the first dawn, still quite dark; returned to hotel, and went to bed again, and now wait around for a train at noon, walking by the river in the town and buying cherries in the great market in all the main places—real country town marketplaces with all kinds of fowl alive in baskets, heads sticking out but lying still. . . . And rabbits still running, skinned, stretched out as in a last great jump, eyes fixed forward still, and the fur feet left on (for good luck!); and skinned geese on their back with their heads hanging down, bent over the edge of the table, upside down, as in real reflection of themselves still floating on a lake; and great fish of all kinds; and great medieval cheeses; and sheep's heads skinned, eyes still in place, six of them together on a plate or plank, skulls broken, red. The patrons of the stalls in Basque berets, red-faced, with thick brogues; and a great murmur of women, bargaining. . . . Elles achêtent la vie . . . c'est pourquoi elles discutent. . . .[7]

A cluck now and then reminding me of another bird, strange one that woke me in the dark dawn in hotel room with window open over rooftops—a trill ending in a series of rapid taps as if it were hitting lightly and sharply a glass piano key at the very high end of a crystal piano. . . .

Train to Bordeaux, then to Irún & San Sebastián, then on in the night to Madrid. Cross the border, see the Guardia Civil just as thirteen years ago. Dinner on train full of pudgy be-ringed Spanish businessmen with little moustaches, French rich bourgeois couples, German couples, all sitting avoiding each other's faces & eyes, glum, expressionless.

June 10—Madrid

Do the dead know what time it isn't? In Spain, they do not. . . . Arrived in Madrid 9 a.m., full sun, hot out on the boulevards, passed thru a great park where Don Quixote rode on his horse, in stone, lance in hand, followed by Sancho Panza on his mule, also in stone . . . wandered up side streets, found sidewalk café, sat drinking coffee & watching crowds go by. . . .

So thru all these countries, all the same, all the pouring people, lips eyes & teeth the same; the moon sails by in the daytime, everywhere the same, the people making ashtrays of their mouths, butts stuck in, little exhaust pipes exhausting them, the remote possibility of a mass turn-on (pot visions of true identity & love with others) becoming always more & more remote, especially in a place like Madrid with its Guardia Civil everywhere watching to make sure the populace

does NOT turn-on . . . thousands of stranded men sitting over *glâces* in the open-air cafes, empty eyes with hopeless hunger. . . .

At the Prado, the Bosch paintings with their people all sinking or burning or caught by weird machines or animals. . . . "El Bosco"—his world one huge Gothic Hell, a medieval inferno of people & creatures *doing things to each other* (So too William Burroughs "unlocked his word horde"). The world of the Bosco Kid: a woman being eaten by a blue insect with hairy beak as blackbirds fly out of her asshole . . . a hand like a fish skewered on a plate holding a dice on one finger. . . . Naked soldiers in World War II German helmets being threaded onto a long sword and an armored knight laid on a pallet being eaten by yellow & silver metallic wolves with long snouts like knives, and a couple of human legs as clappers in a bell, and annotated music written on a bare ass, the torso hidden in a lute with a harp over it upon which is stretched a spreadeagled boy or young woman, the harp-strings thru the crotch & thru the entire body, and a green pair of legs with feet like branches of a winter tree and with an ass made of a round mirror in which is reflected a head with eyes closed. . . . All this (and this only the beginning of one detail) in *El Jardín de las Delicias*. (One thing about Bosch's people I never understood: Why none of them have erections. . . .)

And Goya's Monstre Panic (huge man figure) in the skies, towering over fleeing people & wagons. . . . Fire!

Juin 11

Train south to Algeciras at dusk. . . .

June 12

Slept stretched out in the *coche* for several hours until two Guardia Civiles came in, ordering everybody around & throwing a valise on the seat on top of my feet. From then on the bastards kept me awake with their various imbecile activities. . . . Goya's *Disasters of War* go on, everywhere, and there are no countries except the second-class coach & the wagons-lits. . . . And Hieronymus Bosch & Breughel, Hitler & Franco, and you have the whole Creation, boiling. And it all ends up in the Naked Lunch. . . .

Tangier, Juin 12

The cities are all the same, everywhere, on their hillsides, by their seas, by rivers, by mountains, by bottomless skies, all waiting, with pigeons & caravanserais. And where do they go, with us, where do they take us (those celestial taxis, rollercoaster places under the horizon, over the rooftops)? They take us nowhere, no time. . . . And, as Camus believed to the end, there is no sentient creator or creature au ciel, *qui s'intéresse à nous*. . . . It's obvious.

Tangier—fantastic world, strange city. . . . Overheard conversational mummeries in six languages, the kif-pipe everywhere, veiled women making eyes & cruising, the medina & casbah, the skin of sun, the vaccine of dreaming, came to the edge clear and bright, several scenes I passed thru (the celluloid streaming) which I can't at all remember. . . .

June 16

Marrakesh, strange muttering Arab civilization, horses that never went to the dentist, cream feet of tartar in the foothills on the brown dust plain, flea flaminia, procop of carnivores, gleam in the mind hut, mishmash hashish moan on radio, Casa static, over towers with gallows where the muezzins called, and fast birds flitter as down comes sun, clapt in the clear flat sky, with mountains in it, over the plain, thru mud huts & muezzins, hotter & hotter, rapt people wrapt in cloth turbans, sandals under, slip the eardrum, slip the scrotum, balls out of bag, kif in bulls' balls' sac, sun beats down & down, swelter the Kopek Moroccan Himalaya, boom boom, sun beats its skin drum, true drums too, in the great Place, crowds around the squatting drummers, mummers, horse-drawn carriages, women in them, suckling babies, babies into Berbers in turbans on Le Grand Balcon-Terrasse Panoramique by the CMT Hotel, one old Berber with silver-headed cane, embossed fantastically, like his face; more carriages, bicycles, farm trucks, country buses with baskets & rugs on top, spavin horses, few dogs, little burros bearing great men & panniers, sad creatures, most men in their robes of all stripes & colors, like monks' gowns, with white or brown turbans, dark red fezzes, tassels of truth, hardly any women in sight, and those veiled, noonday now, drums beating still, faint kif smell on air, drums faster, on & on, clip-clop horses, over & over, booths all open under sheets & tin awnings, drums faster & faster, crowd bigger & bigger, as I watch from the rooftop, all kinds of fantastic acts going on—men making monkeys & lizards perform, beating drums to draw the crowd, shouting, others making great hairy speeches, striding back & forth or squatting or sitting on ground, one with three-foot lizard he keeps letting run into the crowd before pulling him back on long cord, as one white mummy body wrapped completely in white is carried thru Djemaa El Fna Square by two men holding wooden rack with body above heads as they calmly pass thru, no one noticing, and the acts go on all over the huge L-shaped Place, preachers in white robes with big open Arabic books in hand, exhorting, haranguing. And four Gnawa dancers (Arab-Muslim, black tribe) in white pantaloons & white headbands with black metal dumbbell cymbals in each hand dancing & gyrating & squatting & bouncing up & down & whirling & whirling to drum beaten with big curved sticks, faster & faster, whirling in circle of four, close up, then each backing off, upright, moving only feet & hands to rhythm, on and on, whole troupe in white, except for one little cat with yellow overshirt, two drums

fakir.....

beating separate rhythms, as little black-yellow cat squats & bounces & whirls & whirls. . . . And now tall white cat taking over, tumbling & turning & stamping with his feet & beating his dumbbell cymbals. . . . Fakirs' reeds sounding & kif smell again, white Gnawa dancer whirling his tassel by swirling his head as he dances, sun coming down, shadows over hills far off all around the town (impossible to describe whole scene, hopeless to catch more than an inkling of it without tape recorders & Goya eyes—hopeless to catch it, hopeless, hopeless!). Like an enormous jam session that no one is aware of, separate groups going together unaware, wailing separately down there, but together when seen from above. . . . Group of six with gray robes & skullcaps turning slowly in a closed circle, clapping solemnly & then playing violins & blowing on reeds, as Gnawas pick up beat again, two drummers with sticks beating more & more insistently. . . . A fantastic bell man in lurid red hat covered with hanging brass bells & cups, selling water. He carries a big skin full of water slung around his body—the skin of a whole animal hollowed out—maybe a sheep or a goat—full of water, which he sells in shining brass cups. . . . Now dusk coming, long shadows on the roofs, cry of some lone chanter the only sound. . . . Tumblers & clowns in scarlet pantaloons, a bicycle stunt rider, two turned-on bearded & turbaned cats screaming & singing at each other, kif-pipes (*sebsis*) for sale, etc., etc. . . . Night now & the night scene different, with yellow flickering lights on carriages and the big minaret illuminated above all. Autos & thousands of people still filling the square, the booths & cafés still open under bare yellow bulbs. . . . Took a *coche* for an hour's drive in the night city, and found a strange Alas had come to pass. We ride on four rubber-tired wooden wheels silently over the cobbles, the driver in his turban with tall whip calling to the horse something that sounds like "Keen, keen!" for turn left, and *"Hélas, hélas!"* for right turn, thru the casbah streets, thru the old arches, broken walls, all sealed away, no other paradise, dreamt battlements, residences of earth, all stowed away, world in a honeycomb folded into clay houses, as we go keening on, clip-clop, stoned into darkness, and the *coche*-man calling out with his tall whip, "Alas! Alas!" On thru the only paradise, cloth figures falling past, rags of figures sleeping curled on curbstones, pointing at them with my whip crying Alas! Alas!

Back in the Place again, wandered among the dark booths. The watermelon seller cuts up the melon with a Kriss, holding it in his crotch & cutting in with the long knife as if he were cutting himself open; so that I see in the darkness the so red soft watermelon guts of him. . . .

Later, on midnight rooftop, night figures with lamps, still preaching and drumming. . . .

Next morning—came out on the café terrace—9 a.m.— Same scene all over again— All resumes— All goes on. . . . A fantastic clairvoyance is what is needed— to clarify existence— So hot in the sun, in the Place, that it's empty by noon— maybe 120° F. . . .

People have become nothing but solid black shadows shimmering against white walls. In the evening the drums begin again, the Gnawa dancers start again & dominate the scene again, six of them and two boys all in white. And now there is also a snake-charmer with a cobra raised up—a long black slick body, half a foot thick. . . .

And a group of gypsy-looking mummers putting on a kind of crude commedia dell'arte, with a big crowd gathered round on the ground, one wearing a horse-head, another riding him, another man playing a woman's part, with a veil, and a kind of clown-ruffian in pantaloons. . . . All this and all everything in this flat of hot earth beside the Grand Atlas mountains, instigated by the Animator, he who Animates all, the same Animator who brought me here in this dark night, for some obscure reason, just as if he were interested in us personally. To what end? The Animator Animates, and that is all. And after a time, he Animates us no longer. . . .

There is something horrible about places like this and Cuzco— Suppose one could, suddenly, never *leave*? What a strange & stupid, dirty end to all. . . .

Tunis/Carthage, Juin 19

Went to Carthage ruins. And, upon leaving, came upon a very black small beetle very quietly & steadily making its way alive around the ruins, like some small hardblack Ghost of Hieronymus Bosch dans son *Jardín de las Delicias*. . . . And on the broken stage of the Théâtre Romain, a man and his woman making love, very passionately. In the dust, in the dusk, which continued to be eternal.

Juin 21

Left Tunis by air, there being no bateaux for a week. I wanted to see Sicily, but no transportation for several days except to Rome. So Sicily will remain, along with *les îles grecques*, among those last wild places one might still go & live. There's always a farther place, one stage farther away from everything, one farther port still untouched or underpopulated, etc. . . .

So I find myself in Rome on a hot night in June 1963.

June 22

Rome—nothing, Firenze—nothing, Pisa—nothing (all because of some nut who constructed a tower on soft ground), Rapallo—nothing (Ezra never made a dent in it)—all caught up in the Great Tourist Disease—the imbecile plague of the epoch (*voir les Guides Michelin pour ces conneries touristiques*). Finally—Genova, on a sunny Sunday morning—in an old square wedged in next to the docks on the edge of the port—three or four young types making music—two accordions, one sax and clarinet, and a singer—at a table in the little café garden—drinking and singing. In the South they are sunnier—here the accordion music catches the strange sadness of Genovese faces. One at the table, happy drunk, raises an upturned straw-wrapped bottle to his lips just as the clarinet lets out a loud clear high blast, very sweet—creating the illusion of the blast coming out of the end of the bottle . . . little pockets of life, made of illusions . . . moments caught out of darkness, in a curious Italian journey in which I spoke to no one, the phenomena of existence continually passing.

Juin 23

Rentré en France & bien heureux de la revoir . . .

I find St.-Tropez at midnight so full of tourists I cannot find even a bed— At last, about 2 a.m., I fall into an alley where there's a hotel by the name of Au Bout du Monde, find a room on the top floor, after making a tour of the waterfront cafés & hotels where a fantastic Dolce Vita seems to be in progress—the whole little port rocking with all the elegant hipsters & svelte beatniks of Germany, Scandinavia,

France, etc.— All night long in the hotel, doors opening & closing, feet pattering, English chicks into bed with trilingual Latins & Huns, radios & beat guitars over the rooftops, laughter under the eaves muffled, someone being screwed in the shower, cats meowing like jeunes filles being deflowered in the first dawn. . . .

So happen upon Albert Cossery[8] on the terrace of the first café I come to in the morning, in search of him—there he is, just as I suspected I would find him, without telegram or rendezvous. We go to beautiful wild plage at the other end of island & spend day sunbathing & swimming with several French couples, friends of his, all young (he's forty-five or so, but looks like a young Jean Gabin)—all à poil—except for one bitchy American *Vogue* model who refuses to take off her clothes "in the presence of men she doesn't know"—or rather, says she doesn't like to see "men she doesn't know" without their clothes. All the French chicks and their men consider her a pain in the ass— She goes off & sunbathes by herself somewhere—bien habillée—and finally returns, since the men & women have by then all put on their trunks (not for her, but because of police helicopter & some teenage boys who keep hanging around & spying from nearby cliffs). Cossery tells her that she can now disrobe like the other women, since the men are proper, and that he has made the other women very unhappy by putting on *his* trunks, but she still won't disrobe, and the women really get sarcastic when her back is turned, all of them lying there with no tops on, etc. . . . I leave Cossery there, in bright sun on a hill above the beach & return to town—to St.-Tropez & St. Raphäel & train to Marseille in the night.

Marseille, Juin 24

Comme Cossery m'a dit, *il y a un esprit qui reste—en France. Tout est changé*—but there's something essential that remains—it seemed evident in the somewhat brilliant, sometimes satiric, sometimes caustic, always sophisticated & somewhat jaded repartee of all those French on the beach, with Cossery's own libertine wit spurring all on—while the *Vogue* model lay there silent (even though she spoke French very well—with nothing to say). . . .

I arrive at Toulouse, ville morne, after riding all night in a couchette from Marseille. When I entered the compartment on the train, there was a body in the opposite bunk, wrapped in a blanket, bald head out, jaw a little open, like a cadaver. Next morning, it's alive, dressed, smiling and saying Bonjour, monsieur—a commercial traveler of some sort, the great Animator having activated him for another day of "life," he falls out into Toulouse, dead city. . . . One sees where Lautrec got his name & the black shadows in his paintings—each walker in this drear place a shadow of himself. . . .

Rodez, June 25

If "God" still exists it's here in the great brown cathedral of Rodez with its huge mass of Gothic glowering, its huge high square tower, its huge high dark interior at sunset, with the late brilliant light flooding through its high round rosé, the great Gothic vaults soaring inside, like any other old cathedral, yet with a gray presence in the high air, as if some Animator were actually still there—a medieval God it is, still existing, in the wrong century, cornered & refuged here, in all its illiterate, dark, tongue-tied peasant being. As if this huge dark fort of a cathedral were in reality a stone madhouse prison zoo of Dark Ages animals, lizards, reptiles, gargoyle primeval hounds & hyenas penned up here forever, still all screaming to burst out. . . . And those gargoyles outside. . . . roaring lions and ravens, like crying women extended from "windows"—flesh birds on them perched forever, very high up, and one great scream/roar heard from all these "blind maws," medieval animals half-sprung out of high cages, croaking beast-women torsos sprung half-escaped from dungeon battlements in air, night zoo of Dark Ages trying to escape its eternal night, those speaking gargoyles, articulated primeval, blasted out of the Stone Dark, mute mocked-up humanity bleeding gray. . . .

Just because some madman named Antonin Artaud once wrote some incomprehensible letters from here, I have to come & stop for the night. . . .

There's an eternal street fair going on in a great empty space at the bottom of the main boulevard, all the town out in the first dark of evening, wandering about among the lighted booths & barkers with their shooting galleries & spinning wheels of chance:

À Tous les Coups On Gagne
[A Winner Every Time]

And

Attraction
Réservée aux Enfants

Sign over a kids' merry-go-round with little cars going around with children in them reaching for the big rag doll on a string the man in the booth keeps dangling on a rope over their heads.

LE POMPON ARRACHÉ

donne

un tour gratuit[9]

as they go around, reaching & screaming for it, as the merry-go-round turns its valse triste of organ-grinder music in the night. While now, into the crowd in the center of the *place*, humps a hunchback, very well dressed, having jumped down from behind a barricade between two wagons in the dark at one side, and now hunching along in the crowd, surveying it with a proprietary air, which gives me the idea that He is the manager, owner and/or Animator of the whole show (so detached and dignified he is, as he hunches along, swinging this way and that)—le Patron of life itself directing all and calculating as he goes, having earlier planned out and planted the whole show, staking out the Fair Grounds like a great Trap & Lure, himself escaped from some gargoyle tower—*bossu* of the world, turning the whole show in his head like an organ-grinder turning a manivelle, a hump figure of Death himself, waiting & watching. For: "À Tous les Coups On Gagne."

June 26
Voyeuristic Tableau Flashed By
The Tour de France bicycle riders in the rain, pedaling thru twenty miles of immense military cemeteries . . . followed by hordes of cars with windshield wipers, which beat out interminably the "time" of sadness . . . while some monsieur in beret mounted & descended & remounted my hotel stairs, his feet making piano tunes on the keys of the steps, the sad valse of his illusions turning in his head. . . .

And returned to Paris again, this time its image in my head already that of three weeks ago, rather than thirteen years ago, as with someone one hasn't seen in years and yet in a few minutes you think his present face looks just as it did those years ago, the old face vanished into the new. . . .

July 2

Reading Krishnamurti with a hard-on in a room full of red spiders with black legs which turn out to be black iron chairs with woven plastic backs & bottoms & black iron legs. . . .

It's the auditorium of the American Centre in Montparnasse and a poetry reading is in progress. Our own. Ghost chairs clap.

July 3 & 4

Fantastic last two days in Paris, beginning with poetry reading at American Centre in Montparnasse—Harold Norse & I introduced by Jean-Jacques Lebel; Lebel & I come on wearing gas masks—it's a Gas—big crowd—and then afterward at Alain Jouffroy's everybody high on grass and dancing around, Harold Norse in a bolero hat making like a bullfighter prancing around with a shawl for a cape, and I pull off his hat from behind, intending to skim it across the room, but his unknown wig comes off with it, showing unknown bald head, and he immediately jamming hat & toupee back on head while Lebel and others collapse laughing & crying & Norse continues dancing, subdued—and I have a flash picture of Dr. Matthew O'Connor in *Nightwood* bedroom wigged & rouged, Norse an echo of the old queen; epiphanous. . . .

Then later we all float down long narrow stairs from Jouffroy rooftop rooms, two or three a.m., kissing everybody on the dark stairs, nearest chick from Atlanta falling into English playwright's arms on way down, and then ten jammed into a small car, everyone on top of everyone else, lips glued together on long crosstown ride to who knows where, I dreamt it all, me solitary, digging it all, a shadow collé against the car seat, dawn coming up in the Rue St.-André-des-Arts where I find myself marching into light, forever.

July 4

So left Paris in late afternoon sun, TWA jetbird rising up so swiftly in the clear, brilliant air over the city, turning in the clear blue sky over it, Paris stretched shining below—turning away now, all gone.

Hard to, impossible to "describe my feelings" now. Strange what happened down there. Heart full, eyes too, looking down & back, all gone again. For . . . dark is a way & light is a place . . . where am I . . . snatched away. . . .

The plane purrs & glides, out from France. . . . I wake up eight hours later, we are over some strange wasteland, ocean behind already, great puddles in a black mammoth swamp or plain and the figures of friends at Orly Airport have suffered a curious diminution, shrunk all at once into a far perspective, figures lost at the far end of a telescope, someone having turned the telescope around as I slept, faces close-up, touching, now gone away, taken away, shot still, forever.

LONDON
1963

Visit to Wm. Burroughs working on his & Allen's *Yage Letters* for City Lights to publish.

The tulips are in bloom in all the public gardens—I sit outside in Russell Square and have tea among the pigeons who alight on the round yellow tables. . . . They'll be drinking the tea next. . . . I have been in the British Museum and seen the Famous Books under Glass—Keats, Shelley, Byron, Swinburne. . . .

I go to see Wm. Burroughs underground. He too under glass. Two floors down, in a subbasement with no windows and a French door leading into a concrete triangular area like an air shaft. He says it's convenient for his cat who craps there. In the little room there is only a couch, a small table, a portable typewriter, no books in sight. The cat is there. There is an alcove. He serves me some tea out of it.

He receives me like T. S. Eliot. He is alive. He comes up the winding basement steps and lets me in, saying he doesn't hear much "down here." (I'd had to knock many times.) He's perfectly dressed, with a British accent. . . .

I look around & ask him what he does down there "all the time." He looks at me straight & says, "Just work." "It's cheap," he says, and explains to me his money difficulties and adds that he's soon going to Tangier via Paris, where he has to pick up some money. He doesn't say "bread" for money, or any of that jazz. Talking about people in Tangier, he says so-and-so are always Bad News wherever you run into them—always getting "arrested." He doesn't say "busted," etc. . . . When he replied, "Just work," I forgot to say, "Why?" I'll have to remember to ask him that

next time. If such a time exists. . . . He gets up and closes door to concrete outside area & lights a joss-stick of some kind of cheap incense & sticks the end of it in the tapestry or wallpaper, saying, "The cat crap gets to smelling out there." We agree to publish a book. I talk to him about anything that comes into my head, which isn't much. I tell him I never really dug his writing until *The Soft Machine*. . . . He agrees to come to a party. . . . I leave. It's dusk outside in Lancaster Terrace. There are lilacs in bloom in the great park. Burroughs is underground.

TIJUANA—LA PAZ

January 4-7, 1964

South from Tijuana by plane. . . . Hopeless landscape, dreamed in a wind-tunnel, slag mountains, desert wastelands, endless barren coasts, windswept & rockbound, not a tree, not a lake . . . no water visible anywhere on the peninsula . . . a thousand miles of it, south to the Tropic of Cancer . . . lost horizons bound by two seas . . . nothing . . . lost world nobody has any use for . . . cast-up end of creation . . . La Paz ("Peace") at the end of it: palm trees, a long *malecón*, beach hotels, 30,000 lost undersouls . . . with nowhere to go but back. . . . Some things are just too sad, too tragic to write about . . . sold age . . . dead lives . . . death by puking. . . . Mother fallen apart. . . . Mariachi music on a radio thru the hotel window at night, across a courtyard. . . . Then silence . . . then laughter, then voices . . . and silence again . . . and music again . . . an accordion waltzing . . . sad voice, singing, above it. . . . Vague sense of having been here before, along the *malecón*, under the palms . . . lonely in a courtyard hotel. . . . Life so very sad when it comes in a window across a court at night . . . like desire itself . . . the whiney trumpets and screechy violins and wailing voice singing . . . clash thru the jungle underbrush with a small moan. . . . Ah. . . . Life as she is breathed. . . . Trópico de Cancer. . . . Two months of rain a year . . . seven women to one man population. . . . The sea, stone mountains & cactus. . . . Life goes on for the taxidriver who has been here thirty years. . . . He takes us to a deserted beach, and leaves.

LOS ANGELES—FRESNO

January 1964

C January 8
ame upon Los Angeles by bus at night. . . . Ah the crazy hotels, crazy
streets, sad signs of America—Jesus Saves!—Tom's Tattoo—"The Electric
Rembrandt"—Snooker Parlor—"Acres of Autos"—Hotel Small—Ice Rink—
Greyhound—Los Angeles Street—TV in Rooms—EAT—Barber & Beauty
Supply—PAWNSHOP—"Shave Yourself"—

Might as well be on the Trans-Siberian Railway. . . .

Strange people . . . waiting in Greyhound Bus Depot: One all-leather cat with
cowboy hat—tight motorcycle pants with zippers on slash pockets and little pad-
locks on each zipper—same on tight jacket—all black leather—& leather gloves
stuck in shoulder strap—more locks dangling here and there on extra zipper pockets— Animated, talking to a Negro also in cycle suit only much less flashy. . . .

And lonely the hotel doors, gaping. And lonely the lobbies, lonely the beds!
Forever & ever. . . . Lonely the lunchrooms, lonely the cars running in the streets!
Lonely Los Angeles, lonely world! . . .

Sure are a lot of defeated people in this here America. . . . Across from me in
waiting room, an old lady, skinny, orange hat, white hair, knit skirt, keeps twitching all over, tries to lie down on seat (wooden arms on seat prevent it), squirms
continually, face & neck full of tics, keeps rearranging and retucking towel around
her legs & lap & closing eyes & then twitching some more & getting up & sitting
down again & trying to lie down again, finally falls asleep sitting up, head on paper
bag on top of suitcase, head almost *in* paper bag. In same row, a Chinese or Filipino-

Chinese continually gesturing & laughing to himself. . . . Next to me a Mexican in U.S. Army clothes without insignia, reading *Reader's Digest* in Spanish, young hard face, good-looking, going somewhere, waiting, not defeated, only just started. Farther down the row, a Negro in jazz felt hat, no brim, check jacket, moustache, head bowed, asleep . . . where off to, bright stud?

Intelligent old Negro faces in midnight lunchroom, two blocks from Greyhound, *watching everything* . . . watching the rotary stirrer turn in the orange-juice dispenser . . . watching the Nickelodeon lights on the counter. . . . The Coca-Cola clock says ten to twelve. . . . Songs on the Nickelodeon: "Grass Is Greener," "Sweet Impossible You," "Don't Wait Too Long," "Heart of Ice," "Limehouse Blues," "When You're Young & In Love," "Busted," "I Gave My Wedding Dress Away." . . .

A man comes in with a new magazine. On the cover a picture of General MacArthur—"An Old Soldier Looks Back." The Negro faces across the counter are watching the white face read what the General looks back at. . . . I am waiting for midnight. . . . A little man in rimless glasses says, "Hello, bud— Say, gimme a . . . cheeze sandwich on white." He's reading next day's paper. There's a strike at Santa Anita racetrack. It's not the horses. The headline says "Santa Anita May Close Forever!" A black man in a blue baseball cap comes in on the stroke of midnight, and the old white waitress says to him: "Hello, Robert." Somewhere the horses are still running. . . . There is no stroke at midnight. It just "goes past."

As it does, "Hold the cheese sandwich!" shouts the skinny woman with the little man. "I got it," shouts the black cook in back. The little man & the skinny dame rush out into the night of America. . . .

I go to midnight burlesque show—the Morosco— Original standup comedian in baggy pants & strippers bumping & grinding to staccato drum rolls—in pink spotlight which also catches face of drummer in orchestra pit just below stripper on apron of stage—he looking up at her to synchronize his drumbeats with the movement of her pelvis, boom boom, bump bump, now jerking spasmodically, her face detached from the whole scene, having nothing to do with her body, trying to get as far away from it as possible, trying to keep her face as far as possible from the audience, at the same time trying to get her legs & pelvis as close to the front row boys as possible, shooting it at them with a boom-boom, and the drummer staring up into it in the circle of spotlight, looking like Gauguin in a jungle landscape, moustache twitching, the whole works against a painted backdrop of huge palm leaves and tree trunks twined . . . all as in Henri Rousseau's landscape in which "tiny human beings move in terrible isolation across the scene. . . ." The strippers, one after another, moving thru the jungle haze of the smoky spotlights, thru Rousseau's Aztec landscape where "little creatures wander, lost and anonymous" . . . "the only surviving creatures semilegendary dream figures, animals, and aboriginals" . . . (Shattuck on Rousseau in *The Banquet Years*). While all the while Gauguin looks on from the pit. . . . The Girl with the 56-Inch Bust grinds her final bump into the curtain, her lost face finally hidden in it as in a huge brown bedsheet. I am alone in the balcony with the spotlight projectionist. Smoke rises from the seats below as in an Inferno. The houselights come on. The stage is empty, the curtain fallen over the jungle backdrop. Gauguin looks up at me thru the houselights.

Next day set out north by Greyhound, to see what happened to the San Joaquin Valley, land I dreamed in Saroyan. Where gone, now, among the powerlines & freeways, the country still there, after all. . . . The great Angeles National Forest, for miles & miles & miles. Then the plains . . . cotton fields with oil pumps in them . . . fruit trees . . . huge trucks full of oranges bowling along the highway to L.A. . . . U.S. 99 North, to Bakersfield. . . . Great plains, more fruit trees, fields of vines; and then a field of abandoned cars, like Rousseau's Sofa in a Virgin Forest. . . . Dream trees in the distance, in morning mist, furrowed fields ten miles long, straight freeway through it. We zoom by . . . palms & eucalyptus, pepper trees by a river . . . a canal full of flat water and clouds . . . tumbleweeds in a fenced-in range. . . . Far horizon hung on heavy-headed trees . . . flat world here in morning light, great land. . . .

Coming toward Fresno—hay baled up, Holstein cows, boxcars going by on the rails, a livestock auction. . . . Tulare—yellow schoolbus, full—Trailer Park—Moto Rest—Chamber of Commerce—Truck Route ⟶ Bowling—Doherty's "Since Repeal"—First Assembly of God Welcomes You—Turkey Growers Co-op of Central California—Kingsville—a yard full of used toilets—a field full of rusty farm machinery—a field full of used dirty white refrigerators—a filling station backlot full of yellow trailers—a freight train at least a mile long; Fresno and Sunset by five p.m. & a perfectly round red sun falls into a tree and sets on a Last Armenian. . . .

NERJA JOURNALS

February–May 1965

WLisbon, February 17

hy can't the world be free of tyrants, why can't all live free? Everywhere the people walk around with serious closed faces instead of laughing like Zen fools; all suspicious, afraid of strangers and of each other, guards of themselves, their own Guardia Civil. . . .

February 21

The family's settled—Kirby and I, Julie (just turned four), and Lorenzo (age two)—in a tiny house in Nerja, an hour and a half east of Málaga, over a wild beach . . . white walls, tile floor, dirt street full of big rocks and broken cobbles, on cliffs over the beach. . . . Saw a dead brown huge dog in a deep gorge under a manzanita tree, so large I thought it was a deer . . . then a dead black cat down a drain . . . and a huge Sancho Panza burro let out a great bellow of a roar from a wooded bluff high above and then came out along the high path, bellowing and looking down at us, very intelligent with his enormous ears. . . .

February 22

I came here looking for City Lights books to publish and to really learn Spanish, and I'm reading Orwell's *Homage to Catalonia*, about the political alignment of the Communist Party in the Spanish Civil War, to the Right of such parties as the

Anarchists, the Communists' position much closer to the Fascists than to the humanitarian and libertarian Left. I am struck with the similarity to the position of the Cuban Communist Party at the time of the Cuban Revolution 1959 or earlier when the Communists were much to the Right of the Revolutionary Party (25 of July Movement) of Fidel Castro, whose *barbudos* were true revolutionaries in the sense that the working-class militiamen in Barcelona were in the early days of the Spanish Civil War. As in the Cuban Revolution, the Communist Party was actually a *reactionary* force working to prevent actual revolution and in favor of working thru existing capitalist structures. . . . As one who was in the Boy Scouts in the thirties, I am going only by Orwell's account. . . .

What is more striking is the curious juggling of political labels which, in the USA today at least, are completely reversed in their alignment, so that all parties of the Left, civil libertarian, liberal socialist, anarchist or otherwise, are stupidly classed with the Communists in the public mind, as specifically promoted and proclaimed by the Committee on Un-American Activities and the FBI, whereas in fact such still extant philosophies as the anarchist and the civil libertarian are still diametrically opposed to the Communist dogma, etc. . . . from all of which it is too obvious that the FBI has very conveniently thrown the old Red Flag over all the Leftists in order to discredit all but its own Rightist, Fascist position. What is curious in relation to this is the point of intersection in the position of the American Goldwater Right and the American Libertarian Left: *both* want less State Control, less super-state and more "individual freedom." The difference however is that the Right wants *economic* freedom from the State while the Left is most concerned with *intellectual* freedom or freedom of thought. The Right is not afraid of thought control but wants no economic control; the Left wants no thought control but is generally sympathetic to some form of planned economic control by the State, but coupled with the fullest possible free thought. . . .

February 26

Couldn't have gotten off to a dimmer start in Spain. Cold, dismal weather, wind and rain. Tiny cold stone house. And the dirt street being torn up, pneumatic drill going all day every day, plus dynamiting to blast the rock for sewage drain being laid down middle of street, terrific racket all day. And too cold and windy to do anything but huddle in house over smoky fire of madera wood & charcoal. . . . This goes on for all of first week, finally a little warmth on the weekend. . . . One of those days we spent the sunny midday in the adjoining town of Maro (maybe two hundred inhabitants): a dozen dirt streets, two bars, no restaurants, no houses for rent—all white houses, one or two stories—tile roofs, friendly small-town peasants— Then I walked back to Nerja—three or four miles— Tried a short cut thru steep hills irrigated by a high aqueduct. Had to go back, since the aqueduct was so constructed that man or animal could not cross it without being an acrobat. Came into Nerja on the highway, passed the Casa Cuartel of the Guardia Civil. The Guard out front did not return my greeting. (In Orwell's *Homage to Catalonia*, he noted that the Civil Guard was generally distrusted by the working class and peasants, the Guard traditionally having "guarded" the interests of the landowners and government, etc.) This week I have not heard a single greeting passed between a local citizen and a Civil Guard, in Nerja. . . . Perhaps this is just a local phenomenon. . . . On the front of the Guardia Civil Headquarters is the motto (or the admonition): *Todo por la Patria*. Franco rules.

February 28

When the house shutters are closed at night and fishermen pass in their very heavy boots their voices resound between the heavy stone walls of the narrow street, deep, rapid voices sounding like small round boulders being rapidly knocked together or big hollow marbles bouncing against each other. . . . We sit & grumble at one another, mostly miserable, waiting for the sun which will no doubt arrive in a glory one of these weeks. In the meantime, our dirt street is a muddy streambed. Calle Carabeo, 72— Mud is king this season. . . .

March 1

The rain in Spain continues. This is no "Homage to Andalucía." The drilling in the street outside continues, steadily, day after day, six days a week. They've been at it some three months & have advanced perhaps a hundred feet, half the length of the street. Some ten men and one puny pneumatic drill, daily boring long thin holes in the very hard volcanic igneous rock, then inserting six-inch-long cylinders of dynamite, placing a heavy wire screen over the excavation, piling big rocks on the screen, then blowing a kind of goat whistle telling everybody to take cover, then letting go with three or four blasts which send rock & dirt flying over the rooftops.

March 2

Today in the Correo I noticed the Postmaster (absentmindedly?) put a stamp on an envelope upside down & cancel it. All the stamps have Franco on them. I had been wondering if my letters would reach their destination if I did the same. . . . I have yet to hear His name mentioned. At least in the streets of Spain there is a conspiracy of silence. . . . Though every day the lead story in *Sur* (Málaga paper) is about El Caudillo in public ceremony with some prince, king or cardinal. It would seem he is preparing Spain for some *monarchist* rule after his own departure. . . . He is already about as remote and elevated from the people of Nerja as any monarch is likely to get.

March 3

Do they smoke pot here, chew peyote or anything? Doesn't look like it, even though it's but a day's journey from Tangier. The fishermen & farmers chew sugarcane. What else do they do for kicks? Certainly not go to church. On Sunday the men stand outside in the plaza, while the women go. Last night, during a great rainstorm, the lights went out in the whole town, and in the dark bars along the Carretera Principal the men were jammed by candlelight, drinking and clowning & talking in their fast guttural voices. One little fellow about sixty was imitating animals. Their tight, shrunken berets make them look almost like French peasants, except they're rougher-looking, they're louder and more boisterous when drinking, given to sudden shouts and bursts of humming or angry imprecations . . . and probably kinder and more attentive to children and dogs than any other race. Town full of stray, friendly mutts of every description. Same for the children, urchins of all sizes in ragged smocks or pants, with sharp eyes, quick smiles & smirks. . . . Men with Goya faces, especially in the night streets and dim-lit bars. Toledo and its El Greco fade into the Spanish landscape behind these Goya faces, leaving the impression of El Greco as one who painted specially chosen cardinals, *dueñas*, *doñas*, and kings and inhabitants of a certain Toledo madhouse but did not touch the "low" people the way Goya did. The "robe" (of one sort or another) seems always present in El Greco; in Goya, one is not conscious of any dress but only of the eternal face and the wracked or racked body.

March 4

There are bright blue flowers all along the way to the beach, on the high cliffs. How "far away and long ago" seems today the American Hygienic Male commuting to Palo Alto or Marin, narrow snap brim felt hat perfectly unsuited to the quirky climate, much like the climate here, given to sudden winds, sudden & brief rains, sudden sunshine, a climate perfectly suited to the beret. But, no, the *norteam-ericano* has to stick to his silly little monkey hat, in the windy canyons of the San Francisco financial district. His pants grow tighter and tighter too, perhaps for fear he will lose them in that tight district. (When money is tight, pants should grow looser. . . .) But the climate here in Andalucía, at least in this season, is even more erratic, more volatile, more temperamental than Northern California with its strange winds & fogs pouring through the Golden Gate. Here the weather's temperament is a furious thing, so fiercely changeable that a perfectly calm blue sea & sky changes into a roaring storm in an hour, then changes back again to calm sunny aquamarine, then storm again, all in the course of an hour or two—as it did on our recent trip to Maro where, walking in green fields of sunshine & mesquite, we'd suddenly find ourselves in a windy downpour as on a Scottish Shakespearian heath. . . .

The Spanish or Andalusian character certainly set by the weather it grows in . . . where the sun shines all is beautiful, to an extreme; where the sun is not, all is dark and cold, windy and tragic, the streets run with mud, the poor folk huddle over their tiny panniers of charcoal. In Nerja, these little braziers, pans about a foot & a half wide, are the only source of light & heat in the fishermen's & *traba-jadores'* white stone houses. They cook over them, carrying the pan out into the street to catch the winter wind (which sweeps from the sea and up the stone alleys—*viento malo*, blowing from the south, out of Africa), then when it's glowing, bringing it back under the kitchen table where all sit over it. . . . But when the sun shines, even for a minute, the air is so clear that there's an immediate summer warmth in the direct rays, though ten feet away in the shadow of a wall, it's still icy cold.

Early this morning, in bright sun, passing some skid-row types squatted against a stone wall, I caught the unmistakable smell of some rough kind of kif in the air, for the first time here. . . .

March 5

Storm at sea, huge waves pounding the stone boulders below our house, and the fishermen hauling up their wooden open boat, out of the clutches of the enormous mad ocean with guttural cries in the night. . . .

How close the savage sea of Aeneas is here with the same kind of boats, the same voices, the same nets & rocks. . . . Remnants of the Natural still remain in the world. The source is still here. I expect any crepuscule to find a Golden Bough thrust from the Sea. . . .

The fishermen row out their nets at night in open boats, laying one huge net down in a great semicircle, and the net is next morning hauled in from opposite ends of the beach, a line of men and boys pulling the rope at each end of the net & coiling it at the uppermost point of the beach and moving gradually toward the center of the beach, so that the two parallel lines of men & boys approach each other, continually narrowing the gap between the two ends of the net. When the net is almost upon the beach, the two ends have come together and the fish are hauled up onto the dry sand as in a big sack, and just as the bulky bottom of the net with the fish in it is dragged out onto the dry upper beach the men & boys form into a small perfect circle around it, each taking part of the net and drawing it back at once so that the whole catch, sometimes pitifully small, lies revealed at their feet. I can see the little fish shining from forty feet above where I sit on the craggy terrace. One day there are tiny sardines, tiny one-inch slivers of silver and black. Other days there are the larger *boquerones*, about three to four inches long, at the most. Within no more than half a minute from the time of the "opening" of the catch, a single man runs forth up the steep path to town, carrying the first full basket of fish direct to the *mercado*. On many days there are no more than half a dozen basketfuls, the end result of the night's efforts of some twenty men. . . .

March 6

Beautiful hot sun & sky today, aquamarine clear calm crystal sky and sea, limitless seaward, open fishing boats skating far out in it as on glass. Close in, a fifteen- or sixteen-year-old rows by in a five-foot rusty ancient metal skiff, stops and shouts "Julio! Julio!" at a cliff ashore, then points ahead of him shoreward and shouts some message. His voice, already deep, already very strong from much sea shouting, carries ashore and up the cliffs with the timbre of a sweet goat's horn. He rows out of sight, his voice still echoing in the great rocks. "Thus Ulysse."

March 8

One of those nights you stay awake hour after hour, after an early sleep, thinking of everything, sea sweep, old men and women, early remembrances, bad deeds, wash of time, terrible the toll of it, on and on. Flesh cargoes, motionless, horizontal, coasting through sleep, gunwales awash, into eternity. . . .

March 9

One of the most spectacular mountain ranges, though of no extreme height, hedges in Nerja and its highlands to the north and west. Ragged, steep, close-up, with one high sharp peak very much like Pico Blanco in Big Sur, California— with the same kind of vegetation, flowers & trees, even eucalyptus—only sugarcane standing in sheaves in every gulch valley bottom making the land itself look different. But the buildings very different, coastal and mountain towns all painted bright white, now and then a pink or blue one, all with Indian red tile roofs; narrow bumpy stone streets, burros and dogs in them; the stone walls of the houses all two feet thick, the only protection against the piercing cold that freezes dogs to death on the plains at night. Went up by bus to the tiny mountain town of

Frigiliana today, came back on foot, twelve kilometers down over the hills, before dusk, passing muleteers, burros loaded with faggots or sugarcane to the point that the poor beasts were almost hidden from view; water coursing down in from the mountains (through the orchards of olive trees and almonds and sugarcane fields) in stone gutters. . . . Noted a Bundle of Arrows bound together by a kind of oxen-yoke, pointed heads up, painted on the route sign at the entrance to Frigiliana; then noted the same emblem upon reentering Nerja on the main highway—and realized it was no local symbol but the national Fascist sign. . . . A Guardia Civil stood waiting for a bus, stern-faced rugged young kid, about twenty, but he smiled and waved a greeting.

March 10

The other side of Nerja, the modern side, is something I haven't touched, and so am in danger of giving no more than a picture-postcard portrait of "picturesque old Spain," a Spain of flamenco and beautiful women with fans. The reality today, however, is of the blight of *turismo* actively promoted by the government, with government-financed *paradores* or resort hotels being rapidly built up and down the Mediterranean coast; one in Nerja, looking like a harmonica, is almost finished on the cliffs above the biggest beach, with a colony of modern Miami-type duplex houses rising up behind it, where lonely widows with two children will come hoping for a duty-free fuck by a Dark Spaniard and with the hope of putting their personal finances on a firmer basis with Fundador cognac at one dollar a fifth. Down the coast, on the other side of Málaga, is Torremolinos, another picturesque fishing port which has already been turned into a junior version of Miami Beach. This is probably the last year for Nerja and its old way of life, with smiling people who will take you across town on foot to show you where some store is and may take it as a semi-insult if you offer them money for going miles out of their way in a rainstorm. But, in fact, the townspeople may well be happy to get rid of most of the features of their "old way of life"—poverty, not enough food and clothing, no plumbing, open sewers, charcoal braziers for cooking, little wood to burn, unpaved streets, no more than a hundred really good houses in ten thousand. In fact, that old way of life has already gone way down the drain. I have not heard a guitar here except on the radio or TV. On most days the town open-air *mercado* has only food (of which there is not much) and none of the basketwork, silverwork, blankets, pottery, etc., etc., which make big Mexican *mercados* lively places till late at night. The native culture is now 99 percent gone, at least on the surface, which is all a stranger can observe. Except for the production of wines, cognac, etc. . . .

March 12–14

Trip to Granada, by bus. The coast northeast of Nerja changes abruptly. The flat coastal land (on the sea side of the mountains) suddenly ends and the mountains rush closer to the sea, hedging in the coastal highway against high, steep cliffs. There are hairpin and even figure-eight turns which beat anything for sheer drops to the ocean below, and there are views, suddenly appearing around sharp turns, more spectacular than any coast I have seen, small white sugarcane & fishing villages suddenly flashed into sight way below or on a far bold headland or spit in the sea. . . . Motril, a dirty, larger town & junction of the coast route and the road inland up thru the mountains to Granada. . . . Orange groves high-up, lemon groves in the valleys of the Sierra Nevada, of the Sierra del Águila, along the Río Guadalfeo and above it, groves & groves of small orange & lemon trees, small bright oranges & pale yellow lemons thick in them, olive and almond and pomegranate trees, flowering peach and apple and quince, big gray olive trees. . . . Higher up, towns on far steep slopes, with sight of snow glaciers beyond them, the highway still winding up; then the great *vega*, a long flat plain, from Talaré, with cloud-covered great jagged peaks & snow mountains ringing the southern & northern horizon . . . then Granada suddenly on a slope above the great valley floor, ahead thru straight lines of alder trees to each side stretching away to the high mountain city. . . . What did God have in mind? . . .

The Alhambra or the Great Cathedral?

Being a diverted Catholic myself and having been aware of the great Real Estate Religion & how it always aimed at the hilltops (if not higher), at the real estate position in any town or city which dominates the rest of it, at the sunny side of all plazas and places, etc., etc., I had a good horse laugh to see how in Granada the Church had been able only to occupy a downtown location, way below and really in the shadow of the huge Moorish Alhambra with its mosque, Arab palace, fort and gardens which dominate the city from a high hill within it. Here the Sultan had set up his great Dream on Earth long before the Catholic King & Queen (Ferdinand & Isabella, who were much more occupied with Granada than with Columbus in 1492) reconquered these domains from the Moors (and drove out the Sultan from his Alhambra, and the Sultan, once out, sat down under a tree & wept). So that the great Catholic cathedral sits like a monster squid with tentacles cut off, after having crawled & squirmed & groaned its way almost to the foot of the Alhambra, and lay there swelling up like some huge dead medieval monster or crab, where it sits today—the most monstrous, ugly, grotesque accretion of Romanesque baroque that ever perpetrated itself upon a light-seeking, death-seeking, love-seeking, blood-seeking populace. This huge stone monster occupying a whole block & centered around a huge block-like central dome (which houses the central altar, so that one walks all the way around it, with small chapels all the way around on the other side of the building), the inside enormous, high & empty, the whole thing a monstrous indoor catacomb-tomb, cold as death itself except in the hottest weather (so that no doubt the piety of the populace increases enormously during the burning Andalusian summers, a thing certainly the Church counted on). But the hideous ornamentation & decoration of this huge Stone Cave one of the ugliest creative acts of an envious perverted medieval mentality: the great central altar ("in the round"—the Church having recognized long before dramatists how effective "theater in the round" could be) rising to maybe two hundred feet of gold-encrusted baroque candelabra, organ-piping and statuary, loaded with the heaviest stone & metal embroidery of every kind, rising up from the stone floor like a petrified gorgon caught about to take off from earth, its tentacles caught congealed & writhing in the air, and in the side chapels all around the center apse the florid excrescence of gorgon wings & tentacles flattened against the back walls of each chapel gilded gold and silver, with oversize statues in each niche, some twined about each other, straining upward or as if trying to escape the tentacles of the Central Gorgon, hideous groups of figures in the round here and there, sometimes nude, sometimes bloody, and a sleeping Virgin in a glass case reclining on a hard pillow on an altar, eyes closed but lightly as if in a sleep from which any small prayer may still awaken her (though centuries of mumbling have not yet succeeded). Perhaps someday she will actually blink and jump out, look around wide-eyed and say, "Man, what have you done to poor Jesus! You really have him strung out in this Horrible House—" Here indeed they've got

Poor Christ Strung Out. The medieval imagination, working through its most barbarous & death-seeking instincts (what Freudian dreams that Sleeping Beauty Virgin must still be having!), produced here the very opposite of what that sweet young cat with a Beat beard must have yearned for—a "house of God" which is the most graphic realization possible of Hell on Earth, the groaning populace here passing through all of Dante's Nine Stages. . . . Black-bat, meat-faced priests with thin lips scuttle back and forth, and out the dark boxed doorways, blinking their small eyes in the hard outside light. . . .

I stole an orange from the gardens in the Alhambra. On the bus back down to Motril and Nerja, I attempted to eat it, but at the first touch of my tongue to the overripe fruit meat inside, my whole mouth shriveled up as if I had taken a mouthful of hydrochloric acid, as if some ancient curse locked up in the royal bitter orange had been released upon me when I dared to violate it and its Alhambra . . . the Sultan's final revenge. . . .

March 15

Moved to larger, older house today, at Calle Carabeo, 68.

March 16

The press in Spain ought to be given a Pulitzer Prize for dullness. For plain boredom & droning grossness there is nothing like it anywhere in the world. The dullest is probably *Sur* (Málaga), followed very closely by *ABC* (Madrid). I have yet to find a masthead in any paper, giving any indication of who is running that paper, who its publisher(s) or editor(s) might be, though now and then there is a signed article. Most news stories are duplicated in more than one paper, and they all seem to emanate from the one news agency—"Efe" or "EFE"—which is the Spanish word for the letter "F." And "F" doesn't stand for Fun. . . . In a big new Spanish dictionary I have just purchased, published in Barcelona, a point in grammar is, prominently, illustrated by the phrase "El amo y el criado están contentos." ("The master and the servant are content.") When I was talking to a sugarcane millworker in Frigiliana two days ago, he looked uneasily toward the manager or owner (who was standing about fifty yards away) when I used the word "sindicatos" (unions) in answer to a question of his about working conditions in the USA. Knowing only what I can see on the surface of things, I may be making up a false picture of this world.

March 17

It also occurs to me that I may have applied traveler's paranoia to what I have seen of the Guardia Civil, Franco environment, etc. It is true, as has often been said about foreign correspondents, that we make up our own picture of things to suit our own ideas. We see what we want to see (re: most reports in the U.S. press from Cuba), the would-be revolutionary sees the Revolution as a glorious, euphoric fulfillment, the conservative or reactionary sees it as a tyranny & police state (which is robbing the vested interests). Were this Revolutionary Cuba here, I would no doubt have reported that there were fewer Guardia Civil in evidence "than there are police on the streets of San Francisco" (which is what I wrote from Cuba in 1961) and that they were on the whole clean-cut, innocent-looking, friendly fellows, rather like the young & goofy-looking guard in fatigues I saw guarding Fidel in Havana 1961. He too carried a little machine gun over his shoulder. . . . The difference is the Revolution here never happened.

March 19

Paco is the twenty-year-old son of a goatherd, and he sharecrops the garden for the owner of this house who lives in Málaga, a haughty *dueña* no one likes. Today Paco took a little gray-and-white rabbit from the rabbit hutch in the corner of the garden. He held it by the hind legs, and the rabbit stood straight out from his hand, stiff and motionless but with big scared dumb eyes looking every way. Paco held it up and gave it a quick short "rabbit punch" behind the head, at the base of the neck. Some very red blood dropped from his mouth, just three or four drops. The rabbit had in an instant soundlessly died, his eyes still wide open. Julie said, "What happened?" A drop of blood fell on Lorenzo's shoe. "The Spanish are cruel people," Kirby said. "No," I said, "just closer to nature." The sun shone & we were still alive. . . .

The Spanish must be tougher than Americans today, being still in primal battle with the elements. In America, Nature has really been Beaten, if not vanquished. Yet Americans retain a kind of primal freshness, directness and spontaneity which seems long to have departed from the Iberian peninsula, if Spaniards ever had it. It would seem their primal element has always been Darkness. Lorca's plays are naturally tragedies. Yerma's breasts have always been blind.

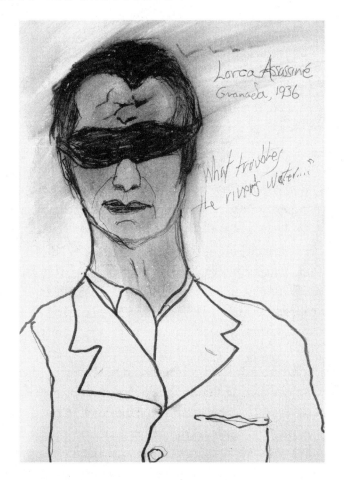

March 20

The Revolution never happened here. "La Señora" and "la mujer" still represent two classes of women, "tú" and "usted" two different kinds of people, equals and inferiors. One wonders how any Romance-language country can ever get around this built-in classification. The French Revolution stopped short of it. In the first months of the Spanish Civil War in and near Barcelona, at a time when a true Revolution was about to happen, everyone or most everyone (George Orwell reported) used "tú" to each other, and "usted" was unheard. So in Revolutionary Cuba 1959. As soon as the Spanish Revolution was aborted "usted" came back to stay. No one knows, even the most advanced linguists of the Spanish Royal Academy, how much longer it will stay.

March 21

I suppose generations of Spanish writers, as well as Cervantes, have tried to describe the sound of a burro's bellow. And unsuccessfully. It is a strangely human sound for such a loud if not raucous bellow. It has a sensitive tone, sometimes plaintive, sometimes angry or upset or impatient. It sounds most like a big hollow coal shuttle being opened by its grate. At other times it's more like a huge wooden farm door being opened on loudly groaning hinges, the wood a thousand years old. Other times it sounds like a big man in a cave drunkenly trying to holler thru a bullhorn after having lost his voice. Other times it's a bull about to die, after being enraged and stuck by a bullfighter *a las cinco de la tarde*. . . . I believe it is the voice of the Spanish people.

March 22

The Calle Carabeo is a long, crooked street "paved" here & there with small round stones, as are most of the streets of the town. It begins near the Paseo (the town's esplanade) and obliquely approaches the cliffs overhanging the stony beaches, so that the houses at the upper end of the street have long narrow gardens while the houses toward the end of the street have none at all, until one comes to the big Casa Cuartel of the Guardia Civil which occupies a big plot of land on a small promontory over the sea. At this point the Calle Carabeo has become a dirt road, and a little farther on it becomes a goat path, with a steep stony trail leading down to the biggest beach. It is lined with two- or one-story stone houses with pitched terracotta tile roofs, the walls plastered and whitewashed inside and out. The floors are all of a common terra-cotta brown tile, sometimes in the biggest houses spaced with small squares of *azul* tiles—white squares decorated with the one blue color that is in everything, wherever there is decoration—a pale Mediterranean blue, color of the limitless transparent blue the sky & the sea take on in good weather— brilliant yet pale & fathomless. Most of the houses in the Calle Carabeo are too poor for any blue except the sky's, and there are goats, chickens & burros stabled in and behind the smaller one-story houses, with the animals led in and out thru the house's front door. On the side of the street away from the sea there are fields stretching across toward the mountains, sugarcane fields studded with cactus. Old crones in black sit in doorways or can be seen fanning their *braceros* of wood or charcoal. At dusk in cold weather you can see the *braceros* burning fiercely in the wind in the middle of the street, where they have been placed when first lighted to get them burning. Wood is very, very scarce, and the one small pannier, under the *mesa camilla*, must furnish the heat for the evening under the table, in the poor houses. (A very few houses in Calle Carabeo have portable butane heaters.) The two-feet-thick stone walls are very effective in keeping whatever heat can be generated, but without any sun the rooms quickly become damp caves. In the spring and summer, it is a whole different matter, for as soon as the doors, windows & shutters are opened to the sun (which is very bright & strong) the houses are immediately flooded with warmth & light. The sun shines, sunflowers turn, and the world is changed, life smiles the hot smile of a *señorita* in sunlight. In another season she will take on the Black & so again goes the world into shadow.

March 23

In the Calle Carabeo there is a young legless man who propels himself up and down the street in a three-wheeled cart with a little motor on it. He is not exactly legless; the stump of one leg above the knee is visible, while the whole of his other leg dangles from the seat, shriveled and crooked as a limp root. His torso is about two feet long, with a hunched back and large head. He is dressed in fishermen's clothes, and when there is a good catch in the nets on the beach he sometimes is carried on the back of a fisherman down the steep cliffs to the sea. They put him down almost in the nets and I saw him yesterday sitting there on the ground fingering the tiny silver fish like some strange huge crab which itself had been drawn up in the nets. Later I saw him being hauled up the cliff-path again, piggyback, his shriveled foot dangling, and a few fish clutched crab-like in a hand. . . . The Legless Man motors up and down the rocky Calle Carabeo in his little cart, helping the motor with his powerful arms on the wheels. The Legless Man has a smile on his face when the motor runs. His voice is deep. He is young and good-looking, from the waist up.

March 24

This is my birthday and as good a day as any other to describe the house at Calle Carabeo, 68, in which we are living on this birthday. It is two stories, with six big bedrooms, all except one without furniture, a big dining room & kitchen, a single bathroom with cold water, a big long empty studio upstairs and a tile veranda downstairs opening onto a vegetable & fruit garden that takes up all the land of the houses on each side. The ceilings are very high throughout the house, with log

her tragic side ....

rafters holding up layers of thin sugarcane matting, on top of which the roof tiles are laid. Walls and ceiling all painted white, plaster flaking off constantly, since the house is ancient. The rotted wooden overhead trellis on the veranda is about to collapse but will probably not do so for another twenty-five years. All the rooms have big French windows with broken wooden shutters on them that open inward. These shutters can render a room completely dark in the middle of the day when the sun is beating down. The garden is planted with lettuce, tomatoes, cauliflowers, leeks, cabbage, mint, chamomile, roses, sweet peas, huge sunflowers, margaritas, chrysanthemums, tiger lilies, peach and fig trees and a lot of other things I don't recognize. (There is plenty of room to grow a little kif but I've yet to see any growing anywhere in this country. A year or two ago you could buy all you wanted in the streets of Málaga, but a new trade agreement was negotiated with Morocco, and one of the conditions was that the illegal flow of kif, hashish, etc., to this coast should be stopped.) The peach tree is now in bloom. The house itself, with its blue furniture, and its blue colored tiles, its slanting tile roofs at various angles and its huge empty rooms and its cracked white plaster walls, stands open under the "torrid truth of the two o'clock sun"—Van Gogh's sunflowers turning in it. . . . The old twisted blue wood tables & chairs with straw bottoms have their own mad life. . . .

March 25

I have forgotten to record my Málaga trip some days ago, in search of books and bookstores there. I found only two bookstores worthy of the name, in the entire city. Both pitiful! One, the Librería Cervantes on the Plaza José Antonio, is a one-room affair. . . . The other, the largest in the town, is in the Calle Nueva, and it is one fairly long and high room with smiling but pathetic clerks who pointed out to me the one little rack of English books and the one little rack of French books and a wall shelf about two feet long & five feet high which counted all the "serious" books in the store—mostly the Colección Austral which we get from South America & Mexico in San Francisco. There was one literary review on a table, the old *Revista de Occidente* (founded by Ortega y Gasset), and there was one other that looked like a pedagogic journal of some sort. I asked the clerk if it was "political" in nature. He shook his head in a frightened way and started backing off. By the time I asked him if there were any political journals he was already ten feet away, shaking his head and mumbling "No, no." By the time I said "Por qué?" he was in the doorway, drawing down the shutters. By the time I asked him where did one find political journals, he was waving his arms and pointing toward the newsstands on the Alameda. By now I was on the sidewalk. He disappeared behind the descending shutters. It was siesta-closing time, all right. . . . I walked about town for two hours in the sultry sun, looking for the Arab quarter or an amiable whore. . . . I hoped I might run into Shushtari, the 13th-century Arab poet born in the Persian quarter of Guardix near Granada. No one had heard of him in the bookstores. . . .

March 26

Drunk on Fundador cognac at a dollar a bottle and eight cents a glass, I got home OK but got up to pee at 3 a.m. and damn near fell out the window. Made it down to the garden, peed on the lettuce, staggered up the stairs to bed, rose up again, damn near fell down the stairs, made it to the garden again, peed again, and then suddenly passed out standing there, and tumbled into the tomatoes, lay unconscious there for a couple of hundred years looking blindly up at the full moon, then came to and got in a sitting position and observed the sound of the sea for another century. Kirby came to an upper window and looked down. I heard her voice far away. "What are you doing down there?" she said. "I am just sitting here looking at the moon," I said, "I am digging the stars."

March 27

A French poet (Claude Pelieu)[10] in San Francisco writes me—"Ne me reste que le junk et les lentes masturbations d'automne." How far away all that junk-scene seems out here! Dispatched the following to San Francisco: TELEGRAMA FROM SPAIN NEWS FROM NOWHERE FALSE WAR RECORDS FOUND AND LOST INHABITANTS CARRYING CHICKENS UNDER ARM COCKS LIKE TAILS BETWEEN LEGS STEALING SURVIVAL ORANGES OUT OF ALHAMBRA GARDENS AMONG INVENTORIES OF WORN-OUT POLITICAL SLOGANS SOWN IN VEGETABLE GARDENS OF THE GUARDIA CIVIL SLUSHPUMPS GUMMED WITH NESTS OF FEATHERLESS BIRDS WHOSE BEATING WINGS WON'T MAKE THE WHEELS TURN BACKWARDS WITH SKELETONS OF STONE LIBERATORS FLOWN OFF THE TOPS OF IMITATION MONUMENTS ON GRAND AVENIDAS DOWN WHICH RUSSIAN TRACTORS ONCE RAN INTO SUGARCANE FIELDS BURNING WITH ANARCHISTS AND FUCK YOU CRIED THE QUEEN WHEN FERDINAND FOUND THE SULTAN IN HIS SACK SAME YEAR COLUMBUS DISCOVERED AMERICA AND POUM! POUM! THE GENERALISSIMO ROSE AND SANK FROM SIGHT UNDER THE WEIGHT OF HIS OWN MEDALS MADE OF MERDE AND IRONY POLITI-

CAL VEGETARIANS FORCED AT LAST TO FEED ON THE GREAT PORKER HIMSELF AND SO THEMSELVES DEVOURED AT LAST BY CENTURY PLANTS OF THEIR OWN SOWING. . . . Signed LORENZO MONSANTO

March 29

A visit on Sunday by two Malagan poets, Alfonso Canales, born 1923, and Rafael León, somewhat younger. Canales just appointed Malagan member of the Spanish Royal Academy in Madrid. They are both academicians, scholars, professors—which they told me most Spanish poets are, "except for the generation of García Lorca" in the twenties—although, as opposed to poet-professors in the USA, they tell me they are "innovators" in poetry. Well, I learned a lot from the visit of these two probably "typical" Spanish poets who are only slightly younger than myself and were very young at the time of the Spanish Civil War, which they remember with some horror. At least, Alfonso Canales remembers it and told me that they realized they were now living in a "tyranny" (the word he used, *"tiranía"*) but that it was necessary and better than the Spanish communism which would have engulfed Spain, and still would engulf it, if Franco had not taken over. He remembered the horrors of the Spanish Civil War when the Spanish Communists almost took over—*"mucha sangre"*—much blood—and it touched every family. He also added that the Anarchists in Barcelona "were all Italians" (at the time of the Civil War). Today they (poets, intellectuals in general) were more or less "laying low." Earlier in the conversation we had fallen on the subject of Freedom by way of my asking whether they did not voyage abroad "because of money or politics," and it was obvious that they were used to such questions from foreigners, León began by telling me that no doubt I had a very distorted picture of Spain from the non-Spanish press, which was engaged in anti-Franco propaganda far from the truth. They both assured me that the poets in Spain, the writers and intellectuals in general, could publish what they wanted, could come and go, abroad or at home, exactly as they wished, and that no one was disturbed, much less arrested. But, I said, what about Carlos Álvarez who is today still in jail, according to a letter I have just received from an important editor in Barcelona? Who was he? they asked. They said they had never heard of him and that this was obviously a propaganda story. They said they had been editing books in Málaga for years and had met many, many poets, but had never even heard of him. (Álvarez was jailed in Madrid last year for publishing a letter of political nature which disputed an official inter-pretation of Julian Grimau, an executed Spanish Communist.) I was in any case impressed by their sincerity and conviction that they themselves were in fact Free. But, later in the conversation, when I asked them where in fact I could get a true, nondistorted picture of Spain and asked if I could get it from the Spanish press itself, they raised their hands "in despair" and said that their press too made pro-paganda, for its side, and that it was a completely government-controlled press. When I asked what literary revues or *revistas* were the most interesting, they said *Ínsula* in Madrid, strictly nonpolitical, was by far the best, followed by perhaps *Índice*, also Madrid, but that even these had to pass the censor each time before going to press. Which was a little point they had forgotten earlier in our discus-sion. They asked if I were a professor and seemed a little surprised when I said I wasn't and that the academic life "no me gusta" and that I thought it was bad for a poet. They came to my house laden with over two dozen books they had written or published—all beautiful letterpress editions published privately or by small presses in Málaga, mostly very small editions (by North American standards) of two or three hundred copies, much like poets' self-published books all over the world. They gave me all these books, and they represent a whole post–Civil war period of Málaga poetry. So thus the state of poets in Málaga today anyway. They were both very nice, kind men, very well-dressed and polite, full of charm, polish, and wit. When one gets past the draggy political scene of the world, there are the people still everywhere, humans with smiles, gold teeth or warts, full of sound and blood, thinking and crying. . . . We inscribed books to each other. Rafael León's inscrip-tion reads: "Con el deseo de que mi amigo Lorenzo Ferlinghetti conozca a España de verdad, no en los periódicos. Nerja 1965." . . . The Spanish postmark on a letter from these poets reads: "25 years of Spanish peace."

April 2

A herd of she-goats lives in the fields behind the house across the street. Every morning they come out through the house into our street, let go bunches of raisins from their bungs, and proceed up the street, their little bells making hollow music. The boy goatherd follows. The goats are brown, white, black, and shaggy with long slightly curved flat, spatulate horns. What could be in these goats' mad little heads, with black raisins coming out continually at the other end? Grapes. . . .

April 4

The great feat of Franco is to have persuaded the great majority of the Spanish people that without him communism would have long ago taken over their country, just like J. Edgar Hoover in the States, using the same line to build up his FBI. And the people just as paranoid about it. . . .

April 7

"The world is in a terrible convulsion," I thought, sitting in the barber's chair in Nerja & looking up at a tranquil postcard landscape of this coast painted by the barber's son. The world is in a convulsion, but it hasn't yet touched the people or the painting of this backwater . . . while expressionists, surrealists, cubists, lettrists, abstractionists, nonobjectivists, James Joyce to William Burroughs and the final cut up and Extermination of language & communication all a part of the Great Breakup & deterioration of the Image, of the word and the World itself.

April 8

Discovered a dark little store today, in the Calle de Generalísimo Francisco Franco, which at first sight seems to sell nothing but toilet paper. There is *papel sanitario* all over the place, stacked up all the shelves from counter to ceiling. White toilet paper, pink toilet paper, and brown toilet paper. The common brown kind predominates. It is the cheapest of course and has a glazed surface, making it particularly impermeable & hard on non-Spanish anuses. It may be that impermeability is a quality particularly sought after in Spain. The Government seems impermeable, the Guardia Civil seems impermeable, if not hard on the people. There are undoubtedly plenty of Spanish ass-holes around who positively *need* impermeable paper. It is the *extrañeros* that want the soft white paper, in the white or tinted shades. Neither the white, the pink, nor the common brown is perforated. This can lead to almost endless complications. Or at least endless ablutions, which is perhaps what the manufacturers had in mind. . . . The man who runs the toilet paper *tienda* is a very serious type, about sixty, dark green sweater, half-bald, dark jowls, thick glasses. He keeps you waiting a long time while he makes calculations with a stub of a pencil on newspaper. Three rolls took him about five minutes to figure up, at six pesetas the roll. If I had chosen three different kinds of paper we might have been there a couple of hours. Then the three rolls had to be wrapped in newspaper on inside page, *not* the front page of the newspaper with the Generalísimo Franco on it, as he is on it most every day. . . . When I was leaving I discovered the man did sell other things—stamps—which he however kept well out of sight under the counter. The stamps were made of paper. They were brown, white & pink. They had Generalísimo Franco on them. They were perforated. I asked if any stamps had other faces. He said: "I've got nothing but Him."

April 12—The Caves at Nerja

Las Cuevas de Nerja are situated about four miles from the town of Nerja, up in the foothills along the coastal plain, with the tiny town of Maro next to them. Today I went along into the caves, descending a hundred feet into the hollow earth. They were playing Wagner down there, over a loudspeaker system so that the sound filled the huge, high caves like water lapping everywhere. Floodlights illuminated grottos and crenellated walls reaching down into deep chasms and up into cathedral-like apses lost in darkness, the colored lights creating stage-like altars and lost chambers, organ-like piping of volcanic stone towering up on all sides. Through which I descended, one of a wandering band of sufferers descending thru nine stages of Dante's Hell, other bands of other nationalities being led by guides speaking *their* language, so that way below I could see lines of these pilgrims being led slowly onward & downward, on and on through mazes of huge stone auditoriums overhung with stalactites, Wagner blasting out as if thru the giant stone organ-pipes, souls in tourist clothes stumbling quietly on thru the illuminated gloom, cameras slung in leather cases not allowed to be used down here as if such a vision of hell were not to be brought back to the surface and to look back at Eurydice would be to be struck dead. . . . So passing onward toward the Exit, I passed a huge band of Spanish boy scouts being led in by two black priests, each scout with the Fascist emblem on his breast, flower of Spain.

April 15–16

This is Agony Week in old Spain. Everywhere they are dragging out the old Misery Images, dragging the Bleeding Christs and the Weeping Virgins and the Holy Ghosts through the streets, through every town and village. Holy Week is Holy Pagan Agony Week and the monster images sway forth in their pagodas from crypts and back alleys, carried by gangs of men. Slowly they move up the great boulevards of the great cities and up the Paseos of little towns, each carried by at least a hundred men, the huge float carrying the cloistered ghouls swaying sideways with the dead slow pace of the men in unison as they march to funeral drums. Where else but in old Pagan Spain would they have a bullfight on the afternoon of Easter Sunday? Ex-Falangist generals announcing & describing the Holy Week parades on TV, senior commentators talking gravely to each other (yet with a sparkle and a fat chuckle in the eye) like Huntley & Brinkley, ex-hatchet-men describing processions heavy with ghosts of the centuries and led by generals wearing Iron Crosses and white-hooded figures looking like grand masters of Ku Klux, preceded by embroidered priests with heavy jowls and small eyes, and lines of girls and grown women carrying candles along each side. . . . In our little town of Nerja, on the night of Good Friday about 10:30 p.m., they have their little procession, consisting of one float bearing a figure of the Weeping Virgin, Her tiara blazing with candles, carried by about two dozen village fishermen and tradesmen and sugarcane workers, preceded by a thin line of girls and mothers in black carrying long candles, followed by two medieval knights in tin armor with tin shields and swords. The church bell tolls and tolls, and the Weeping Virgin appears swaying on its float in the open arch of the church, and slowly, very slowly, comes forth into the dark town plaza, to the funeral beat of two drummers right in front of the float . . . to God knows where. The Weeping Virgin sways ahead, the street crowded behind with people following, off through the night. Where are they taking Her at this late hour, in the Spanish night, in Pagan Spain? (I never found out.)

MÁLAGA—The woods are full of German barons (met one smiling with long teeth who'd been in the Wehrmacht ten years) and retired British majors (all in the real estate business) and every sort of human ostrich you can imagine. . . .

April 24–27

Trip to Seville and the Las Escobas bodega built five or six hundred years ago and frequented or visited by Cervantes, Lord Byron, and many other famous cats. Las Escobas is what a Spanish tavern should look like. In the front room there's a long dark wood bar, and in the back there is a big, high-ceilinged room with elegantly carved rafters overhead and dark wood paneling all around. In the corners of the ceiling ancient wood gargoyles "stare" down upon great heavy oak tables and baronial chairs. About ten p.m. the place began to fill up. I had been brought there by two American students (studying flamenco guitar) whom I had picked up in my

borrowed car on the outskirts of Málaga, hitchhiking to Seville. They were standing out there waving a big American flag. They had been standing out there for
hours, doing tricks with the flag, holding it behind their back in an upright position on its pole and then flicking it out sideways like a railroad signal as a car
approached, or draping it around their bodies, wearing it like drawers or a skirt or
shirt or bib or otherwise disporting themselves with it. They were twenty years
old, tall and thin, with long Spanish sideburns and fairly long hair—which made
them look like handsome Spanish Don Juans but with the American flag on its
pole also made them look like U.S. Civil War soldiers on bivouac in the Deep
South. Their names were Michael Kerson and Dwight Porter. . . . At Las Escobas,
Kerson brought out his guitar and started in and soon had everyone turning to
him, including several flamenco singers, who began to sing "against" each other in
blasts and retorts of song & shout— At one end of the hall was a party mostly of
theatrical-looking types. One, a very handsome homosexual, wrapped his suitcoat
around his shoulders and started a torero dance with a handkerchief for cape, circling the other who put a handkerchief around his head becoming at once an old
woman and a bull, as the first dancer circled him, twirling and strutting in a burlesque of flamenco and of bullfighting. Several guitars joined in & the comic con-
tortions of the two dancers broke everyone up, roaring with laughter. When this
scene finally fell apart & there was a lull in the room, suddenly a young dark handsome skinny cat, sitting with a girl and another couple at the table drinking, burst
out with a deep cry as if he had just received a mortal wound through the heart,
or as if in conversation with his girl he had suddenly been struck, and he burst
forth in a *cante jondo* cry. The room had filled up with a series of young rich-
looking, elegantly dressed, aristocratic cats who would have been fraternity men in
the States, and one of them in an affected way now answered the Wounded Lover
with a bit of elegant, mocking *cante*. He wore dark glasses & was very vain, strutting and smirking at the other singer and at the audience. Then the first singer
burst out again, without turning around but remaining seated with his chick, an
American college girl—very Vassar-looking, with stereotype long hair hanging
over one eye—who began to get pretty worked up over him; she kept putting her
hand on his back and stroking him as he sang his shouts of passion or grief, the
cante jondo being more like a combination groan & a shout than a song, each verse
of it seeming to lead the singer to a new depth of despair and loving. (Someone
whispered to me that this was the way most American girls "learned" flamenco in

Spain—getting themselves "injected" with it by sleeping with such a Spanish stud.) But now had entered the room, and came to our table, a short, tough-looking, ill-dressed, belligerent singer, and Kerson told me that he was a waiter from a small town south of Seville and that everybody hated him. Indeed this waiter's face was full of hate, his squint eyes casting vicious glares at all the elegantly dressed young aristocrats at the other tables, his neck bulging in a too-tight shirt, hairy arms stuck out of frayed clean cuffs, his lips curling in a snarl as he started up with a burst of *cante*, as if spitting into those handsome, fop faces around him. His accent was hard and rough, and his *jondo* violent, as if he defied and challenged that whole upper-class world to try to put him down. One of the fops, the one with the dark glasses, made a satirical, mocking pass or two at him, but the waiter turned on him with such pure hate & fury in song that he was silenced; then the singer at the table with the Vassar chick cut in with a riposte of his own, without turning to face the waiter—whose name was not Paco de Antequera, but was a peasant name like that— And "Paco" cut into him with a harsh burst & a shout of song, casting his hard eyes around defiantly at everyone as he sang— It was as if he had come deliberately here this evening as into the bullring—to meet and put down his mortal opponents (who were everyone in the world who was better-born and better-dressed and better-looking than he—he the ugliest man possible, almost deformed with hate & fortune, giving the effect, although he was not, of being a *bossu*, a hunchback). Between bouts of song he smoked steadily & deliberately in great inhalations which made his *jondo* voice ever hoarser and more brutal. And then, when someone had finished a riposte of song, he would turn on that person with his great voice, murderously blasting out his attack in hoarser & hoarser cries of passion, disgust or despair. (Kerson whispered to me that "Paco" had a *novia* (girl) in his hometown of whom he had just heard rumors which he chose to interpret in the wrong way, and his singing was thus tonight very bad but true.) And "Paco" ended one *canto* with a disgusted cry of "I have had enough!" ("Tengo bastante!") . . . when I left at two a.m., Paco's voice was cracking and veins stood out on his neck and temple—but there were others in the room still singing against him—and he would keep singing as long as Kerson's guitar would back him—and he would sing them all into the ground—and he would keep singing after the guitars were gone—he would shout them all down, the whole world against him, life itself against him, and he would beat them all down. . . .

May 5

So leaving Nerja for good, I turn and look back down the Calle Carabeo, white in the morning sun, the dirt street bone dry now, dusty under the bright clear blue sky, urchins running in it as always, a black goat with fat milkbags settled in a sunny corner, a squid hung up to dry, women at the public fountain with their water urns, the bellow of a burro in some garden over the sea. . . . Bag in hand, I turn & look back, not exactly leaving with that "sigh of the Moor" looking back at his lost Granada one last time, but still with that strange feeling of never-returning, never-to-pass-by-there-again-in-this-life. . . . One more familiar wrinkled peasant woman's face tells me "vaya con dios"—which is still not a goodbye as much as a greeting.

JULIE'S POEM

The sun was a burn ball but the sun fell down
around the other side of the world
and the night went somewhere else.

ITALIAN JOURNAL
June 1965

O June 27

I am not Jean Genet walking through wheat-fields into another country. . . . Yet it is strange sitting in this Italian landscape, watching the swallows wheel over a back garden in Spoleto, the morning sun over the hills in the distance, the sky hot white-blue, stone houses & tile roofs, fig trees, washing hung out on the iron railings of the balcony upon which I am sitting. Singing birds in cages in the garden awoke me. . . . Last evening rode on the train from Rome thru a hushed yellow dusk, the whole traincar of Italians, men & women, looking out silent at the darkening hills & trees & sky, roads lost in it, all that car-load contemplating the landscape, unconsciously, in a strange kind of reverie or spell, hurtling forward together. Soul in their eyes, more than the French or Spanish. And I see my brothers' faces in them always. (If I had known my old man, I'm sure I'd see him everywhere.) And it's happened to me before in Italy, as it happened yesterday at the railroad station in Rome: an old woman comes toward me with hands upraised, recognizing someone lost in me, then laughing & speaking to me anyway, as she sees her mistake, yet still wonders, shaking her head a little. . . .

A canary twitters down below, white doves or pigeons fly up, with a great flapping, to my balcony. Sunday morning. Lord lord this Roman landscape sinks into me. And I am wondering if D. H. Lawrence sat like this writing, somewhere on a balcony in Italy. . . . Well, I am not D. H. Lawrence nor was meant to be. I am an American poet who flew here from London with cold weather clothes and a satchel full of paper to read poems in American and hear them translated into Italian at the Spoleto Festival. Lord lord this Roman landscape sinks my soul. . . . Should I project such an image of myself? To what purpose? I am no wanderer, but a fixed place. A fixed place in myself. Self which knows its own hunger, its own longing. (Inchoate throat! Not mine. . . .)

June 29

There is an awful lot of bullshit being passed about at this Spoleto Festival. First the gossip had it that Yevtushenko had refused to come because Ezra Pound was coming, and he considers Pound still a Fascist. (But he did come, performed & left immediately—before Pound arrived.) Yevutushenko arrived in a diplomatic limousine from Rome, read with great histrionics (which caused me to dub him "the Discus Thrower of Muscovy"), and then immediately split in his limousine, without making any contact or establishing any communication with poets from other countries. This is pretty bad, considering that the most important thing to be accomplished by any such international meeting is the establishment of personal rapport & communication with other intellectuals normally unreachable behind the obscene boundaries. . . . Then, to continue with the bullshit, it was rumored that Pound would not come because he didn't want to meet Ferlinghetti who had recently published in *City Lights Journal* an English translation of an interview Pound had given to the Italian picture magazine *Epoca* several years ago which Pound considered bad or upsetting. . . . Yet Pound is now coming on Friday, according to a telegram received from him today. . . .

POUND AT SPOLETO

I walked into a loge in the Teatro Melisso, the lovely Renaissance *salle* where the poetry readings and the chamber concerts were held every day of the Spoleto Festival, and suddenly saw Ezra Pound for the first time, still as a mandarin statue in a box in a balcony at the back of the theatre, one tier up from the stalls. It was a shock, seeing only a striking old man in curious pose, thin and long-haired, aquiline at eighty, head tilted strangely to one side, lost in permanent abstraction. . . .

After three younger poets on stage, he was scheduled to read from his box, and there he sat with an old friend (who held his papers) waiting. He regarded the knuckles of his hand, moving them a very little, expressionless. Only once, when everyone else in the full theater applauded someone on stage, did he rouse himself to clap, without looking up, as if stimulated by sound in a void. . . . After almost an hour, his turn came. Or after a life. . . .

Everyone in the hall rose, turned and looked back and up at Pound in his booth, applauding. The applause was prolonged and Pound tried to rise from his armchair. A microphone was partly in the way. He grasped the arms of the chair with his boney hands and tried to rise. He could not and he tried again and could not. His old friend did not try to help him. Finally she put a poem in his hand, and after at least a minute his voice came out. First the jaw moved and then the voice came out, inaudible. A young Italian pulled up the mike very close to his face and held it there, and the voice came over, frail but stubborn, higher than I had expected, a thin, soft monotone. . . . The hall had gone silent at a stroke. The voice knocked me down, so soft, so thin, so frail, so stubborn still. I put my head on my arms on the velvet sill of the box. I was surprised to see a single tear drop on my knee. The thin, indomitable voice went on. I went blind from the box, through the back door of it, into the empty corridor of the theater where they still sat turned to him, went down and out, into the sunlight, weeping. . . .

Up above the town
     by the ancient aqueduct
the chestnut trees
     were still in bloom
  Mute birds
     flew in the valley
         far below
  The sun shone
     on the chestnut trees
and the leaves
     turned in the sun
  and turned and turned and turned
     And would continue turning
  His voice
     went on
       and on
         through the leaves. . . . .

Some other people reported to me another tableau of Ezra Pound which I had missed at the noon concert. The first event, before the chamber music in the *salle* itself, was a performance of modern experimental music by an American composer, performing his work on improvised instruments—all percussive—strings & things like Harry Partch's "cloud chamber bells." This was set up in the entrance hall to the theatre itself. The hall was full & Pound was ushered to a large chair, center, close to the performer. He said nothing as usual, and sat motionless as usual, looking nowhere. The performance began, the performer bent over his bells & strings & cymbals & timpani & xylophone, barely touching them here & there, his ear close to whatever he touched. One heard nothing at a distance of three yards. Pound, sitting in the pose of that prophetic portrait by Wyndham Lewis (done at least thirty years ago & showing him as he is today—like an old Chinese sage), showed no sign of hearing anything. The performer continued, very silently, intent on his work; not a sound in the air, not a sound in the vacant ear, in the vacant eye of Pound, silence meeting silence.

ANDREI VOZNESENSKY / YEVGENY YEVTUSHENKO

1966

I.

NOTES ON ANDREI VOZNESENSKY
April 11

Published poems of his in *Red Cats*, City Lights Pocket Poets Series, 1962.[11]

Met him in London summer '65 after reading with him, Ginsberg, Corso at Architectural Association, Bedford Square. He told me he liked my "Underwear" poem.

He called me last Friday, April Fool's Day, 1966, from Berkeley where he had had reading with Louis Simpson as translator at U.C. He said he'd like to have reading in San Francisco before leaving for N.Y. in five days. And asked me to read the translations at the meeting. He then took off for country retreat & did not return until the day before the reading I scheduled at Fillmore Auditorium April 7. . . . When he got first look at handbill announcing reading, he called me up and said, "Lawrence, what is Jefferson Airplane?" When I told him it was a rock group, which would come on only after the poetry reading was finished, he said, "Lawrence, just you and me. No Airplane." But later he thought about it & said OK, don't cancel the Airplane. . . .

Took him on a short tour of San Francisco, with his interpreters (two women from U.C.) and Shig. . . . We passed gun shop & someone indicated he was inter-ested in guns. (We didn't stop. I remembered he was inactive Army Reserve lieutenant or something like that.) At interview with Michael Grieg of *San Francisco Chronicle*, he also allowed talk to be recorded for KPFA but requested that Grieg ask no political questions. Grieg agreed but then asked him, as final question, why he didn't want to be asked any political questions. He said he would answer but Off the Record. One of his translators "explained" to me that as a good Soviet, he was expected to answer all political questions at home but that, in foreign countries, this was liable to rebound against him. She said he was a very courageous man operating in a very delicate political situation, treading a very finely balanced line. (This was the same thing someone pointed out to me about Yevtushenko at Spoleto last summer.)

Full house at Fillmore Auditorium: maybe 1500. Maybe two-thirds of audience there for Voz, others for Airplane. Voz quite nervous before reading, in upstairs room where they left him alone, at his request. A narrow, dark, decrepit stairway led up from the ballroom-type main auditorium. The auditorium itself large and not too beatup-looking, if not exactly elegant. But the little upstairs suite looked like a set out of Dostoevsky. I went up just before the reading to find Voz alone in the back room up there, sitting on a broken-down divan as if he were waiting to be interrogated by the magistrate in *Crime & Punishment*. When I came in, I noticed he very quickly checked to see if I had a necktie on. (I did, for a change.) In the other room, a couple of the Jefferson Airplane were warming up their electric engines, their long Beatle haircuts making *them* look like Raskolnikovs in Siberia. (One might elaborate on the goofy political parallels ad infinitum.) Two or three little windows overlooked the auditorium itself which was still filling up. Bill Graham, the house manager & promoter, came up to say we'd have to delay opening for fifteen minutes, since there was a line outside around the block. A little later Voz, looking through the window toward the back of the hall, said, "It's full, full." . . .

He rearranged the order of the translations I had stapled together. After he'd established the new order, I said I was going down to the office to staple the loose, odd-size sheets together again so that they wouldn't fall out onstage. In telling him this, I made the motion of stamping the sheets together with my fist, since his comprehension of spoken English wasn't too good. He at least partially misunderstood me & said, "You're going to get the 'police stamp' on my poems?" I couldn't tell if he meant this seriously or not. (As if this "police stamp" were common routine in Russia before poetry readings?) . . .

At the end of the light show that was flashed on the walls behind the stage (to the sound of rock tapes interspersed with Bach & Vivaldi) before the poetry reading itself, a huge Buddha was projected, filling the entire wall & dominating the platform where we were to recite. Voz saw it and asked me to have it removed before we came on. "Lawrence—just you and me—we don't need Buddha!" We removed Buddha. . . . On stage I introduced him: "This is the first poetry reading City Lights Bookstore has ever actually sponsored. But City Lights was the first to publish Andrei Voznesensky in this country, four years ago. The translations used tonight are not the ones in the City Lights book *Red Cats* because we were naturally accused of 'beatnikizing' the Russians. So the translations we are using are mostly by famous, respectable British & American poets. I now give you my friend— Andrei Voznesensky." He came on to thunderous applause & the reading was a blast. Afterward, the psychedelic light show resumed, the Jefferson Airplane took off, and a thousand dancers vibrated in white strobe light. Voznesensky did dig it, after all. Actually fascinated. He went up to the back balcony where the light show was being projected & talked to the cat doing it. He said he had a theatre in Moscow & was going to do the whole scene there. (Where would he find the rock in Moscow?) Down below, the place was jumping with Freedom. The Wild West rocked onward in the night. . . .

A half hour later, he said he was ready to go. After an hour at my house, with a dozen people we'd picked up at the reading, he cut out for his hotel: the San Francisco Hilton. . . . This was probably his only reading outside of academic circles this trip in USA. He was a little afraid of the wide-open non-academic scene, I believe. His translator in New York, Max Hayward, and/or the publisher of his forthcoming *Antiworlds*, Basic Books, certainly were frightened by what might happen to him in San Francisco. One of them called a professor at Berkeley with whom Voz had been staying and was upset about the possibility of Voz getting mixed up in "some sensational beatnik scene," "with drugs," "at parties after the reading," etc., etc. . . . I assured them that the Chief Beatniks were in New York these days & they should rest easy since I hadn't seen any "drugs" go by lately, etc. . . . I had a good laugh after that. Christ. . . .

I did the best I could with the translations which I considered basically very pedantic & dull. I doctored them up a bit—especially the very British overrefinements of W. H. Auden—and read them loudly & dramatically—though still not as loudly as V. himself. . . . The translation preceded the poem in Russian in each case, so that I was at quite a disadvantage. *Afterward*, I found out how the poem was supposed to sound. A couple of times I guessed wrong, other times I hit it right. Nevertheless this was—I felt—better than giving a "flat" reading of the English & leaving the interpretation to him, in Russian that hardly anybody there understood. This is what all the academics—like Louis Simpson—had done with him. In fact, Simpson advised me not to try to imitate him. I took the risky course. But I think it was worth it. After all, Voznesensky, at least in the best English translations available, is not really a great genius poet. He's good but he's no great genius, at least in English. There are *at least* a dozen young poets more interesting & exciting than him in American non-academic circles today, maybe more. . . . But he's a fine reader aloud, a real spellbinder. It's the loud, histrionic Russian tradition—after Mayakovsky—the poem as oration—which no one really follows in the USA. Yet there's a heavy-handed, banal side to it. For instance, in the final poem of the reading, "Fire at the Architectural Institute," the next-to-last line is "It's only the beginning!"—a line that calls for a roaring interpretation. But the last line is, "Let's go to the movies." Voznesensky roared this line too, though the context didn't justify it. . . .

We paid Voz three hundred dollars capitalist love money for Fillmore reading. (I took a hundred.) I gave him a copy of my *Coney Island of the Mind*, inscribing it, "My Goya speaks to yours," since the first poem in my book parallels, or contrasts with, his Goya poem (which he has read everywhere in public & is probably his best-known). . . . Looking at the City Lights booklist, he asked how many copies of *Red Cats* there were, and I said about 5000 in print, adding that we'd made no payment to him as author since we hadn't been able to establish any contact with him or his Russian editors. To which he replied, "I know—no copyright." (Russia doesn't observe international copyright laws. I've heard there are Russian editions of Ginsberg and others we've published though I've never seen them.) When I told him there were 100,000 copies of *Howl* in print, he was civil enough to wait a minute before writing 300,000 in large figures & saying, "My next book: 300,000. . . ." "That's published by the State Publishing House, isn't it?" I said. . . .

To someone who asked him how he liked the audience of our reading he said, "In Russia, they're larger." At the *Chronicle* interview he'd said, "But these large readings aren't new or at all unusual in Russia. In our country, poetry, not painting or music or something else, is considered the *first* art. . . ." I would have unkindly interpreted the huge sale of his (and other young Russian poets') books a bit differently: the Hunger for Freedom will not be denied, even the thinnest, smallest voice picked up avidly, each ear in the dark like a crystal-set picking up the faintest tapping of distant signals. . . . When Voz first called me from Berkeley, saying he'd like to have poetry reading in San Francisco, he added something about seeing "our political friends," which was a bit of a surprise. I certainly considered myself at 180 degrees from him ideologically, the *anti-totalitarian Left* being about as far from him as possible. Even though I recognize that some form of supra-national "planned economy" is a life or death necessity for the peoples of the world, I am still an enemy of the Police State, *per se*, totalitarian or democratic. If he met any of "our political friends" during his visit in S.F., I didn't see them. . . .

Generally I would say Voz in America was on the defensive, of course very careful about what he said, never really opening up except in his own poetry in Russian, onstage. And even his poetry could not be said to be really "open," forthright or "uncompromising," and certainly not "revolutionary," certainly not "radical" by American *non-academic* standards. It's ironical that the poetry of young Soviet poets such as Voz & Yevtushenko is officially approved in Russia today. Except for Yevtushenko's "Babi Yar," their poetry is not radical, except in the sense of its being a brave attempt at a free breath in a stifling atmosphere. Let us hope they are not made to choke on it. Their poetry is closer to certain of the best British & American academic poets or poet-professors than it is to young American poetry outside the academies, whether Beat, Black Nationalist, or New Left. Both Yevtushenko & Voz have shown some personal interest in & empathy with certain Beat poets but it was notable that in all his interviews, Voznesensky avoided mentioning any single American poet by name when asked what modern American poetry he had read or been influenced by.

It would seem that, on this American trip, Voz felt more at home in the universities he visited than in San Francisco. I have the feeling no one got close to him here, he opened up to no one—an extraordinarily well-defended, nice, "clean-cut young man," rather like an Ivy League undergraduate in his tennis sweater (under his suitcoat), a quiet poet with a loud voice, no madman, no Mayakovsky, no Rimbaud in a drunken boat on fire. He was Pasternak's protégé, no other. . . . It is the *heroic performance* of his poems (as with Yevtushenko) that makes the difference. The stance & the loud, sometimes gentle, often bellowing voice, are *heroic*, and the voice literally lifts the poem from the printed page. (Here is certainly the greatest point of affinity with American Beat poetry which also has had its emphasis on the spoken message, though not "heroic.") But mention of the "printed page" is itself irrelevant since it is the Russian tradition not to *read* the poetry onstage but to recite it without printed text. The Gutenberg Galaxy never encompassed the Russian poetic voice the way it did the American voice. The American voice was engulfed by that galaxy & is only now emerging in the electronic air on the far side of it. The newest songs (i.e., Bob Dylan) rock with poetry. . . .

Frankly, the radical difference between American non-academic poetry and the poetry of Voznesensky & Yevtushenko boils down to this: the Russian poets are not clearly & unequivocally telling *their* government, *their* State, to make love not war, and to go fuck itself with its atomic bomb. . . .

II.
NIGHT WITH YEVTUSHENKO
December 18

Yevtushenko in San Francisco night of Thursday December 8, 1966. Called me at home shortly after arriving from Chicago (he'd flown from N.Y. to Alaska to Hawaii, & back to Chicago, then to S.F. for his reading at U.C. on Friday night December 9) & we made date to meet at Attic Studio in the Marina where Joe Lomuto was to recite poems by various poets including Voznesensky, Yevtushenko & myself. (Lomuto read my poem "The Situation in the West, Followed by a Holy Proposal"— which includes the lines "Why are you so puritanical comrade, kicking Allen Ginsberg out of Czechoslovakia, Let's turn on together comrade," etc.) Yevtushenko showed up with a beautiful young blonde he'd met along the way. After Lomuto, I drove them to North Beach in my old VW bus (which he said was "good for parties"). We stopped at City Lights, left word that we'd be at New Pisa, and went there, since he wanted dinner, having not eaten "since Chicago." We drank three bottles of red wine, and the conversation between us, mostly in English (his English was not quite as good as Voznesensky's at this point), lasted about 2½ hours, until the place closed about midnight. He also spoke Spanish & Italian. While raising many toasts over the wine, he mentioned that Voznesensky "liked dark glasses"— not eyeglasses but dark drinking glasses—in which one couldn't see how much liquor there was inside when drinking toasts—said Voz didn't drink, and said he never could warm to anyone who didn't drink. So we drank & drank. . . .

The discussion eventually got around to politics. He said he was very worried over the effect of John Steinbeck's forthcoming trip to Vietnam & about what Steinbeck would undoubtedly say about Vietnam & the war. Yev said he thought it might be disastrous to the cause of coexistence between U.S. & Russia— disastrous to those who were trying to keep a dialogue open—such as himself. He felt that Steinbeck could only come up with a position similar to that of his letter to Yevtushenko months ago, which amounted to the U.S. State Department position on the war. I agreed, but added that Steinbeck hardly represented any point of view but the Establishment anyway, and that he certainly didn't speak for any of the "dissident Left," radicals, or even American youth in general, and that no one I knew considered Steinbeck as *their* spokesman. . . . Yev also mentioned a "very important" interview with Fidel Castro coming out in *Playboy* this month, which got us onto the Cuban Revolution, and I told him I'd been to Cuba several months before the Bay of Pigs "invasion" (he seemed to know I'd been there). He'd spent a long time there—perhaps a year?—more recently. He told me my friend Pablo Armando Fernández (whom I'd last seen summer 1965 in London where he was Cuban cultural attaché) was now back in Cuba, which I was glad to hear—so many of his former friends having defected. Yevtushenko said he'd heard of the big Royal Albert Hall Poetry Festival in London 1965. But when I said I thought Pablo Armando had not been able to participate because of political pressure, Yev denied this & said no, it was certainly personal—that Pablo Armando must have been sick or something. (My feeling at the time, when Neruda failed to show up—and when Voznesensky refused to read, although he was there—was that the Communists had gotten the word from their embassies not to associate with the American "beatniks," etc.—Ginsberg, myself, Corso, others there.) . . . At one point, when I was telling him that, due to the lack of any hard & reliable information available to us on Cuba today, I had no solid grounds for being disillusioned with the Cuban Revolution or to conclude that Castro had become corrupted or had finked out, I said that "the Cuban Revolution happens to have been the Spanish Civil War of *my* generation." This was overheard by a Spanish waiter I know named Manolo who happened to be at the bar, and he came over & sat down, saying he could not resist asking me what I had said about the Spanish Civil War. Manolo eventually tried to get us to go on with him to the Tosca Cafe, but Yev wouldn't move & said vociferously that he was "against any planification" ("Five Year Plans," etc.). The only other time in the evening that Yev showed any such vociferousness was when I was twitting him a bit about having—like Voznesensky—been captured by the academics in America, traveling almost exclusively from one university circle to another in the USA, translations done by professors, etc. To which Yevtushenko replied, "Don't prick me—I have a sting."

I didn't hear his translations read aloud until the following night at the U.C. Berkeley reading, and they were read by a British actor traveling with him. This actor had a most refined "stage speech" accent, & I found it highly unfitting for Yev's poetry. There was one sharp exchange with a Russian professor in the audience. Yev had just read his poem about the Colosseum and the victims led to the slaughter—with a political parallel—i.e., the Soviet writers, Daniel and Sinyavsky, jailed by the State.[12] And the Russian professor had interjected from the audience, "But you were a spectator"—meaning that Yev had done nothing to defend them. Yevtushenko replied from the stage, "Don't bother a man when he's working." But at the party after the reading he said he *had* written & published a strong letter of protest on the imprisonment of the poets. He told me that these writers were arrested after they had been reported to the Russian government by the "American secret police." And he said he knew this "as a fact."

At the party he was surrounded by masses of students, and there was no getting near him—although at one point, he spotted me across the jammed room, raised a jug of red wine, poured me a glass, passed it to me, and shouted, "To the poetry of Lawrence Ferlinghetti." To which I replied, "And here's to you, Zhenia." And drank.

BERLIN BLUE RIDER

February 1967

Berlin Blue Rider,[13] sequel to Berlin Poem written October 1961 in San Francisco, never having seen Berlin. . . . Now January 31 1967 getting out of plane from Cologne. . . . Great esplanades & plazas. . . . A window of cigars of all kinds & sizes under the S-Bahn. . . . Two days after arrival—taxi to Lake Wannsee and the great Victorian Colloquium Literarische, where I read tomorrow.

Like a lost Wuthering Heights— Swans on the lake in the dusk . . . *brown leaves like toast* on the trees by it. . . . Lake "Swansea." . . . A little summer house on the end of the boat dock, in which a window stares in the gathering dark & in which I stand, leaning out, arms raised, and shout to those on the shore—"Behold! The Prince of Darkness comes!" . . . En route, between Wannsee & central Berlin beautiful woods all along a long straight highway, white birches in the gloaming. . . . Forest of Grunewald. . . . Dark nymph-woods. . . . This a surrealist-expressionist novel, starting here in *cauchemar* Berlin. . . .

Meer, rette mich, ich ertrinke am Ufer.
Sea, cover me, I am drowning on the shore.

February 6

Heiner Bastian shows me the sights. I first met Heiner when he was a student in San Francisco a few years back, and now he's my interpreter and translator. I've decided to go on to Moscow and then cross Siberia by train, take a ship to Japan and return to San Francisco that way. Heiner's joining me for the whole trip.

Berlin a very uptight city, everyone nervous. Dark winter city, though not cold now. The sun has shone only once since we arrived. Very square city, no lightness or gaiety left in the people. . . . Wooden scaffolds which you can mount just inside the Berlin Wall to look into dismal East Berlin & see nothing. At Brandenburg Gate the same. Unter den Linden, approaching the gate, the Russian monument guarded always by two Russian soldiers. I am lost in the landscape. . . . For new surrealist prose book = Absurd capers to be written up some later date. . . . Title: *Berlin Blue Rider*:

1. The Great Shoe Exchange— Heiner & I changing all the shoes outside the rooms in our hotel corridors when we come in at 3 a.m. . . . If we did it in the Hotel Metropol, Moscow, it would be a real test of communism—the people waking in the morning must, if they are good Communists, put on whosoever's shoes they find in front of their door & walk off, happy & interchangeable. . . . Disruption of Capitalist & Communist systems by the Great Shoe Exchange at 3 a.m. in every hotel. . . .
2. The Stepladder in the Bathroom Caper. At Renate Gerhardt's I find a tall ladder next to a high window in the WC. . . . I climb out of it & away, over the rooftops, returning hours later to the party still going on, with everybody all that time saying, "He's in the bathroom."
3. There is a great tall ladder, fifty feet long, leaning against a bare tree in the birch & linden woods leading to the Brandenburg Gate. What is it there for? To catch birds. . . .
4. In Zoo Park leading to the Brandenburg Gate also a small wood sign, pointing off into a thicket, & it says in German: GOLDFISH.
5. On the S-Bahn (elevated railway that runs into East Berlin) the passengers are bound up in plastic bags with tags on them, like Beckett characters, or the Schmerz in Boris Vian's *Empire Builders*.

6. Lake Wannsee waterfront by the Colloquium mansion, the brown leaves like toast shake in the night. Except for one brown leaf I took the other dusk & saved from darkness. This saved leaf now wings its way in a letter to West Coast, America. Brown leaf left in the toaster too long. It is possible this Brown Leaf will never arrive in that house in San Francisco in any recognizable condition. Brittle, it will be crushed and fall out of the envelope in fifty tiny pieces. Is it a symbol of Berlin or of love? Can it stand such long, high flights around the world? . . . and "where are you tonight, sweet Marie?" . . . A riderless horse wanders in a sea of swans & brown leaves. The river of brown leaves rises & engulfs the horse, its head becomes a huge leaf with a brown eye still looking for its Rider, Sweet Mary. The brown leaf horse is swept under a bridge upon which I stand. "And it is not the river which flows, it is the bridge which moves over the torrent." . . .

7. The Brown Leaf falls from the scaffold & blows away, the birds are abandoned in midair & don't know which way to fall, the rice is thrown, the brothers are departed, someone takes the flag down, it is black & is buried before it could turn red in anybody's sunrise if left flying, my passport flips its pages in the dawn wind, vaguely green & perforated with my name & number. . . .

8. I am lost in the dark landscape. In this strange place, surrealist city—thru the dark cellars full of jerking dancers to old Beatles records, crowded rock clubs—(the Eden Salon—etc.)—something out of *Steppenwolf*, I go off into the desolate night streets at 3 a.m. among the monster buildings. . . . Where now? And to what end? Time passes, and love persists. Life goes on, time passes, and nothing changes.

9. Writer Reinhard Lettau[14] tells me about the gallery owner who was going to exhibit paintings by Alexander Kinsky in his Berlin galley but that Kinsky came and made remarks about his dog & insisted upon feeding the dog. The *gallerista* informed the artist that he would have to stop feeding his dog, since only he himself could feed the dog, and that he was canceling the exhibition of Kinsky's paintings. And he did. The next day Kinsky came back & tried to get him to change his mind. He would not & there was no exhibition. . . .

10. Berlin Brown Leaf—Death City—the Peace Symbol is a Death Symbol, the Germanic rune for Life being . This used by the Nazis for their Department of Health. And someone asks me why I am wearing the Nazi symbol upside down. . . .

11. Le Reportage du Lapin Libre = Renate, Heiner Bastian's girl, goes out for a walk at 3 a.m. and meets a gray rabbit free crossing the street against the light. She told him Don't Be Afraid. He went down the sidewalk & around the corner "into the American bushes." Senseless dream!

12. Man in Thick Eyeglasses goes to kiosk & rips up *all* the newspapers on the racks. (Not senseless).

13. Macduff's Pony—Weltangste—Polska Vodka—Fasching Fucking—Dancing in the Art Museum—Berlin Epilepsy—German Batman—Checkpoint Charlie Chaplin—Valse Triste in the Sports Palast—Bank Für Handel und Industrie in der Bundesrepublik—Berlin Flugplan—

14. Schnurre—Snorer?—reported dead by famous woman poet— Not true— He lives. Two years later his wife takes her life in the Grunewald Forest. They don't find the body for two weeks. The Snorer lives on. . . .

15. The Red guard doesn't drink tea.

16. East Berlin February 8— Walking in Treptower Park with East German poet toward great Russian monument & side monument made of marble from Hitler's house, down great wide formal esplanade gardens, suddenly a troop of French soldiers in British type berets appears on the horizon, marching down a great walk toward us & suddenly they're directly behind us like a parade, with us the leaders, and a French guide explaining the park & monuments to them. It's a surrealist Happening with the soldiers paid by German Happener Wolf Vostell? A herd of American soldiers & tourists appear, taking pictures & gawking. We go off in the woods to take a photo of the East Berlin poet for the album of the West Berlin Colloquium to which he was invited but to which he wasn't permitted to come. (Someone else read his poems at the Colloquium.) In the freezing cold I find a couple of real *plastic* roses in a bush. I "pick" them & give one to the Marxist East German poet, about to say "Rose of Revolution." But I don't say it . . . back at his flat they engage in a long argument on the recent actions of the Red Guards in China, some maintaining this is a historic development, a classic example of a new revolution, with Mao not controlling it, *not* carrying on a "purge" of the cadres that brought him to power, etc. . . . . . others maintaining the opposite. . . . Earlier, we passed thru Checkpoint Charlie, having to change license plates, have passports examined, etc. It took an hour to get thru. . . . Then we go to Metropol, press café in East Berlin & meet others from West Berlin & then proceed to the East German poet's flat farther

out in town . . . whole second half of Brown Leaf Berlin here lost in the world, drab & lifeless, the people solemn in streets & cafés, 1940 buses, smell of cheap cigarettes, stale food. . . . Dante's *Inferno* illustrated by Hieronymus Bosch, when we return after dusk thru the bare night streets at Checkpoint Charlie. Joyless Civilization. Wow, where is ecstasy gone since the Creation? Man & Woman placed in the Garden of Eden speaking many tongues but meant for Ecstasy—or Misery? East Berlin a sewer of sufferers left on earth, washed-up remains of Creation, bodies tossed up, lost in the landscape. Checkpoint Charlie. They roll mirrors under the car with floodlights to see if anybody is strapped under the chassis trying to escape to freedom. The Blue Rider does not appear. They put measuring sticks into the gas tank to make sure there's no false bottom in it. They raise the hood of the car and inspect the motor & the compartments, looking for propaganda literature. You get out & go thru a long low building where they check your papers, money, passports, etc. East German sentries & soldiers wearing World War II German Army uniforms, and Goose Step still practiced in the Changing of the Guard at the Tomb of the Unknown Soldier. The Blue Rider does not appear.

17. Berlin Wall monster serpent running thru the city, like some kind of barbaric medievalism, dividing the city into two grim camps. East Berlin camp infinitely grimmer— Incredible they're still running thru these disgusting Checkpoint Charlie routines twenty years after! 1967—and it still goes on. Incredible & disgusting to see it. The Wall runs on, barbed wire over concrete & brick, whole endless streets on the borderline abandoned, streets of houses abandoned, boarded up & made a part of the Wall. Along the river the factories boarded up on the side facing the west, though work still goes on day & night in the factories. Every once in a while a new ruse to escape to the west is uncovered & put an end to. Swimmers shot down in dark midnight canals, bodies found strapped under country wagons, anything for freedom. The human spirit will out, no matter where. Still the Blue Rider does not appear. . . .

RUSSIAN
WINTER
JOURNAL

February
1967

Lawrence
FERLINGHETTI

RUSSIAN WINTER JOURNAL

February–March 1967

S February 9

oviet Air Flot, Berlin to Moscow—an enormous bunch of furry citizens flood out onto the dark field to take plane at East Berlin airport, crowd looking like they just were de-mobbed from the *Battleship Potemkin* crowd scenes, 1917. . . . They all succeed in getting on jet and we're off, in sunny clear weather, Berlin tilted below as plane climbs & banks north & east. . . . No announcements at all on P.A. system, no oxygen masks stowed anywhere to be seen, cabin very bare, circa 1950 U.S. plane. . . . But jet works & it's two hours to Moscow above the clouds, an excellent cold lunch served with white wine & caviar. . . . German students, twelve to fifteen years, from East Berlin on excursion for six days in Moscow, some teachers, Soviet businessmen, no beards but fur hats and heavy coats, women all hefty & healthy, ready for any scrimmage. . . . A price list of articles available for purchase on plane includes recordings of "Lonely Accordion," "Evenings in the Moscow Woodlands," "Sevastopol Waltz," "Song about Leningrad," "Kiev Waltz," "Field, Wide Field," "Ensemble of the Soviet Army," "Snowball Tree," "The Volga Flows," "Flowers Were Blooming in the Fields," "Song of Russia," and "Do the Russians Want War?"—the author of the last being E. Yevtushenko. . . . Also, available for purchase: a memorial medal of Gagarin's space flight. . . .

Light brown flatland visible clearly below. . . . We fly over what history? We'll be coming down soon, into what snowland, thirty below zero . . . snow & frozen tundra below . . . limitless weightless fields & fields of snow lost in some Klondike, windswept ice plains in white sun glimmering. Ivan spurs his White Steed somewhere still & gallops into Siberia, thru Tashkent Nowheres . . . almost sunset here now while the West still freaks in afternoon, great forests visible, small cities banked in snow, straight railway into nowhere, snowhere, over the horizon, forests washed back stand frozen like islands in dry-ice seas . . . sun gone, dusk down, still we swoop across the land-escape, and so down now at last, smoothly, into Mockba, Mock-haven. . . . Fall out, in Russian winter light, balled in fur, looking for igloos & cold men, find self in same old body instead, passport extended, a would-be *moksha* in Mockba, lost in his *samsara*. Transported? We take our selves with us wherever we go.

Thru Intourist & customs and out into a car to Metropol Hotel, thru the first darkness midwinter snow landscape way outside of the city, great snow world and white birches in the gloaming, on both sides of straight single highway, snow farms & crossroads, no billboards or roadsigns anywhere, finally more houses, then huge housing developments stretching for miles, then the beginning of long straight boulevard into the city, streetcars & buslines, lighter waiting rooms glassed in, and the black figures of the people against the white snow under high street lamps, Gogol night-scene, Gogol night-tale, black figures against the white landscape, "eternal Russia." . . . Life still noble and tragic. . . .

Two days in Moscow, full up with sound & sight of strange city. . . . Went to Writers Union & made contact with people Allen had told me to look up,[15] Yelena Romanova, Frieda Lurie, and Andrei Sergeyev, the latter Allen's & my translator here. Zoja Voznesensky, Andrei's wife, took us to see the production of *Ten Days That Shook the World*—a Brechtian dramatization based on but distant from the John Reed book. This was at the Drama Theater on Taganka Square & the director was Yuri Lyubimov. Really brilliant direction with many great scene effects, devices such as banks of spotlight-footlights raised to shoot a sheet of light from downstage edge of stage. At one point, an anvil was placed close to the light & hands waved behind & above it, looking like flames, with men hitting the anvil with great sledges. . . .

History of the Russia Revolution, with Lenin speeches woven in (using his voice); then very satiric characterization of Stalin, very sharp & caustic & really laying him out; ending of course with triumph of the Revolution (in the future & in the past) with handbill dated October 1917 showered down on the audience at play's end & Brechtian crowd scenes of masses rejoicing & dancing. . . . We met director in his office at intermission, were invited to write on his wall & I wrote "To a great Director & great 'Ten Days That Shook America'?"

On the walls of the Writers Union Café I saw Allen's three-fish symbol drawn by him here in summer 1965 & I drew woman nude with inscription "The door to the invisible is visible." . . .[16]

Impossible to get Moscow down on my paper, of course, or to give any real idea of great cold city in Russian Winter Light. . . . Walking in Red Square at midnight with young Russian poet Pietr Vegin and his beautiful wife, Marina, we go past the huge night Kremlin, and past the fantastic Arabian Nights Basilica built by Peter the Great, the whole square a kind of surrealist night-dream in the snow, dark fur-hatted & fur-coated figures going by silently over the hard snow & cobbles, a big Red Star illuminated on a high steeple against the ink sky, the buildings inside the walls of the Kremlin floodlighted and yellow, not black & forbidding as always imagined. . . . Red Star over Russia. . . . The metro here the deepest in the world, 450 feet underground in some places, and one metro station at a great depth having a *salle* filled with dozens of great bronze nude heroic statues, in alcoves & niches, on balustrades, etc., as if the whole station were peopled with bronze figures. . . . The Writers Union at 52 Vorovsky Street a big complex of handsome old buildings with offices, reading rooms, libraries, and the club with restaurants & cafés & exhibition rooms with portraits of great Russian writers & a big auditorium. (Pasternak's portrait had been removed & not put back yet.) The functionaries of the union seem to be such kindly old, tough, gold-toothed ladies as Yelena Romanova, probably widows of writers of the first years of the Revolution, generation of 1917. . . . Lunched at their club with Yelena Romanova, Frieda Lurie, Andrei Sergeyev & Zoja.

They really quizzed me. What was my opinion of Steinbeck & his report on Vietnam? (A reactionary, who does not speak for young American writers & especially not for the poets.) What party did I belong to? (None. Registered as an Independent.) What is my opinion of Hemingway? (Worse than that of Steinbeck, intellectually & morally bankrupt by the time he committed suicide. Lived in Cuba all during the second Batista regime & never opened his mouth in public on the subject. Went fishing instead. Result: *The Old Man and the Sea*.) What American poets do you consider great since you are so critical of Ciardi, Lowell, Wilbur, etc? (Whitman, Dickinson, Hart Crane, E. E. Cummings, Pound, William Carlos Williams, Kenneth Patchen, Allen Ginsberg.)

Zoja Voznesensky concluded, after a discussion of Ginsberg (who had visited Moscow summer '65), that Ginsberg was concerned with the interior world while I was concerned with the outside world, and therefore my poetry was "more comprehensive" (or something like that—this was thru an interpreter). I asked why, then, was his poetry so much more universal than mine? She replied that because the interior was more important than the exterior. . . . Later I reflected that, if she knew Allen better, she might realize that it was Allen who is in fact the extrovert, I the introvert. . . .

Sergeyev said he had translated Allen, myself and Richard Wilbur, Denise Levertov, John Ciardi & Robert Lowell, and I told him he was more broadminded than I, both poetically & politically. . . .

ON THE TRANS-SIBERIAN

February 11

Got the romantic idea of crossing Russia on the Trans-Siberian Railway after picking up Blaise Cendrars's book *Sur le Transsiberien* (1913). I'd take a Soviet ship from Nakhodka to Yokohama, and after a trip to Kyoto to stay in Gary Snyder's house and visit Zen Institute and temples I'd eventually take off for San Francisco.

Heiner and I are picked up by Intourist at hotel on night of February 11 & deposited in our car on the train, which leaves right on time, 8:50 p.m., off into the night. . . . At the same moment that the train starts up silently, the compartment lights are switched on & the loudspeaker in the compartment comes on very loud with Russian music sounding like an opera of the Revolution about to happen, interspersed with heavy Russian voice making announcements, the speaker in our compartment very old & scratchy, the sound coming out as through a wall of gravel & static. Four berths in little compartment but only one other man beside Heiner & me. A silent type on his way to some midpoint in the wilderness. . . . A nice old Russian lady in train uniform collects our tickets & serves us tea. . . .

February 12

New day, we wake up late, the train gliding on smoothly over flat snowland. First glimpse out the moving window shows beautiful birch woods (the taiga), tall thin white birches all along the track, to the horizon on one side, bare snowfields on the other, single big birds perched on the very tops of trees. Freight train, very long, passes in opposite direction, loaded with all kind of wood. Birch logs on end, planking, split wood. No people. Finally come to a small town & see one small boy on skis, then a larger town, also made all of wood, with many children skiing on low slopes by the tracks, then about noon big freight yards & big town-city of Kirov. Ten minutes & we're out of there, gliding eastward toward the Great Siberian Plain, the sun a faraway lost small dime disappearing in white winter sky . . . our compartment flies along the ground under it, four comfortable berths, and the conductor-porter-maid of our car an old Russian woman looking like she may have been a countess before the Revolution. She's now shoveling coal into the hot-water stove at the end of the car. . . .

February 13

Great Siberian Plain. It's like the sea. Too huge to write about. Nothing but birch trees like the froth on endless white groundswells— Sometimes thin lines of black forest on the horizon. Forlorn wood towns, rail junctions, with switchmen standing outside of sentry houses holding up woodsticks from which the signal flags have long since worn off—a horsedrawn sled or two. . . .

Our train full of five-feet-tall dark men & women in dark clothes & serious faces, hardly any smiling, the whole huddle of us rolling on, past the white birches of Russia. Five days to go, to Nakhodka, east of Vladivostok, where we'll sail for Yokohama. So far we've passed through Kirov, Perm, Sverdlovsk, and will reach Omsk this afternoon. . . . Our Babushka Countess brings us tea in glasses set in silver holders. . . . A man in a soiled white coat comes thru the car every once in a while selling buttermilk in bottles, and other men come thru selling hot meat-dishes. . . .

We arrive at Omsk at 3 p.m., stay thirteen minutes, and off again. By quarter of four the Siberian night has already settled in, and a thin crescent moon shines down. . . . Babushka brings us tea. . . . Pete Seeger recording of his concert in Moscow (1965?) comes on over the compartment loudspeaker, interspersed with applause & Russian interpretation, including Russian audience singing "We Shall Overcome" with Seeger. . . . It's getting colder—it must be 35° below outside—it's about 45° in our compartment. This trip may get rough yet—a trip for fools & poets. . . . I have the strange feeling we're going to freeze to death in the Mongolian mountains. . . . (We have two maps—a Lufthansa flight map showing the topography, mountains, etc.—and a "General Map of Asia" published in England, in pretty colors—the Siberian part all in green. The Lufthansa map looks much colder & dangerous. "Better we should use the friendly green map," says Heiner.)

The Face of Siberia has ice eyes and a beard full of icicles. . . . In order to arrive where I am not, I must go by a way I have never been? But is this route necessary? I believe Mount Analogue is a long way from this part of the world. . . . Taiga and tundra flash by in the night, ghosts of shamans and Tungus flash by over the landscape.

February 14
Woke to the sound of a heavy Russian voice singing over the loudspeaker:

> "Madame, I would buy you silks and laces,
> Madame, I would be your lover,
> Madame, will you marry me?"

In English. And then a Russian chorus replying,

> "Oh no, no, no—no, no, no—no—no—no"

This is repeated with many verses, all with the same sad answer. In the passageway, Babushka is standing still, looking out the window. She does not understand English, but it is a sad song on her face. . . . So we ride thru Siberia on a first-class train with white tablecloths in the dining car over the land which bled & bled its white blood & its red blood. The Decembrists do not know us, neither does Kropotkin (though we know him), neither do the sailors of the *Potemkin*, neither do the twenty-seven-year-old workers on the Bratsk Hydroelectric Project, south of which we will pass tonight. . . .

February 15

There are no red flowers in the taiga in winter. . . . Raunchy, upland country here between Zima and Irkutsk, snow piled up everywhere, sledges full of wood drawn by black horses, fir replacing the birches a bit. . . . Three days to go, to east coast of Asia . . . out on the station platform at Irkutsk, where it must have been 40° below, our female porter was working with a crowbar, breaking ice off the big shock absorbers under our car. Call her Nushka from now on, in honor of the girl who worked at Bratsk in Yevtushenko's poem. . . .

Late afternoon, train running along Lake Baikal now, great frozen lake with snow mountains high on far side, fishing boats pulled up along the near shore, by hamlets and double-ended black dories. . . . Kids skiing on the ice, offshore. . . . Mountains on both sides now, could be the U.S. Pacific Northwest. But they turn into huge forbidding glaciers, on the other side of which is Ghost Gobi . . . while the frozen lake goes on & on, on the other side of the train—a frozen sea. . . . The great white snow mountains, rising up steeply, sun on their western faces, the other sides in shadow—their sunny sides bright as mirrors. . . .

February 16

Sometime during the night the electric engine was changed to steam, and we awoke to blue sky filled with white smoke from up front, mountains still to the east & south, desolate wooden hamlets on the other side, on a long plain. . . . Six & a half days from Moscow to the east coast of Asia, twice as long and far as the fastest train across the USA. Endless Siberia!

Under the continuous white cloud of our steam, we proceed quietly eastward & north, skirting the northernmost province of China. At one station approaching Mogocha, we jump out & run up and down the platform & buy postcards with stars & sickles on them & Red soldiers against a background of Soviet planes, tanks & submarines. Heiner sees one small very beautiful girl with slightly oriental features. He wants to kiss her, pick her up, and carry her onto the train; but there is no time. The train is sounding its warning whistle. We dash aboard & off, leaving love on the platform. . . .

February 17

About five hundred miles from the Pacific now, we get out at a station at noon, and suddenly it's almost spring. It's warm in the bright sun, and the snow is melting on the eaves of the station house which is painted red & decorated with clusters of little red flags. There is a little permanent display with pictures of Lenin and a postcard machine which dispenses photos of Soviet heroes. A three-star Russian general arrives with his staff and much saluting, and disappears into a first-class compartment. He is pretty tough-looking, to say the least. No one is smiling as he goes by. . . . Huge, with a pig's neck and a pig's face, with small eyes, wearing black knee boots and riding breeches with a four-inch-wide crimson stripe down the outside of each leg. A tunic to match, in dark blue, breast covered with ribbons— several rows of them. The expression on his face is what is hard to describe. It isn't hostile, it is indeed pleasant enough when he glances at you, but it is imperious & hard. He is like a ram standing there. A certain large imperiousness certainly elevates him above the other officers, probably filling them with unadmitted fears. You get the feeling he has been in command a long time & wouldn't hesitate to blow up the whole train in an instant if it would further his ends. He would not stand for any foolishness on any account. He would kill you if he could. . . .

We have had little communication with the Russians on the train. We don't know any Russian and didn't think to bring a phrase book, and none of them speaks any other languages. All we can do is gesture, nod & smile. Although they're shy with strangers, after they get to know you a little, they are liable to break up with laughter quite often. In the dining car, they sit very strait-faced and serious. Plain, square faces, straight hair, brown or black eyes, seldom a very good-looking young woman, though the old ones are often beautiful. . . . *Figaro* in Russian blasts out of the 1930 loudspeaker in the car corridor. It's like listening to a stuck bull roaring . . . meanwhile the eternal white birches fly by. . . . The last night of the six days & nights on this train, two Finnish boys in the diner get drunk on four bottles of champagne they buy to use up their meal tickets. We refuse to join them, calling them "decadent capitalists." (When Yevtushenko came to San Francisco fall 1966 he was going to the topless joints to see "capitalist decadence.")

World's longest train ride coming to an end. . . . I leave behind on the train

Blaise Cendrars's book. (Turned out he never went?) As he said, "Il y a des trains qui ne se rencontrent jamais."[17]

We have one more night's train ride from Khabarovsk to Nakhodka, then to Japan and back to San Francisco.

"Ce que je perds de vue aujourd'hui en me dirigeant vers l'est c'est ce que Christophe Colomb découvrait en se dirigeant vers l'ouest."[18]

February 18—Khabarovsk—on the Amur (Blue) River (now frozen over)—

RECIPE FOR HAPPINESS IN
KHABAROVSK OR ANY PLACE
One grand boulevard with trees
with one grand café in sun
with strong black coffee in very small cups

One not necessarily very beautiful
man or woman who loves you

One fine day

Main boulevard, tree-lined, with cafés, etc., is Karl Marx Street, leading from waterfront park up to Lenin Square. Bright town with beaches, art schools, "Houses of Culture," theaters, broad esplanades. . . . We spend the day walking in Khabarovsk & sitting in its cafés & walking in its big parks, then get kidnapped again by Intourist at 5 p.m. & put on night train to Nakhodka, train winding south slowly in the winter dusk.

And we have come to the end of Siberia— The Sea of Japan rises up.

February 19

Thinking of Nagasaki today as I wait for a ship to Japan—Nagasaki which I saw in August 1945. I was navigator and third-in-command of the attack transport *AKA-47*, the USS *Selinur*, and we had docked in Sasebo, a few hours south of Nagasaki.

Sasebo was completely deserted, not a Japanese in sight anywhere. A ghost port, a ghost town, the Japanese all fled to the hills. After we had unloaded the troops for the Occupation, we had shore leave for a day, and three or four of my shipmates and I took off for Nagasaki by train which somehow was still running. In my memory now that train trip was a blur, as are my comrades, whoever they were . . . rapt faces in a moving landscape.

Nagasaki itself was no blur. The site we were allowed to see had been totally "cleaned up." That's all there was—scorched earth. Sickening to see how the city of Nagasaki seemed to have just vanished from the face of the earth. . . . Except for one tea cup with bottom melted-out . . . skeletons of trees on the horizon. . . . Not a soul in sight. All souls melted too.

And what the hell did we know about it, walking about in our neat Navy uniforms? We had been at sea for a long time before Sasebo, and we were permitted to know only that some huge new kind of "nuclear" bomb had been dropped on Hiroshima and then on Nagasaki. We walked around on the scorched earth, wondering if we were getting radiation from the scorched earth.

Now years later I can only see our bombing as a monstrous racist act which probably would never have been committed if the Japanese had white skin. . . .

February 20—Sunday—"Day of Doom"

I was complaining a day or two back that we were hardly even scratching the surface of Russia, of Siberia on our uninterrupted train ride from Moscow eastward, and that our journals wouldn't be worth much, confined to what we could see from train stations on ten-minute stops. This day I got beneath the "surface" in a big way. . . . We sailed along on our overnight train from Khabarovsk to Nakhodka, arriving at the latter part at 10 a.m. & transferring to a bus that took us to the dockside of the SS *Baikal* which we were to take for Yokohama. There we spent an hour getting thru Russian customs etc. & boarded the ship itself. (Heiner got slowed up behind me & got held up by the customs who went thru all his luggage & took down all the Moscow addresses he had, while he yelled at them.) When I got on board, I went into the main lounge & gave the official my ship ticket & passport. "Where's your Japanese visa, please?" This was a flabbergasting question to get, since in the West Berlin Intourist agency we had inquired about this & had been told that no visas for Japan were required for Americans or Germans. (Heiner had a German passport.) I told the official this & she went to confer with someone & then with the captain. Then they motioned for me & I stepped up & told the captain my story. No go, he said . . . He shook his head & went off. He would not take an American who did not have visa. It was a Russian ship & the last time he arrived in Japan with visaless Americans, the Japanese police were hard on him. He had since received a written notice warning him not to take abroad for passage to Japan anyone who was required to have a visa & did not have one. He had a list of countries whose citizens did not require visas, and the USA was not in that list, and that was that. German citizens did not need visas. So Heiner was clear. But I had to get off the ship!

It was sailing in thirty minutes. I had all the money for the two of us in traveler's checks & I couldn't transfer them to Heiner. So I rushed ashore to cash a $100 check for him, carrying my luggage with me, including my new UHRE tape recorder, which I had forgotten about, slung over my shoulder. I got the money & brought it back to the ship & Heiner came down the gangway for it & I handed it to him, but when I tried to hand over the UHRE, the captain of the Russian police at the dock at the foot of the gangway shouted that he wanted to look at whatever I was handing up. When I opened the case, he literally roared "FORBIDDEN! FORBIDDEN!" and I slunk away. . . . Stood there & waited for the ship to sail without me, waving feebly at Heiner on board. . . . Awful sinking feeling. . . . Finally, I said the hell with it & went back into the custom house & sat dully waiting for the Intourist woman to come & take me to the same hotel— Finally the ship did gaily sail away & she came & an Intourist car took me to a big stark hotel & gave me a small top-floor double room, my partner turning out to be a twenty-year-old Japanese youth hosteller with knapsack covered with those international camping emblems, etc. He had lost his Japanese passport in Moscow & they took him off the ship too. He was gone off to Japan a day or two later, but in the meantime he served me in good stead.

I was feeling sick, with a bad headache, and I thought it was just a hangover from a bottle of bad port we'd drunk on the train, combined with the depressing effect of having been booted off the ship. But no. By 9 p.m., my head was splitting and I had the chills. I put on flannel pajamas, bathrobe & two very heavy blankets, took aspirin & antihistamine and I still shivered & shook. By then, I was getting alarmed, realizing I must have a high fever. The Japanese kid was in his narrow bed sound asleep—I debated for another hour whether or not I should get him to call a doctor for me. It got so bad, I was beginning actually to feel afraid of falling asleep because I might not wake up!

I had awful visions of L. Ferlinghetti's biography reading "Died suddenly in Russia," and of being buried there in, of all places, forlorn Nakhodka, wife & children never able to take the body home, etc., etc. . . . That did it. I called my friend. No answer. I called much louder & finally aroused him & told him I was very sick & would he please call a doctor. He did it willingly, and in ten minutes two doctors came & examined me thoroughly, consulted over me in Russian for some time, & then said I should be taken to hospital at once. I agreed, got up, dressed & went down with doctor who took me in ambulance, at midnight. At night the hospital seemed bare as a prison, though the Russian nurses were pleasant enough. They unlocked the ward doors to let me in, which also gave my already-morbid mind a prison impression. They immediately gave me another complete examination, then put me back in the ambulance, the original doctor still with me. They drove thru the night to another hospital nearby & there I got a four-by-eight cell. It was a very bare room, with a single bare bulb. The whole thing was like a bad dream. With the Russian voices incomprehensible to me, leading me on thru the night from hotel to hospital to hospital, and then to this bare room. I undressed & lay down shivering under the blankets. They immediately started the full penicillin treatment for influenza. (I would have called it the Mongolian Grippe.) They gave me injections & at least six pills to swallow at once. I went to sleep. . . .

Next morning, dark dawn on bare ceiling with seven cracks in it. Nurses & doctors, more injections, pills, talk I can't understand. Nothing to do but stare at the ceiling, still with high fever. . . . Thinking . . . I am being punished for my sins at last! . . . All day lay there, looking at the ceiling, the bare walls, the bathtub, the toilet with a clean white cloth tied over it so it wouldn't be used (across the hall is a row of usable toilets). Lay there thinking & thinking. So this is my Mount Analogue? Come this far around the world, all across Asia, to Pacific far shore, and my Mount Analogue turns out to be this bare white four-by-eight cell, with seven cracks in the high ceiling, bare floor, bare walls, silence. And if that Mount Analogue exists only in ourselves, then mine is a low mound, or at best a bunch of detached vague pinnacles hanging in air, baseless. . . . Thinking of that. . . . All that poetic bullshit about setting out in search of my Mount Analogue & the door to the invisible visible . . . all nothing. Nothing but sick me & my body in this bare room. Monotony. Absolute, interminable boredom. Every minute is an hour. . . .

No books, no paper or pencil to write with, no tongue to ask for some with. Too foggy and feverish to read or write today anyway. But the mind nevertheless lying there, awake. . . . That first day a real eternity. . . .

Second day, a small miracle. One young nurse they bring is able to understand a word or two of English. I ask her for books in English, French, Spanish, anything. And for paper. Late that day she brings some magazines, the next day paper & a pen . . . and I also receive a visit from a friendly Korean interpreter from Intourist who brings me books in English. Russian authors published in Moscow by the Foreign Language Publishing House. Chekhov & Tolstoy. I begin reading Tolstoy's *Resurrection*. For three days I read *Resurrection*. . . .

The room, however, has gotten less & less bare, by very gradual stages. The first day, a little rug is brought in, then a table & a table-lamp. Next day, I get more pillows & coffee with breakfast. (The Russians seem not to know what coffee is for, certainly not to be brought steaming hot & right away in the morning.) Then a radio is brought in & hooked up. Then another day, a mirror is installed over the sink. The kind nurses have warmed up to me & all come in and gawk at me & smile. So they keep making the room better, and by the fourth day it is very warm-looking. I came in on a Sunday night & I'm discharged on a Thursday morning.

February 23

Thursday and I'm installed in the hotel. And a wire comes from Intourist Moscow saying they can do nothing for me about getting a visa & that I'll have to do that myself directly with the Japanese! But here in Nakhodka there's no Japanese Consulate or any contact with Tokyo, and the only way to get a visa is to appear in person at the Japanese embassy in Moscow! Insane! Unless I can get a Japanese ship to take me to Japan without a visa, I am going to have to go all the way back across Siberia to Moscow! I can do it by plane, but once in Moscow, I might as well continue on that direction & go back to San Francisco via Berlin! Absolutely insane. The Korean interpreter, Kim, is getting a Japanese businessman with ship connections to go on board various Japanese freighters & ask the captain to take me on. . . . Now it's Friday night & no luck so far. There's one due tomorrow 4 p.m., and there's some hope. Purgatory continues. My Siberian exile!

Nakhodka—a new town the government decided to build seventeen years ago. Big harbor surrounded by hills & mountains similar to San Francisco. But the town is forlorn. . . . Muddy at this season. . . . In hotel dining room at night, couples dance stolidly to 1940s-type Western "jazz." I go to the hotel barber, and he finishes the whole job in less than five minutes. Lonely & extremely depressed I lie on my bed in my little hotel room, writing this. . . .

February 25

In the stores, offices & restaurants, the abacus is used to count change and make calculations. Waitresses carry little abacuses with them. . . . This workers' city really seems a joyless place . . . busy building a new city, a new world, not much time for frivolities or refinements. . . . In the Buffet in the morning, people line up for their tea, looking glum. There is an insufferable heaviness & drabness about life here. Where's the happiness? It must be in the intimacy of the private home.

February 26

Sunday & no church bells ring in this town. Nothing but silence. Still waiting to hear if any Japanese ship will take me aboard for Japan. The suspense is terrible. There are three Japanese ships in port this morning, and Kim has gone out to them on a boat with the Japanese businessman to help him persuade a captain. . . . Last night, in the hotel dining room, the administrator of the restaurant, Anna Gordeyevna, a buxom woman of about fifty-five, brought two pussy willow twigs to my table, saying she had picked them on an excursion to a river outside town where the first spring was stirring. The *Moscow News*, published every day in several languages including English, is replete with stories of "cultural interest" each with its propaganda slant—even stamp collecting and match-box-label collecting are attuned to the October Revolution. The article concludes: "Matchbox collecting is very exciting!"

The answer is no! Not a ship captain will take me to Japan without a Japanese visa, fearing I would have to remain on board & go on to other ports indefinitely, etc. . . . So I must return via Moscow & Berlin, what a fucking farce! Tomorrow morning, by train, first stage, back to Khabarovsk. . . . The Trans-Siberian redoubled.

The hotel dining room should be described at greater length. A long narrow ballroom-type scene, graced by a five-piece Western-type "orchestra" in the evening. (It doesn't deserve to be called a "group.") Sometimes it sounds like Tommy Dorsey warming up & running down, sometimes like Guy Lombardo about to get constipated, accompanied by a Russian Jean Sablon bellowing into a mike.

The musicians are all very serious in public, though they look like they might be "cats" if allowed to escape for a few years. . . . The couples get up to dance when the music starts, very sedately, face each other straight & put their arms up, expressionless. Usually the man puts one arm around the woman & the other he rests on her shoulder. She puts both her paws on his chest, and they march & wiggle around, avoiding eye contact. Some one or two daring types try the "latest" Western style of dancing without touching each other, even whirling about a bit, really wild. (Now I understand what Voznesensky must have thought when he saw the "free-form dancers in ecstatic clothing" at the Fillmore folk-rock dances in San Francisco, with psychedelic light show, the dancers rocking in strobe light, and Buddha projected on the wall over the stage where the Jefferson Airplane was taking off.)

Underneath the glum exteriors (no doubt the result of years of public paranoia) the people I've had contact with all turn out to be very warmhearted and generous, and when they decide they like you they start giving you presents, anything they have. (We found this out in Moscow where a young Russian poet & his wife gave us everything in sight off their shelves at home when we were leaving—dolls for the kids back home, books, drawings, photograph of Mayakovsky. . . .) Kim has knocked himself out trying to get me a ship, spending most of his Sunday off on it today. . . . Everyone's very apologetic & sorry for me . . . but the closest consular services of any kind are in Moscow. So off into the night again, lost in the land-scape, as ever. How many machines, in the ground & in the air, have to function perfectly for me to get back to San Francisco safely again. Japan & its orange blos-soms never to be seen . . . except someday from another direction. . . . In order to arrive where I am not, I must go by a way I have never been before? . . . Impossible to realize the absolute isolation of this particular northeastern province of USSR—no planes to Japan, Hong Kong, or anywhere eastward—one plane a day from Khabarovsk to Moscow— No airmail to Japan, except via Moscow! Two weeks for an air mail letter this way. Telegrams go the same route & take two days.

Anna takes me to the movies late Sunday afternoon. There is a crush of people in the big hall. It has a floor slanting forward to the stage—about 15 percent slope—but the wooden seats were put in without putting them on levels, so that the seats slope downhill too. The film is Russian, about Nazis and Partisans fight-ing them in some port like Riga. The Russian Partisans keep blowing up ships. The Partisans get killed one by one. A grim film. Everyone sits silent throughout it, never once a laugh or a shout or a clap or a cry. At the end everyone files out perfectly silently under their fur hats & fur-collared coats.

One last look at that "dance orchestra" in the dining room. Asia's first & last hope. It is my last dinner. I sit alone, as usual, staring at the band. The drummer is an older man with thick glasses & an implacable beat he must have picked up from a grandfather clock. He starts. It's "Melancholy Baby," believe it or not. The sax man gets right in there. He wouldn't call his horn an axe, not he. The Jean Sablon–type singer probably can't face it: he doesn't get up & sing "Melancholy Baby." The pianist holds up his end. You wouldn't call him a piano player. He's a pianist, and he's Melancholy, Baby. When it is all over he actually hangs his head over the keys, puts his arms up and cradles his head in them. There is a middle-aged, plain waitress sitting alone at one of the tables, looking at the musicians and then away with a sad, sad look. She just sits there unmoving. There is nothing to be done.

SIBERIA REVISITED
SIBERIA RECROSSED
SIBERIA RETRANSITED
SIBERIA DOUBLED

February 27

Voyagers on a certain old passenger train on the road to Khabarovsk and over the northern steppes of Russia in the long winter of 1967 might have noticed one lone passenger in a foreign-looking fur hat and a long Navy raincoat & scarf sitting silently, bundled up & staring moodily into the landscape as it crawled by under the lead sky. This same passenger was of course none other but that same L. Ferlinghetti, poet & fool, sinner & absurd traveler, contemplating nothing so much as the insanity of his present return voyage across Siberia, all of which might be fittingly made into a stupid book entitled (beginning with the Sunday a week ago when he was taken off the Tokyo ship) *Ten Days That Shook L. Ferlinghetti*.

On February 20 he was removed from the Tokyo boat— On March 1, if he had any luck at all he would have flown back to Berlin—and one more day by plane would land him home in San Francisco. That's the plot of it. We'll see how it works out. It takes great fortitude & stupidity to undertake such a journey. Dark Night of the Soul Backward. Descent of Mount Carmel. Circumrenavigation up Dante's fire escape. . . . Mount Analogue never even glimpsed. . . . The train starts up from Nakhodka on time, 9:10 a.m., bright sun over the harbor & Sea of Japan. Farewell, miserable, brave new town of Nakhodka—may I never come back to your literally godforsaken, joy-forsaken shores. . . .

Missed all the mountains coming down here at night. Going back now, north, surrounded by beautiful open country with high hills & sharp mountains rising up on both sides, filling both horizons. . . . Look like California mountains but closer in, steeper, all brown & rust in winter, the ground still frozen, marshes & ditches frozen over, no birds, some high mountains still full of snow . . . glacier peaks glistening in sun. . . . Lost land & lost people. . . . This is the milk train, stopping at every little dump, north into the snow country again, birches again. People are amiable & eager to please—but—they try to be understood by repeating the Russian phrases louder—and then writing them down. I've no inkling of what they're trying to say.

In the dining car, the waitress steers the natives to other tables. Mostly rough looking men, the kind that you used to see on the trains of the Pacific Northwest. But instead of lumberjacks, these are mostly seamen & soldiers in civvies. . . . Purgatory, this journey. This man needs time to reflect on his life, so we'll give it to him; let him have it! Days & days & days & days waiting for time to pass, unable to write anything except this lame journal, nothing to do but think & think. A kind of enormous Paranoia takes over. Will I ever get out of this country alive? Will they search my papers at the border, read my journal for subversive passages, will I end up really in Siberia? . . . Out of desperation, I am reading the only book I could find in the Intourist library which was not hopeless to open: Gorky's *Tales of Italy*. Such sentimental corn! Not a very original mind, this great Gork! Hymns of praise to Mother, Work, Labor, Love. . . . I believe these Russians are in another world. About thirty-five years back. In everything but science. . . .

I am sick still, my body aches, around the kidneys, I have a stopped-up nose & a slight fever again. I miss my friends & family, especially the family. I feel so very far from home. It is as if only a miracle will ever get me back. What is my forty-eight-year-old body doing, crawling over this far, snowbound landscape on the other side of the world from Home? If I ever reach home again alive, I don't think I'll be leaving for a long, long time. . . . I want to live in the woods in Big Sur—but not alone. . . .

Night outside now, train stops in some big rail-yard on a snow plain. It is snowing lightly & the flakes drop into the white rail-yard under platform lights & floodlights. On the ground, walking along at the same rate as our train, is a man in a fur cap & railway greatcoat. He is a young man, striding along in the snow night, holding a little flashlight. On the loudspeaker in our train some old Russian music is coming across, something slow & reminding one of long winters and the Russian steppes— maybe Prokofiev— The young man keeps striding along in the dark outside, hearing only the sound of our train. I look at him thru the Prokofiev— He looks in at me. I am standing in the corridor. He keeps striding along, abreast, not hurrying or alter- ing his stride. He keeps coming on in the night. The train picks up speed & he drops out of sight. He is still striding along, eternal, over the steppes. . . .

Thought I was really going to die about four a.m. on the train. Woke up with the cold sweats, thinking I had a ruptured kidney or something, thinking what an awful place to be buried—Khabarovsk—the bright town we passed thru coming down, never thinking here I might leave my body, halfway around the world from home. Took two aspirins & went back to sleep. In the morning, it's all cleared up, my body feels better than in weeks—the fever all gone, etc. . . . Blue sky with fields of cumulus outside, and the train going thru birch woods under snow. The white smoke from locomotive billows thru the woods and along the ground, threading the trees. . . .

The morning radio intersperses music with lectures on Marxism & Imperial- ism. . . . There is an enormous emptiness in Soviet life that stares out of people's eyes everywhere. . . . All this senseless retracking of Siberia back to Berlin because no doubt one little rat-faced German-Russian in the West German Intourist agency didn't double-check our question as to Japanese visas. He'd taken a dislike to us anyway—and I'm not being paranoid— He had a cold, unpleasurable look on his mug when we first spoke to him—he wouldn't let us use his phone—and Heiner had a short argument with him. Result: L. Ferlinghetti retracks Siberia, vowing he'll never come back to this miserable country.

I find I have a reservation on a flight to Moscow. Then to Berlin pronto and, I trust, out! Into life again.

Arrived Moscow after nine-hour flight on strange Russian passenger plane with compartments like a Pullman & a load of Russian foot soldiers. Plane had about eight propellers on each engine, with four engines. It looked and sounded like a nest of frozen white butterflies taking off. . . .

Poetry has more than once
'saved my life?'
Now it has done it again. →

MOSCOW IN THE WILDERNESS,
SEGOVIA IN THE SNOW

Midnight Moscow Airport

      sucks me in from Siberia

   And blows me out alone

          in a black bus

     down dark straight night roads

        stark snow plains

         eternal taiga

           into monster Moscow

    stands of white birches

       ghosted in the gloaming

Where of a sudden

     Segovia bursts thru

        over the airwaves

They've let him in

      to drive the dark bus

Segovia's hands

       grasp the steering wheel

Yokels in housing projects

   drop their balalaikas & birch banjos

Segovia comes on the bus radio

    like the pulse of life itself

Segovia comes on thru the snowdrifts

       and plains of La Mancha

   fields & fields & fields

 of frozen music

     melted on bus radios

Segovia at his instrument

     driving thru the night land

   of Antequera

      Granada

        Seville

    Tracery of the Alhambra

in a billion white birches
born in the snow
trills of blackbirds in them
Segovia warms his hands
and melts Moscow
moves his hand
with a circular motion
over an ivory bridge
to gutted Stalingrads
Segovia knows no answer
He's no Goya & he's no Picasso
but also
he's no Sleeping Gypsy with Guitar
Guarded by a Lion
He knows black condors fly
He knows a free world when he hears one
His strums are runs upon it
He does not fret
He plucks his guts
and listens to himself as he plays
and speaks to himself
And he keeps driving & driving
his instrument
down the wide dark ways
into great Moscow
down the black boulevards
past Kremlin lit & locked
in its hard dream
in the great Russian night
past Bolshoi Ballet & Gorky Institute
John Reed at the Drama Theater
Stalyagi & heroin at Taganka
Stone Mayakovsky stares
thru a blizzard of white notes
in Russian winter light

Segovia hears his stoned cry
   and he hears the pulse in the blood
      and he listens to life as he plays
   and he keeps coming & coming
         thru the Russian winter night
He's in Moscow but doesn't know it
He played somewhere else
         and it comes out here
     in a thaw on an airwave
        over Gogol's Dark People
     stark figures
      in the white night streets
    clotted in the snow
He listens to them as he goes along
He listens for a free song
       such as he hardly hears
        back home
      Is Lenin listening
        after fifty Octobers
Segovia walks thru the snow
       listening as he goes
    down Vorovsky Street
  to the Writers Union
He meets the old hairs that run it
    They dig him
       & they know what it means to dig
        in mahogany cities
Segovia teaches them open-tuning
    with which they can play anything
     freely and simply
    This is not his Master Class
He leaves them humming and goes on
Segovia plays in the loose snow
   and digs a bit alone
      under the free surface

                                with his free hand
He strikes softly as he listens
He hears a dull thud
            where something is buried
                        a familiar thud
            such as he sometimes hears
                        back home
He turns away & goes on
                        down Vorovsky Street
His music has a longing sound
He yearns & yet does not yearn
He exists & is tranquil
                        in spite of all
He has no message
He is his own message
                        his own ideal sound
And he sounds so lonely to himself
            as he goes on playing
                in the iron-white streets
And he is saying: I say all I know
            & I know no meaning
He is saying
            This is the song of evening
            when the sphinx lies down
            This is the song of the day
            that begins & begins
            The night lifts
                    its white night-stick
            The ash of life
                    dries my song
            If you only knew
He is saying
            My love my love
                    where are you
            Under the pomegranate tree

He is saying

    Where is joy where is ecstasy

    stretched out in the snow

    where only the birds are at home

He is saying

    There's a huge emptiness here

    that stares from all the faces

    All that is lost must be

            looked for once more

He is saying

    Far from me far from me

    you are the hour & the generation

    they marked for result

He is saying

    I am your ruin

        unique & immortal

    I am your happiness unknown

    I am light

        where you are dark

        where you are heavy

He is saying

    I am an old man

    and life flowers

        in the windows of the sun

    But where is the sun the sun

        Soleares . . .

On the steps of a jail

    that looks like a church

        he finds a white bird

What is important in life? says the bird

Segovia says Nada but keeps on playing

    his Answer

And he cries out now

    when he sees a strange woman

        or sees a strange thing

And he hears many strange women
    & many strange things
    after fifty Octobers
    & fifty strange springs
And Segovia follows them
    down their streets
    and into their houses
    and into their rooms
    and into the night of their beds
And waits for them to make love
And waits for them to speak
And waits & waits for them to speak
And he cries out now
  when he hears them speak
    at last in their last retreat. . . .

MOSCOW—SAN FRANCISCO

HIGH NOON, HIGH NIGHT,
SALOME, ARIZONA

October 9, 1967

Two days' hard driving from San Francisco in a VW bus not built for these wide-open ranges— Staying tonight in big old stucco-adobe motel in middle of high desert, a hundred miles northwest of Phoenix— Adobe buildings and woodroof veranda and a swimming pool full of leaves, green water, algae, bugs and cigarette wrappers. A few soggy cigarettes with cork heads agape float about like waterbugs leftover from some other civilization. 1:30 in the hot afternoon—too hot to continue in hippy tee-pee over the fried horizon— High noon lasts all afternoon out here. Nothing moves in the white sun, shadows black wherever there are any, and there aren't many. Highway 60 stretches away straight in both directions. "Salome: Where She Danced" is the full official name of this spot on earth, pronounced Sal-oh-m (as if the discoverer was Jewish), altitude 1875, home, according to local guidebook, of Dick Wick Hall (1877–1926), "Arizona's first widely-known humorist who credited the town with an annual growth of 100 percent a year: '19 people in 19 years.'" Looks like they've been adding one a year ever since. . . . Yuma Indian country, gold rush country—Harquahala gold mine discovered by Yumas high on peyote. That high netted $15 million. State Narco Agents take note. . . . Sheffler's of Salome the name of the motel-inn-restaurant-bar I'm at—the main restaurant room a barn-like affair with about a hundred dusty horned heads of all kinds of animals mounted high on the brown board walls. I ask the counter lady, "How long those heads been up there staring down at everybody, lady?" She says: "Don't rightly know." "Know anybody rightly who ever shot any of these animals, lady?" She gives me a strange look and goes away, looking very sorrowful. When she has to come back past me I hit on her again. "They been up there looking down at you maybe a hundred years, lady?" She gives me another strange look. "Anything else you want, mister?" "Yes, ma'am, I'll take two of those glass elk's eyes on toast," I tell her. They look like they're about to fall in my plate anyway. She looks at me like I'm John the Baptist or something, but doesn't start dancing, even though she looks like she'd like to have my head to hang up. "Who danced for all these heads?" I fling at her as she retreats to the kitchen where I imagine her unsheathing a scimitar. Antlers sprout from my head and my hundred predecessors stare down at me. . . . Oh, the weird conversations that have gone on here under those dusty antlers. Five men in cowboy hats, just piled in out of a pickup truck, line up at the counter, laughing and joking and slapping each other on the back, Haw-haw-haw. A drunk, silver-haired Los Angeles tourist staggers out of the dark cabin-like bar, with a good-looking young chick in tow, and the cowboys eye her. They've never seen a woman before. And they'll travel all the way to San Francisco to see what Salome looks like topless. The chick steers her silver-haired friend to the counter and they plunk down next to me. She whispers in his ear and he points to a door in a corner and she gets up and goes. He shrugs and leers at me gaily—"Been stopping here every week for six months so guess I oughta know where Salome's crapper is!" Now it's my turn to regard a tourist darkly. I catch myself asking, "Anything else you want, mister?" . . . The dusty wagon wheels overhead, hung with dim lightbulbs, turn and turn in the dusk of eternity. . . . I get up and walk around reading the various inscriptions, plaques and doo-dads around the walls. Quotations by Dick Wick Hall all over the place, including a postcard of an awful poem about his Thirsty Frog who wears a canteen in the desert. Horrible way to be a poet. . . . In the lobby, on burlap walls, old canteens and branding irons hung up, along with "Black Bart's Boots." Gad, what big feet he had. Evidently passing through Salome one hot night, he took them off to dance with you know who, and—bye bye, Black Bart. . . . (Where's his head?) . . . When I fall out, it's dark and the town has come alive in the desert night—all the daytime signs are neonized and blare out down the straight highway—"Sheffler's Motel"—"Your Cafe"—"GAS!" A half-moon, very white, hangs over, and the "Vibrant Mysteriousness" of the desert seems to close in on all sides, reminding me of Camus's phrase about night's "primitive hostility." A great gleaming silver aluminum truck roars out of that night, flashes thru the four blocks of neons and plunges back into the darkness of the universe. . . . Salome danced thru my night. Woke up very early, hearing voices thru a wall, and thought of a woman's deep Spanish voice heard thru a wall in a hotel in Málaga, years ago. She was moaning and moaning, coming in the night. She was a long time coming, now still heard on great Southwest plain in the heart of another world. And will go on, the primitive inchoate nightlife of the world: life against the night, voice shored up against Darkness: and "what has been, will be."

S D. H. Lawrence Ranch, October 22

teve Durkee told me a tale a Taos Indian told him about how the tribe was gathered in its kiva & the cacique's spells weren't working & something was wrong in the air & they looked up & saw a white man in a niche who was writing everything down & this was the end of the Indians' power & the beginning of the White Man's takeover (the Indians' Intuition rendered powerless by the Written Word of the white man)— And the cacique threw a bolt of lightning at the White Man in his niche which caused the White Man to have a complete loss of memory so that he remembered nothing of what had happened & had no intuition of it & had only the Written Word to remember it by & this is where the Indian considers the White Man to be at today—intuitionless & depthless. And the White Man ran away & the Indians chased him & that is where they consider themselves today, still chasing the White Man—trailing him—not really wanting to catch up—

October 24—El Rito, N.M.

Arrived just as darkness descended, lights in broken houses just coming on. Drove once thru the one street of the town, turned around & came back to Coffee House sign, dismounted & knocked. No one there. Saw light in back house & went around there & knocked on screen door on veranda, intending to ask whereabouts of friends. Thin, bearded man, about fifty-five or sixty, comes to door, peers at me thru screen, in back of him a warm kitchen with open fire, a boy of eleven with flax hair, and an interesting-looking woman of about the man's age. I have a strange familiar sensation when the man peers at me with his faraway visionary eyes, as if I had awakened him from a dream or a sleep—as if I had known him before—a strangely familiar look, Rip Van Winkle look. . . . No, that was not it—rather a fleeting sensation that I had unexpectedly come upon B. Traven, or the ghost of B. Traven—which was strange, seeing as later he gave me a review of his painting to read in which the critic called him "the B. Traven of painters." The man was Wilfred Lang & the critic was Richard Ogar in the *Berkeley Barb*. . . . Wilfred Lang asked me who I was, as if I looked familiar to him too, and then asked me in—all this in a few instants—and I gladly entered into the warm home & met his son, Skipper, and his neighbor—not his wife—Ingeborg Lorenz. They gave me a glass of white wine & invited me to supper, which I most gladly accepted (contributing a bag of carrots I had in the car). . . . I had heard of Wilfred Lang ever since I first came to San Francisco in 1951—had seen his painting from time to time—in friends' houses, etc. Remembered he'd been living in the '50s up the Sacramento River somewhere—but had no idea where or what he was now. . . . Turned out he was an old friend of all the San Francisco poets & artists of Rexroth's generation[19]— Bill Everson, Dick Moore, Jim Harmon, Lewis Hill, Dave Koven, Marie Rexroth. Was at C.O. camp at Waldport, Oregon, where they had designed & printed all those fine poetry books—Everson the printer, Lang often the designer.[20] This was where Patchen's *An Astonished Eye Looks Out of the Air* had been printed. (Lang asked how Patchen was now & I told him he was somewhat interested in moving to the Southwest, if a warm house close to a hospital & stores could be found.) . . . A delicious dinner & then we retired to another adobe room (where Lang's easel was) & I read them my poem about visiting the D.H. Lawrence ranch—Lorenzo in Taos— and Lang brought out his first editions of the Waldport poetry books & reviews of his painting, etc. . . . I asked if I could sleep on his porch that night in my new sleeping bag, but Ingeborg Lorenz offered me her house down the road, since she was leaving for Santa Fe & Annapolis, Md., for a few days (which I most gladly accepted, wanting a place I could rest up for a few days & gather my thoughts & write a bit, before taking off for San Francisco) and they went over with me & built a fire for me with *piñon* logs in the living room stove & left me & here I am!

Maybe this is the place. . . . Nowhere to go from here. Bring the family out? Or—? Strange, open, isolated feeling here. As if I've already disappeared in the great land, lost wilderness, gone over the horizon, followed a line in my palm, branching off in a great division, the final big turning-point & change? . . . Horde of blackbirds now talking in the yellow aspens out back. . . . In the late afternoon sunlight the fields around the house stretch burnt yellow to the hills which are sandy & dark green with scrub growth. It is a little like New England in the fall, brittle leaves on the brown dry ground. The backs of the bright yellow aspen leaves are pale white. There is a stillness even when the wind blows across the mesas. . . .

Three days later I'm still here, sitting in the bright sun out back. The wind blows the brownest leaves off the fruit trees, in bunches. I write a letter I've been trying to write for three days. We go on. . . .

SANTA RITA JOURNAL

January 1968

SANTA RITA REHABILITATION CENTER, JANUARY 4, 1968—What are we doing here in this dank tank? Probing the limits of legitimate political dissent in this unenlightened country? Nonviolent gesture of blocking the entrance to war at Oakland Army Induction Center hereby judged beyond that limit. Rehabilitate us, please . . . First rough impressions of anybody's first time in jail; suddenly realizing what "incarcerated" really means. Paranoid fear of the unknown, fear of not knowing what's going to happen to your body, fear of getting thrown in the Hole. . . . Routine of being booked, fingerprinted, mugged, shunted from bullpen to bullpen itself a shock for any "first offender" . . . Naïve vestigial illusions about the inherent goodness of man fly out the barred window. . . . From Oakland jail, shunted through a series of sealed boxes, the first on wheels—long gray bus, windows blinded, fifty inmates behind locked grate, the freeway where yesterday we rode free now visible only through holes in grate. . . . Prison sighted half hour later on a forlorn plain at Pleasanton. . . . Barbed-wire fences and watchtowers. Poor man's concentration camp? . . . Shunted through another series of holding cells, several more hours of not knowing one's immediate fate, just as likely you'll be put in "Graystone" maximum security pen as in General Compound. . . . I take the easier way out: I don't refuse to shave or work. Reforming the prison system is another issue. Rather have a pen than a beard (and so keep this journal). Pen mightier than beard. Opportunity to infiltrate general prison population with nonviolent ideas? Another naïve liberal illusion!

The prison is about two-thirds black, and the other third is Mexican, Pachuco and white North American. They've got their own problems and their own enemies, and they've no use for "nonviolence." The jungle is full of felons and, as for the war, most of them have the attitudes of their jailers and think what the U.S. is doing in Vietnam is great, violence being one way of life they fully understand. This sure deflates the myth promoted by Our President equating antiwar demonstrations with "crime in the streets" and with ghetto wars. If there were any blacks busted this time at the Oakland Induction Center, I didn't see them. (And if I were black, in Oakland, I'd stay away too.) . . .

JANUARY 5—There's not a political prisoner in my barracks. The most "uncooperative" of the demonstrators are in Graystone, two in a cell or in The Hole on bread and skimmed milk. A larger group is in Compound 8 with no privileges and a meal-and-a-half a day. A little incident happened today when they were marching back from the mess hall. The last in the line suddenly went limp and sat down in the middle of the Compound street. He was a kid of about twenty with medium-long hair he'd refused to cut. One officer ran up to him and tried to make him get up. He would not. The officer made a signal and four other officers wearing black leather gloves came at the double up the center of the street from the gate. They had no guns or night sticks. Each took an arm or a leg of the boy and started dragging him. He was a big kid, and they couldn't get his tail off the ground. They got him out of sight in a hurry. When I got back to barracks, someone had an *Oakland Tribune* with a photo of four Marines carrying a dead Marine buddy away from a Vietnam battlefield in the same style. . . .

JANUARY 6—I told them I had printing experience, and they put me stencilling pants! "Santa Rita" in pure white on every pair. "Gives us something to aim at!"

the deputy told me, laughing, sighting his fingers at the stencil marks. Very funny. Holy prison, named for a Spanish saint. . . . Goya should have seen a place like this. He did, he did. Goya faces in the morning chowline, a thousand of them sticking out of blue denims, out of Goya's *Disasters of War.* These are the disasters of peace. Down rows and rows of long wooden tables, half of skid row mixed with Oakland ghettos and the backwash of various nearby penitentiaries, long-term cons now here hung up on short-term crimes—petty boosters, bad check artists, child molesters, freeway drag-racers, car thieves, armed robbers, mail frauds, sex-freaks, winos, hypes, pushers, you name it. And political prisoners. . . . Sit swine-like at the trough, gobbling the chow from metal trays. Great place to keep from getting too refined; dig these myriad beat faces. . . . Here comes "Orfeo"—very handsome young Negro dude with a fine great black beard. Walked out of a Genet prison novel. Just stood there smiling like a black angel without wings when they told him to shave or get thrown in The Hole. They came back later and took him away. Now he shows up again in the mess hall, looking as wild and gentle as ever. I believe he is truly mad and they know it. I don't believe he understood anything they told him. They let him keep his beard. He'll fly away over the rooftops one day, to a shack on a hillside above Rio and live with a beautiful mulatto and tend goats, blowing a wreathed horn. And the horn full of grass. . . .

Another face in the gallery across the table from me: enormous ragged gray head, with hogshead snout, on a two-hundred-pound body in ragged jeans. Great hams of white hands. But the face, the face: white stubble from shaggy hair to throat, rum-pot eyes. Small pig-eyes, but not mean-looking. Just dumb and staring. This is what has become of "The Man with the Hoe." Long, heavy jaw with great, protruding rows of white teeth. Grunted and snuffled as he slurped his pancakes. When he called for the coffee pitcher, his voice came out in a thin squeal. Man, what have you done to this man? Man, who made you like that? Man, has Mother ever seen you, seen what has become of you? Man, you still alive inside? (I hear your stentor breath.) Man, are you to be born again? Live again, love again? Man. Who is there to redeem you. Fidel Castro? The true revolutionary, Fidel said, is one whose first concern is the *redemption* of mankind. . . . Faces fallen out of wombs somewhere, long ago. Now rolled down streets and come to rest among writhing bodies in a painting by Bosch, Garden of Paradise. . . . Feed and shuffle out, doubles of models Goya used in a Toledo madhouse. "By Graystone's foetid walls." . . . One doesn't eat here to consume food; one eats to consume time. And time is life. . . .

JANUARY 7—Sunday in the Compound, and "religious services": let them explain away the existence of evil here. The older one gets, the more one learns to believe in the very real existence of evil. This place proves it. The making of criminals. The redemption of mankind? The rehabilitation of man? They put nineteen-year-old Judith Bloomberg and Joan Baez on bread and milk for three days. (On the men's side, Gary Lisman fasted for twelve days.) These kids are the greatest. They are busted for disturbing the "peace" and are hauled away. They plead *nolo contendere*. They do not wish to contend. They are telling their elders they can have it. They are telling the Establishment that they want nothing to do with its power structure and refuse even to dispute the legal terms of that evil. . . . As long as there are guns, they will shoot, telescopically. . . . At the weekly movie tonight, the inmates spy Joan Baez through a crack in the curtain hiding the balcony where the women prisoners sit. A hundred felons turn and raise their hands in the Peace Sign and shout, "We love you, Joan!"

JANUARY 8—The Enormous Room of my barracks: a black inmate is reading *Synanon* (the place is full of junkies). He doesn't realize what an elite place Synanon may be. Diedrich, the founder, must have read Hermann Hesse's *Magister Ludi* (The Bead Game) and seized upon the conception of an elite world-within-a-world depicted by Hesse in Germany—Castalia being the name of the German intellectual elite created to govern society, with its own special *esprit de corps*, its own hierarchy, its own pecking order—a self-contained world of its own—Synanon also having developed its own cadre of first leaders framed on the wall, approval and status in its society dependent on length of residence, etc., the drug user rejected by the outside straight world here able to reject that society himself in favor of Synanon's own hierarchy: the Bead Game on its own level. And the prison system with its own Bead Game. . . . Shigeyoshi Murao[21] comes to see me during visiting hours and tells me it looks just like the prisoner of war camps they kept Nisei in during World War Two.

JANUARY 9—Obscenity: violation of the Penal Code: today in the commissary line when I tried to exchange a word with Dr. Lee Rather (a political prisoner), Officer Dykes hollered at me: "Get your fucking ass out of here, you motherfucker!"

JANUARY 10—Back in the barracks, the sealed life goes on. We are on some blind ship, all portholes sealed. Siren sounds and loudspeaker barks. Up for the count. Then down again, felon shipmates stretched in their bunks, staring at the overhead. . . . You spend a lot of time staring at nothing in a place like this. Great place to develop the Tragic Sense of Life. "Lucy in the Sky with Diamonds" comes over the barracks radio, and I picture myself in a boat on a river, where newspaper taxis await on the shore, waiting to take me away. . . .

JANUARY 11—Awakened at exactly three a.m. by a guard with a flashlight and told to get up and stand by my bunk. "You're going to court today." From three to eight a.m. I wait in a bullpen with over fifty other inmates going to court. The cell is twenty by twenty, and over half the inmates have to stand up all that time. I talk to one black felon who has been gotten up like this three days in a row, and if he wants to fight his case this is the way he can do it. . . . Life goes on at Santa Rita. Or death. . . . I got the Santa Rita blues. . . .

Afterthoughts and vituperations: Really realize how a hole like this literally makes criminals: eighteen-year-old first offender thrown in for disturbing society's deep sleep now making his first hard connection with hard drugs (they are shooting it up in the john!) and enforced homosexuality (bend over, buddy!) . . .

Guards with hard-edge voices careful not to show any human feelings for inmates, on the watch for the slightest lack of obsequiousness on the part of prisoners, now and then goading them a bit with a choice obscenity . . . a slip of the tongue in return, and you're in The Hole with your tongue hanging out. . . .

Plus mail officers with German names withholding mail and books at will, first-class letters opened and censored. . . . Working in the mailroom I note two books (sent directly to an inmate from City Lights Bookstore) withheld: Debray's *Revolution in the Revolution?* and *Black Power*. . . . Burn, baby, burn—but in here, baby, it's you who'll be burning. . . .

Unhappy Dehabilitation Center, man-made excrescence befouling the once-beautiful landscape in the shadow of distant Mount Diablo: Devil's mount!

If only revolution can blot out such scenes, let there be revolution; but not a revolution of hate leading in the end to just another super-state. . . .

I t was Paris 1968 and by the eternal corner where the Boulevard St.-Germain cuts across St.-Michel, by the tall iron gates of the Cluny gardens, a band of three violinists, each with his cup, fiddled disparately. The separate screeching strands of music fell upon the curled iron gates and wound around them like snapped violin strings or rubber bands, only to dissolve at once in the swelling carnival sound of the street, while just inside the wrought-iron gates, three silent stone-winged griffons sat in darkness, unmoved.

Meanwhile in the real world of May '68, the artist Jean-Jacques Lebel had invited me to perform (along with many other Happening poets from various countries) in the first of his Festivals of Free Expression at the American Centre in Montparnasse. Lebel was the very first to stage Happenings in France, and we were among his first performers, and when the '68 student uprising at the Sorbonne begins to happen, here I am hanging out with Lebel on the fringes of the anarchist group Noir et Rouge, which was the very mother yeast of the student revolution begun on the Vincennes campus of the University of Paris before spreading to the Sorbonne.

And now at the Sorbonne just up the block from the Cluny in its medieval dream, a huge crowd of students and workers was forming in front of the Café DuPont-Latin, some waving signs reading Tout Est Con Chez DuPont. They were beginning a great parade proclaiming a new ideal society of liberated youth and total freedom from the chains of the status quo. Streaming down the boulevard, they gathered momentum, carrying off stray bewildered tourists, Sorbonne professors, concierges, dowagers, streetwalkers, dance instructors, pale poets and artists with easels, guitarists, street sweepers and girls with books and flowers.

And the horde turned right onto the Boulevard St.-Germain, heading toward the Place Maubert, now thousands marching and singing in the street. But when they reached the Place Maubert, suddenly hordes of black-helmeted gendarmes descended from squad cars hidden along side streets and threw themselves upon the students and workers, firing tear gas and wielding horned truncheons and swinging leaded capes, the Establishment descending with all the blind brute force of the entrenched state. Students fell like tin soldiers before the assault, but many rose and started tearing up the paving stones of the Place Maubert and making barricades with them. Still, the armed *flics* kept coming on and on in waves, some hiding behind huge shields emblazoned with coats of arms of the imperial state.

Meanwhile *le grand général*, President Charles de Gaulle, was on the radio, calling for calm and for *grandeur* and for *la gloire*, for the eternal glory of *La France*.

MAY '68 GRAFFITI
Be Realistic, Ask for the Impossible
Under the Paving Stones Lies the Beach
I Declare the State of Permanent Happiness
Boredom Is Counterrevolutionary
Death to the State
I'm a Groucho Marxist
The Liberation of Humanity Is All or Nothing

THE HONORARY SHERIFF OF
KEYSTONE HEIGHTS, FLA.

August 1968

The sign along the road around Lake Geneva said Tropical Fish Farm. There were two old VW sedans in the farmyard, one with a bumper sticker reading "Support the Boys in Vietnam," the other with the largest American Legion emblem I had ever seen on the front windshield—a full two feet in diameter. The driver would have to see through it to drive. There was an outside pool with large goldfish and a greenhouse full of tropical fish tanks & a strange decayed tropical smell—a generator groaned somewhere & water flowed through the murky tanks filled with brilliant tiny fish of all breeds. Then the owner & keeper (& driver of those cars) appeared. He was about five feet tall, about sixty years old, naked to the hairy waist, and wearing one of those plastic green eyeshades that can be sprung out horizontal to the face, under which he wore a pair of thick rimless smudgy eyeglasses. He was myopic, pudgy, hairy, and mostly bald, with a squishy watery voice, sort of indeterminate in tone & with no particular accent. The voice groaned or growled out, as he fished out our selections from the tropics. He was very gentle with the little fish as he worked with the net, telling me exactly how to care for them. His baggy pants hung down below the belt, revealing colored plastic underwear. His stomach hung over in small hairy rolls. When our transaction was through, we went out in the yard again, and, looking at the VWs with the stickers, I said, "You the retired sheriff around here?" He hesitated perceptibly before he answered. "I'm honorary sheriff— First World War," he told me finally. He went off with his life, & into the farmhouse, where a gray woman awaited him, the screen door slamming behind him. . . .

MASSACHUSETTS—BIG SUR

August-October 1968

G ot up early, clear & windy & blue, down across the dunes to the white beach, ran along it, throwing off everything, and dove in, ice water, salt shivering, gasping, clear deep, ran back up the beach & lay in sun on terrace, dried, went in, took up first book at hand, bringing to it what I wanted to read, no matter what, almost, it would say the same, what I wanted to see— So—*Sonnets to Orpheus*! Rilke spoke to me—

Wellfleet, Mass., 8 a.m., Thursday, August 15

She was almost a girl and forth she leaped . . .

And—

. . . To what deeps
does she sink from me—where? . . . A girl
almost . . .

And another poem—

A god can do it. But how
shall a man . . .

A new life begins, clear & high this morning. It will be.

August 16

This fortnight sleep on four corners of ocean: Big Sur, Baja California, Florida, and now Cape Cod. . . .

August 22—Bixby Canyon Big Sur Again

Looked at a yellow rose all day—Pete Spears gave it. Long stem, long yellow phallic flower, bud still firm, far outer leaves large & *fanées*, six fronds of green leaves on stalk, in afternoon sunlight, thru west window of cabin, on red-checkered table. When will the lower leaves fall away? During "the recurrent ending of never ending night"? Before the dawn, when "the dark dove with flickering wings passes below the horizon of our homing"? The leaves, the petals do not move, in the later afternoon sun. They are not giving away any secrets.

August 23

The first petal of the yellow rose still has not fallen. The bud has completely opened out, its bright yellow silk leaves flat almost, and the very lowest ones bent back down, one pointing straight down to the table. And it will fall, it will not last the night. So it is with relationships. Is it too late to move the flower already to a safer place? For the petals may fall if moved at all. And, then, is there any such thing as a "safer place"? The petals will fall in no matter what place. And which woman does the yellow rose represent? The green tall stalk and the still-fresh green leaves will remain green still for some time. But even this is illusory. It is a cut flower, after all. Rootless, cut from its plant, some distance from the ground, in a wine cruet on a checkered table in the sun which is itself about to go down. . . . "The leaf that moves the entire tree never falls off"? It is hard to remember that the world is ours only once.

August 25

The flower fooled us: three days later it has not dropped its petals; instead, it folded upon itself & half-closed, half-shriveled, but still yellow & lovely, it sits upon its stalk, dried, its green leaves still green & open. . . . (Kirby told me, "I am just a daisy, leaves open, waiting for the rain." . . . This touched me deeper than anything else she's ever said.) I believe Pete Spears, the "drunken bum" who used to be in North Beach, is an angel-messenger sent by some Good God—turning up here with that yellow rose for Kirby—no matter how drunk or broke I've ever seen him, he always was carrying fresh flowers— This time no exception— Ten years ago he'd stumble into me in S.F. & hand me flowers for Kirby— Then here he comes, stumbling through the woods with a rose for Kirby— And now three days later, here he comes again, this time with a bunch of very beautiful big chrysanthemums which he lays on me with the admonition to be sure to give them to Kirby. He's sent by an angel of some kind, to keep me & Kirby together. (He's driven down into Bixby Canyon by a young cat who digs my poetry & turns me on as we're standing by the gate waiting for Pete to gather himself together for the ride back to the highway.) The flower makes me think of K, the turn-on of something else—

> Tell me, tell me, o cock, must I give up love
> at the fourth level of enlightenment? (A. Ginsberg)

San Francisco, Much Later: Labor Day weekend

Flash during the night of our old wood house giving one small almost inaudible groan or heavy creak, very short & deep & almost not heard, in the midnight dark, as if it were some lost abandoned hull drifting & now suddenly foundered awash in the dark & wind, and then down out of sight, fallen suddenly apart undersea, timbers & beams letting loose & all parted now in darkness, gone forever, incredibly sad. . . . All the lives it held too all foundered away forever. . . .

October 7—Big Sur

Curious how I reverse the roles of Eros and Reality Principles as given in Marcuse's *Eros & Civilization*—the Reality Principle, one would think, would dominate in the daytime and the Eros Principle naturally dominate at night, in dreams, visions, subconscious, etc. With me, it seems to be just the opposite: at night, in sleep, the Reality Principle seems to take over my being—so that when I awake, at the very instant of awaking, as in "reentry" from a "trip"—coming back to earth—I have a flash dictated by the Reality Principle—that everything I am doing, actually, is "wrong"—that I am acting at the command of Eros which is the voice of irrationality and of unreasoning blind desire, even of madness. As if a flash voice whispers to me at the very instant I am regaining "consciousness" (at 5 a.m. when I've been awaking, "before the recurrent ending of never ending night")—as if a flash whispers to me, "That way lies madness"—as if a little Reality Hammer tapped me lightly but solidly on the skull, "awakening" me, recalling me to "Reality." Then, during the day, I build up my vision again, and by nightfall have persuaded myself again that my vision & way are not mad. . . .

PARIS AND ROME

December 1968

L eaving England, after four gray days, British European Airways to Paris Le
Bourget, a long wait on the ground buckled in at London Airport, then
the jet takes off and suddenly we are riding in brilliant sunlight and out over the
Channel— England back down there in the dense fog, locked in its dreary winter
climate— Still the tight little island it always was. . . .

Then planing quietly to the ground at Le Bourget under cold gray skies. Lights
are on in buildings, and evening is descending, 5 p.m.

But how bright everything is, coming into Paris on Air France bus; the light so
clean & bright, windows shining. Paris still exists despite all . . . I still wander . . .
a figure in the landscape, disappearing over the horizon, as darkness descends.

We cross a lighted bridge on the Seine, bright & light all along the rise of night.
The lights are on in the restaurant in the Eiffel Tower. The traffic streams by the
illuminated monuments. . . . Took a taxi at Invalides, fell out into the Place de la
Contrescarpe, looking for the Hotel du Carcassonne, found it, a real dump, and the
shrew concierge told me no rooms for single nights, went out & down the Rue
Mouffetard, behind the Sorbonne, a street-fair atmosphere, strings of lights over the
narrow street, booths & hawkers, the stores open onto the street, music on loudspeakers, street choked with evening crowds, down the steep hill on the cobblestones, freezing night air, pheasants & other birds hung up with their feathers on

outside butcher shops, good-looking chick at counter giving me the once-over, students & people of the quartier pouring by. . . . Out at last into the Boulevard St.-Michel and then St.-Germain and the Rue de Seine, the clock in front of the Pergola across from the Mabillon reading exactly 6:03 p.m.

How many years after my first long transit here. . . . It's good, it feels good to be back. . . . Or does it, really?

Décembre 5

Gray day, temps morne, pas de chance, "la vie continue," tout est beau et con, et les dieux ne me voient pas Rue de Seine dix heures du matin petit déjeuner au lit et le téléphone qui ne répond pas. Tant pis, on arrive pas trop tôt ou trop tard. Je fais des calculs sur mon miroir. . . . Je fais des calculs en savon sur mon miroir, et mon verre s'est brisé avec un éclat de rire. Une vieille tricoteuse mémé-volante arrive avec mon café-au-lait, dit bonjour dans une voix sépulcrale en me jetant un coup d'oeil douloureux, et part. La vie-de-tous-les-jours ne change pas et les vieilles tricoteuses et les vieux ne changent pas; les jeunes changent; les vieux font les gestes obscènes, les jeunes font pipi comme les vieux, et alors deviennent vieux. Et tout recommence, tout tourne, et la vie continue si belle et si conne. . . .[22]

December 6

Chez Jean-Jacques Lebel—I'm not a windmill—I don't have two wings for arms, I am not prophesying the end of the Eternal, I do not content myself with working for the end of immobility, I won't put a cork life-ring from a shipwreck in my grave "just in case" (though on second thought I might, except that there are no second thoughts in the grave). We are kidding each other but I don't kid myself, No, kid, No, señor, my tree is the most beautiful & wouldn't you like to climb in its branches. You can't fall. The blanket my grandmother knitted all her life unravels in my soup I'm not hungry but I'm always coming back to it. I see the woman hidden in the forest where someone hid the gold pieces of time I am still blushing to have uncovered them so bare so shining those hours and so perishable subject to both inflation & deflation Deux francs cinquante s'il te plaît c'est tout ce qui reste de la monnaie I'll eat flowers instead even though they give me a toothache, I will return to myself and reenter myself by my right ear which is open and waiting for instructions The sea of time is lapping me but I'd be very happy to die so young

I've got talent and thirsts still undeveloped I'd like to sing some more and where is the wandering singer lost in memory on an isolated farm someplace not here not now gathering sapphires on an island off Ceylon a kite made of silk stockings dances in the void and I have made this text from the Manifestos of Surrealism. Parents, tell your dreams to your children.

December 8

Histoire des Mains—Hands partout: Hands of the rich in the Alsatian restaurant, at the corner of Rue de la Sorbonne. Soft, bejeweled, pudgy hands on the women, and their men's hands also soft & pudgy, as one of them says to another at the table, "Eh bien, which of us hasn't been president of something!" and shrugs his shoulders with a laugh. These are the rulers of France. *Et tout de Gaul ne se divise en trois parties.* There is only one party, only one part, and it is the party of the rich & soft & fat, eating twenty-five-dollar dinners with their elegant wives & grandmothers & associates & sons, ruling de Gaulle's kingdom.

The thirty-five-year-old son of one of them, obviously the present manager of one of the family enterprises, dressed more or less like a senior executive American, has the same hands, only they are not yet so advanced in decomposition, not yet so pudgy, not yet so soft around the rings, though already Pure White. . . . Down the street, in the Rue St.-Séverin, up an alley where the Arabs eat, the nails are black.

December 9

Histoire de "I Love You": there are days I see all too clearly but also there are days when I love everyone I see or meet or touch or know in any way. Strange how in these last full-blown years of this vie errante et déracinée, vie flânée, I should have this profound, almost pure feeling or attraction or affection or even love for everyone, for the most casual acquaintance, even for people passed unknown in the street or in a café. . . . As yesterday in a tiny couscous restaurant in Rue St.-Benoît, the fair-looking forty-year-old waitress was sitting still in a corner with her face in her hands, either with a hangover or sleepless and exhausted or with her "period"—I felt like saying to her, "Je t'aime." And I did, walking out. . . . Or maybe it is just a huge lust for everybody's bodies, as if as middle age progresses my own body develops more & more of a solitary hunger to be close & in contact with other bodies—a sort of runaway voluptuousness, a runaway sensuality, even licentiousness, for everybody & everything in sight, or within reach. . . . Though with men it's not the body thing at all, yet I still feel great affection & openness to certain male friends, including ones I haven't seen for many years— There is a desired Identity or Oneness of being, all pulsating together with the universe itself, an entity of all . . . which is also the predominant feeling I get from grass, hash, or LSD. . . . A sense that the whole universe & creation is whirring around & throbbing together, all living & dying parts of it, animate & inanimate, all being & existing together, all conscious together, as parts of one huge sentient organism, the leaves on the trees or the brown leaves on the ground & men's & women's bodies all quaking together, no end to it, no end, no end to it all, "no end to the withering of autumn flowers," and no beginning either, all wrapped up in one huge Breath of Being. Om. Back to some source, some silence of silences, where all ends and all begins. There is nothing to fear. . . . Where the dots begin. . . . .

December 12

Driving thru the old streets of Paris, from Invalides to Orly Airport in the Air France bus . . . beaux quartiers, boulevards, mazes of traffic & streets, immense stone churches with unknown names (of saints, no doubt), metro entrances. . . . Kiosks and stores illuminated for Christmas, 12 noon now, the sun like an illuminated gold coin in a gray-violet sky, now above bare plane trees—Porte d'Orléans—Boulevard Périphérique— And we take the auto-route out—thru a tunnel. . . . Farther out, the remains of great fields, still bordered with knotted plane trees, now intersected with auto-routes, fences, modern housing developments, now smokestacks & factories & great power lines carrying in the current for Paris; cut those lines on their great steel poles (each astride the landscape, like an Eiffel Tower) and all of Paris goes black. We arrive at Orly. . . . We take off to Rome. . . . Looking down, I see the famous "Map of Paris as Seen by a Bird in Flight." Great buildings and boulevards lost in time, solidified nostalgia! Three-quarters of an hour later, the most fantastic sight appears: a solid layer of clouds, cottony but dense, and suddenly out of this vast snowfield appear the tops of all the Alps like great brown stone pointed islands, the cloud fields surrounding the mountains like some great white sea with fluffy waves lapping, the whole like some frozen landscape on another planet or the moon, a lost archipelago, no roads, no houses, no trails, no signs of human presence or passage, Man never there. And then down toward Italy, down to the Mediterranean shores, past Turin, past Genoa, and out across the blue flat sea, and in the far distance to the rear the white frozen Alps on the horizon, remote as another planet now, the whole crossing or passage a panorama such as Ruskin never saw or imagined in his famous passage in *The Nature of Gothic* (or *The Stones of Venice?*) or that some great bird of passage saw migrating southward over those great mountains or the Apennines.

Rome, 3:15 p.m.

Changed my money at the airport "Bank of the Holy Ghost" (Banco di Santo Spirito) and took off for the city. . . .

December 13

Fell as if into an Inferno of Hieronymus Bosch, thru his Doors of Paradise, into this *fourmillant* Rome, thrown headlong as it were into the midst of an enormous ant-hill, where millions of creatures walked & moaned & laughed & ran & coughed &

smoked & squirmed & sang & lay down & rolled over & struggled for an inch of space, digging their ant-elbows into their neighbors, gesticulating wildly. The only thing that seemed to be missing from this Bosch world was the funnels up people's assholes or vaginas into which others poured boiling oil, wine, or hot sperm. . . . Leonardo's faces still walking the streets, and Marco Polo need never have left home to do his *Description of the World.* . . .

December 14

Via Bocca di Leone, the fruit market in the narrow streets, street hawkers, men shouting from window to window, the full bright life of the street, "theater of the streets"—more a commedia dell'arte than guerrilla theater or Living Theater's *Paradise Now.* The street scene is still the Italians' "paradise." . . . Upstairs, behind closed blinds, on a brass bedstead, an intellectual takes sleeping pills and uses the telephone to call his psychiatrist who also answers in a darkened room in another city in another country where civilization is also continuing to repress Eros, where those who recognize this repression and act upon it are known as anarchists, where even "revolutionaries" say "drugs" and revolution are incompatible . . . the attraction of anarchism today especially among the young (Black Flags in the barricades of Paris & San Francisco) being the attraction of Eros, rather than its political qualities. . . . In "The Mouth of the Lion," the intellectual turns over in his bed & switches off the light. His sleeping pills are taking effect. He escapes again into his own Eros.

The line in my right palm (which a month ago I saw suddenly for the first time, as if it had appeared overnight) just as suddenly seems to be gone. Looked at my palm tonight at dinner in some hotel in Ostia (waiting for a plane) and it just wasn't there anymore. This hard, sharp line, on the left side of my hand, cut vertically all the way from my heart-line to the base of my life-line. Very strange, how it has disappeared completely. At first I thought it must be the light; I looked more carefully, but it just was not there, the line which a month ago had shocked me by its sudden appearance. Ah, now I do see there is some bare trace of it, as if some threat or great threatened change in my life were now somehow disappearing—not to happen after all. This could very well be. But is this merely a prophecy or a sign of what I should do about my life? The other night, lost as I still am in this Italian Dantesque landscape, I asked whatever supreme power there is in the sky, "for a sign." "God, give me a sign," I said, using the word as much as a curseword as for a deity. Maybe this is it. Telling me to "turn back."

Ingeborg Bachmann,[23] the Austrian writer-poet resident in Rome, also lives in the Via Bocca di Leone, in the quartier of the Piazza di Spagna. I give her Ginsberg's new book, *Planet News*, with an inscription to her: "Alive in Rome / in the Mouth of the Lion."

December 16—5 a.m.

Flight from Fiumicino, Rome to Catania. The mouth of my palm has closed again. The big line cutting vertically across head-, heart-, & life-line is there stronger than ever as we taxi in darkness to takeoff. In the bright cabin light, the new line is stronger than ever, and there is another even stronger vertical line, which cuts all the other ones, this one having been noted for the first time maybe six months ago. It is now as heavy as the three major lines & strikes directly down the middle of them, except for the bottom life-line which it shies off from "at the last moment." The "new" line off to the left of it intersects it & comes right down to touch the base of the life-line. All very strange, the meaning of the ancient book à la main— hidden in what superstitious inscrutability? The DC-9 takes off, also inscrutable, into the old inscrutable darkness. . . . Engine whines its Om. . . .

Catania—Taormina

Passed Mount Etna very close up on the port side, snow slopes & peak & then immediately to the Sicilian coast, black land with yellow lights in first dawn, listing over now to some coastal city, probably Catania, Etna on the horizon, filling it like a white ghost in first light, "just another goddamn snow mountain."

Driving to Taormina, the bright landscape a little like the north of Málaga going to Nerja, only cleaner & more beautiful, with Etna's top on the far horizon, beyond green hills & olive trees, untrimmed plane trees along the narrow road, and on the other side the blue sea close-up, with a red sun just cleared the horizon, and as soon as it gets clear it turns gold-white. Now gray stone walls & fenced-in orange orchards, small yellow unripe oranges & lemons the size of ping-pong balls on them, with Etna suddenly loomed up huge & close ahead. A Roman pine, with umbrella head, standing out here & there on the coast side, and cactus too & a few palm trees, onward toward Taormina.

Bright, bright, bright in early morning sunlight, bright & green, small stone towns, stucco buildings painted pink, with tile roofs, as in small-town Spain, villas with scarlet forsythia, olive-colored lower slopes of Etna dotted with hamlets. . . . Taormina on a very high bluff in the sky . . . what a place to read poetry aloud!

For
Lorenzo
should he someday
come upon himself
in that labyrinth
of solitude

7/83 ?ferling

re.

Marrakesh

April 22–27, 195?

Pardon me if I disappear in Mexico, wearing a mask and strange suspenders. Puncho Villa. Wandering about, speaking my curious 'spagnol. The trees are coming down, we'll to the woods no more, mad mind and black sun, we'd better find an island quick. Though there's no longer any "away." Southbound through the Toltec debris, the dark horse still a free runner. Under what volcano. . . . My soul in various pieces and I attempting to reassemble it, mistaking bird cries for ecstatic song when they are really cries of despair. And poetry a procession of waterbirds in flight

mixed with motor accidents, O drunk flute O golden mouth, flower in the bung-hole, kiss kiss in stone boudoirs. Voice lost & dreaming, door floated over the horizon. Where am I? Leaving Alamos on a local heap of a bus, full of vaqueros in hard cowboy hats, smoking Sonora Gold on the backseats, stoned blind in the dusk. One hombre passes me a huge joint, size of a Brown Bomber. Setting yellow sun slants through the bus. Gone now. . . . Thus did he see first the dark land. . . . Dark trees flash by, white leaves nested in them like birds. . . .

"LOWER" CALIFORNIA

October 24, 1961

A visionary journey without visions, in a stone blind land—the new Mexico still the Old beat Mexico—that huge dark foodshit smell still here (which I first smelled in dank woodwork of a Mexico City pension, 1939) . . . in Ensenada, on the blank Pacific, there's always a wind full of sand at this season, and you don't get the Smell on the long dust crud street by the bay—but stick your head in some cantina and you get it full in the nose. . . . Ensenada, baja California—bah on this baja—who stole the sun? where's love? Brown Hades! Dig the native inhabitants, groin streets, mud people. Only the kids and dogs have anything left in them—and the dogs can't stand it—they lie around stretched out with flies all over them in the gutters, a curious race apart. I saw one dunghill dog go in a church, up the center aisle, looking for his *pugh* (that's a smelly pun), he scooted out a side door quick, no place for him in there, he scared maybe by the wood confessionals like doorless phone booths where priests sat listening to penitents on each side hidden in curtains, each by a little lattice window through which whispers went—priest listened to both at once, answered both at once, or confused the two? Were those phoners getting thru to any Central? Daddy, I've been disconnected. Stagger out into the dust land. Perhaps I could learn to love this land if I stayed awhile—though it's the third or fourth time I've been to Mex already—if Los Angeles is the asshole of America, what is this brown appendage down here? Lost Ensenada, existing only by the force of gravity—stuck in the earth forever. . . .

. . . I arrived at night, on a creaking bus, among devious faces. In the morning, all's different. There's palm trees and sun, street sweepers are out, sprinklers go by to lay the dust, the bay is calm with fishing boats, mountains rise up. . . .

The day before in Tijuana—I walked around with McGilvery and Floyd Damon from La Jolla, digging the jumbled streets, eating roast corn from street-vendors, drinking Cerveza under arbors in back gardens of crazy hillside restaurants, stopping to watch local celebration at Mexican Lions Club of United Nations Day—a little Mexican municipal band struck up its mournful flourish when officials arrived in open limousines, an enormous racket of trumpets and trombones and drums sounding as if some truck had just blown its muffler. It's a full minute before the blowers get together on the tune—and stumble on into the Blue Danube. A dead dog lay on its side by the entrance, flies in his eyes, up his nose—the Lion that didn't make it.

October 25

Hotel Plaza, Ensenada (town without a plaza), room on roof I look two ways out of, to sea and mountain, over flat rooftop town—I hear roosters before dawn, see the light growing, headlights of junkheap cars coming down hillside, a little brown bird on windowsill seems about to take off—no, it's a tiny halfbuilt house with frame of roof like wings on top of hill outlined against first windowlight. . . . Up before dawn, writing, I'm some faroff hungup Hemingway character waking in some small Spanish hotel alone, counting my marbles. Or the ghost of Elliot Paul contemplating the life & the death of a Spanish town. I see myself ten years ago in Majorca, in Andraitx port, lost fishing village, where they fished up those mute Phoenician urns. . . . From which way will the fascists come this time, baby? I can almost hear their minutemen machineguns in San Diego. . . . *Can I survive another transplantation?*

I ride on the beach on a brown horse, rented from a caballero called Alfonso. Horse is called Elefanto. Alfonso rides along on his horse singing a slow Indian song, points out a stucco shack beyond the dunes where he has two wives. We gallop past. Dusk is falling, night creeps up out of sea. A gaggle of dark fishermen struggles past onto a pier with nets; under great hats like turtle shells, they scuttle into dark ocean: the distance between man and primeval mud measured from below sea level.

October 27

Three days here, and I can't stand it any longer, I'll leave in the morning. Dirt streets of shitcity! It's like dying; suppose there were no escape—yet the people here smile at each other from time to time & act as if they still had some great slur of hope somewhere. While consuls drink themselves to death. Help! *No se puede vivir sin amar?* Let the ocean come in and cover it.

October 28

Ensenada to Tijuana to Mexicali by bus. Rode all day, contemplating the earth, saw nothing. Endless riprap roads, hills, mountains, hopeless houses, trees, sagebrush, fences, dust, burros, dry land. Dry people stuck to it. . . . Passing thru Tijuana, I see legless man at downtown dirt corner sitting in backseat of antique sedan from which doors have been torn. He has stained felt hat on center of head, rimless eye-glasses with cracked glass, a huge old typewriter propped up before him on wood box. Typing, he has butt of cigarette stuck to lower lip, burnt-out. Signs hung on car say:

ESCRITOR PÚBLICO

A *campesino* is speaking to him from the curb, he writes what he hears; a great writer, this here Public Stenographer, Public Writer giving people back true images of themselves. Legless, he holds the mirror up. . . .

Tijuana to Mexicali, approaching town of Tecate, bus passes thru hill country strewn thickly with rocks from road to horizon, nothing but rocks, rocks, millions of them covering the landscape, in place of trees. Nature has tried everything! There's beautiful country farther on, other side of Tecate—rock mountains, Tibetan peaks (one of those border mountains north of Tecate, on U.S. side, inhabited by American translator of *The Tibetan Book of the Dead*). We roll on between hills of small rocks, pepper trees and sage and twisted fir growing out of rockhills, rock mountains beyond, sunset coming, bright sun flames close over, bright blue sky with rock holes in it, whole fantastic mountainous landscape of nothing but stone. Then suddenly, at turn of highway high up, a great dry brown plain stretched way below, eastward and northward for a hundred miles, North America. . . .

Arrived at Mexicali, another dust town, only worse, in midst of flat brown plain I saw from above, at nightfall—bus station crammed with *campesinos* looking grim, tough & hungry, under enormous hats & ponchos, waiting for country buses and revolutions. These are the Front Teeth of Latin America. . . . I walk out into the mud boulevard & vision of utter Desolation, Dung & Death in the image of crowded streets and dark people. Everywhere I walk & look, the same! Later, found the tourist part of town, and the American border: big sign over it saying UNITED STATES. Showed my California driver's license and went thru to the American Zone, saw an American movie with bingo advertised with double feature. Went in. Bingo just starting, American on stage with mike announcing numbers drawn out of whirling basket, says number in American and in atrocious Spanish. . . . Came out at midnight, walked back thru border station, no one on Mexican side to check—completely open in *that* direction. Sign said in English: Narcotics Addicts & Users Are Required by U.S. Law to Register Before Leaving Country. Also: Warning: Cats & Dogs Leaving U.S. May Not Be Allowed to Re-enter. Do not pee on the wrong side of the fence. Show your dogtags. Borders must be maintained! An insane fluidity & deracination surely would prevail without them—no countries, no nations, nothing at all to stop us anywhere, nothing to stop the hordes of the world still starving and howling like Calibans at the gates, no customs, no wars, no protective tariffs, no passports, no immigration and naturalization papers, none of the old protective barriers protecting everyone from everyone else, even the oceans dried up eventually, leaving us no alternative but to recognize Indians as brothers, the whole earth only one continent, under it all, after all, all colors of skin at length blended into one skin with one tongue. It'll only take five thousand more years to do this, Indian, even after wasting two thousand mostly in the wrong direction. A very simple little revolution could accomplish it in no time: declare an immediate moratorium on all liaisons, partnerships, and marriages between all people of the same color, everyone immediately to seek union with someone of a different color, all national flags made into snotrags or bandages to be used in maternity hospitals giving birth to nothing but a new generation of babies of nothing but mixed colors & race. . . . In the meantime, I wander about the landscape, making like that American Indian whom Henry Miller wished to have at his side when he crossed the continent in his unconditioned *Nightmare*, the one he wanted to have with him when he viewed the smoking steel mills by roadbeds of Pittsburgh in an *Inferno* Dante never dreamed of. I am ready to return to the Cave at any moment, carry a flint arrowhead in my pocket, just in case. Cro-Magnons carried stones for books.

October 29

My last night in Mexico I spend in Mexican border hotel overlooking the wire barricades. This hotel advertises "Clima Artificial"—but the air-conditioned night in Mexico is different—the Clima Artificial doesn't work. In the middle of the night I tear open my hermetically sealed window which is about the size of my head. A fine dust sifts in from the street. . . .

I sit writing this in the pay toilet of the Greyhound station in Calisco, across the border again next morning. Suddenly my sixteen-cent ballpoint pen slips from my fingers and falls down into the john. Here I make a grave mistake. I flush it, hoping to clear the muddy waters and retrieve my stylo. When the waters clear, my stylo is gone, forever. Perhaps it will reappear centuries later in the alluvia of the Rio Grande, and some strange-colored descendant of Americans come upon it, wondering what strange weapon is this, and how many it killed with what ammunition. Words? So drowns my Journal.

THE ROAD TO TOPOLOBAMPO

May 1962

> "I owe to such evenings the idea I have of innocence. . . ."
> —Albert Camus, *The Myth of Sisyphus*

Sitting at a table in the Parque de la Cruz Blanca, Chihuahua, Sunday afternoon, bright sun . . . I write in a marble notebook with rainbow edges,

We were born
                under the mulberry trees
        From which drop
                        the mynah birds of madness

Someone is playing an accordion, it is Sunday in a Seurat garden.

> Fish float
>
> thru the trees
>
> Eating the seeds
>
> of the sun. . .

The crowd I came with has gone back to Las Cruces. I've two days to wait for the train, to Topolobampo. I walk around town, aimlessly. A storm is coming, sky clouding, wind rising. I lie on my back in the middle of another park, a great grassy park full of willows & palm trees & fountains. Couples lie scattered on the grass, as in pointillist painting, dappled. Laughter muffled. Pieces of voices drift by. I see the tops of the palms shaking, with huge swishing noises, sweeping the sky. Yet the wood clouds do not move. High school boys come by joking & tumbling behind the circular bandstand. "Imbeciles in neckties drop from the trees." The ghost of Malcolm Lowry skulks from behind a bush carrying his sign:

> Le Gusta Este Jardín?
>
> Que Es Suyo?
>
> Evite Que Sus Hijos Lo Destruyan![24]
>
> . . . et cetera.

In coal night, black train starts up at last, noiseless. Reaches westward for the Sierra Madre, upward. Thru black solitudes, green nowheres with the light turned off. *Au pays du Tarahumara*, that wild junkie landscape Artaud apprehended. Still I'm not with him, I'm with Camus who also rushed too fast into his unknown, in this *cama alta*. . . . In this upper berth of being, there is a slight noiseless rocking, as of the universe, and we advance only in darkness, no windows upon the mescal landscape, a bunker in space. In the night of earth, *the unreasonable silence of the world returns*, night a kind of barbaric tongue-tied mongoloid sphinx who will never speak. No answers there! *The primitive hostility of the world rises up to face us across the millennia.* Thru it, we dream onward, skull blind. Wrapped in our own skins. It is an old story.

> Suplicamos
>
> QUIETUD
>
> En Beneficio de Los que ya
>
> Descansan[25]

I am indebted to the young German playwright Günter Eich whose radio play applied the image of the closed train (hurtling faster thru night) to the postwar German situation—a boxcar with an old couple & a couple of kids closed in, hurled to an unknown destination thru a landscape the young have never seen and the elders find impossible to describe. . . . *The world comes to a stop but also lights up.* Our consciousness is the projector, the moment of attention, which focuses on successive images, and each is a truth yet there's no Truth discernible as a whole. Consciousness is merely the act of attention; it understands nothing in itself. There's no *scenario, but a successive and coherent illustration.*

My projector is being hurled thru the dark. If my mind is strong enough I can liken it to one of those Cyclops searchlights mounted on flatcars, piercing the sky yet reaching only so far and no farther, no matter how powerful. Fortunately I do not have that kind of mind. I have a flickering little halfass projector that must resort to all sorts of improvisations in order to function. And no live God discoverable except consciousness itself. And that consciousness itself an improvisation, a drug or a dream. So that, passing thru the stoned country of the Tarahumaras, we continuously improvise our existence, make up our lives as we go, improvise our present, our future, make up our own Topolobampo.

Topolobampo itself is a bleary little fishing port on the Pacific, one of those rag ends of native civilization, half in ruins, harbor like a lost pocket in a canvas poncho, ringed with strange barren islands and lonely juttings of Topolobampo Bay. The road from Los Mochis (flyspecked inland Tortilla Flat) ends suddenly at the base of one small treeless hill, and by a bumpy stone rut one passes up and around to the main pier at the foot of the center of the town which fills the seaward side of the hill and leans over it almost into the water. Two or three small rusty coasters are tied up at the pier like stranded cockroaches.

Ragged hollering urchins of all sizes are running and jumping and swimming off the dock and off the lee side of one of the listing cockroaches, the dark water at least twenty feet below stirred with great splashes and wriggling bodies as in some flailing shipwreck at sea, tattered cries echoing.

Above, in the town itself, screenless, glassless shacks & houses stare down, everything open, as in some Italian hillside village, with a tiny plaza no bigger than the inside of a stone church, the people barefoot, itching with *chinchas*, sitting on beatup open terraces or in big bare swing-door bars hanging from the hillside. And the whole dive creeping with babies, brats of all ages, teenage *muchachas* (already women) in torn cotton shifts laughing & chattering, mud-hut whores among them and old fishermen sitting silent with grandmothers in shawls like reaper deaths. Sundown, 1962. Come back in 1972 and it'll be transformed with gringo hotels on the waterfront, stucco cafés, guides, post-cards, pluribus dollars. The railroad just opened from Chihuahua will see to all that.

There's an Indian fishing village on one of the islets in the bay which is also being considered. . . .

The road to Topolobampo runs ten miles south-southwest in a straight line from Los Mochis. There is a *camión* that runs every half hour or whenever the driver wants to travel. I take one of these jitneys a little before sunset. It is filled to bursting with: two or three young hombres in huge hats, a couple of old hags in kerchiefs, several mothers and little boys and girls, babies in slings, baskets, wicker birdcages, shopping bags, burlap bags, and an ancient phonograph and a stand-up microphone carried by one of the men in sombreros, the whole works jammed into four rows of sprung seats. At the helm, the *chofer* is a young cat with the usual sexy little Latin moustache. As soon as he gets off the dirt streets and dust ripraps of Los Mochis and onto the paved one-lane highway to Topolobampo he turns the radio on full blast with mariachi music and relaxes. He's a *mancarrón*, a one-armed man, but still is able to wave his arm about in great gesticulations & oaths any time any animal happens to get in his way on the road. There's a little lace fringe strung along the top of the windshield to shade the eyes from the sun, there's a metal crèche and a plastic Madonna in a little metal altar stuck to the top of the dashboard so that, sitting in the back, low down, you look thru holy objects to see the road and the horizon way beyond. Later, more than one peak sticks out of the flat plain, but for most of the ten-mile straightway you see this one peak rising up at the very end of the road at the very end-point of the endless perspective, and, looking back, you see another very similar cone-shaped peak rising up behind Los Mochis. Between these two weird cones runs this perfectly arrowlike narrow highway upon which the setting sun, yellow-red, streams, the *camión* seeming hardly to progress down that long perspective, even as it rocks along steadily to the howling of the robot radio tuned to one of those crazy Mexican stations emitting a hilarious mixture of dramatic advertisements for shows, American jazz played by violins and cornets. Church bells thrown in to punctuate special announcements, sexy male announcers sounding as if they were simultaneously seducing a housewife and reporting a fire in the studio, all mixed together with mariachis (who must be kept handy at the station at all hours to be thrown in like shock troops whenever the slightest threat of silence presents itself).

Or maybe it is only a recording of life, played over & over, the whole trip like some weird little record or film running on & on, some kind of comatose dream in which the film withers and slips and the *camión* keeps rolling forever on into the *sol poniente* and into the infinitely narrowing perspective, yet does not advance, everyone strangely silent, all together listening absently and intently to the crazy outpourings of the radio tuned to the world, and digging the sad marcescent landscape of trees, huts, *campesinos*, slatterns at windows (cow-eyes stare out), donkeys, dogs, dry land, sea where coelacanths swim. . . .

It is *innocence*, it is their seeming *innocence* which presents itself incessantly, as you see the *camión* passengers so gravely taking in everything the hotrod announcer throws at them (the announcer himself knowing just whom he's talking to, in fact can see them all in every country backstreet in dustbin Mexico). He's talking to them in person, and they are listening, laughing, smiling, gawking out windows, peering ahead thru Madonna fringe as radio blasts on with rock-and-roll played by nothing but trumpets borrowed from hockshops in Mexico City (*monte de piedads* of leftover life). And the whole absurd Gestalt of the *camión* bowling along like some flippy total caravanserai-symbol, wheeling into space with all the ancient trappings, shawls and superstitions, hunger & flocked beauty (the young dark girl's eyes on the road) carrying along with it all the claptraps and fandanglements of microphones, phonographs, plastic madonnas.

All sit there still groping on into the falling dusk. Innocence persists, insanely intarissable, in spite of all. The road does not end. It is as if the radio were not playing at all. There is stillness in the air, in the light of the dusk, in the eyes fixed forward, in the still end of life, an intolerable sweetness. . . .

Cinco de Mayo, 1962

> Passing strange mountains
>   & dropping pine needles
>   in an envelope
> I send you
>   some of my bones. . . .

Mayo 6, '62

> Morning mocks its flowers
>   by becoming
>   Afternoon

Mayo 7, '62

> We have our moments
> > of ecstasy
> > and then the bird
> > > falls into
> > > > the absurd. . . .

OAXACA

September 6, 1968

Mad, a hole in my shoes, under the jacaranda trees and the great Indian laurels, roots still in the Ganges, in the plaza de Oaxaca. . . . And then at night by the circular bandstand listening to the marimba music, everyone out strolling or on the park benches in the semi-dark, the high lamps shining through the trees. . . . A wandered statue myself . . . where my pedestal?

MITLA

September 7

"Jesús mío misericordia"—one of those Bleeding Christ churches one stumbles into in all the small sad towns of adobe Mexico: entered at thirteen minutes after twelve noon & dropped a big copper Mexican penny into the plaster box held by a five-foot-high plaster altar-boy at the side entrance, startled by the big clunking noise the coin made as it fell through the false bottom of the plaster box & down through the plaster statue itself into a hollow wooden stand upon which the statue stood—the heavy coin hitting the hollow wood base with a loud empty thud. Inside, not one but three bloody bleeding Christs—one stretched out under a garden-green trestle like a birdcage—not a trestle but a sort of bier with handles at each end and a cage of green bars over it—like some kind of stretcher used at sports events to carry victims off the field, take me out coach I've had it, your turn on the gridiron baby, your turn on that cross, what's these nail holes in me hands, fer Christ's sakes? This Christ not more than five feet long, with wood head and hands, stretched out under a white muslin sheet, only his head with crown of thorns showing—like an invalid in bed asleep, blood on the forehead & the lips dripping with it, the green bier trestle like some garden-house trellis with white & blue paper flowers strung on paper vines over His Head; and on the side of the bier in handwritten scrawl—"Jesús mío misericordia." . . . Stumble out into the sun, daddy, and make it among the Mexican tourists just disgorged from a tour-bus, blinking through sunglasses & cameras. . . .

OAXACA

Night of September 7

Corner of Avenida de la Independencia in front of the Science Institute of the University of Oaxaca just off the main plaza, a student revolutionary rally going on in the floodlighted little square with a wooden speaker's stand set up, the front of the Institute hung with huge cloth and cardboard signs: TIERRA Y LIBERTAD, OLYMPIAD DE HAMBRE, VIVA LA JUVENTUD, A LA VICTORIA POR EL ESPÍRITU JOVEN Y LA ACCIÓN REVOLUCIONARIA, LIBERTAD DE ESTUDIANTES PRESOS, EL GOBIERNO LLAMA LEY A SU PROPIA VIOLENCIA, HASTA LA VICTORIA SIEM-PRE—VENCEREMOS.[26] The square filled with standing townspeople, dark and quiet but not hostile, listening to the shouted speeches bounced off the walls by gravelly loudspeakers, the student speakers fired up, gesticulating into the micro-phone, crying out great revolutionary phrases into the Oaxacan night, dense Indian dark. . . . And around the corner, squatted against a wall of the Institute, just out of the floodlight, across the street from a big bank, a blind guitar player squatting in the dust, playing & singing very quietly in the semi-dark of that side-street, his steady low voice an undertone beneath the shouted political voices, the end of his guitar wrapped in torn plastic, he picking at the guitar with a sure calm lively rhythm, his voice going on & on, chipped white enamel tin cup, empty, clamped between his knees, beneath another sign: PUEBLO ÚNETE A TUS HERMANOS. Applause for the speakers, the singer's cup empty. He's bearded but not old, his straw sombrero on the ground next to him, he barefoot, ragged all over, with calm handsome face, maybe part Indian but not much, his low voice clear & strong & calm under all, his gut-string guitar going on & on, below the shouted speeches, below the radical resolutions, beneath the eternal cries for Progress & Liberty, across from the bank, on the ground, hermano, not exactly "united" with the pueblo, yet he its old voice under all, behind & under all, still coming through, sounding through, he's like part of the tierra, rooted in that earth, the song going on under the night, his voice coming in again & again under the speeches, like some kind of revolutionary rejoinder, echo & contre-temps, answer to all, the guitar driving on under his voice. People come & go, crowd applauds, cars roar down the side-streets blowing dust in his face, shined shoes brush his dirty feet, and his song goes on, no part of him moving but his strum hand on the guitar, a full moon above winging thru the clouds, no expression on its face or his, as his voice comes thru again in a pause between speeches. His head is cocked to one side now, as if he were even listening to the speeches the whole time. And answering. 1968: Year of the Mexican Olympics. "Olympiad de Hambre." Olympics of Hunger. . . .

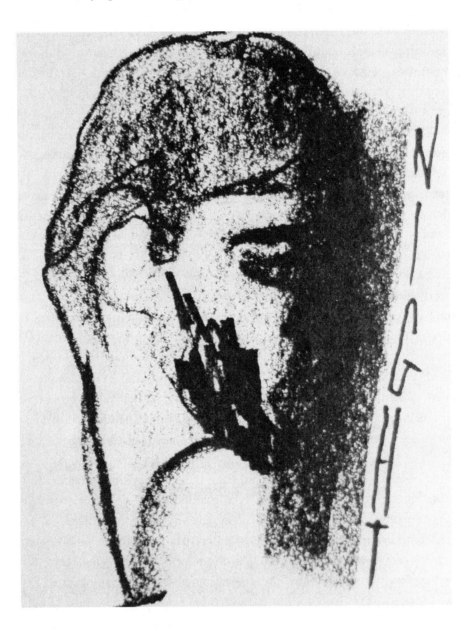

September 10

Shoe *cauchemar* in the streets of Mexico City—millions of shoes, tongues agape, coming at me, a sea of soles flapping—all Latin American countries curiously filled with millions & millions of shoe-freaks— Ever notice how many shoestores there are per block in Mexico City or Havana or Lima Peru? Or La Paz Bolivia? . . . I am wandering thru the Zócalo, Mexico monster city, past the Monte de Piedad (National Pawnshop) and across the enormous plaza at midday, & here come the millions of shoes, tongues in all of them, dusty in the burning sun, all kinds of them, all shapes & sizes, coming past me & past the Monte de Piedad with its national hopes in hock & revolutions in pawn; then on thru the twobillion four-million city, down the great boulevards, Avenida Hidalgo, Avenida Juárez, and the Alameda Central, great central park, hot in the afternoon siesta sun, no siesta, señor, but noon nightmare streets & shoes filled with foreign feet, on sticks in pants & skirts, faces fixed to the upper ends of them, pouring past me where I sit on a wrought-iron bench in a corner of the great park, and then the traffic flooding round me later where I stand on an island in the middle of Avenida Juárez, trying to snare an impossible taxi, all full, all careening thru the massed screaming traffic, pedestrians crossing against all the lights, brakes screeching, horns stuck, me too swimming in the crowds from island to island, shoes a-flap, where am I going? Suddenly a sharp cobblestone strikes through my left shoe sole & the forgotten beginning of a hole, and I understand in a dumb flash how revolutions die on foot, die afoot—a shoe wears through and falls apart a long way from home—foot soldiers limp onward—a donkey needs reshoeing—a guerrilla *camión* wears its tires bald & there are no spares—Che Guevara ties together his shredded boots & goes on, shifts to rough sandals, *abarcas*, and staggers on thru the jungle. . . . The city jungle at midday just as thick & hot, full of just as many hallucinations, noon nightmares & lost tongues. The shoes come at me, all tongueless now. And the big hole now in the bottom of my left shoe, only my right shoes now capable of effective action, the second stage of any revolution when it is easier to go to the Right than further Left. My kingdom for a horse? Nevermind the horse, nevermind the hole in my soul. . . . I go to the occupied University of Mexico campus in late afternoon—with some poets and editors of *El Corno Emplumado*—and pass through the barricades into the buildings held by the students, like Cuba 1960 with young cats in fatigues guarding the entrances & chicks with rifles.[27] A calm prevails today. In the Med School the students have embalmed the bodies of some of their comrades killed by the government of the people. The army is a mile away, cooling it for the Olympics. Soon it will happen. It does. Still Che Guevara goes on, through the jungles. . . .

THE MIND OF CHE GUEVARA A DAY AFTER HIS DEATH

September 11, '68

AH ACA LA VIDA GONDOLA PUERTA
ESCONDIDA REVOLUCIONARIA ACA PALMITO
ACA CHOCLOS ZAPALLOS YUCAS ACA CHACO
HAMBRE EL ELEVADOR ESCONDIDO AYMARAS
Y CAMBAS ACA ARMADILLO PERDIDO NO
REVOLUCIONARIO ACA TAPERAS PALMITOS
DE COROJO PERDIDAS TRANSPORTES DE
ANIMALES FORRAJES Y SEMILLAS ADONDE
ADONDE ESTAN   ADONDE ESTAN
GUARIJOS   ADONDE ADONDE ESTAN
ADONDE ALEIDA   ERNESTITO   CELIA
TANIA HILDA CELIA   CHICOS Y CHICAS
HERMANOS   ADONDE   EN ESTE CHILCHEO
NADA   NADA   NADA QUE CHANCHOS
TATUS   NADA QUE NADA   CHILCHEO EN
CHUCHIAL Y DONDE DONDE ESTA DONDE
PACHUNGA Y DONDE ESTA BIGOTES Y DONDE
ESTA PAPI Y DONDE ESTANISLAO   NEGRO
ANTONIO   JOAQUIN   APOLINAR
RICARDO CHINCHU   JORGE EL LORO
PACHO PACO PACHUNGO   OLO VILO POLO
MORO   MOROGORO   MUNGA
MUGANGA Y EL MEDICO   FELIX EL RUBIO
IVAN RENAN Y PEDRO   PAN DIVINO

MAURICIO PAN DIVINO   EL PELAO

CARLOS LUIS CHEPACO   CAMPANEROS

CAMPANEROS   GONDOLO

REVOLUCIONARIO   TATU Y   TANIA

Y CELIA   Y ALEIDA   Y ALEIDA

ERNESTITO NADA QUE CHOCLO

HUMINTA BAGRE   SED Y HAMBRE   JOCO

CHARQUI   ADONDE   ADONDE

GUARIJOS   ZAPALLOS YUCAS HOCHIS

CARACORES   CARACORES

CARACORES ANTAS   CAMBAS

GUERRILLAS   YANQUIS

NADA QUE   BOROS   CHANCOS   Y

CHINCHAS   Y PULGAS   CHINGA MI

MADRE   CHINGA   QUE   QUE

PASA QUE PASA SEÑOR   QUE

ES   QUE   PASA AQUI

TIENEN SED HAMBRE   ADONDE

ADONDE   CACARES CACARES   CARAJO

NINGUM CACARES AHORA AQUI

AQUI AHORA ADONDE   NO CHANKAKA   NO

CACA NO CARACORE CHINGA

HAMBRE ADONDE CACARES   NADA AQUI

NO SENTINAL RADIO BEMBA ABAJO EN

BARRANCO PIERDAS NO REVOLUCIONARIOS

PERO   PERO   ESTAN   ADONDE   MIS

ABARCAS   ADONDE MIS BOTAS SI

MIS BOTAS   EN ELEVADOR SIEMPRE   ACA

ALLA   ALLI   VAMOS PA'LANTE

GRITA CACARE   MIS ABARCAS

            LLEVALAS

            PA'LANTE
              SIEMPRE

MIS BOTAS

LLEVALAS

SIEMPRE

AL TERRITORIO LIBRE

AL TERRITORIO LIBRE

AQUI

ACA

PA'LANTE

Y

Y

GRITA

GRITA

CACARE

GUADALAJARA

Marzo 7, '69—Revolución Directo

Up and out early, into the bright plaza, first morning, white sun flares into plaza and park, church on plaza rings its skinny bell, a man hands me a free newspaper, a heavy bell tolls in another church of the same religion, the traffic flows through the middle of the long plaza, an avenue put right through the middle of it since I was here ten years ago to the month, quiet little square transformed into a downtown thoroughfare; still the birds sing in the high trees, twitter in the jacarandas. And the trees dance. . . . A beatup bus made in 1917 full of dark workers, mostly Indios, creaks through the plaza, its destination-sign reading REVOLUCIÓN DIRECTO. One doesn't have to wait long for this bus to that Plaza on mornings like this. I jump on, then jump off and run into two churches, one on each side of the avenue, mass going on in both of them, under the high stone naves and the gilt, only half a dozen old women in there, in their black shawls, kneeling, but the service goes on, the priests and their acolytes making their eternal holy mumble; in the first church the wall behind the altar is maybe one hundred feet high, completely gold-plated, with maybe fifteen life-size statues of old dead saints in niches at various levels up to the ceiling itself encrusted with flying sainted creatures. I mumble obscenities and rush out and into the second church. Same mass going on & on. In a side aisle is a glass-enclosed bier, and inside lies the statue of a dead monk or Christ himself on a trip, eyes open, hands folded. Down by his feet lies an old skull, eye-sockets gaping out of the 16th century, and for some reason there is a brass ring affixed in the top of the head. For some reason! To swing the Cat from Heaven, to hook him back up to Heaven when life on planet is finished, to swing from the top of the huge high dusty nave above the altar on a long string, like a pendulum, swinging slowly the whole vast and terrible distance in the upper air over the pews, like a huge clapper, clapping for God, a real swinger. I rush out and grab the next bus marked REVOLUCIÓN DIRECTO. . . . I am sitting in the back, toying with my skull, eye-sockets staring out at the massed humanity on crowded avenues, awaiting *its* bus along the route of Hidalgo's March for Freedom. In the bus everyone is smoking cigars, and I see now they are not Indios at all; they have been transformed into *mestizos*, and now they are all diplomats in morning coats, and they are blowing their noses on various flags. The most popular flag for this purpose seems to be North American. One diplomat is even just using one to wipe up the semen he has just succeeded in ejaculating. Some of it has even gotten into his good eye, and he is using the flag of the United States of North America like a pocket handkerchief, dabbing at his eye with it, and I am not so sure he is not crying, for this is a political-parapsychological parable, and there is as much salt in semen as in tears. A star falls out of the flag, and I pick it up and put it in my pocket. I can always use an extra state. I notice now that it is not an American flag at all which this particular star has fallen out of; it's the flag of some small Latin American mañana republic, and the stars weren't sewn on too well, which I as an Americano del Norte was the first to notice. There may be other used stars to be picked up at bargain prices. New Mexico was cheap enough, practically nada, but the loose stars on the flags on this bus may prove even cheaper, the bus fare being cheap enough if you've got real money rather than these perishable paper pesos and other misery-notes. The diplomat who didn't even notice me pocketing his star now is engaged in wiping the eyes of the bus driver who is an Indio with shades in a vaquero hat. He keeps singing out, "Gracias, señor!" and hurtles the bus onward, displaying his *machismo*, through the crooked city streets which seem to have gotten narrower and more and more crowded all the time as the centuries wheel by. The bus itself gets absolutely jammed with citizens hanging out all the windows and onto the sides. There is one cripple who can walk only on all-fours, but he now succeeds in keeping up with the bus and hollering epithets at it, for the bus now has to go slow through the crowds. Every once in a while this deformed creature raises up and sticks his so-called face through a bus window, right into mine. He has a small monkey on his back, and the monkey carries a small parrot, and the parrot has a small jade stone in its mouth, and the parrot screams at everyone in Portuguese, which is the language of all good parrots, according to a guidebook I am reading on Revolución, noting also that the "second language" of all good parrots is Spanish, no matter what dictator they are living with, and that to try to teach them anything else like Russian is useless, even an adulteration. The last time the monkey swings the parrot into the bus marked REVOLUCIÓN, the bird jumps off and perches on the driver's head, and the driver starts using the parrot's voice, calling out the various localities and way-stations through which it seems we are passing, followed by names of Mexican or Indian or Latin American heroes that happened to pop into his weird head, much in the following manner: "Calle Constitución! Juárez! Zapata! Hidalgo!" The bus now becomes so crowded that the diplomats in their swallowtail coats now have at least one *campesino* or Indio or beggar or vaquero sitting in their laps, and there are a few old crones thrown in on top of all, cackling and toothless in their shredded shawls, some carrying babies wrapped in flags. The diplomats have now taken to picking each other's noses, and there is now also quite a bit of backward fellatio going on between the old crones, who turn out not to be so old as all that, and the diplomats, who turn out not to be so young as all that. Every once in a while a diplomat lets go of his diploma and lets out a curious cry and zips up his fly and then proceeds to mop up again with his flag. I look down now and see that my own flag, I mean my own fly, is open, and a huge snake now raises its head out of it, and looks directly at me, winking its one eye. It has a jade head. The bus suddenly careens to a fullstop in front of some Latin American embassy or national hockshop, and a flock of gaviotas flies up pronto out of a cupola and lets go with a shower of guano on the busload of revolutionists & hangers-on. The flags are pressed into service spontaneously in a new great mopping-up operation gumshoe. While this is in progress, a very *macho* Madonna of Revolución flies or falls out of a stained-glass window into my lap. I proceed to introduce her to my snake. "It won't bite!" I tell her. But it does. And when I squirm out of my striped pants to really screw her, I notice the stripes are no longer Red White & Blue, and my top hat with the Red White & Blue stars & stripes is suddenly blown away over the heads of the cheering crowds still now rushing together at last in every Plaza de Revolución where a bearded man whose name is not Quetzalcoatl mounts the wooden stage. . . .

UXMAL, OR THE FLIGHT TO THE SUN

March '69

At Uxmal, in the rain forest, I am climbing up a great unfinished pyramid, its base hidden in jungle. Through the mouth of the rain-god Chac I entered the Pyramid of the Magician and now climb up & up, dragging a huge basket of stones for the construction of the pyramid. I am wearing a loincloth and a hat of pineapple leaves. My skin is dark brown with green tints, and it glistens with rivulets of sweat. The sun beats down from directly above the pyramid where it seems to be stuck in the meridian. The stones I am carrying are round as sun-stones and do not stay in place when I get them at last to the top of the pyramid. They go rolling down the stone steps of the pyramid, like stone eggs. I climb down and begin over. It is another day and the sun is rising again over the pyramid. My basket is full of sun-stones, and they are incised with curious circular calendars. The sun turns in its white sky like the loose wheel of some sun-chariot. I crawl higher with my sun-stones, place them on top, at last, and lie down on top, with a jade stone in my mouth. The sun itself rolls down on top of me, spinning. It is made of peyote and white-hot sperm, jism of the universe. I am a part of "Space Odyssey 2001" but I am also a bloodshot Indian maid being impregnated by a bronze Indian prince seven feet tall. The white hot sperm falls in showers. The moon rises and drenches us in pulverized peyote. The jade stone, which had been destined to be set at the very tip of the pyramid, is still on my tongue as I suddenly stretch my arms and take off into the sun, to catch the Sun Bus, a sun slave who needs to be liberated, revolución directo. I am a strange bird flying up, straight up into the great sun, my wings are yellow with it, they flame into it, the top of the pyramid spouts liquid gold, a gold volcano, floating me away on the wave of it. In the mirror of the sun I see my gold face, gold teeth and hair, I see sunflowers sprung up huge & turning with the sun, covering the sunburnt landscape from horizon to horizon, I hear sun adazzle through a silkscreen overlay, a near moon wings by, a Quetzalcoatl phoenix fills the upper air, dripping yellow sperm of light, there is no other paradise, there is no other consciousness, no other ecstasy, there is no death or dying, there is only change, there is only revolución in the Territorio Libre of the Sun, there where the light pulses, the universe rings like a gong, I have discovered its tongue, light's clapper, there is no god but light in the flowerless fields, Territorio Libre del Sol where there is no god but life, but life turns out to be a Sonata in *Miao* Minor for an Indifferent Cat, where Toltec strangers dance together to a singing somewhere among the peyote blossoms through which life freaks into being, the true timeless life of ecstatic consciousness interrupted impromptu now by U.S. roman emperors of space in which my skin dissolves and drifts away beyond the spaceship, earth a very distant small blue ball lost in lonely time disappearing now through a crystal crack. . . .

SAN MIGUEL

March 8, '69

The policeman's traffic whistle in the dusk in the plaza of San Miguel de Allende, sounding like hollow bird cries, the trees of the jardín full of boat-tailed grackles, beautiful blackbirds crying out all at once in the last of the sunset, flocks of them swooping down upon the jardín from other parts of town and crying out joyously (no other word for it) to the dying light. . . . The cooing of turtledoves under far eaves. . . . The grackles in the Indian laurel and jacaranda trees, and the sound of armadillo guitars. . . . The Conchero dancers in the dusk under the jacarandas. . . . The Conchero dancers with armadillo guitars under the Indian laurels in front of La Parroquia. . . . The Aztec dancers with armadillo mandolins under the Indian laurels in the late dusk in front of the cathedral. . . . A tall young Indian prince, very bronze and very beautiful, with long bronze legs, dancing with an Indian maid in feathered headband, her eyes bloodshot. He plays his armadillo guitar as he dances, shellbells on his ankles. . . . A circle of older dancers surrounds them. They look in each other's eyes as they dance, unsmiling. A feather blows out of her headband into the center of the dancing circle where it lies on the cobbles. They dance around it, hooking their ankles together, slowly. They are smiling in each other's eyes, very beautiful. . . . The faint rattle and whir of their ankle bells, echoing hollowly, fills the sweet air.

Marzo 10, '69

Lizards with flickering tongues on the broken stones in the ruined gardens of Marfil. . . .

Marzo 11, '69

Out at Atotonilco in the hot spring swimming pool of a half-built resort, the Incredible String Band (British) coming over the tape recorder of some butch gringos from New Jersey, the music blasting out over the pool: "Through mangos, pomegranates, and flames . . ." "There's a monkey coming to stay tomorrow. What's that paraffin stove on your head?" "I don't need a wife to live the timeless life." "I'm Buffalo Man, I'll do wrong as long as I can. . . ." A mountain breeze blows & blows the willow trees.

Marzo 12, '69

There's a story to be wondered about the roofless room in my semi-ruin of a house at 27 Recreo, San Miguel. A *criada* (a housemaid) was killed in this room when the old wood & stone roof fell in a few years ago. (It's been cleared away now and at night in that room you can see the stars, pure & brilliant as through a wide telescope.) I don't know who was living here back then, nor whose *criada* she was, but I found the room at noon in blinding sunlight furnished only with four large, flat, square stones arranged in a square on the stone floor around a stone head with blue eyes. The sculptured stone is light gray, almost white, and it is the aquiline head of a young woman. The head is upright on a kind of altar-stone. High on the broken gray & mottled white plaster wall are two oval spots, each about two feet high, painted Indian red, resembling the high oval windows that let in light in some great rooms. I drew a face with closed eyes in each oval, and high up on another broken wall I hung an Indian God's Eye. . . . The room is about twenty feet high, and the sun beats down directly into this room at noon as into some ruined temple. The stone head looks out into the fallen dry sunlight with its blue turquoise eyes, its speechless mouth half-open. Someone has stuck a thick, short, dark blue crayon between its lips. The sun slips behind a windy cloud somewhere and the sharp shadow of the head disappears from the floor. The wind stirs pile of dry green cocoa leaves in a corner. The sun comes up hot and burning again, and a brown hornet lights very slowly and drowzily on the lips of the silent woman, and she is the *criada*, with blue tongue, stoned to death. . . .

Saturday night, Marzo 15, '69

Barbarous night— At a party and someone passes me a pipe & I take several tokes & almost immediately find myself on a bad trip. First time that ever happened on grass, I remember saying to myself, someone must have slipped me some shit; but everyone around me had toked the same pipe, and there they all were, oblivious, sitting up in the semi-dark, watching color slides of Rembrandt in black stroboscopic light, laughing and grooving with it. Only it is super-stroboscopic to me. Rock on the recordplayer in the dark corner where I sit, and the whole room begins to rock, not only rock but move around sickeningly. I am in a cold sweat & feel the drops of it on my cold forehead. The room has closed in and I am trying to keep my mind working and then I zonk out completely. I am out for two or three minutes maybe and then I come to, gasping for air, people shaking me and asking in scared voice Am I OK? I say Yes, Yes, as if everything were normal, and someone hands me a plateful of spaghetti and brings me a glass of water. I can't hold them in my hands and I put them down on a low table so I won't drop them and a dude next to me says, "He forgot to breathe, that happens sometimes. He's OK now." And everyone goes back to Rembrandt and rock, most of them stoned & oblivious; but I'm not OK, I'm shivering and covered with cold perspiration, and I sit there in the semi-dark, trying to hold on to consciousness, trying not to zonk out again, calculating if I can make it out of the room to the fresh air, afraid if I get up I'll pass out en route. Rembrandts pulsate in the dark. What is happening? Someone turns up the music, who is someone, I begin to feel sick to my stomach and begin sweating again. I know I am going to throw up; but where, I have to get out at once, I do get out, somehow, threading my way through the bodies sitting strewn on the floor, leftovers from an experiential orgy, blocking the exit. I make it into the courtyard and keep going on out through the courtyard streetdoor, and as soon as I hit the dark cobbled street I throw up very violently, blah blah blah blah blah, leaning against a stone wall, retching in the dark black, then stumble on down the narrowing, very dark street, homeward, missing a turn, going back, passing over a stone overpass, on up to the other end of town, better in fresh air but still in a cold sweat, still stoned stumbling a bit on the rough cobblestones, I remember everything, nothing, throwing up a few more times here and there en route in dark streets, thinking of "that great dark Thing—primitive Mexico" in black *pulque* night. . . . A couple groaning in a doorway, he into her, at it, heavy breath coming, coming. Blah. A *pulque* drunk lurches against me, white corn teeth gleaming under broken sombrero, Indian eyes blind, glazed, primitive night upon us, he in his dark world, I, mine; lurching past each other, *almost* like lost humanoids, awful, beasts abroad. Out of that alley and up "my" street, into my door, unlock it, fall through it, into the veranda-court under arches in the moonlight, how calm all, how peaceful, moonlight like white water filling up the court, lapping. Light a candelabra, high up, rubber shadows strumming, bullfrog gloat, crickets in a far place, the moon is no angel, it only paints mescal freakscapes I swim through, where is someone, the Mexican night blots out silkscreen overlays of reptiles run through an Osterizer, puree of brownjism bleached out, I walk very quietly and slowly around the cloister in moonlight, in silence, still high, afraid to lie down and never wake again, walking and walking round and round that square courtyard, by the ruined walls, trying to come down, no place for a landing, air clears my head, still up there, still high, trying not to breathe or trying to breathe, so cold I put on a *jorongo*, keep walking, fancy myself pulling myself together, very funny dude in *serape*, stopped short and go to bathroom, pee on funny wall through a silkscreen underlay, catching looks at myself in dim mirror hundred years olde, in my *jorongo*, Quetzalcoatl and the fucking flapping Plumed Serpent, sperm prince of darkness, the fairskinned blue-eyed "god" named Lawrence come from across the sea to fuck the dark peoples, a phoenix on my brow, I return to the cloister and continue walking flapping in *serape* around the square of it in broken moon, pieces of it falling off, there's a man on it turned reptile, fuck him, gringo man-in-moon waving plastic flag, I still here walking through the shadows of the great arches, still listening to the primitive night, crickets in it, somewhere, far off, I a strange bird flapping, wearing leather, creaking sandals. I keep creaking forward in them, I not Neal Cassady who died here in the rain at night along the railroad tracks, counting the ties to Celaya, this year, still high on life, he never walked but ran to wherever he was going, and so arrived there first, I not Neal whose lostandfound manuscreeds I'm here deciphering. . . .[28]

All this had been going on a long time. And would go on. The night had no dawn attached to it. Or dawn had a lot of night still stuck to it, still hung on it, and couldn't get off the ground. The blackness, dark tar, pitch of night, black mescal, still stuck to everything. I had to be careful not to step on the lizards with flickering tongues in the cracks. I was still high. I couldn't come down. I kept walking. . . .

BAJA REVISITED

Sometime in time south of Rosarito—the Beach of the Small Round Stones—
when sea's rollers recede, the round stones tumble over each other, with a rumbling
tumbling undersound, a deep clacking—sea grinding its teeth. All night in the
sea's jaws, under the sea's roaring— Smoked some strong grass and fell off into that
roaring—the round stones like tumblers in some great lock whirring around and
tumbling at last into place—sea and earth's great combination-lock—"life's lock"
fallen open—sea grinds its teeth and moans *Ah, ah, ah*—I float on, a small island,
made of bodies attached by the lips, floating, hair streamed out, body stretched
out—"détendu"— Houses rise and fall, with the tide. Morning beach in fog, scorpions on the rocks, half-smoked "roaches"—the sun again and sea's roar again over
gray rocks, stretching away miles on the Mexican strand—distant fisher figures on
it—and dried kelp, dried bulbous rubber sea tubes—"sea's inner tubes cast up"—
among bent beer-cans, rusted tongues alack, bleached white twigs, sea-flowers cast
up, dried stiff, all baked now in hot Mex sun—"Never later in the memory will
these flowers fade"— Transcription of organ music—sea-tune to hurdygurdy billion round small rocks, sea full of gulf streams, floating all eternally away. . . .
Golden field on distant mountainside, "sending its signal to heaven." . . .

VW bus stuck in sand up to hub on right rear side—deserted beach at Colonia
Guerrera, sixty miles south of Ensenada. Get it out finally by jacking up rear and
putting rocks under wheel. "Could Purna Das fix a flat?" . . . Got up in the 8 a.m.
fog and addressed the sea—shaking my fist—"You—you—monster moitherer!
Great groaner! Big blabbermouth, roiler and despoiler, roarer and rocker, you—
you—talking asshole of the blithering world—you, world washer, eternal loudmouth and blabberer, cantor to the universe, answerer to Allen Ginsberg, Om-singer
& Om-maker, you, blind, moithering, roistering, rabble-rouser! You, you, you mad
monster flippy fric-frac faceless palaverer! Washer of the world's intestine, laver and
looter of universe's underwear, death driver, life lighter, gargoyle-wave maker, salt
bathtub of creation! Salter of sailors' wounds, embalmer of dead seagulls in sand,
eternal embalmer, you, you stupid, ceaseless, slaphappy, shiftless shouter and sham-
bler. You, intoner of Nothing! You, answerer of Nothing with Nothing! You, obscene
old daddy sperm-spurter of them all, frothy foam-phallus of earth! Roaring and

roaring all night! Crying Nothing! All! Alway! Never! Forever and ever! And ever! You! Om! Fuck you! Fuck *you!*" . . . Two silent waterbirds wing by, very close together, holding wingtips. . . . A huge dead seagull with wings outflung and bent back as if still hurtling down through air lies stiff on a dune, sandy wild beak still outstretched, empty eye still fixed in skull, transfixed flat upon the sand as upon a shield, emblematic, plumed serpent phoenix, life . . . in the ocean's long withdrawing Om. . . .

Tiny, brilliant dark red sea-roses on the dunes, just beyond reach of the sea— raspberry-like small red roses, but made of sea-rubber, brilliant red amber & green, glowing, in great low clusters, glistening as diamonds. "Never later will these flowers fade. . . ."

Arrived just before nightfall at great wild white sand beach ten miles south of San Quintín near San Simón & Sky Ranch, over dirt roads running into sand. . . . Bright red ball of sun down behind rugged mountain promontory, great dunes hiding the roaring ocean; and the VW bus gets back wheels stuck in sand down to the hubs. Took a chance and raced engine, and dug it in worse, so abandoned bus for the night, took sleeping stuff & food & moved into abandoned adobe shack, onto which had been added an old trailer, with corrugated tin roof laid over old adobe brown wall; inside, a big adobe fireplace with metal hood and grates; and a porch made of sugarcane stalks also covered by tin roof. . . . The beach: huge sculpted hills of sand, sensuous, enormous breasts of smooth, scalloped pure-white sand, each over twenty feet high, and these great forms running like immense waves from the shrub-ridge at top of beach to the sea itself, the whole width of beach at least three hundred feet, stretching in both directions to bay horizons, sand scalloped hills casting long shadows as the red sun fell down into night. As if the mountains had allowed the wind to come through and make these shadows of themselves out of sand.

Walked through wild dunes to Rancho Santa Maria & got tractor to pull VW out, then settled in sugarcane shack on beach at Sta. María (two dollars a night for the privilege) looking out over wide white beach, cobalt sea, succulent green seagrass, could be South Sea island, deep red sun falling down behind distant volcano-like mountain down the coast, in a sudden steep plunge, red fire sun absorbed in the black bold headland of mountain. . . . Woke to the seabirds' sound, cawing & crying over the dunes, far off. . . . One solitary small beach bird comes to perch on roof corner of grass shack & goes through his repertoire—a half-dozen different songs, or more, infinitely varied, trilling, calling, warbling, whistling—then flies away, not to return. . . . Long lines of big silent fisher-birds wing in single formation low, over the dunes at water's edge, dipping to the waves, very slowly. . . . And at the edge of a blowing meadow above a bluff, three great white horses, *sitting*, looking out to sea, motionless, white manes blowing in wind, each a white bone statue, but alive, heads up, eyes fixed forward in the wind, perfectly unmoving, under white noon sun. . . . Two strange insects, two inches from my nose where I lie on the beach alone, buzz and roll over on each other, their many legs wrapped around each other in a frenzy, making love or war, killing each other or in trance-like rotor orgasm. It is love, not death, and a warm wind blows; in a few seconds, which could have been their eternity, one bug flings itself off & goes straight away, fast, not looking back; the other lies dazed, then moves slow in small circles, no longer knowing where she is, if she ever did, alone in a white sand land, stretching before & after. . . .

Curious how I hang on here, day after day, or is it year after year, in my sugarcane shack on the dunes. He who travels on peninsulas must expect someday to turn back. It is as if I were waiting for the sea to stop its absolute incoherence. . . . I see myself in the dark distance, a stick-figure in the world's end. . . .

March 24, '69

La puerta escondida

            no está escondida

La puerta al invisible

            no está invisible

The door to the invisible

            is visible

The hidden door

            is not hidden

I continually walk through it

            not seeing it

And I am what I am

And will be what I will be

Sobre las playas perdidas

            del Sur. . . .

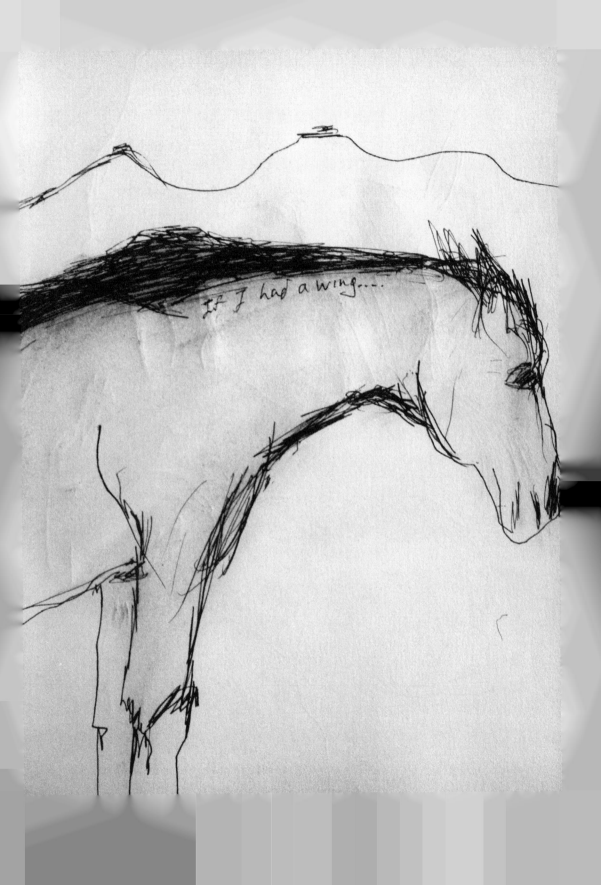

Journal

de

Baja California

October 1961

FLORIDA

July 1970

July 10

Delta flight to Atlanta. The white Anglo tradition: wristwatch & cigarette & short hair—deodorant air & nylons & uniforms—the Vietnam vet returning reading *Peanuts* all the way across the United States—deodorant & shaved legs—you "can't tell the mothers from the daughters"—be-ringed dowager belting down two bourbons & smoking filter-tipped Kents. . . . We are crossing the Rockies? We are crossing the Mississippi? At 37,000 feet over the Great Plains Xerox executives scribble the death of three thousand Indians below . . . wagon-trains creak over the Last Divide. . . . Thirty minutes to Atlanta, and the lady switches to Salems. Every time the engines roar we swallow another American Eagle. . . . Atlantis.

July 11—8 a.m. Downtown Jacksonville, Fla.

A half-eaten stale brown waffle on top of a mailbox outside Mayflower Hotel— The "Floridian"—Trailways Bus Station (still Separate but Equal, though no more signs)— Headline in *Florida Times-Union* on rack: "Nude Barmaids Must Wear Pasties"— Bus drivers fraternalizing over coffee, all White, middle-aged, crew-cut. Bus out into the flat country: Florida a thousand miles long, a hundred miles wide, and a foot high. . . . Straight highway down thru it. Young new pine forests, clay side roads—American flag waving on a post— Colonial gas signs—Swanee River crossing, overhung with live oaks heavy with Spanish moss—Route 218—"Thus

did he first see the fabulous dark land." Old "country" Black preacher on bus, wearing both belt & suspenders, panama hat, rimless glasses, and carrying *two* rolled
plastic umbrellas, talking about how "the further out I get into the country, the
better I feel." And he speaks of "way back yonder," gesturing over his shoulder to
the 1920s—"back in Prohibition times"—hums a fragment of an old song about
"leaving whiskey behind"—like leavin' the city for the country, he says—"Trust in
the Savior, and ye shall be saved, Trust in Him and ye shall be led into Salvation,"
he repeats to the Black Sister with him. "I got that," she says. Then, after a minute's
silence, she begins humming to herself "I Wonder as I Wander." . . . The image of
the labyrinth, even in central Florida.

July 14

Had a very beautiful dream, very clear: sitting in a yard in the back of a brick
building where I had a ground-floor apartment, its location about three or four
blocks south of City Lights Bookstore, down Columbus toward the old Monkey
Building and the Black Cat and Iron Pot.[29] A lot of the buildings had been torn
down, as if for redevelopment, maybe year 1980, so that there was a feeling of openness, and my rooms were large & airy, with sun. I was maybe sixty, and I had a visit
from Kenneth Rexroth who had some great books with him, and I showed him
some kind of hieroglyph message on a printed form from Russia which he knew all
about of course, saying the message referred to the big books he was carrying, great
wise tomes which we never opened but talked about until a *very* young girl—no
more than thirteen years old—walked out of one of my inner rooms as if she
belonged there. Kenneth said something like "So" or "Aha," and after he was gone
this very young girl nymphet sang and danced for me, looking directly at me and
beating a light gong now and then as she pronounced certain words inscribed on a
transparent tapestry with golden & silver rings woven in it. It was very beautiful
and she sang lightly and spoke goldenly with a great purity, great simplicity, in a
vibrant small voice, the sun behind her shining through her hair as she danced, and
who it is or was I have yet to find out, someone I have yet to meet, someone's child,
still song, sweet life. . . .

July 16

Reading Ginsberg's *Indian Journals*[30] for the first time in book form, after reading it in page proof, which was like reading Angkor Wat with a magnifying glass & missing the meaning. . . . Fantastic passages, genius true. . . .

July 17

Julie found a box turtle walking down a road & brought him home. He's about six inches in diameter & maybe six years old. He hardly ever moves. He has a completely different sense of time. Every week or so he says, "I think I'll take a step."

We're staying here at Kirby's mother's tin-roofed fishing shack, with its wide screened-in porches, like a set for a Hemingway Key Largo story. The house sits sheltered under palms next to a shrinking Lake Geneva, the water table sinking. . . . Julie and Lorenzo also have their completely different sense of time. In the later years of their childhood, they run lilting to the water, alive in their endless summer.

July 27

Passing over the Mississippi at 30,000 feet, I see Yevtushenko down below, making like Tom Sawyer, floating down the river, trolling for catfish. When he gets to New Orleans the Russian consul will be waiting on the deck with a basket of hushpuppies, in case he caught anything good, kind of like the commissar who took Voznesensky back to East Berlin in his black car after our poetry reading in West Berlin (after allowing him an hour—observing him from afar!—across the Wall).[31]

SPAIN REMEMBERED AT A DISTANCE

1971

Julie, do you remember when you were four years old we went to Spain and got that little tiny house in Nerja on the coast near Málaga and the name of the street was the Calle Carabeo which was the same street where Lorca's living brother had a house and we stayed about two months in that little house and then moved into a much bigger one down the street, an old house with two stories and high-ceilinged rooms with sugarcane rafters and Mom couldn't sleep because she claimed the sugarcane shed a fine pollen to which she was allergic and there were fleas which bit her in the bed all night but I was trying to be happy and was studying Spanish & reading & translating and trying to be happy and I was.

FERLINGHETTI–GINSBERG
AUSTRALIAN TRIP

Hawaii/Fiji/Australia/to Adelaide Festival of Arts

March 1972

W Honolulu—Fiji, March 1
ith Lorenzo (age nine) and Allen— Wild sunrise above a plateau of clouds fragmented upward in towering headlands & peaks— brilliant crimson-pink streaks on the horizon—white ranges stretched everywhere below like huge blown-up snowfields and avalanches—shattered, shredded endless fields—eggshell blue delicate now over crimson streaks at world's edge—sun almost up. Lorenzo draws sunrise with trees on hills: red sun, red rays, blue hills, black trees, clouds with birds in them. Sun brighter & brighter, piercing iceberg clouds—towering snowfields & pinnacle of clouds, with veils of lighter cloud streaming downward from them, like sheets of sea-spray off white plunging bows of icebreakers. Suddenly the round ball orange sun burns free of the horizon— crimson, yellow light thrown horizontal onto cabin walls—fireball roars in the gloaming, purpling the snowlike fields and shredded peaks and ranges of white air—bright, burning eye of sun blinding the eyes—fields of flame— And sun eats earth—eats the world and its consciousness of nothing. Plane banks and descends to sound of cultured British (BOAC) voices, as I remember last night's dream of descending thru some huge high apartment house or warehouse with Lorenzo, only all the stairways & doors were closed, so that we had to descend tortuously floor by floor thru various forgotten windows trapdoors or back escapes—across rooftops and down, thru apartments and lofts, past a final goodnatured "caretaker" guard or night watchman—out into daylight street—

Sun has turned white, as Lorenzo sights a "teeny island down there." Down close now—tiny islands in bay, all green, beautiful winding river up close, palm trees & grass huts, down onto runway in brown green savannah. . . . "On behalf of Captain Cook and the crew we bid you goodbye and fair journey" (British accent). And Allen saying, "Here we is in Fiji, here we is in Fiji."

Crossed equator like a dark horizon in the sea and crossed International Dateline and it is March 2 here. Change for Fijian dollars in airport & off in people's bus, for Sigatoka and Suva on other side of island. Three hours ride in open bus—first into Nadi, then on out into green open country. Bus open all around—wood bank seats, full of Fijians & Indians (from India as laborers in last fifty years, now outnumbering the Fijians). Women in saris, some with marks on forehead, men in very clean white shirts—Fijians in colored shirts and dresses, very different in every way. Bus roof keeps sun off and bus motion keeps cool air going—no need for air-conditioned taxi tourists ride in. Bus zooms on single winding road around island, thru jungle trees into open farmland, lush deep green everywhere—we are sunk into deep green dream of life with no sense of history to be fulfilled. . . . Palm trees, cattle, goats, mynah birds, sugarcane plantations, thatched houses & huts. Whole thatched villages with babies on ground as in aboriginal photos in *National Geographic*. . . . Bus roars and rocks on through the photos, leaving a thin smear of pollution on the virgin unexposed film. The film, however, has been exposed already and is already in the process of being developed—by chemical developers, outside agents. . . . The emulsion on the film in a state of very delicate & vulnerable suspension—soft with tropical humidity. Anything can happen to it in an instant of light or darkness or clap of thunder—the whole picture wiped out and only a print of it left, mounted in a museum.

Riding backseat of bus, Lorenzo up forward in seat next to Indian woman in sari— his delicate white body surrounded by dark skins—his very sensitive face looking out at the country flashing past— Life in an instant caught. Then he moves back nearer Allen & me, now next to very black Fijian woman-girl, in colored print dress. She's got her head buried in her arms against seat in front of her, to keep dust from road out of her eyes, her upper back and arms exposed. Dream of Gauguin— the pure black breathing flesh, alive with its own warm life—a sudden overflowing sense of direct tactile empathy—not sexual but deep feeling of the pure skin—the overflowing life & breath, deep, deep in the green, in a thatch hut in shadow on a mat—dark, enveloped, pulsing—smiling face, white teeth, full breasts—Gauguin's deep dream.

Koralevu, March 3

Afternoon—very hot—
Lay down with a fever
And dreamt I was Gauguin
Dying of syphilis in Tahiti

Déjà vu—beach hut & palm tree
     wind in it
Lady in red skirt and black skin
crosses brown beach
     thru small
          frame of door
Wind whips the palms
     and sea white caps
dash on coral
         brown breakwater
          rocks
The high palms shake
     their heads
  but do not drop
     their nuts
The brown volcanic ash
     pulverized stone of beach
porous in the sun
     as brown skin
pockmarked,
     breathing
Overhead punka-fan
     whirs round

Long palm-frond arms
            wave in door
    turning brown in
                    burning sun
delirium of pulsing
            heat waves & sun
Red lady passes and repasses
A brown sail at sea
            waves back
The little boat
            in trouble in
    high wind rising & sky darkening
gives up and runs
                    before it
full tilt
                onto the
            brown skin beach
Single man jumps out
            at instant of impact
and falls flat full-length
            onto the brown pulsing flesh
                kissing it
            arms spread-eagled—
Storm breaks and sky opens
            with thunder roar
and hot rain suddenly descending
            steams the brown earth skin
and sea's lips utter Ah, Ah, Aaah
and sea lips close
            with a soft licking
                    at the brown skin
folding in man
                    vulva in terra
            later under brown moon

Night of March 4

Firewalking Ceremony at Koralevu by Beqa Island tribe— At sundown—small three-sided bleachers set up in woods just off beach, around fire pit where wood fire has been burning over foot-size rocks since 3 p.m. Kava-drinking ceremony first, with local chief offered first cup of it, sitting in wicker armchair next to white "guests of honor"—man in Bermuda shorts and his lady. Bleachers full with maybe four hundred white tourists in Fijian bright colors—director of Hotel Koralevu on microphone in British voice introducing the firewalking, and saying guests may sample kava after ceremony—"a mild diuretic, mild soporific"—actually kava numbs the lips (and perhaps firewalkers soak their feet in it, as well as drinking it, before walking on the red-hot rocks?). Some say it has a mild aphrodisiac effect— but that may be like weak marijuana—we put into it what we would like to get out of it—

After more cultured accent talk explaining Firewalk, the braves from Beqa parade out and circle fierce fire and with poles with loops on them pull out great burning logs with great shouts, dragging the burning wood off into the woods, running together with whoops and cries—until nothing but red-hot stones remain. Then do they come forward in line two by two, holding hands—and walk slowly onto stones, picking their way carefully—a few paces only, then off—the whole pit maybe six feet across. Then do some of them do it by themselves, with deep shouts. Then do all the rest of the braves throw green palm leaves and fresh long grasses onto the stones, in a few minutes smothering the fire, the braves all standing now on top of the leaves and stones enveloped by thick smoke—which gradually dies out—and the Firewalk is over, leaving all in darkness. The white man files out with his ladies. Walking back thru the dark by path near beach, we hear the constant lowing of a Brahmin cow tied near a *bure* beach hut where two Indian women earlier sat on grass in their saris drinking tea in late sun—

But the native rites have just begun.

They are roasting a huge whole pig in another fire pit, and a gourd of kava is being passed around. It's a religious ceremony, and Allen asks an old man with a headband if eating pig is part of the ceremony. Assured that it is, Allen the vegetarian says, "Well, I'll have to eat some pig so as not to offend the elders!" The smell of the roast pig is overpowering.

Omnivorous Allen! He has to experience everything. Omnivorous mind must devour everything. Everywhere in Fiji he had this spiral notebook out, taking down the names of trees, plants, roads, people, in conversation siphoning up people's minds!

March 4

Koralevu to Suva by open local bus at noon. We lie under huge boca tree waiting for bus, as tropical rain falls lightly. Two buses go by, too full to stop, but we manage to get a last one, jammed into the last seats with Fijians and Indians going to town. It's Saturday—seventy miles to Suva— Bus plunges almost at once through tropical downpour into jungle and wet side of island—huge fan palms thirty feet high, coconut trees, breadfruit, mangos, magnolias, great fern leaves & deep grasses. Deep lush green hills with single gravel road winding up and down thru them, no houses for miles & miles—then single thatched farms & Indian hamlets. Tropical rain pours down, then clears up as we go on thru the deep green landscape. Now and then someone on bus pulls the cord and a tinkly bell rings and the Indian driver puts on the brakes and lets off a passenger with his or her baskets. And amazingly out of the jungle thatch come singly very beautiful Hindu women in lovely, fresh saris, with gold earrings and bracelets, carrying straw hampers—to mount the bus for town—red dots on their foreheads and red paint in the part of their hair—Saraswatis of the jungle! *La vida es un sueño real.* Life is a very real dream, it goes on everywhere . . . at once. . . .

Late that night, Lorenzo and I sit on second-floor terrace of South Seas Private Hotel, on a hill overlooking harbor of Suva—great old wood building with deep porches running length of it. We sit in darkness in old wooden armchairs, looking out thru the wooden railings and bamboo—tropical birds screech in the darkness in the jungle park between us and waterfront—over the tops of the palms we can see the harbor lights (like from a hill in Port-au-Prince, Haiti). "Silence comes back like a thought," and I have the distinct feeling I have been here before—déjà vu again, at this porch in this hotel in this darkness. I tell Lorenzo about it and about how these moments may be memories or dreams of a former life. He says he's dreamed things a lot that later happened. . . . We sit on in the real dream. . . . Those are clouds which once were islands. . . .

March 6

Afternoon plane to Nadi, over rain clouds and uninhabited jungle mountains, rivers flooded & roaring down thru the lush green, brown waters, no roads, thatched-hut villages isolated on terraces, coral reefs off coast. Jitney into town, free, for the night, baggage checked at airport—wearing shorts and Fijian sandals. Fall into Nadi hotel—tropical rainstorm hits—downpour with thunder & lightning. We go up on hotel roof in rain where there is straw-roofed pavilion with wicker chairs. Lightning & thunder strike close by—whole sky lights up—we take pictures of each other with Allen's camera, with backdrop of rain, rain clouds, and great mountains. . . . Thunderclap, thunderkavaclap (before and after drinking kava, the ceremony is for the server to clap).

NIGHT OF MARCH 6, IN NADI MOTEL—So noisy couldn't sleep all night. Like a train station: trucks roaring past, people talking in hotel, doors slamming, etc., etc. Bad dreams. . . . 7:15 a.m. we fly out to Australia. Possible that our waking psychic states are mirror images of our sleep & dreams, as the branches of the tree mirror the pattern of its roots? So that the profile of our dreams transfigures our waking moods preceding or following that sleep? The depressions or euphorias of dreams carried over into our daytime subliminal feelings. . . . A bad dream may blight our day, a dream of desire carry over into waking sexual aggressions. Of course, it is all in Freud, all in Wilhelm Reich. . . . He who farts in sleep will go on to realer, more solid things upon awakening. The moon is my undoing when the sun comes up, the midnight sun gathers us in, our dream siblings signal us thru the flames.

RIVER MURRAY LOG
SOUTH AUSTRALIA

March 15

I wish Julie could have been on this houseboat trip! At Blanchetown, eighty-four miles from Adelaide—14:00, March 15—shoved off aboard *Sea Queen #9*, paddle-wheel houseboat, headed upstream with Lorenzo & Sam Dutton (publisher Geoffrey Dutton's eight-year-old son). River about two hundred yards wide here. Five knots, one knot current setting us back.

16:50, passed SS *Coonawarra*—big Paddlewheel Steamer, about 135 feet long, passengers on deck, going downstream. We waved and took pictures. Flat country each side: eucalyptus and scrub—yellow sandstone cliffs—high grass riverbanks—lagoons & swamps with huge dead eucalyptrees standing in water. Taking it very easy, we tie up for night on sanctuary side of river. White wild cockatoos float in the sky. A great wind comes up & blows our houseboat around into rushes, still tied securely to trees. . . .

March 16
10:00, passed small houseboat who gave us position eleven miles up from Blanchet-own, and time, which we carry only in our heads. . . .

11:00, passing *Sea Queen Seven*, calls us on radio-telephone for help, stuck on beach. Try to pull them loose, no luck— Proceeding up river— A dream settles in. . . .

> Eternity turns over
> > another tick
> Two days pass
> > between the banks

March 17
Last night on river, we tie up across from high white-yellow sandstone cliffs. Geologic ages sculpted down, layer by layer of stratified cliffs (maybe a thousand feet high)—Murray River burrowing down all those eons, Australia's Mississippi—but got no Mark Twain. Tom Sawyer Lorenzo rows a punt along beneath the cliffs in the swift stream, looking for calm still place to drop his fishline in the swift coursing waters. There is none, and he ends up trolling with his worm & sinker. The dusk is falling, yellow sun flaming on the cliffs far above where white cockatoos circle & soar in the white sky—hundreds of them, huge, white, looking so very beautiful yet filling the air with their black cries & hoarse chatter. Clatter of creation, still, out here—the Great Chain of Being rattles its links, the Food Chain chatters, into the dark, cockatoos dive on swallows, hawks upon cockatoos, huge cormorants sail above all, their beaks agape for any lower creation. Only fish-shape clouds make a mockery of it all, huge sky whales drifting over, flipping their tails

in the rising night wind, hammerheads driving over the high cliffs, tiny eyes pierced with slanting sunlight. Huge overhanging cliffs tower over the small boy in the skiff where he hovers in the lee of a log, pulling up some local's fishline from a deep pool. He finds the line is baited with a live foot-long redfin, hooked fore and aft through its back with two huge hooks—so that it swims eternally around and around at the bottom of the food chain—helpless terrified all-vulnerable victim for any passing underwater predator, for an *eternum* of days before the fisherman returns to check his traps. All along the deep pools close-up to the cliffs are set these live-baited lines. You can see the slender poles bobbing & bending with the struggles of the still-uneaten baited fish—huge hooks, impossible to unhook their backs without destroying them—avaricious food links. The swallows have built their hive-like nests under overhangs in the cliff's sheer face— Cockatoos alight in cave-holes near them, then fly to the very tops of tall bare white eucalyptrees to catch the very last rays of setting sun, setting up a final agitated non-ecstatic yawking— Shadows fall down the cliff— Bare huge trees standing stark inside lagoon swamp-water turn black— Black water rushes by— A white egret fights against it— A shining boy in a white skiff rows against it.

Strange experiments in survival nature tried!

March 20—Sydney Zoo

Koala bears zonked out in the eucalyptus trees, stoned on eucalyptus leaves, hanging there, eyes open, against the trunks, in crotches of the trees. . . . Not a kangaroo in sight.

SYDNEY AT NIGHT—Drop into "Wayside Chapel" and get involved chanting (with Allen) in middle of Hare Krishna group on stage. Allen asks Stand-up Comedian associate pastor how Krishna is related to Christ. He says "Jesus Krishna!" and "Hairy Krishna!" (Australian Liverpool cockney accent)—

Drove thru Sydney district where D. H. Lawrence wrote some of *Kangaroo*— looked like London in Eliot's *Waste Land* or *Prufrock*. Dead mythos!

Great Barrier Reef, March 21

Great Keppel Island—almost exactly on the Tropic of Capricorn. Back in tropic climate again. Coral isle, off-season. A single dark brown horse on the island—goes swimming off the coral sand beach—at dusk he runs up & down the beach, and gallops off inland when we approach. . . .

March 22

Marzo sobre el mar— The horse is still running up and down the beach. Saw the moon last night, either in dream or waking—*relaying its signal from the sun*— reminding me of the tiny lakes & ponds & puddles we flew over yesterday, each flashing for an instant a reflection of the sun, like turning mirrors. Even at night the universe employs these moon-mirrors to send us some trace of the sun—the signal saying, "Even if you turn away from me, I will come to you from the opposite direction." . . . "Only in old, old age shall you escape me, Earth Man." . . . Sweet early mornings here, on the inside of the Great Barrier Reef—*douce* air and breeze moves the palms & fern-like trees. Already the tropic sun beats down on the tin roof verandas. A young Frenchman who works here walks by in tropic shorts, shirt open to the navel, straw hat, probably thinking he's a Beach Boy Gauguin. He twiddles his moustache. . . .

Allen went inland to the center of Australia, Alice Springs, Ayers Rock—I to the sea instead. Once a sailor always a sailor. La Mer: ma mer: ma mère—reading the sea charts—off Queensland—Keppel Island—Capricorn Channel—Coral Sea—Cumberland Islands—Flinders Passage—following the coast inside the reef, northward—Cape Melville, Cape Grenville, Turn Again Island, Deliverance Island. Note in chart: "Great Barrier Reef—stretching 1250 miles, measures 12 miles at narrowest & 150 miles at widest. A seething line of surf marks its outer ledge, where seas beyond abruptly plunge to depths of a mile or more. Containing the widest variety of marine life found anywhere. . . ." Didn't go to all those places above, just read them on the chart, which saves me many days beating windward with Melville? And Captain Cook, who charted this east coast of Australia to Cape York very thoroughly but ran out of time or tide on the other sides of the continent & didn't chart but sketchily. . . . The skipper of a little tour boat here said he'd never been able to figure out why Cook hadn't charted *all* the islands on this particular stretch of coast, having missed a few good-sized ones. I suggested as an old navigator that perhaps it was because you can only be certain it's an island by sailing right around it. So with women & men. None an island; even those apparently cut off on all sides have underwater underground connections with the mainland, the manland (or womanland) . . . so send not for whom the sea-bell tolls?

March 23

El Mar continues its incessant slow stroking & agitating of the shore. The sense of the sea here is very strong indeed. "The sea is the land's edge also." Oh, I am a seaman & will always be. Yesterday, on the fish boat to another island (where Lorenzo found live wild oysters on the reefs, and we ate them) I climbed out a boom & down a cargo net into the water, while the boat was underway, and clung to it in the surging water (Lorenzo climbed down too for a short while, then climbed back). And felt suddenly one with the ocean and sky—the surging swell, spray & waves breaking over. Hung there for a long time, as the boat boomed on between islands, washed between earth & sky. . . .

This morning went out with Lorenzo and others on a speedboat rigged for deep sea fishing and caught a seventeen-pound two-foot golden trevally in deep water close to Barren Island, ten miles from Keppel Island. It took fifteen or twenty minutes to get it reeled in—a ton on the line, and the big outboard pulling it all the time, as I reeled in. Finally she came up, floating almost flat, the rod still bent in an n. The skipper gaffed it in with one stroke & lifted it aboard. It was a beautiful animal—poor fish—so naïve—innocent-looking—fat. Not a chance against the outboard. It had gray sides but golden fins & a tail—and golden eyes with large black pupils—so large that gold just ringed the eye—unblinking, of course. A kind of jack fish. I'll carry the sin of killing him on my docket, biggest animal I ever caught & killed. . . . Shade of Ernest Hemingway. The boatskipper broke its skull with a wood bludgeon. The blood from the hole made by the gaff ran red on the deck. I was surprised, as if I had expected it to be green. . . . Strange to look at that fish in the blind eye of creation. Here was one attempt at consciousness. And it rose to the surface. And took the bait.

March 24

My birthday, I believe. Today there's a storm at sea, and a hurricane offshore a couple hundred miles. Here sky is heavy with storm clouds and wind whips the wanderer palms and poinciana trees. A single gull flaps by over the beach, and the wind blows fiercer: the nerve of him. . . . The fish boats rock at anchor. . . . "It was my [fiftieth? thirtieth?] year to heaven"— Woke to the heron cry— It was all long ago and far away, and I am not W. H. Hudson, D. H. Lawrence, Malcolm Lowry,

Somerset Maugham or Gauguin or Dylan Thomas. . . . There are white caps way out, almost like snow on the eastern horizon. And, farther east, on the Barrier Reef itself, the sea crashes in great white sheets, spray thrown up fifty feet in the air, with a huge, voluminous, mothering roaring and thundering . . . the huge, unwinding white sheets of ocean rolled out, beaten and shredded on the white coral teeth of reefs. Light shredded. Falling in foam. Into aquamarine. Into the fish's eye. Into the lightless black depths where the ocean floor plunges almost straight down off the continental shelf, at reef's outer edge. Into the black fish-eye of creation. . . .

O the myths we lay upon ourselves, over the sea's desert. Cook, Grenville, Darwin. . . . Melville, Maugham, Hudson, Lawrence, Lowry, Gauguin. The French Foreign Legion, the British Empire, itself a myth, lived out here, in pure white Australasia, in Keppel Isle Resort air-conditioned cold Dining Room, white couples and foursomes seated at table as if eternally ready for a hand of bridge—high watermarks of the Empire, left here dying out as the tide receded. . . . A single white drunk, about my age, bleached hair askew, weaves among the palm trees, early morning, two bottles of beer under arm, sits down heavily at beach's edge, and throws up. The myth continues, the ghost of Malcolm Lowry stumbles on. Out at sea the white caps drive upon each other, unconscionable. . . .

March 25

Back to Sydney and off to New Zealand. In the *Auckland Star* I read the Maori proverb:

> Ka mate kainga tahi
> Ka ora kainga rua

> *The first home dies,*
> *the second home lives.*

And:

> Ka mate he tete-kura,
> ara mai he tete-kura.

> *A fern frond dies,*
> *a fern frond lives.*

"Even a casual observer of the countryside can see how, after a fire has swept thru the fern, the blackened tree-fern stumps are left standing forlornly amid the ashes and charred branches. Then, with the first rains, come the soft brown curling fronds, life arising from apparent death."

We fly on a small plane to what tourists are told is the original Maori settlement. But all the artifacts are already carried off to mainland museums, wherever.

March 27

On the traces of Monsieur Paul Gauguin—Musée Gauguin: not a single original painting by him in the museum. American tourists padding through, cameras and Bermuda shorts, colored shirts. Some fine photos of Gauguin's ancestors, wife and children, the last of whom died in the 1960s (all white, conceived and born in France before he split for Océanie).

Papeete is already eaten up by tourism. But there must be an island farther out that is still pure. Moorea is an island farther out. There's a Club Med. . . .

March 28

The Crown of Thorn Starfish is eating the coral reefs of Océanie and destroying them. It is impossible to kill it—dismember it, and the parts crawl back together, or grow new parts. Nothing kills it, short of burying it far from water. So with the tourist industry, which also is destroying the South Pacific— The U.S. government became interested in South Seas real estate during the Second World War, closely followed by the U.S. business and Australian business. The Crown of Thorns pressed onto the native brow. Eating all before it. And thou shalt have no other gods before you.

March 28-31

Out to Moorea by boat—to escape the cars, motor scooters & smog of the Papeete waterfront where they cut down the palm trees a few years ago to make a two-lane boulevard. Moorea—fantastic, dramatic peaks—no town, just three or four hotels. Jim Boyack, editor of the *Tahiti Bulletin*, the only English-language paper in Tahiti, gets me a house on the beach and a Citroën beach-buggy/jeep to use. The first day Lorenzo cuts his foot on coral and can't go swimming again until the last two days. We finally do go skin diving then, with Lorenzo's new snorkel and fins & mask. I have just a mask & I find I can still stay down for five minutes without breathing, like the time I swam across Hilo harbor (Hawaii) when I was in the Navy, three hundred years ago. Fantastic sea-life, underwater universe, two-thirds or seven-tenths of the earth covered by water—and we are able to see into only the fringes. Just a few feet down on the purple, yellow & crimson coral reefs around Moorea, unimaginable life—strange sea-slugs like black inner tubes inert, yard-long striped snakes with feeler-heads, striped angel fish flat as leaves, trumpet-fish with mouths like medieval hunting horns, sea urchins & starfish, corals like pincushions, like huge feather-boas waving in the water, like beds of *crenellated brains*. Swimming close over the sea's bottom, we signal to each other, pointing out astounding objects of Creation. Watch out for the yellow coral—it's the sharpest here and will cut your feet up like razors (when you do get cut, wash the wound well with fresh water & soap, then squeeze lime juice on it—the live creature which is coral will live in your skin & infect it, if you don't wash it out. And in the tropics you bandage any wound—nothing is left open to the teeming air). Undersea, all breathes together, pulsing with the waves, the true model of the universe in the Buddhist sense—all living sentient beings part of one breathing whole. When the Crown of Thorns Starfish engulfs its coral prey, the rest of the universe quivers, the sea anemone stretches. There is one little fish the anemone allows to swim in and out, because the fish feeds him. There are tiny purple flowers which the coral lets grow on its body, since those flowers act as sensors, folding up in a flash at the approach of any other creature. And it's not true what Apollinaire or Cocteau said: "les fleurs arc-tiques n'existent pas." Fantastic & unimaginable the wild experiments Creation tried—all some kind of blind, groping attempts at Consciousness. Flying fish burst into air in schools as our bow cuts thru the waves back to Papeete. There is a wind blowing the sunlight. We drop our fins and climb higher onto the land.

MEXICO, AGAIN

May 1972

May 19—Bus, Manzanillo to Guadalajara
—9 a.m. to 3 p.m.

M exican middle-class women's hands like hens' feet—crooked or curved fingers like hens' claws, hooked, with painted nails, pointed, hands bent down from the wrist, gesturing, like hens' feet raised, brown-white wrinkled skin, with gold rings, forearms stringy, veined, ringed with gold-plated wristwatches, hands clutching handbags when not gesturing, palms heavily lined; somehow all conjure up the word "conchita" and the sound somewhere of hens clucking, mixed with now and then the cry of a rooster, or even a goat, a *cabra* crying in a stubble field behind some house. . . .

Mountain towns, north of Tecomán, Tecolotlán, and Ciudad Guzmán—upward, toward Guadalajara—all day the dry, brown landscape floating by—a certain sadness in the landscape, on the brown plains, in the adobe and brick houses—lone burros, cows and men, a dead horse just fallen at a crossroads, harness still on. . . . From where, this loneliness on earth? Of course, the floating landscape is symbolic of time itself. It is only as we pass through it, as through a stationary wave, that time seems to flow past. Otherwise, it exists without us, immobile.

Everywhere on earth, for endless centuries, man and beast struggling away from this solitude in time, toward some Community— And yet today a book can be written on the Search for Solitude in North America. . . . Why do I voyage so much? . . . And write so little? The travel between the lines is enormous, whole *passages* left unsaid. *On the Road*, eventually the open space takes over, the white space, where all is silence . . . travel being a form of meditation. . . . This Week's Road led to:

Saturday—Mexico City
Sunday—Morelia
Monday—Pátzcuaro
Tuesday—Uruapan
Wednesday—Manzanillo and Barra de Navidad
Thursday—Guadalajara
Friday—San Francisco

Reading *Snow Country* by Yasunari Kawabata, I feel as solo as Shimamura in an empty landscape from which the light has been drained. I think of crossing Siberia by train in the winter of 1967 and reaching the Sea of Japan in the dead of winter. The train moves slowly into the station of Nakhodka in the last light of evening. Everything is solid black and white—the snow banked high, the horse-drawn sledges, the iced cuts in the roads, the dark figures scurrying past in the zero cold. There is a movie house showing a sea-battle in the Russian Revolution. There is a queue waiting to get in, standing silent in the snow. At a great round deserted traffic circle, on the tops of flagpoles fifty feet high, great long brilliant red banners stream in the wind. There must be fifty of them spaced around the great circle, under a long banner below, proclaiming the Fiftieth Anniversary of the Revolution. The crowd outside the movie has disappeared into it, leaving the real snow-world behind. I feel like the confused hero of Tolstoy's *Resurrection*, a novel I never finished reading, though it was the only book in English in Nakhodka. . . . In the darkening fields along the tracks, butterflies—flying about in the middle of winter! Couldn't be butterflies—but small white birds with paper wings, like Japanese rice-paper, blown over. They flitted about, these tiny snowbirds, as if afraid to be drawn into the night as it darkened after sunset, drawn into the great dark along with the bare trees, the people, the city itself. During that night the movie house burned down, as in *Snow Country* across the Sea of Japan a movie house cocoon-warehouse had burned down in the final catastrophe of love. And during the night it snowed on the white Chijimi skin of that land.

May 20—Dreamt This Whole Letter:

Dear Sir: Since I am without friends in France, England, or the USA, I am taking advantage of the chance meeting with you in Mexico several years ago to put forward my rightful claim to recognition as the true son of the French poet G. Apollinaire. Perhaps you will not easily recollect the brief chance meeting ("rencontre au hasard") with a dark stranger in a poncho who accosted you in French on the railroad platform of a hamlet high in the Sierra Maestra whose name I would rather not remember and which in any case I think it more discreet if I do not reveal to you or your readers at this moment. I say "your readers" since I write you in the fervent hope that you will do all you can to publicize my rightful claim to my true parentage and to the literary estate which, in the absence of any other true descendants of G. Apollinaire, should rightfully devolve upon myself. I suppose it is quite usual for a great publisher such as Gallimard in Paris (present publisher of my father's works) to receive spurious claims to the royalties of their authors from fraudulent persons claiming to be legitimate heirs, etc. . . . It happens, however, that my claims are neither spurious nor I myself fraudulent in any way, and I hereby call upon Gallimard & Cie. to immediately forward to me ("au soin de City Lights") all moneys which have accrued and will accrue to the estate of G. Apollinaire from the proceeds of his books published by Gallimard or other publishers controlled by Gallimard. Since I hold no brief or affection in general for the French as a nation—

a true "nation des cons"—I harbor no illusion or expectations as to the response of M. Gallimard to my rightful claims, and yet I beg you to at least bring to public recognition my true inheritance & blood relationship to G. Apollinaire.

Lost here in this morbid, wild country of the Tarahumaras for the major part of my life—I am now forty-seven years old and arrived in Chihuahua in swaddling clothes, never to leave—I have long meditated on returning to the "outside" world, or at least revealing my true identity to that world in such a letter as the present one— Thus you see, dear sir, that this letter is not something I take lightly, and I hope, sir, you too will treat it as something of first importance, not just the ravings of "some nut."

[unsigned]

HAWAII

March 1974

S Kona, March 10
ix a.m. and the voice of the dove, the morning dove, mourning dove, turtledove, trilling lowly, a bell-like tolling, rapid lolling, somewhere by the still pool, in the underbrush, by the magnolia, in the palm, soft and faraway. . . . Life slips by. . . .

A lot of rainbows on Maui, across the bay on the north side of the island, with one end of the rainbow on each end of the land, the southern end right in the little town of Paia, which I take as a good-luck sign of a place I shall revisit. The inside of a rainbow is its subjective side, its colors from the inside out being violet, indigo, blue, green, yellow, orange & red—the sun always on the outside, red side of the rainbow, the fire side. Inside all is protected, calm, subjective. The wind does not touch it. Outside the clouds fly by—torn to shreds in the mad sun— On the calm inner shore the morning dove calls—on the high ragged mountaintop, the great eagle's head raises its greaved beak above the rim of the canyon, the high cliffs on each side stretched like wings, as in the Magritte painting, with a rough nest of white eggs on a stone wall in the foreground. . . .

March 11

Reading Cervantes, and sallying forth each day. . . . I am both Quixote and Sancho Panza, both his horse and his ass. His hack, that is. . . . And poetry the bridle. . . .

"Ah, that is the truth— And if I do not speak of my sufferings, it is for the reason that it is not permitted knights-errant to complain of any wound whatsoever, even though their bowels may be dropping out."

Let us neither, then, dwell upon the miseries of just the opposite—constipation— that scourge and constant malady of reclinant writers, sedentary scriveners, and other drooping dromedaries of the leisure class—the constipated poet being no exception to this Marxist criticism. The Constipated Poet being in fact the very exemplar (more than even the Professor) of that leisure class *existencia*, living off the effluence of the affluent society, the true fat of the land, Fat City itself—and what society but our own can so fully and flatulently afford it?

So many Dons and their fat asses riding over the land in VW buses or Greyhound buses with portable toilets wherein sit those true knights-errant reading *Portable Cervantes*.

Pull the chain and all goes down. Still on the Road. The dawn comes up at a crossroads in North Dakota. I rein in my nag, being no Easy Rider.

Is this a centaur I ride upon? Why so many buckings, joltings, false starts and sudden gallops, so much rearing and rolling . . . ? Last month I rode with my shining daughter Julie over Mount Tamalpais and down over the foothills to Muir Beach and up the valley to Green Gulch Ranch, now become the Zen Center, where a Hundred Days ceremony was being held to commemorate the death of Alan Watts.[32] Sat on a fence post outside the Zendo listening in sun to the Great Paramita Sutra being chanted in shade, remembering Alan Watts once said humans are the only ones who hoard their dead, keeping them in boxes in cemeteries, all other animals abandoning their dead to their natural biodegradable fates. And on the way back up Mount Tam a drag-racing dirt bike roared up behind my Arabian stallion, and he reared up, into the sky, no Mobil Pegasus reared on gas fumes.

"Time, that devourer and consumer of all things," including myself. . . . In a week I'll be at Grand Forks, North Dakota,[33] which no doubt will be an "affair of the crossroads," whereas here & now we have an affair of islands. And an affair of mountains, rather than of plains. On Maui there's a mountain upon whose slopes resides one Ira Ono, né Ira Kaufman, turned ceramicist; and he gave me a ceramic mirror he had made, small enough to fit in my palm. I set it on a ledge on an open window of a cabin on a beach, and while I was away, a wind blew it off and cracked the mirror, wherein I then glimpsed a cracked vision of myself; and this being one of those rare trips on which nothing happens without significance, I am wondering where that crack in eternity may fit in. . . . .

March 12

Town of Captain Cook—who turns out to have been a real estate man— They are covering over this big island with a golf course. Pax Romana = Pox Americana Tourista in flowered Hawaiian shirt. (Not the island Don Quixote promised Sancho Panza.)

Off a wild beach, Lorenzo, spear-fishing underwater, came upon a barracuda, close-up, jaws half as long as its body. Lorenzo sped away on his flippers, really scared, and came ashore. . . . What is the significance, if any, of this barracuda entering our lives? Somehow Lorenzo avoided that bad karma which has fallen upon me these past few months: my old dog Homer, over sixteen years old last month, had to be put to sleep while I wasn't looking; and two days later, my daughter's much-beloved young dog Wolfie was run over in the street in the instant I was turned away talking to a neighbor. The car sped away, and there he lay, perfectly still, and dead.

Konane or Hawaiian checkers is an interesting game, strange in its resemblance to life: the loser is the one who finds himself unable to move. It is played on a board with one or two hundred holes, using white and black stones. All moves are made by jumping your opponent's pieces. Your object is to live in such a way that your "opponent" finds himself or herself unable to move. . . .

March 13—Hilo

Returning to San Francisco tomorrow, I find myself in such a life-position that I am no longer able to move. Or, rather, think I can't. And he who thinks he can't, can't. I stop thinking. And move.

BEATITUDES VISUALES MEXICANAS

October–November 1975

Autobus on Avenida Reforma with destination signs: BELLAS ARTES INSURGENTES. *Exactamente.* Just what's needed: Insurgent Arts. *Poesía Insurgente.* This is not it. . . .

1.

Bus to Veracruz via Puebla & Xalapa. . . . Adobe house by highway, with no roof and one wall, covered with words: LA LUZ DEL MUNDO.

2.

Passing through Puebla late Sunday afternoon. A band concert in a plaza next to a ferris wheel—I have passed through many places like this, I have seen the toy trains in many amusement parks. When you've seen them all you've seen One.

3.

Halfway to Xalapa a great white volcano snowpeak looms up above the hot *altiplano*— White god haunting Indian dreams.

4.

A boy and three burros run across a stubble field, away from the white mountain. He holds a stick. There is no other way.

5.

Deep yellow flowers in the dusk by the road, beds of them stretching away into darkness. A moon the same color comes up.

6.

As the bus turns & turns down the winding hill, moon swings wildly from side to side. It has had too many pathetic phallusies written about it to stand still for one more.

7.

In Xalapa I am a head taller than anyone else in town— A foot of flesh and two languages separate us.

8.

At a stand in the park at the center of Xalapa I eat white corn on the cob with a stick in the end, sprinkled with salt, butter, grated cheese & hot sauce. The dark stone Indian who hands it to me has been standing there three thousand years.

9.

I'm taking this trip from Mexico City to the Gulf of Mexico and back without any bag or person—only what I can carry in my pockets. The need for baggage is a form of insecurity.

10.

Two hours in this town and I feel I might live forever (foreign places affect me that way). The tall church tower tolls its antique sign: PRAY.

11.

In early morning in the great garden of Xalapa, with its terraces and immense jacaranda trees, pines & palms, there are black birds with cries like bells, and others with hollow wooden voices like gourds knocked together. The great white volcano shimmers far off, unreached by the rising sun.

12.

Brown men in white palmetto cowboy hats stand about the fountains in groups of three or four, their voices lost to the hollow-sounding birds. Along a sun-lit white-stone balustrade, student lovers are studying each other, *novios* awaiting the day. The sun beats down hot and melts not the mountain.

13.

On the bus again to Veracruz, dropping down fast to flat coast. A tropical feeling—suddenly coffee plantation & palms—everything small except the landscape, horses the size of burros, small black avocados, small strong men with machetes—each still saying to himself *Me Llamo Yo.*

14.

Indian women in Veracruz with yellow-brown hair like the fine silk of a shredded coconut.

15.

Along the *malecón*, ragged bums living in overturned old wood hulls with beds under them—*mariscos* cooking on a beach fire by their driftwood palaces.

16.

By the maritime union, two huge stone fishermen hauling in a stone net in which Venus is being wrested from the sea, clutching one stone breast. She does not look at the fishermen, nor they at her—one looks down at nothing, the other at the sky, she at a tourist ship arriving. A strange trio.

17.

In the Mar-y-Tierra Hotel, shed my coat & shoes. Set out on the beach southward, past Macombo—and Veracruz no longer visible. . . . Panama down there somewhere. . . . Shall I shed my final pants and disappear into the jungle?

LOOKING AT A MAP OF MEXICO

October 23

Where's the lake that was Tenochtitlán? Is that it, that little pond with goldfish in Chapultepec? And that great Cathedral? Are they lined up there to learn their Cataclysm? Here's a zone called Madero—must have been a tree there once. Here's ten or twelve million sufferers & lovers & haters in various stages at various levels of Dante's Inferno—the true landscape of Hell in the Seven Lost Cities in Mexico City—miles & miles & miles of dust streets & *avenidas* choked with cars & clouds of monoxide—millions of pedestrians' lives threatened every instant, saved only by their enormous intrepidity, the fantastic ambidextrous resourcefulness of the human biped so adept at saving his own neck by the most original & daring improvisations. It is the vast murderous landscape of William Burroughs's *Soft Machine* transposed onto the paradise-inferno of Hieronymus Bosch—millions of willing sufferers walking, climbing, crawling, crying, laughing, eating & sleeping in their clothes, or naked on the rack of industrial civilization à la Mexicana, on the rack of the infernal combustion engine—the great meat rack upon which all groan in the *distritos ricos* & in the endless Tepito barrios of Mexico DF. All caught in the clutches of the mad machine monster that eats all before it—Moctezuma himself dying in the poisonous fumes of its bad breath as the great old Mexican *muralistas* are put down by new critics working for the State, who really don't want the walls of Mexico covered with new "arte-acá" depicting the final apocalypse of the city as it sinks farther & farther into the dried-up lake-bed and, like the tilting church of Santa Veracruz on the Alameda, someday soon capsizes completely, like a ghostly Spanish galleon tossed upon cloudy seas, going down with all hands singing.

Tepoztlán, November 1

Took about a dozen "San Pedro" mushrooms—very small, dark ones picked on Popocatépetl—tasted gritty. Very mild and gentle trip, "blissful." Friendly presence inside me—very strong little fellow, definitely masculine—"myself inside myself." It's Nothing, nothing at all—San Pedritos out of the gritty volcanic slopes of Popo— Sacred mushrooms, Flesh of God, *Carne de Dios*, in a house in Tepoztlán. On a feathered wing, a translation dimly perceived, something trying to contact me—sun-stone going round with lights on it. Aztec Wing creaks open like a door flying. The land is very strong here—men & small horses surging from it, riding over it— The snow top of Popocatépetl seen at sunset clearly without clouds, a heart-shaped snow face on its westward side and on it the sign of Aries in black, the whole under a mantle ten miles high.

We rode on small little horses down a valley into the sunset. But the sun never set. We rode on and on into it, never tiring, sun never setting. Endless day, endless night. . . .

PACIFIC NORTHWEST
July 1976

July 14—Near Anacortes, Washington

J ust in off the *Scorpio*, twenty-eight-foot sloop, after cruising the San Juan Islands with Lorenzo (fourteen years old) for nine days. Started on Vancouver Island (benefit poetry reading against Trident nuclear submarine in Victoria July 5, Lorenzo's birthday), cruised to Salt Spring Island, then to Bedwell Harbor, sailed south a day to San Juan Island, then to mainland Bellingham, Washington, where we delivered the boat. . . .

A fourteen-year-old boy is a thicket of contradictions, energy and lassitudes, full of internal strife, longings & boredoms, irrational, intemperate, selfish, affectionate with animals, tender, kind and cruel at once, fresh & lovely, sweet with small children & women, respectful and rebellious at the same time, impudent, arrogant & intolerant of his elder's failings & opinions, incapable of admitting he does not know everything about subjects that interest him, with a super-sensitive ego very easily wounded, upset easily by the smallest slight to it. . . . Yes, and yet—a Boy like this is a precious thing—still in a kind of dormant, lovely state, between childhood and manwar, innocent and yet not innocent, clean and open to everything, and not open to anything but himself, complete in himself, in a sense the Whole Being more than adults are, sufficient in himself (though still needing parents), ready to go in an instant, without baggage (like a dog, up & wagging, ready for the farthest trip, no toothbrush or extra pants required), his necessities very few materially, his needs very simple, give him his head and a fishing-line & he'll do better than you, a fourteen-year-old Boy, beautiful to behold, not broken like a colt, carrying in his blood all that has gone before, through the ages, Italian, Portuguese Sephardic, English, Welsh, French, whatever, all in his face, asleep still, late in the morning, the bright sun coming in on his tousled hair. . . .

July 18–21

Camping three days & nights by the Deschutes River, near Maupin, Oregon, with Lorenzo & Pooch, fishing for steelhead & trout—only one trout in three days, but beautiful weather & river & New Mexico–type hills like mesas—tent & VW bus on lovely greensward by the river, with fireplace of piled river rocks—Lorenzo now in bus sleeping (in new green down sleeping bag, for fourteenth birthday), me in mini-tent writing this, 7 a.m., sun on high hills brilliant on yellow dry grass, flooding down now to other bank of the river, fifty yards away, river rapids running all night like a distant train, and actual trains running along other bank, long freights rumbling, whistle blowing, two or three times during night. Pooch sees cows for first time in life up close & chases them off, hounds them away, with ferocious barking, skirting them, zooming away when they turn at him, performing ancestral sheepdog function . . . when an old bull lowers his head and charges a stumbling foot or two, Pooch runs off squealing & crying as if he'd been run through, tail between his legs. . . .

Full sun now, 8 a.m., a little open railroad car with four men on it, dollies down the grade across the river. Their yellow hard hats gleam in the sun. Some birds flitter above the white water rapids, two small dark-blue swallow-tailed birds flittering close about a swooping gull whose eye scans the running waters for fish. Good luck, gull, may you have better luck than we had with the fish. Our luck was elsewhere: in having the whole landscape, river, trees, and you, to live among, dreaming by the riverrun, for three days. . . . In the stillness of Lorenzo's childhood eternity.

MANINA

Kohala, Hawaii

August 1978

Awoke alone in the dark dawn on the Big Island Kohala dreaming I was still on the sugarcane coast of Spain and heard a roost of tin silver birds shaken awake all at once by some great hand Their silver beaks tangled together set up a cry by the sea *Manina*

And single small birds somewhere undercover like elephant bells shaken slow A hollow wood knocking A small low calling *Manina*

And the dawn came up on the great uplands sweeping to the sea as on that seacoast south from Granada long ago The great green meadows The long grasses blowing in the tropic wind The great uplands sweeping sunlit to the sea The soft warm wind blowing toward the sea High palms bent and blowing coco fronds waving signals to the sea *Manina*

The long green plains The lush fields with far dirt roads and long grasses running down to the high bluffs above the sea The seabirds cawing and calling *Manina* the dark birds in the high palms sounding like scissors above the sugarcane fields The red rutted roads lost in them through the trees where the waterbirds called and called *Manina*

The long hair of the fields blowing in the dawn wind down to the high bluffs *Manina* your face upon the sea Body of longing The long plains lush with sugarcane and stone watercourses through them The green uplands between Granada and the sea where gods slept in the mountains and the mistral wind blew and blew Where now *Manina*

Imaginary woman loved by the blown sea Loved through the blown years Her face upon the fields Fair body upon the landscape when the wind sang in the arch of heaven in the first dawn *Manina* away back then when the dark birds all at once cried out *Manina* The hot wind blowing Sun upon the slate sea High clouds scudding over Dappling the land with their shadows between two palms and the brittle fronds moved like scissors above the longhaired fields the goldhaired fields cut down when the warm rains came in dark torrents Her face upon the fields Upon the dark land Eyes closed Hair blown back *Manina*

BISBEE POETRY FESTIVAL

Bisbee, Arizona

August 1979

Bisbee in Cochise County . . . an Old West ghost town, famed for its rich mines in the Mule Mountains, as well as for its outlaws & combative miners . . . now the site of an annual poetry festival. I read poetry here last night with Drummond Hadley in a deconsecrated church, and during my reading Drum (known as the Cowboy Poet) shot off his six-shooter thru the roof, an event reported this morning in the *New York Times*.

MULE MOUNTAIN DREAMS
1.

The white hot sun fallen over the stone rim of the steep hills of Bisbee—the tops of the hills still aglow in white sunlight—the little weather-beat hillside houses incandescent with leftover sun fade like filaments in turned-off lightbulbs and await the desert mountain night—windows agape like mouths to breathe the first cool air. In my memory somewhere a donkey brays. No border exists—the Mexican night closes in.

2.

Stood on the roofs of Bisbee watching Pancho Villa galloping by down Zacatecas Canyon—Apaches hunkered up in gullies—Cochise holed up—Yaquis run out of Sonora into the Mule Mountains, hiding out in the rocky mountain passes thru dry eternities, skulking into town on black nights for women & liquor. Years later finally run down—shot down in dry arroyos and buried head-down—their small drums left swinging in burnt-out trees.

3.

An Apache in the back row during a Hopi film showing their desert lands at sunset suddenly lets out a wild warwhoop and hurtles his tomahawk over the heads of the all-white audience straight through the screen.

4.

Heads and drums, birds and hands drawn on an adobe wall come alive in the night. Drumbeats & hoofbeats echo among the dry yucca, raising the dust along the canyon roads. From the desert plain comes the hard sound of wagon wheels and the harsh cries of drivers flicking their whips over wagon-trains. Prairie schooners into Pullmans—their dark saloons sheeted in oblivion—flashing down the desert roads of the future.

(Continued from page ①)

——— VOYAGE ———

Under grey skies, due East from
Paris, from the Gare de l'Est —
the brown fields, the bare trees
the green fields stretch away
small brooks + streams twisting
away, rows of peuplier bare
against the sky, flatlands, and
small hills on the horizon, black +
white cows impastured, all
so calm through the sound-proof
window.... Now a small
one village, ochre-colored

AMSTERDAM AND THE RHINE

September–October 1981

S Amsterdam, September 29
tepped out in the late dusk 7 p.m., in the beautiful center of town, by the museum park. Absolutely splendid to be here, feeling absolutely great. . . . I go to a "Concert Café" and order a beer and an espresso and sit on the terrace watching the European dream go by in the dusk. . . . Quiet traffic, bicycles and trolleys with big clean arched windows; now headlights on the bicycles come on, and there are neighborhood people walking their dogs, streetlights coming on, candles lighted in glass lamps and the café tables in the enclosed terrace. . . . Inside the café, musical instruments suspended from the ceiling over the bar . . . a sax, clarinet, a violin, a drum; the bar is lit with suspended lamps in glass shades. . . .

It is cool outside now, like San Francisco at night. The terrace heater comes on. . . . The lights in the buildings across the boulevard come on, I can see the cigarette smoke rising peaceful behind the big windows of a fourth-floor flat. It rises above a lamp. A man in an elegant smoking jacket comes to the window, smoking, and looks down.

War and thunder come later. . . . "Squatters" on the roofs of broken buildings, *The Night Watch* still guarding its rich burghers, nights full of blood and broken glass.[34]

October 1

Called Voznesensky and Yevtushenko in Moscow yesterday to persuade them to come to Benn Posset's One World Poetry Festival here. Voznesensky was out of the city, somewhere in Georgia. I talked to his wife, Zoja. Zhenya (Yevtushenko) was at home but couldn't come, having just returned from three weeks in Italy. He told me his new four-hundred-page novel had been recently turned down by two American publishers . . . "on the advice of their Soviet advisors."

Yesterday, on the way back from contemplating the burghers in the Rijksmuseum, sat on a park bench on Museum Plein, amid the cries of blind schoolboys playing field hockey with yellow plastic sticks. It felt like Vienna 1910. Perhaps I was Musil's Man Without Qualities . . . a stick figure on a bench in a great park by a boulevard . . . or a spin-off of Proust. . . . Only my Madeleine a bud of marijuana in my pocket. . . .

The despair of never knowing what's behind the trees in the Vondelpark, behind the screens, behind the elegant windows in the stone house where hangs a Chinese lantern, nor what's behind the face turned away, as in a scene from Vermeer in morning sun. . . .

This poetry festival is a "War Against War"—a War Against that War that keeps all States from withering away.

The biggest brains are walking around in old clothes. . . .

October 3-4

I have a feeling I'm in Vienna but I'm not; it's Amsterdam. The Danube is the Amstel. I have a feeling I'm making love to my sister but I'm not; it's you. Our ancestors are making love in the attic of our hotel up the twisted stairs in the room under the eaves. Their lovemaking filters down through a hundred bedrooms in this hotel of dreams. On the ground floor in the great ballroom of today I meet you, my redheaded sister, my Munch-like sister whom I've never known before except in bent dreams of old Vienna by the Danube, you floated by like Ophelia in an inner tube with the dark of Denmark, the night of Norway, on your brows. But here now the dark is gone and only the light, the blond light of your long hair, remains to fall upon my open eyes seeing you so clearly now without illusion, stripped to the bones of your nightwood voice.

October 8

Head out of Amsterdam on the Lorelei Express 8:19 in the morning, after last night's fantastic blowout of imagination at Paradiso Dance Hall. I recited the Lord's Prayer Parody from a high balcony, wearing a scarlet bishop's robes, after which the globe of the world was lowered with spotlights on it, to wild rock music as naked male and female bacchantes danced around it, and the crowd danced and roared as the world descended to the floor and cracked open, and a great python was lifted out of it, out of white sulphur flames, and the snake wound around the neck and arms of a naked black dancer who whirled and writhed with it to the heavy rock beat on drums. Then, as the fires had been extinguished and the serpent taken out (the Earth cleansed of Evil), the globe closed up and ascended again in night skies.

This past week here has seen a fantastic outpouring of creative energy, a great flowering of it, rushing together from around the earth—for a brief few days and nights, a wild concentration and outburst of the imagination at its most flaming lyric stage. . . .

Now the train heads out over the lush flat green fields between canals, past grazing cows and sheep, bicyclists in yellow slickers, bargemen smoking pipes at the helms of loaded barges moving up the middle of straight canals full to the brim with still water. Under the Rembrandt gray-gold sky, the brown-gold trees of autumn . . . the brown houses, the rows of still-green poplars, the white and brown horses, the yellow-brown furrowed fields, the lush thick green grass under orchards, the dull red tile roofs, the steaming factories by a town, the white birches by a dirt road in dense woods along railroad tracks, the lumber trucks on a paved highway, Eastward toward the German border, in the nine a.m. brown-gray morning. . . . Rembrandt's great round flat wooden palette, autumn palette, is Holland itself, the "Rembrandt-plain." . . .

In the dining car behind me two American girls (aged maybe ten) are laughingly reciting, "Now I lay me down to sleep, and if I die before I wake, I pray the Lord. . . ."

"What?" (laughter)

"My soul to take." (more giggling)

It's obvious that when man's and woman's consciousness emerged from the dreaming dumb munching of the animal kingdom, their new consciousness demanded some literal explanation of why they were there, here, on earth at all . . .

here was the first beast to emerge from the general slough of dumb inchoate consciousness, the first to be capable of reflection on him or herself, the first to recognize its own image in a mirror, and to say who is that and what is it and why and how are we here, when it was obvious that all blind creation merely existed without fore or after—all creatures great and small, all things, rising and falling, from conception to decay, a stone or a dead grasshopper ("nature morte"), a baby or an old crone, a full breast or a shriveled testicle—all one in the general mulch of multiform blind creation— And our "literal explanation" of it all now in the sweet fabrication of a "soul" which we do pray some Lord in the sky to keep. . . . Keep *where*?

So, into Germany. . . . The train flashes thru Andernach, on the Rhine, where Charles Bukowski was born (1921?), a flat dull-looking place, a blunt, hard-looking landscape, with small hills in the distance, on each side, maybe twenty miles across the flatlands; industrial town, known for the manufacture of what hard objects (ball-bearings? billiard balls, hammers? truck bumpers? tire irons? handcuffs?). Certainly not a good place to be born. Leading one naturally to a life of drink and whoring, gambling and horseracing, whoring in shit factories or post offices, or migrating to more of the same in Los Angeles; and "love is a place in hell"; a *helluva* life on this earth; Bukowski's, in fact. . . .

Wiesbaden—Rüdesheim: vineyards interspersed with cemeteries, all behind stone walls on hillsides, brick & stucco buildings with slate roofs. . . . Cross-country, back to the banks of the Rhine. . . .

Rüdesheim: a hillside tourist town, with bulbous church tower way up. I ascend to it thru the cobbled narrow streets. The church bell strikes in its tower. Five o'clock. Rhineland burghers are walking around with their shopping bags. I walk around, under the plane trees and past the shop windows filled with beer steins with medieval frescoes on them, with pewter or silver handles and hinged lids. It is not for nothing *Kitsch* is a German word . . . there are also dirndl dresses and miniature horseshoes in silver in the windows. And in the Tourist Information Office they are selling little LP recordings of the Rhine maidens singing. "In German," the clerk informs me. Should I expect the Lorelei to sing to me in English? Maybe next year. . . .

6 p.m. Went down into a beer cellar and in a vaulted cave saw a lot of lonely people in dim booths listening to a Philippine band of three women wearing India prints

singing about Santa Maria with electric guitars. When it was over a lot of men clapped and beat their steins on the table. It is very dark down here. I expect Peter Lorre to appear, escorted by some Brunhilde in drag. . . .

In the Rüdesheimer Schloss I order bratwurst and liebfraumilch as heavy dancing couples whirl to "Roll Out the Barrels" played on a Hammond organ. Dreadful sound, drowning out the Milk of a Beautiful Woman which I drink as fast as possible. Now they're playing "Red Sails in the Sunset" with marimbas behind the Hammond, and singing it in German. God, it's Chicago near North Side 1941. . . .

The man at the Hammond organ is eyeing me but I am eyeing the waitress with the Klimt eyes. Klimt's Lucy in the Sky with Diamonds. Her eyes are small for the fullness of her face, and they are green with green eye-shadow and mascara. She comes to collect the check a little early, saying "I go." "Too bad," I say. She says "So!"

Man, the predatory animal, always on the prowl. The men sit around the women like toads, then circle them on the dance floor; if they were Spaniards, they would wave small handkerchiefs as they circle them, like matadors around the bull. In Chile they dance La Cueca around them. Here it's slightly less subtle, more like the original cave-man meat-market.

The band, in red vests, is now into "The Blue Danube," very blue indeed. Organ, violin, and sax. I haven't heard anything like this since a bar I went into in upstate New York, maybe 1939. A bar with a dark ballroom in the back, with a crystal ball revolving, and a spotlight on it, sprinkling shreds of light onto the silently moving dancers . . . lumberjacks come to town, paying ten cents a dance for the local floozies in diaphanous evening gowns.

When the band is finished with this here now in Germany 1981, the patrons bat their hands together to signify approval. . . .

Friday October 9

The people here don't seem to be too happy about the coming end of the world. Even here in the lyrik morning by the lyrik river on the terrace of this boarding-haus, it's glum-city, located somewhere between High Glum-stück and Low Glum-stück, not far from the river Styx-stück (One-Two, Button Your Shoe, Three-Four, Open the Door, Five-Six, Pick up the Styx).

Here comes the Rhine "steamer," just as I imagined it. Down the river from Mainz, stopping here to pick up Japanese tourists and at least a hundred others.

Three hours down to Koblenz, where I'll take a train to Köln and Düsseldorf. The steamer is approaching in the late morning mists. The sun just now burns through. You can hear the recorded festive band music on board as the ship approaches, and the sound of the engine-room telegraph bells reversing the engines as the dock comes alongside. Immediately with a great clank they throw the gangway aboard. No time to waste! By the time I take ten steps on board, they are already pulling away from the dock. Ahead of me the tourists, checking out the johns . . . I struggle through them and through a huge dining room where people are eating frühstück and out onto the fantail of the ship in the sun. A steady wind is blowing downstream. You can see the black & red & yellow flag of the German Republic waving gently in the wind. It must be quite heavy to move so slowly in such a strong wind. . . . The Rhine vines are growing on the steep hillsides, the crenellated castles stand on the promontories, high up. "Robber barons" still in them? I wouldn't want to live in one for very long, not even with a baron, or even with a baroness. I might get klapt in the stück, stuck mit the klap.

11 a.m.

The ship pulls into Bacharach, a very lovely ruined Gothic cathedral in a niche of a hill behind the tiny town. There's no roof, and you can see the sun glinting through the very high Gothic windows and architraves. Only the high narrow transept remains. . . . No glass in the windows, but the stained-glass light reflected from the blue-green hillsides filters through. Already the boat is moving away from the dock. . . .

They are playing accordion music over the ship's loudspeakers. In the dining room they're eating cold pork burgers and potato salad washed down with liebfraumilch or Pilsener.

Across from Engelsburg there's a castle right in the river, "built by the Frankenstein family" (according to an overheard lady). You can see little slits in the walls where archers no doubt preyed on passing ships. The Bride of Frankenstein may still be in there, shaving her legs and singing to herself. . . .

The announcer comes on and in English announces we are just about to pass "the famous Lorelei rock, almost five hundred feet high and celebrated in the famous poem by Heinrich Heine, with music by Schumann." The American woman behind me shouts "Down in front!" Slow and stately, the sound comes over the speakers, women's voices, not very lyric except in the stateliness and slow bourgeois grandeurs. This is also the narrowest place in the river, according to the announcer, "making it especially hard for the sailors to get past the Lorelei." The unfeeling ship passes very close, without slackening speed. On one of the rocks halfway up you can see the word "Ghost" in white paint, or it may be GHOT. At the very top of the Lorelei rock, a German flag is waving in the hot wind as the Lorelei voices swell with stately passion.

12:30

A sudden flight of crows over the town of Bad Salzig. The ship's white gulls shear off. The crows flap upward, their black color like shadows on the steep hillsides. The vineyards high up are light green seen through deep turquoise blue netting. Even the ground looks blue through the netting. I have not seen this blue in German painting. The Blue Rider never came this way. . . .

Düsseldorf, October 10

Ufer Hotel. One of the more curious & interesting native customs to be observed by a traveler in Holland and this part of Germany is the practice of eating nothing but ham & cheese sandwiches for breakfast. The breakfast everywhere I've been here consists of these essentially indigestible items (when consumed before noon). Another telling local custom I noted last night here in Düsseldorf is eating raw hamburger with a raw egg on it. This surely would suggest the German is closer to the Wolf than other nationalities. They have not lost contact with Nature, as have so many of us in our skyscrapers. Or perhaps it is the *Wolf* they are eating.

On the way to the train station to go to Wuppertal, in an area with the streets closed off, there are Incas in a booth giving out literature to save the Amazon, a children's mime troupe, a Salvation Army band with a sign:

LAND

LAND

LAND,

HÖRE

DES HERRA

NORT

[Country, Country, Country, Listen to the Word of the Lord!]

A Salvation orator harangues the passing crowd; nobody listens. The mime troupe lady asks if there is a child in the audience who would dare to put his or her hand in the mouth of the bear (a dummy)— One baby is carried up but gets scared and cries— A little girl comes up and does it. Everybody claps. And the lady cries out with joy. (Perhaps it is a Communist group impregnating the young and dispelling their fears of the Russian bear.)

Crossing through a park a little like the Luxembourg Gardens in Paris, we stop to watch mallard ducks fighting with seagulls for a big ball of bread in the long pool. First the mallards have it and run with it, then the seagulls. A mallard with a beautiful green head gets it and heads up the pool, paddling for all he's worth & eating at the same time, then a seagull pounces on him from above and makes off with it. There are maybe thirty birds in all, rather like a soccer game, and it continues until finally a flying seagull pounces on the bread and flies off with it, all the birds crying after him. Walter Höllerer[35] says "In ze end ze flying people has it."

In the Bittner Café the rich bourgeois are feeding on fine cakes, marvelous fantasies in chocolate and colored frostings, strudels and pastries. The well-to-do elderly dowagers sit around like ladies in 19th-century French novels in the beaux quartiers. . . . Walter Höllerer treats us to the capitalist decadence, upon which we gorge ourselves like *marchands de cochon*.

5 p.m., October 10

Back at the hotel, the television shows the Bonn peace demonstration, several hundred thousand in the streets. Coretta King is shown saying millions of Americans are opposed to the arms buildup and the *neutron bomb*. There's a shot of an Uncle Sam figure on stilts with a skeleton walking alongside of him, miming his movements. . . .

Harry Belafonte sings, "Lay down your neutron bomb, lay down your neutron bomb, Mister Reagan, lay down. . . ." Also pictures of assassinated Anwar Sadat's funeral in Egypt. They are carrying a huge picture of him thru the streets, maybe a hundred feet high. The cortege enters someplace with huge marble walls, and the men in black suits press thick around the coffin which seems about twenty-five feet long (due to the TV angle). Then they move with it down into a long rectangular marble hole, and it disappears, as into some great pyramid, for all eternity. Looking like imperial Rome, the troops in their battle garb come on, rank on rank, over the horizon, their helmets flashing in the sun. Violence triumphs again, and innocence is no protection. Having learned nothing in two thousand years, the tribes of the world continue their barbaric antics.

In the Kunsthalle Museum. . . .

Reading this evening with local German poets and Americans David Henderson, Miguel Algarín, and Ed Sanders, followed by discussion which ends with a question from the audience to Ed Sanders: Did he expect his "chanting" would do anything to solve the problems of the world (the questioner referred to Allen Ginsberg's chanting as "romantic")? I ended the meeting by immediately replying that it was not "romantic" at all, that the basic concept of Buddhism is that suffering is the ground of all human existence, and anyone who can alleviate that suffering by any means—including the lyric—is accomplishing a great thing. (A burst of applause for my incisive comments and flashing wit.) Goodbye Düsseldorf. . . .

October 11

It's cold and raining hard when I take the train to Köln, en route to Paris. . . . On the bridge over the river in Köln, there's an emperor or a warrior on a stone horse, with a bird perched on top of his helmeted head—the stone bird has its wings spread, as if eternally about to fly. It never does. The iron rain continues. Köln Cathedral sits right next to the railroad station, dominating it from above. It stands there like some huge ludicrous medieval gray Gothic grasshopper with flying buttresses for legs. . . .

11:12 a.m.

Train to Brussels. . . .

Left the other American poets asleep in their hotel, and split. . . . In thirty minutes the train runs out into the sunshine and the green flatlands, lowlands toward Belgium. How happy I am to be out of all that cold, rain, and steel. Along the tracks are lush green fields, rows of poplars, and mansard roofs. I feel like an escapee . . . I am free!

October 12

Paris again. Staying at George Whitman's Shakespeare & Co., 37 Rue de la Bûcherie, in his upper rooms, my home away from home. . . .

BOULDER NOTES

Jack Kerouac Conference, Naropa Institute[36]

July 1982

Staying at Chautauqua Resort, Columbine House— Rim of hills close-up against the night sky, like Mexico. . . .

> Summer fireflies—
> The moon sails out—
> the old drunk boat!

July 30

At the panel on the Beat Generation and Censorship, I had the effrontery to point out—amid the general eulogizing of Kerouac—that while books like Allen's *Howl* had been busted for what can broadly be called political reasons (writing that threatened the Establishment or made people see deeper into themselves than they wanted to see, etc.), Jack's writing—except for some trouble over *The Subterraneans* (black-white relations)—was never busted. In other words, his writing did not threaten the status quo or the Establishment, and he was "hardly a committed revolutionary writer." This caused some heat from the other panelists and from the audience (which was large). A loud woman down front started yelling at me, "Do you consider yourself a revolutionary writer?" I did not want to seem pretentious and egotistical, and I demurred along those lines. She insisted loudly, boring in with her question. Finally I said, "Well, of course!" That brought a kind of relieved laughter from the audience.

To give some idea where I was coming from in this, I came out of the tradition of the French *engagé* intellectual or writer as articulated by Sartre and Camus—particularly Camus's *L'homme révolté (The Rebel)*, in which he talks about "guilt by complicity" in co-operating with a government engaged in "death activities." In the case of Camus, he was talking about co-operating with the German Occupation of France; but this is applicable to the American situation and to any co-operation with a government which—while funding artists and writers through the National Endowment of the Arts—is, with its other hand, killing millions of people overseas in illegal wars. I went on to point out that perhaps two-thirds of the "supposedly dissident presses and writers in the U.S." had taken government money through the NEA. Pressed still further on the point, I said I had—and City Lights Books had—never taken this money and had in fact turned down an invitation to be a member of the committee that chose NEA grants. William Burroughs on the panel asked what criteria were to be applied, and I said "not co-operating with any government that is engaged in death activities." A questioner in the audience asked if this applied to "local grants." I replied that, so far as I knew, the state governments of Colorado and California were not engaged in war activities—killing people—except in that there were death-related industries in these states, and I could see there was "some equivocation" possible on the state or local level. I then went into the idea that the State was increasingly encroaching on the individual and on his freedom, and that in general it seemed that the State and the modern military-industrial perplex were continually killing the subjective in the individual—the Little Man in each of us—the Charlie Chaplin man—and the poet by definition as the free individual is thus the natural enemy of the State. The poet is the bearer of Eros—the life-seeking, love-seeking being, etc. Michael McClure on the panel then spoke up to say that I "looked richer" than he, and that I could thus afford to refuse NEA grants, etc. Allen Ginsberg interrupted as moderator to steer the discussion back to the subject of the panel, censorship, before I had the chance to suggest to McClure that he had a sliding scale of moral values, based on the idea of being able to "afford" opposition to a death-dealing State, etc. I would have also liked to emphasize that if I was indeed richer than he, then it was *all the more incumbent* on me to take my particular ethical stand against war and for the Individual, etc. . . . So much for my "purist" views. . . . The word "revolutionary" probably shouldn't have been used at all. "Dissident" would have been more precise. To say one is "revolutionary" is a little like saying one is a Zen Buddhist— If you say you are, you probably aren't.

THROUGH THE LABYRINTH
INTO THE SUN

August 1982

M exico City: sunny Sunday morning. A woman in a red sweatshirt and running shoes is clipping her poodle pup on a stone bench on the Paseo de la Reforma. She finishes and puts the poodle down on the ground where the pup's legs start going like a mechanical toy, but she holds it, and then seems to crank its tail as if to wind it up. Then the little white dog scampers away under the little trees with their trunks painted white—aspens and birches maybe five years old. A short bald man in dark glasses comes over from where he was lying down with a newspaper over his face on the grass and engages her in conversation about the dog. It seems he is extremely interested in this dog, the like of which he has never seen before on earth. The dog wants to be picked up, not the woman who holds the clipping scissors in her hand and slowly opens and closes them as she looks at the man. After a while she reaches up and scissors a hole in his crotch. His nuts drop and roll away on the grass like balls in a pinball machine. They careen against a curb and ricochet down the Avenida de la Reforma, bowling over the late morning traffic. Each time a ball hits a car a red signal lights up. After a few seconds the balls fall back down the Avenida and come to rest in the little dog's kennel. The woman picks them up and plants them in the lawn under the trees. After a while another tree with a white trunk springs up from each nut. The dog scampers about under them and pees on their white trunks. The lady is about to mount her white horse and ride away but she cannot catch the dog. The dog keeps circling the trees in a figure eight, barking like mad. The trees grow up, the dog and the lady grow old, the sun and the moon rise and set a million times over the ancient lake of Tenochtitlán. When the lady is an old crone on the bench and the dog lies under a tree like a heap of uncombed wool, another man approaches from under the newspaper where he has been lying. The scene begins again in macho Mexico, and the lady is the eternal *curandera* who will cure modern man with her powerful spells.

August 15

At a late afternoon *tertulia*, I meet Octavio Paz. I tell him that in his *laberinto de soledad*, he's not much interested in psilocybin mushrooms as a way I suggest to get out of the labyrinth. . . . He gives me a strange look . . . backing away . . . I'm a real imbecile.

Agosto 16 (Lunes)

To Oaxaca. On the way to the International Poetry Festival, I join the poets' tour of the Aztec temple ruins found under the Zócalo. In the mud below the torn-up paving stones, the poor *indio* workers are digging, with spade and wheelbarrow. The guide tells me they get three dollars a day for eight hours. Down in the ruins of one temple ruin, an old *campesino* is heating his tortilla on an electrical hot-plate. . . . They are brushing the ancient stones with ammonia, the acrid aroma hitting the nose like the exhalation of a hundred Aztec corpses with wet bloodred burning crotches.

In the temple ruins discovered in 1978 in another part of the Zócalo they have uncovered a huge goddess, three yards wide, with head and breasts cut off, buried in the Hill of Serpents. At another place in the ruins, the omnivorous obsidian head of a huge serpent has been uncovered. His mouth is half-open and between the widely spaced blunt teeth a tongue can be seen, about to flick out, petrified in time. His obsidian eyes glare up at the Anglo women tourists. A low hissing may be heard under the sound of noonday traffic and the tolling of great bells in the tower of the cathedral. It is as if some great underground labyrinthine beast were trying to open its jaws to swallow us all in one gulp. They are digging to free its jaw so that we will be all consumed.

Oaxaca: Five p.m. and I'm sitting in the Oaxaca Zócalo, on the plaza, *al centro*, drinking a *cerveza* on the café terrace. Wanderer! How many times wandered into a plaza, sack over shoulder, looking for a cheap hotel, how many times the pigeons on the paving stones and the iron bell tolling in its stone tower, France or Italy or Spain or Mexico. A character out of Nicanor Parra comes by—dark glasses, a cane, a paper bag, gray beard. "Speak English? Spanish?" He tries to sell me a single piece of sandpaper! It is a new piece of sandpaper. There is a fly walking around on his old necktie, as in the poem by Parra. . . . Since I can't bring myself to buy the sandpaper, he passes on to the next table and a young couple, perhaps Anglo, where he sits down. He is talking to them, very serious. I wish I could hear what he is saying. Perhaps it is a meditation on sandpaper in Oaxaca. A meditation on mescal would be better. There is a worm at the bottom of the bottle, *un gusano de magüey*. After two drinks the worm turns into a butterfly and flutters away to dry in yellow sun. . . .

6 p.m. The late sun powders the plaza. . . . Loneliness is still a curse. Still the people that singly wanted to come on this trip with me must understand: I have to be alone on a trip like this. Or else they are not trips like this.

A break in the weather of loneliness. The clouds part and in the open spaces I glimpse bodies floating by, each like a boat of flesh. They borrow each other's bodies for the night. In the morning they cast off the moorings and drift away again, each to his own unknown unfathomable end. All night long the heavy bell clangs in the cathedral next door to the hotel I'm in. Every quarter hour all night long. It is as if some demented Quasimodo is in the tower, venting his frustration with existence. The plaza at three a.m. is absolutely deserted, the white trunks of the huge tule trees stand about in the total silence like De Chirico ghosts.

Somewhere close by someone starts playing a lonely lovely ecstatic trumpet, free-form slow jazz, improvised out of light in the night. It is as if it were a lantern playing on a dark wall in the night. Rising and falling, it blows on the wind, fading away in the dawn. . . .

Second Day in Oaxaca: One gets very jaded sitting around café terraces by one-self, overhearing polyglot conversations. Everything one hears seeming to be a cliché. I have been there before—an "old Mexican hand" at the next table knows all about exchange rates, *los turistas*, *casas de huéspedes*, and who killed Trotsky and even which hotel Trotsky stayed in the night before his murder (Hotel Montejo, Paseo

de la Reforma, DF)—many times have I passed alone through Mexico like this. I have passed through San Miguel de Allende, bullfights at Carretera (the most critical aficionados in Mexico), Pátzcuaro, Morelia, San Blas, Vaca Cuerna, Mexico City, Oaxaca; stood in endless buslines in broken down stations waiting for third-class tickets and broken-down buses, drunk mescal in dark dusty cantinas in mountain villages, imagining I was the Consul in Malcolm Lowry's *Under the Volcano*; I have *become* the Consul, staggering hallucinating down blind alleys . . . as if one had to live out the literary myths, from Hemingway to Kerouac. . . .

THE VIRGIN OF THE SUN IN HER PUBLIC SOLITUDE

In the grand Hotel del Presidente in Calle 5 de Mayo—in the long, high-ceilinged baronial baroque hall, there is a banquet going on at the far end, about a hundred *funcionarios*, little dark Aztec-looking businessmen or local government officials in stiff suits white shirts and neckties. The banqueters are being serenaded by a band of mariachis, singing softly with guitars. The diners act as if the singers aren't even there and don't seem to deign to hear the singing. A little portable loudspeaker has been set up and the governor of the city or state of Oaxaca gets up to make a welcoming speech. The diners, mostly men with a very few stylish women, are seated close together around both sides of the narrow long horseshoe table. They stare down at the white tablecloths or into their food. The high wall directly behind the speaker at the center of the horseshoe is covered from floor to ceiling with the top halves of wine jugs, on their sides with mouths onward, extended slightly like lips, each jug a clay face with mouth slightly open, red-clay colored. Close, one on another, they are stacked to the high ceiling above the speaker, thirty feet up to the great wood rafters or *vigas*, dwarfing the little figures at the banquet. A sense of the absurd blankets all in the mid-afternoon light. It is a scene from a Buñuel film, or a painting by Goya. The waiters scurry about with little white napkins over their left forearms, careful not to make noise with the dishes. It may be being recorded for some commemorative reason. The speaker drones on in his guttural Spanish. It seems now he is addressing one particular gentleman seated next to him who is engaged in divining the meaning of the wine in his glass. On the great walls, old oil paintings of dignified personages stare down, as if from the ages upon this insignificant moment in time; the darkened oils of the ancient canvasses in their stately frames are full of heavy shadows. The Velázquez-like figures in their magnificent garments seem turned to the little official and his flowery eulogy. But he is addressing the honorable gent next to him—the Honorable Crispin Tickell—British ambassador! The speaker finishes with a flourish, and now it is the ambassador's turn to respond. He rises and adjusts the little microphone, clears his throat, and launches into the possibilities of British economic imperialism in the Oaxacan region; the subject is not named and is indeed finely painted in polite phrases and *saludos* to the local state and its functionaries. It is now that I note for the first time to his side, a big blond lady who must be his wife. Even seated, she seems very tall, and her blond hair falls down her shoulders in a fan of light. Perfectly motionless and expressionless, she seems more like a statue or an icon—an embodiment of the famous local statue of the Virgin of Solitude. Is it the Virgin of the Sun, rather, with gold Aztec headdress, the blond goddess, wife of the blood conqueror who came as prophesied over the eastern horizon? Unblinking, she looks straight ahead as the speeches continue (a heart-shaped face, gold flowers in her clasped hands!). Her divine spouse the British ambassador is speaking in flawless

Spanish with British inflection, and it is quite possible she understands not a word of it. Perhaps she thinks he is ordering the execution by firing squad of all the *indios* in the region. The trouble is, if this is done, there will be no waiters. George Orwell would not wait here. The Virgin of the Sun in her Public Solitude seems lost in her own gold dreams. Through all the speech she never moves nor shifts her eyes. Their depths are inscrutable. She may be dreaming of her British garden, or of a lover in Bloomsbury or atop the Pyramid of the Sun. The local newspaper sent its photographer, a little man five feet high, and he approaches with his flash camera. When he is directly in front of the Virgin of the Sun he flashes it. She never blinks. The photographer suddenly falls back, as if dazzled. It is possible he quite missed the governor and the ambassador in fascination with the true Virgin. The Ambassador finishes his oration and abruptly sits down. Perhaps now they will drag the dark *indio* waiters away and line them up against a wall in front of a firing squad, as in Goya's *Disasters of War*. It is the disasters of peace we are witnessing! There is a clinking of glasses and knives against dishes. Mouths relax and hands pour drink into them. Above their heads the bald clay heads of the wine jugs stare down, each about to regurgitate all the wine that has ever been drunk through the centuries in this great hall, or all the words in all great speeches that have ever been spoken or sung here. The Virgin of the Sun bows her head slightly, for the first time seeming to take notice of the little men around her. Her gold breast-plates quiver. A ray of real sun suddenly flashes down upon her from a high slotted window, turning the aureole of her hair to white gold. The Velázquez standing portrait of some conquistador looks down, arm extended, toward the WASP Madonna, his hand with middle finger raised.

Third night in Oaxaca: In mescal, the Mexican night comes back. It is all in the worm, the *gusano de magüey* at the bottom of every bottle. It turns in the bottom of the bottle. Colorless, inert, it nevertheless is there, a terrible crawling presence, in the night, primitive, waiting. It is the dark of ancient Aztec Mexico. These kids with their knapsacks on summer holidays from the States eating in the Sol y Luna don't know what it is all about. They have never seen the night-worm turn. They don't know what loneliness is, the worm in the bottle, only one worm, never two, bottled darkness, bottled night, the genie in the bottle a dark insanity. Even Kerouac on a Mexico City rooftop long ago in his *Tristessa* had no inkling of it, except as the Great American Night, which is something else. The murderous Mexican darkness is in the hills, in the small lost mountain villages, the Chilchutls the buses don't go to, where the magic mushrooms grow, the dusty hopeless backstreets where all is lost and all is ancient and eternal, *indios* in tattered blankets blind with the mescal, eyes glazed over, nothing but madness in sight in the twisted cobble street, swinging door interiors of dark cantinas lit by candles, shadows of the living death on the dirt walls. It is the ancient Aztec's hallucinated place, but all the desperate of heart know it, and the wandering English, longhair Dutch hippy, Swedes, British consuls, *norteamericano* exiles in their sixties, old *bohemios* in sandals, Carmel ladies wearing *serapes* in hill towns, expatriate poets who think they are poets and live by it, year after year, *en exilio*, their only life in the life of their illusion, on and on, into the night of the earth, the mescal animal primitive darkness.

She was an English-Irish waif (aged forty or more) who called herself Countess Caroline and started screaming at the British ambassador in the Café Sol y Luna that night. She had Irish eyes and an Irish jut-jaw that hated authority and couldn't stand the well-modulated tones of the ambassador across the room. She started screaming Irish vituperations at him, he looking startled and scared. Her wild eyes caught his and he knew what was up. A Mexican folksinger started hurriedly performing, and the tension was broken. Pretty soon everyone was talking and drinking as if nothing had happened. Just then Caroline the Irish patriot pulled a Gaelic harp out of her bag and started wailing. The British ambassador's wife lay down on a bench singing to herself. The British ambassador looked terrified but kept a stiff upper lip and split, abandoning the Little Woman on the bench. Cries of despair and ecstasy are heard, as the British ambassador's wife turns into a mummy. The sound of the Irish sea can be heard rising and lapping as the mummy sinks under the waves. The Irish countess cackles uproariously and waves at me, shouting "Let's fuck!"

Next day: Bus to the airport in morning sun, mist in the far valley high up, through the cobbled streets, up out of the pocket of the town, out onto the autoroute to the airport, past the dirt streets alleys and shacks with donkeys of the old Mexico that still exists wherever the pavement ends, grinding poverty and yellow shit, yet gold sun on hillsides, a white cross high up. Love is the Holy Ghost. In the trees at the farthest outskirts of the city, a heart nestled, and would not fly away. Some strange bird.

August 29

Second International Poetry Festival of Morelia shifted to Mexico City due to collapse of peso which governor of Morelia used as excuse to cancel festival. Director Homero Aridjis[37] claims it was political. So it's on the University of Mex campus on the far outskirts of town, whereas we are all staying at old Hotel Motejo (style *antigua*) on the Reforma, *zona rosa*: about one-third of the invited came, after being informed of the shift from beautiful Morelia to this monster sprawling metropolis of traffic, dust, torn-up streets, millions of poor people like rats or ants in a hive. Ted Hughes, Charles Tomlinson from England. I'm the only U.S. poet (W. S. Merwin canceled out). There were delegates invited from Cuba, Nicaragua, Salvador, revolutionary countries, but none of them could make it. Enzensberger from Germany, Mazisi Kunene from South Africa (in exile), a Romanian (speaking French), a Brazilian, lots of Mexican poets including Octavio Paz. No one from Chile, although Nicanor Parra was invited. Homero Aridjis the director tells me Parra was an enemy of Allende and Neruda and was always *for* the present militarist regime. Aridjis said he has told this to Fred Martin at New Directions, Parra's publisher and mine. I wonder if he comprehended it. It certainly casts a new light on versatile, witty, ironic Mr. Parra. (A fly on his necktie.)

I have seen the best minds of several generations from several countries killed by boredom at poetry readings. No *duende* in any of them, the first night! Ted Hughes had it the second night, with some love poems. The only one . . . I told him so. As usual, he had a very beautiful woman with him. . . . Swedish poet, Lars Forssell, member of the Swedish Academy, was the most unusual, original, and eccentric, personally. Generally appeared late, ruffled, and either shy or distracted. Spoke good English and French, little Spanish. Enzensberger ingratiating and witty in a particularly German way, when speaking English.

MEXICO CITY—Went to visit Trotsky's house, and the museum of Frida Kahlo, wife of Diego Rivera. Turns out she could draw better than he, perhaps paint better. As for Trotsky's house, I was taken there by Vladimir Serge, the son of Victor Serge, friend of Trotsky, a famous poet. "Vladi" is a wonderful painter, and has been working eight years filling a former church (now a library) with semi-surrealist tempera & oil murals—enormous walls covered by heroic modernist figures &

themes, but some looking like Titian & Michelangelo. Huge figures of Freud &
Marx entangled. Children in oedipal wombs. Freud with an erection. God falling
out of the heavens into modern civilization. Adam and Eve fucked up. (I showed
him my sketch for a painting:

Vladi said he'd already painted it in another mural.) Vladi wears a ponytail of gray hair, a moustache, a leather Solidarity cap from Poland, a Russian tunic, and speaks French. Trotsky's grandson, who spoke English & French, gave us the tour of the house, "us" being me & others who had arrived: Charles Tomlinson & wife, delegate from Soviet satellite Romania, Lars Forssell from Sweden, Homero Aridjis & wife. The tour consisted of: the tower that was constructed with gun turrets to protect Trotsky after the first attempt to murder him failed. The tower proved ineffectual, since the second attempt, with the help of someone inside the house, succeeded. An inside job. The bullet holes are still in the wall where the first band sprayed the place with semi-automatic weapons.

A man who introduced himself and his photographer as "doing a story on the Trotsky house" for a Madrid magazine, *Acción* (he showed me his press card), said they were surprised to find poets visiting the house. Was it just tourism or was it a political statement? It flashed through my head that these two men suddenly appearing (in the garden where we were standing) could just as well have been "terrorists" or on one side or another. Which *side?*! I thought to myself before answering that it certainly was not a tourist visit and that it certainly was a political statement on my part (I couldn't speak for Tomlinson nor for the Romanian). Trotsky, I said, after all *was* opposed to the Stalinist totalitarian state, and anyone who stood up against that repression, etc., should be recognized, if not enthusiastically supported for other ideological reasons. That's the way it looks from here & now, anyway. We see how history is really written when we see the myriad Rashomon interpretations of the Trotsky story. History is written with a weighted pen: its point dipped in pure bullshit.

At the festival, Charles Tomlinson was the nicest but least powerful as a poet. Hughes was the most tragic (on TV he said he wrote poetry to hold himself together). A reporter asked Tomlinson what the poet could do for Peace. Tomlinson shrugged & laughed and said, "What can *you* do?" Write about it, I said sotto voce, as if I were some kind of wise-acre wise man.

I missed the last night of the festival. I'd talked about Montezuma on TV, asking why he didn't come back and reestablish paradise in Mexico and the solid peso. Montezuma's Revenge fell on me, and I ran to the bathroom for three days. . . . (Gandhi cleaning his own john so that the Untouchables wouldn't have to do it couldn't have felt worse.)

MILAN

December 1982

TRistorante Vittoria, December 14

hree bald-headed men at the next table speaking accented English, which is native to none of them. I am trying to figure out their nationalities— Maybe two are Italian and one is from Egypt and doesn't know the *bella lingua*. They are discussing deep-sea mining . . . a thousand meters down—nodules! Perhaps I should report it to the Italian CIA—suspicious discussion in English in a restaurant in Milan— It's the Latin of our time, the language of the Conquerors. . . . This is definitely a peculiar situation— We are alone in the restaurant— I decide at length that they are all Italian, putting me on, for some perverse reason. I decide to pretend I don't understand the strange language they are talking, maintaining an inscrutable and urban countenance like some debonair expatriate character in Henry James, putting my meat in my mouth with the fork in the left hand after cutting it, in the continental manner, having read an international spy novel in which the American fugitive gives himself away by changing his fork back to his right hand before raising it to his mouth. I am seriously pursuing this line of behavior, as the three men with bald nodules continue their seemingly very serious discussion of the deep sea off the coast of Abyssinia, though at any moment we might all burst out in riotous laughter at the ludicrous absurdity of the whole charade.

DUOMO PROSE

December 16

On three sides of the Duomo (which takes up a whole city block) a fair has been flung up, with plastic booths full of scarves and shooting galleries, handbags and refreshment stands. Smell of cotton candy. In the shadow of the Duomo they are shooting stick figures on crosses in the shooting gallery. A block away they are doing it in video, Pac-Man. . . . Pac-Man inside the cathedral still evades them. It is a sanctuary.

This greedy business of Christmas (what our world has done to it), not to mention the eternal guilt trip the Church lays on its adherents! Christ died for your sins, you are guilty of original sin, even though you've just popped out of a pure womb, trailing clouds of glory! (And any religion that doesn't allow dogs to have souls is definitely suspect.)

At the War on War international poetry fest[38] here last night in an ancient deconsecrated church, at the very end of the program, I raised my arms to the assembled congregation and prayed:

> Our Father whose art's in heaven
> Hollow be thy name
> unless things change
> Thy Kingdom come & gone
> Thy will will be undone
> on earth as it isn't Heaven
> Give us this day our daily bread
> at least three times a day
> And lead us not into temptation
> too often on weekdays
> but deliver us from Evil
> whose presence remains unexplained
> in Thy Kingdom of Power & Glory
> Oh Man!

Now in the Duomo, the silence of God's response is deafening. You can hear a penny drop. It is mine, into the Poor Box. And another into the box of the Virgin.

After all, they may be right, the Holy Trinity may really exist. In which case, I'm in deep trouble. Blasphemer! I'll drop another penny, even light a candle. No use taking any chances.

The Duomo seen through trolley wires at noon in Milan. . . . The cathedral a huge inedible wedding cake . . . a dirigible flying over it . . . medieval frozen music—white music made into stone—grace notes in flying buttresses. . . . Over the portals a stone sign:

MARIAE

NASCENTI

Coveys of gray pigeons crisscross the piazza in quick short flights in the winter rain and smog. Inside the cathedral huge scaffolds up behind the nave where the knave Himself is hung up high on His cross surrounded by ladders and catwalks in the dim light & dust. Still He gleams through the gloaming over the troupe of little children in Titian red coats clustered around tables of candles lit to the Virgin Mary. The white light falls & flashes on their Virgin eyes as they look up.

Behind the scaffolds and scrims the sound of little hammers and chisels chipping away very slowly as if the restoration had been going on forever and would continue forever.

It is Christmas and in the self-service cafeteria near the Galleria they are playing "Singin' in the Rain" in English over the loudspeakers— Now the rain pours down in the piazza. I am alone in it, with that great hooded creature, the cathedral.

RADIOGRAPHED RESTAURANT

December 17

I look through people I don't know like radiography—the way they photographed Delacroix's *Liberty Leading the People* to tell how he painted it—never a line falsified. I do the same in this restaurant: three well-off functionaries with their fashionable wives right out of a Fellini movie or Balzac or Hugo or Prévert. They are making it, I'm sure, and making it good. Now there are four wives and four plush plutocrats— They are listening to one at the head of the table, a figure from Goya with mouth open—so full of himself I am suddenly taken with fear that this restaurant is much more expensive than I had imagined and I will end up in the kitchen— As I tighten up my tie, I notice there is a winter fly upon it.

The diamond ring on the middle finger of the most important wife sparkles in the light of the chandelier. Her husband twitches his Vandyke beard. They are all so well put together, these solid bourgeois . . . every detail is perfect—the clipped moustaches—the manicured fingers—the coiffed hair—a lot of care has gone into it—not a single hair out of place on all eight of them.

I can see them raising their glasses now in a natural gesture of solidarity— Architects or armament brokers or sycophants of some sort ("Quelle connerie la guerre!"), they all raise glasses again to their solidarity—the solidarity of the ruthless & successful, in every country of the world, Right & Left, not the "solidarity" the workers had in mind, but their own brand of loyalty, as in "When I hear the word 'Solidarity,' I reach for my gun."

The fly on my tie has fled out a window to escape the general rape of the living. . . .

I straighten my tie, realizing this may be my last compromise, deceiving myself as usual that this is a gesture of independence. Charlie Chaplin, Hugo and Balzac look over my shoulder, Camus and Sartre shake their heads, the best minds of the new generations of the world turn back to their video games, their hands on the triggers.

A WALK AROUND MY OLD QUARTER

December 21, 1982

89 Rue de Vaugirard around the corner from the Rue Littré and the Post Office and the old Gare Montparnasse (before they put up the Left Bank's only sky-scraper on its site) where I lived in a two-room cave as a student (cold water spigot in a medieval sink hollowed out of an ancient block of stone, and the WC outside and up the curving stair halfway to the first floor) now gentrified with small trees in the courtyard among the worn cobblestones, and looking through the one courtyard window I now see my old dark cave transformed into a studio with sky-lights and tables with lace on them and armchairs with lace on them and framed pictures under glass on walls covered with dark red velvet wallpaper, the same damp wall upon which I painted a classic odalisque figure of a nude and scrawled Poe's words: *Thy classic face, thy naiad airs, thy hyacinth hair, hath brought me home.* No naiad airs, no hyacinth hair hath brought me here this time, and I turn back to the Boulevard Montparnasse and up past the Académie de la Grande Chaumière where I drew the model and on past the Closerie des Lilacs ever more closed with lilacs and rich diners, and then down through the gardens of the Avenue de l'Observatoire with its fountains of great rampant horses and spouting turtles through which the waters poured into the basins, and the great gnarled winter trees, and the statues of naked intertwined lovers with arms raised, the hands broken off and pigeons turning about on the broken limbs, as the late sun flashed through darkened branches in the Paris of that year.

MARRAKESH JOURNAL

July 1983

S ometimes it is better not to know anything about a country when you visit it. Especially it is important not to know its language or languages. Thus every sound, striking the ear like a small bell or animal cry, without any associative meaning, takes on the immediate quality of poetry, the quality of pure color in painting, with the percussive effect of pure sound in a void. It is only as these sounds accumulate inside us that some sort of composite meaning forms itself. Until then, we are like children newly arrived on earth, with virgin timpani, each a *tabula rasa* upon which all has yet to be written. Herein lies the true fascination of travel, not in the confirmation or contradiction of what we have been led to expect by the perusal of history or the learning of local languages, nor by the recognition of native customs in their similarity or dissimilarity to our own, etc., etc.

Thus it was that I came upon the *souk* in Marrakesh as a space traveler in a time warp, knowing nothing of the place in which he has landed, with only his senses to inform him of the strange terrain.

And strange it certainly was. Night itself, and I arrived at night, casts its mystery even on the most familiar domestic scene, for night itself is always the eternal unfathomable darkness out of which all is born and into which all is borne in the end. We are merely time travelers in between, fleetingly passing in a patch of sunlight, from shadow to shadow. Every day is a patch of light, however somber or bright, every night a patch of that eternal mystery.

The *souk* was of that darkness, and it lay everywhere before me.

CRIES

I must write a little book about cries, nothing but cries, street cries and distant cries of all sorts, of which there are not really many sorts. They are very few in kind, they are all poetic, they are all distant, somehow hooded, or muffled, and their source is often mysterious, even though we know who or what is crying.

There are a very few of them that stand out in my mind, echo in my memory, as fresh and vibrant today as when I heard them many years ago.

One such cry is the street cry of the glazier or window-repairer: "Vitrier!" The cry echoes down the stone streets, down the Rue de Vaugirard where I lived as a student in Paris. "Vitrier!—Vee-tree-eh!" The last syllable accented and drawn out in the dawn or dusk. The man carries his glass on his back, down the dim street, disappearing under it. "Vitrier!" over and over. The cry floats up to your window, distant yet close by, an offer to repair the world.

I had a recurring dream in those days in which the cry of the *Vitrier!* conjured up a distant figure disappearing at the far end of my street at sundown, and out from all the windows of that street hung concierges, each holding a broken mirror to be repaired, as if the man's simple offer to repair windows somehow included all the looking-glasses of the world. The man in the dream never turned back but continued to cry "Vi-tri-eh!" until both he and his voice were lost in darkness. It was as if he were the light-bringer who dealt only in clear glass, keeping his back turned resolutely to the appeals of broken mirrors with their lightless shadows and hidden depths full of mysteries which he and the light he brought could not deal with.

It was years later I learned that, in the infinite mirrored subtlety of the French language, there is a separate word for mirror-repairer (I can't remember it, but will reflect upon it).

MOUTHS

Mouths in different countries are the same and yet very different. (We are talking here only of human mouths of course. Dogs' mouths form a very separate subject, a very distinct category. So with cats. So especially with horses. "Out of the horse's mouth" has a special meaning to us humans. Why words coming out of a horse's mouth, or simply sounds coming out of a horse's mouth, should be given more credence than sound out of any other mouth is something impossible to fathom, unless you have a horse's etymological dictionary. If anyone reading this has such a book out of the horse's mouth, please send it. Such a dictionary would undoubtedly be of much greater worth than ordinary books, books which have not been chewed or eschewed or otherwise masticated by a horse.)

To get back to ordinary human mouths, I should right off say that there are no ordinary human mouths. They are all extraordinary, each in its particular way. Since I conceived of this treatise on mouths, I have resolved to notice mouths everywhere I go, especially when I travel abroad, but also locally, domestically, in every café and public and private place, in bed or in the street. I intend to "zero in" on mouths, like a camera with a zoom lens, like a painter concentrating his eyes with brush raised. I'll report what I see. . . . This could be endless. . . . Let me begin with my own, out of which such absurd sounds often come. . . . It is a mouth for all seasons, I would like to think, a universal mouth, a large and delicate mouth, capable not only of emitting every conceivable sort of sound but also of consuming everything, a kind of omnivorous maw, symbolic of man's universal hunger and thirst. In other words, an ordinary, extraordinary mouth, assuming everyone has the same hungers, the same cravings (some of which there is no mouth for).

I hate lipstick, like any true libertine. (You can imagine what Don Juan thought of lipstick, but that is beyond the scope of our present inquiry.) I hate lipstick for what it does to mouths. It of course paints a "false reality"—but since it is always impossible, even with the latest electronic instruments, to determine what is "true" reality, there is no reason to assume that lipstick reality is "false." Perhaps in fact lipstick is the psychedelic agent that allows us to see the only reality. Why not, and who am I to judge, I whose perception of my lipstickless self is certainly to be questioned.

Nevertheless, a face is a face, a lip is a lip, and the lower lip is sometimes said to be a true indicator of a person's character, sensibility, or psyche. No doubt it is a sensual key to the whole body, together with the clitoris, or the penis. Everything that goes on in between the two can be divined from them. . . .

THE MOUTH OF THE TRUTH

August–September 1983

F Rome, August 28

ourth International Poetry Festival sponsored by the Comune di Roma. My second time at this fest, the first at Ostia in 1979,[39] with twenty thousand European hippies on the beach, the Italian Woodstock.

This year Allen is not here and I am getting the big publicity, a little like Nicanor Parra coming out of Neruda's shadow when Neruda died. (Allen still alive! And good thing, too.) In an interview this week I pointed out that A.G. had functioned as a great literary catalyst for the Beat Generation, just as Ezra Pound had done for his time, dragging a whole gang of writers into print with him, many of whom would never have seen print if it hadn't been for his insistence to editors.

August 30

Antico Caffè Greco, Via dei Condotti near where Ingeborg Bachmann lived, and died in a fire there in 1973. Sitting in this elegant café thinking of her avid self. On my way to Taormina (1968) I met her once here, obsessive, still in love with Max Frisch . . . a strange, hungry creature she was. . . .

August 31

HOTEL WASHINGTON, PIAZZA FIUME—During the night I woke and thought a long time about how I must write the story of my lost brother Clem, now senile in a nursing home outside Baltimore. He is over seventy-five, incontinent and violent. He has beaten up the nurses. The director wrote me a long letter. The last two times I wrote Clem, he did not answer. The time before that was a childish scrawl. The last sentence of my story would be: "My brother had long ago entered the country of silence."

Must go to the Testaccio cemetery and see the illustrious dead. It is said that if you say you're a relative they will let you in free. Suddenly you are no longer a tourist, in the land of the dead, the foreign legions.

September 3

Some curious sexual Italian stories I've picked up on this trip:

1. An Italian publisher, who was blown up when a terrorist bomb he was rigging went off, had a penis so small that he had to change women frequently. When the remains of his body were found after the bomb explosion, it was reported to police headquarters on the phone, and the officer at headquarters—attempting to make sure of the identity of the body—shouted into the phone, "Did you look at the penis?" (There may have been an accident or maybe not . . . some suspected a fascist plot to assassinate him. . . . The general judgment is that the publisher was politically naïve. The fact that the newspaper *Corriere della Sera* published a report of his death, furnished by police, even before he was actually killed, led some to suspect the police were in on the killing, wanting to get rid of what they considered a Left-wing terrorist.) The above story told me by a reputable Italian literary critic and journalist. . . .
2. Pasolini[40] was the unfortunate possessor of a condition called *Eiaculatio Precox* or Precocious Ejaculation. This caused *him* to have many frustrating affairs, naturally.
3. Pavese—another death with sexual connections . . . I was told. . . .
4. And what of Ingeborg Bachmann, that driven soul, always in love with Max Frisch, and unable to come. . . . And then burned up by a fire in her own apartment?
5. And what of Madame Flaubert who complained in a letter to a friend that her husband's penis was too small?

The necrophilia is endless . . . what of Rothko? what of Frank O'Hara? Artaud? Marilyn Monroe? All strange deaths with something unexplained.

All deaths are strange, with something unexplained. As with translation, the poetry is lost in it. . . .

September 6

The Swiftian vision of beings on a much smaller scale, enabling the observer to see them more objectively, as through the wrong end of the telescope: walking through a great piazza, I see everyone as ants scurrying about, or bees buzzing about, or grasshoppers, tiny creatures stirring or rushing about or absurdly gesticulating. . . . The absurdity of the entire picture, the absurdity of the seriousness of these little beings intent on their curious activities, emitting strange little cries or whispers or songs, accompanied by all sorts of movements, signals, "body language," gesticulations violent or gentle, their mandibles furiously at work. Antic ants all! The world a huge anthill with billions of tiny creatures in fervent activities.

"What wild pursuit"! The absurdity of it all, enough to make one die laughing. "This busy little monster man-unkind." Essentially a circus character, putting on his comic little act, his absurd routines! Tragicomic face of a clown. I laugh to see myself crying, I cry to hear myself laughing. . . .

The "world leaders" going through their insane unintentionally comic routines, gesticulating, saluting, shaking hands, bowing, smiling, making absurd speeches with the utmost seriousness, as if they really believed it would make any difference under the cosmic eye. If the sun moved a little nearer or a little farther away we would all die. That's the only reality.

September 7

Visited the Villa d'Este and the Villa Adriana (Hadrian's Villa). . . . Those Roman women weren't free at all. So many of them had to stand forever with heavy broken stones on their heads or holding up whole marble houses. Sometimes they were allowed to lie down—or were seduced—and immediately turned to stone. It seemed a no-win situation, as with many women today still. Either they allowed themselves to be put on pedestals and idealized in marble, or they perished, their flesh melting away in less than a hundred years, which is nothing in geological time. How little we have changed!

On the other hand, it was the same with insects, not a single one of them surviving today, though the race continues. When we see the insects as humans, close up, we see them often locked in embraces, perhaps of love, their legs wound around each other to the death. The fact that they have more legs than humans makes their love-embraces all the more fatal. An amorous spider or centipede is a lover really to be grappled with. However, the idea that it is love and not some other emotion that motivates such grapplings, human or insect, is hilarious.

September 9

Just before dusk, the ancient town of Tuscania, on the border of Tuscany— Green-gold Tuscan countryside— Suddenly, around a turn, a herd of bone-white cattle sequestered in a field as in a lagoon. Herds of bone-colored sheep along the road. . . .

Deep green Toscana, little mountain villages. . . ancient Etruscan hill towns— red-brown stone houses with red tile roofs on steep hillsides or on hilltops, surrounded by gorges of lush green, oaks & olive trees & cypresses. A time of heavy winds and rain. . . . Tomorrow to the coast.

September 13

Boat from Porto Santo Stefano to Isola del Giglio—German tourists—young couples, all blond with backpacks—the afternoon sunlight shines through their flaxen hair— They are all looking ashore, shading their eyes for the Lorelei; the light paints them white against the turquoise sea, the green slopes & rocky promontories, white castle towers, stone houses high up with cypresses, terraced steep farms. . . . A fat ugly priest in a black dress paces the deck.

This is the Tuscan archipelago: Santo Stefano to Elba . . . Napoleon was here. . . . The sun sets, and in its final moment, when only the very tip of it is still visible, it looks like a little car on fire. . . . Perhaps it is: Civilization.

Florence, September 15

1. The old man selling corn to feed the "uccelli capitalisti" outside the Palazzo Vecchio, and
2. The "practice" concert in a great Renaissance hall of the Medici (a Medici pope with arms raised behind the orchestra). A cello competition—with full orchestra—Dvořak concerto—fantastic sound—young conductor, full of fire— Late afternoon— Audience on canvas chairs beneath great wall paintings of medieval battles— And huge struggling statues along each side, in heroics. . . . The oxymoron of the violence all around on the walls in the paintings & the statues, and the calm peace & ecstasy of the music.

typi Fiorentini

September 18

TWA TO BOSTON—A woman in "Ambassador Class" having a heart attack while the people behind her wearing headphones are laughing hilariously at a movie with Dustin Hoffman. They bring the oxygen tank and pump her up. She starts crying uncontrollably when she comes to. The audience continues roaring at the movie. She keeps saying, "I am going to die." She doesn't. The audience keeps laughing. She keeps crying. She doesn't die. The audience continues laughing.

SEVEN DAYS IN NICARAGUA LIBRE
January 1984

I went to Nicaragua in the last week of January, 1984, to give the poet and minister of culture, Father Ernesto Cardenal, a seed from a flower at Boris Pasternak's grave which had been given to me by the Russian poet Andrei Voznesensky at a poetry reading against war at UNESCO in Paris.

When I presented the seed to Cardenal in an open-air amphitheater in Managua, I felt I did not have to point out to him nor the audience that the seed was not only a symbol of the power of poetry to transcend all the boundaries of the world dividing people from each other, but also a symbol (from the grave of that great Russian writer who survived the most repressive period of Soviet life) of resistance to Stalinism. The theater was in the Plaza Pedro Joaquín Chamorro, named after the man who was murdered near the end of Somoza's dictatorship, the outrage over it hastening the end of the regime.

I also went to Nicaragua to deliver the first copies of a City Lights anthology of Central American poetry, *Volcán*, and to see the Sandinista Revolution for myself.

As a civil libertarian tourist of revolution, I hoped at least to probe the supposed limits of what one anarchist member of the Sailors Union of the Pacific in San Francisco had called "Potemkin Village Tours."

I came to Nicaragua thinking that what was happening here was not, in fact, a revolution, not at least in the sense of the dreamed ideal of many intellectual revolutionaries, particularly anarchists. What has happened here, rather, is the overthrow of a tyrant (Somoza) supported by the U.S., and the attempt to overthrow the economic tyrant of colonialism in which Latin America has been for centuries the cheap labor market for North American and multinational business. It is not so much a revolution as it is a crisis of decolonization in a poor country the size of the San Francisco Bay Area in population, devastated by U.S.-financed war, desperately short of supplies, attempting to set up some kind of "democratic" government (in the teeth of a U.S. policy evidently designed to force Nicaragua into the Soviet camp and thus give the U.S. justification to move in and "control" the situation).

In the face of all this, were the Sandinistas now setting up a Soviet-style authoritarian government? As a civil libertarian with anarchist sympathies, I was interested in discovering just how much "authority" is absolutely needed to lift a country out of colonialism into a free society. Was it possible at all, without losing the very freedom revolutionists always proclaim? The answer to that question is the history of revolutions.

Nicaragua is now the focus of passions of the Left, fifty years after such passion and hope were concentrated in Republican Spain—and disappointed; twenty-five years after the same hopes were concentrated on Cuba. Everyone dreams his or her ideal of a perfect society—and is disappointed or disillusioned. The absolute is unobtainable.

In the history of revolutions, the issue of individual civil rights and especially freedom of speech and press has been the pivot upon which all in the end has stood or fallen. So it was in Cuba—to the dismay of many early supporters; so it may be in Nicaragua—whose leaders are trying valiantly, it would seem, to avoid the mistakes Cuba made.

How *libre* would "libre" turn out to be?

January 27

I'm making the trip with the San Francisco photographer Chris Felver. On Aeronica Flight 500 from Miami, we seem to be the only North Americans, except for one twenty-two-year-old student with backpack going to work two weeks with other volunteers in the coffee harvest. The plane flies directly over the eastern end of Cuba. Suddenly, after some two and a half hours, we are over the dark green waters of Lake Managua, circling down into the heart of this Caribbean amphitheater where the fate of Central America is being played out.

The stewardess makes her announcement, first in Spanish, then English; the fifty passengers stir—mostly well-dressed Nicaraguans looking like they've been shopping in Miami—one lady shrugging and saying there's nothing to buy in Managua, and that the only reason she's going back is because she has a big house there. It wasn't taken away from her by the Sandinistas, but she says she'll lose it if she stays away more than six months. She had members of her family on both sides. It wasn't wise to take sides. Her heavy rings glitter.

The plane lets down its landing gear with a thump, and then we are coming in low over the brown-green fields, over farmland with brown and white houses, stone or adobe. The first impression is how small everything is—the whole of Managua seen at a glimpse in the falling sun, the center of it flattened by the earthquake of 1972 and still to be rebuilt—the whole town seeming about the size of Mazatlán or Guadalajara years ago—the airport tiny.

Ernesto Cardenal is there on the apron of the field, waiting to greet us, wearing a black beret and a white short-sleeved blouse, and blue jeans. The plane doors open and we file down—handshakes and *abrazos*, Ernesto beaming, with that angelic smile of his, his head as always slightly cocked to one side. It is as if I've known him forever, though I've met him only twice, once before the Revolution and once since in San Francisco, and hadn't known him at Columbia University or later when he was Thomas Merton's disciple at the Trappist monastery in Gethsemane, Kentucky. Now in his late fifties, there seems to be something childlike and eternal about him; but perhaps all small older men with white beards have that effect. (He guards his inner self, as all public holy men must. There is still enough of a Trappist in him to preserve him even in a revolution. He also guards the inner Revolution, and you don't get much out of him on any dissident subject, at least if you are a journalist.)

Walking to the airport building, I note one big camouflage-colored copter with two guards in fatigues with AK-47s guarding it. There aren't any other planes in sight, military or commercial. (Their commercial air force seems to consist of no more than four planes—two in the service to Miami, two to Mexico City.) A lot of uniforms in sight, but hardly a state of war. We are escorted into an upstairs V.I.P. lounge in the two-story white building. A waiter in a white coat is circulating with demitasses of black coffee on a tray, a napkin on his arm. One would think it's the old days; but it isn't. Two Nicaraguan journalists sit down to interview me, one from *El Diario*, the other from the Sandinista radio station. "Why have you come?" An excellent question. I see it as a voyage of discovery, hoping to discover the Sandinistas are in the right, and that I might take some public stand in their favor, rather than the political silence maintained by many U.S. writers today. (Not exactly with that much-vaunted objectivity of North American journalists, I hope I at least have an open mind, but a mind not so open that the brains fall out.) I also tell the journalists I hope to make some new breach in the wall of enormous ignorance and misinformation and indifference in the U.S. on the subject of the Sandinist government and Nicaragua in general.

We meet Bill Finnegan, from *New Age* magazine (Boston) and Ken Silverman, photographer for Finnegan and stringer for the *New York Times*, both of whom will be traveling with us a good deal. There's a senator from India being interviewed in another corner. (It is Doctor Shri Shyam Sunder Mohapatra, and a story later in *La Barricada* quotes the senator as expressing "the preoccupations of his government with the way the U.S. tries to undermine the independence of Central American and Caribbean countries." He also said India was sending medical aid to Nicaragua and helping in the construction of railroads, as well as other technical industrial help.)

We're soon out of the airport and on the road to town in a standard Toyota sedan (no bulletproof glass?). We're on a newly paved road, behind us a jeep with soldiers pointing their automatics at everyone. Ernesto pointing out the great empty spaces of the city devastated by the earthquake over a decade ago, and then the great park created by the Sandinistas out of that waste in the center of Managua. What's left of the "business district" looks at first glance like downtown Salinas, California, fifty years ago—one high-rise on a hill is the pyramidlike Hotel Intercontinental (where the few tourists and most foreign journalists stay). Our little cavalcade pulls up another hill overlooking the center of town, and we get out in front of the government guest house. The neighborhood has the feel of a rich suburb in any Latin American city. Only in one of those posh suburbs there wouldn't be a big poster painted on a wall across the street with a quote by Tomás Borge, Sandinista minister of the interior, addressed to Carlos Fonseca, a founder of the Sandinista Liberation Front: "Carlos, dawn is no longer a fantasy in our minds but a reality."

We're installed in a mansion formerly owned by *Somocistas*. There are two empty swimming pools. We sit down on a tiled veranda in the shade, and are served by a houseboy in a white coat—Tonya beer in mugs. Ernesto looks through our new anthology, *Volcán*. We rock in big wooden chairs. . . .

January 28

Wake at six to the sound of a bird I've never heard before—a macaw of some kind. I go out in the stillness of the early light and walk around the veranda and walled gardens. Next to the first swimming pool, an old guardian sits, silent, staring into the still water. I wonder if he was sitting like that back when this was one of Somoza's henchmen's houses. . . .

The bougainvillea are in bloom in Managua, in a garden across the street, as they were in the first sentence of the photo book *Nicaragua: The War of Liberation* by Richard Cross, the American photojournalist killed last year at the Honduran front. . . .

At nine, Daisy Zamora shows up to take us to the Museum of the Armed Forces. Daisy Zamora is one of the Nicaraguan poets in the City Lights anthology, and her latest book is *La Violenta Espuma*. She tells us parts of her story. When her husband was preparing to join a surprise attack on a post of Somoza's National Guard, one night at the beginning of the Sandinista victory, she insisted on going with him, though she'd never fired a gun. He taught her how to use one. There were twelve of them with small arms, against a garrison with heavy weapons. When the surprise attack started in the darkness, she felt a "terrible loneliness," realizing that she had no one else to depend on, and had to survive on her own. They were surrounded, but they made it through and took the barracks.

She says her story is typical of many young Nicaraguan women. Over 30 percent of the Sandinista fighters were women. They fought alongside the men, they were all in the streets at the time the Sandinist victory swept the country. (Women fought in greater numbers than in the Cuban Revolution two decades earlier.) They felt that in the fighting they had won equal rights with the men, rights which women were still fighting for in the U.S. Until recently, Daisy Zamora was assistant minister of culture. (I later noticed that there are no billboards showing women's bodies to sell products—the Sandinistas passed a law prohibiting the use of sexist advertising.)

Outside the Museum of the Armed Forces—a single-story building like a gym—a lot of relics of the Sandinist victory are set up. Dominating it is a monumental statue of the dictator Anastasio Somoza García on horseback. It lies where it was toppled over by the Sandinistas on the day of liberation, July 19, 1979. It is as if you could still hear its snorting, as the dust settled in the swirling wind of history.

There is also on display a rusty home-made tank about the size of a VW bug.

There are some little mortars made of stovepipes. Inside, there is a kind of school bulletin board display of the history of the Sandinistas, with many photos of early heroes—Agosto Sandino, Carlos Fonseca, and others who perished earlier, as well as heroes and martyrs of the final victory. There is a photo of poet Rigoberto López Pérez who killed the *first* Somoza at a party in 1956 in León, Nicaragua, disguised as a waiter. He was immediately killed and his body destroyed.

But they did not kill his poetry. Next to his photo is a poem, "Ansiedad," which ends with the lines:

> The flower of all my days
> Will always stay faded
> As long as the tyrant's blood
> Remains in his veins
> I'm looking for the fish of liberty
> in the blood of his death

On the way back across town, we pass the Palacio Nacional and the Catholic cathedral, both heavily damaged by the earthquake of 1972 and never restored. It was as if the earthquake itself were the first great blow against the dictator. It is symbolic that the upper hierarchy of the Church—divided in its ranks against the Sandinistas—doesn't want the towers of the cathedral torn down, though they are dangerously faulted and unrepairable.

We stop for a beer at a wooden pavilion on the edge of a *laguna*, a lake in a crater about the size of a football field. At a *cantina* by the water, we watch kids running and diving and sunning themselves. The noon sun beats down. It is almost as if we were at some peacetime tropical resort. "Up there," points Daisy, "just over that hill, was one of Somoza's villas. People couldn't swim here then."

Speaking of tropical resorts, we are going to one after lunch—Pochomil, on the Pacific coast. It's Saturday, and Ernesto is glad to get out of town—he hasn't been away from his work in weeks. He comes and gets us in his sedan with the soldier-driver. Ken Silverman and Bill Finnegan are in a jeep behind us, and there's another jeep with soldiers bringing up the rear. It's a little more than an hour west to the beach. Small farms and rolling land. Cows and dogs in their eternal present watch the past and the future roll by (in the form of ourselves), the cows munching their cuds and staring, the dogs standing still and barking at the Revolution. They are a little like the bourgeois lady on the plane—ready for anything, they will survive. Dawn is long past, and the sun stands at the meridian. We hope there will be no death in the afternoon.

We roll into Pochomil and the tiny beach resort built since the Revolution—a few thatched-roof beach houses and an open-air restaurant and bar facing out onto the wide beach and sea. A few *palapas* and outbuildings strung along the ocean front, set back under the palms. It's like an unspoiled Mexico before the tourists arrived with their various kinds of pollution, cultural and otherwise. Fishermen and *campesinos* come up and happily greet Ernesto. We sit down at a table under an arbor. Michael Jackson and Paul McCartney blare from jukeboxes. We are soon furnished with *camarones* and *mariscos* and Tonya beer. Ernesto has some clear rum. I've never seen him without his beret before. He's not bald; he's got white hair almost to his shoulders.

Ernesto says someday they'll have tourists, someday this resort will be built up, avoiding the pollution of prostitution and the other forms of *usura* which were so much a part of Batista's Cuba and Somoza's Nicaragua. When your country is an economic slave to Rome, the Romans come, and it is your women that bleed the most. Ernesto's use of the Latin word for usury reminds me that Ezra Pound was one of his poetic masters.

Ernesto has another rum. He would like to kick back and relax; but the journalists bore in with their hard questions. It goes on for hours. He answers them steadily, he never seems to tire. There is a sweetness about him, almost angelic, mixed with a touch of Cupid. . . . *Temperance and fortitude*, he insists, are the distinguishing characteristics of this Revolution and of the *junta* directing it. *Junta*, he points out, doesn't mean a military dictatorship; the dictionary simply says it's a "group." The Revolution is being directed by a group—there is no single dictator, no dictatorship except of "the people." (I'd heard that before—in Havana in 1960–61—in the early euphoric stages of the Cuban Revolution. Ernesto is only the first of the government leaders to tell me they are trying to avoid the mistakes the Cubans made—as Fidel Castro himself counseled them to. Castro was in fact quoted in *La Prensa* as saying, "I am not a follower of Moscow; I am its victim.") And Ernesto went on to say that the Sandinist model for the Revolution is neither the Cuban nor the Soviet, and that for himself as a priest the model is the kingdom of God. And with his vision of a primitive Christianity, it was logical for him to add that in his view the Revolution would not have succeeded until there were no more masters and no more slaves. "The Gospels," he said, "foresee a classless society. They foresee also *the withering away of the state*."

The sun is falling into the ocean, like a great round stone, whirling, the Aztec calendar stone, a roulette wheel in time. We walk along the long beach, our figures casting long shadows, like Giacometti statues, gesturing against the darkening sky, in the soft glowing dusk. The sun of a sudden turns dark red as it sinks in the ocean. Caught in clouds on the far horizon, it becomes a great ship afire—Turner's burning slave ship—and blood "incarnadines the multitudinous sea."

Earlier this season, the ships and port of Corinto on this coast were set afire by *contras* financed by the CIA, that international terrorist group.

January 29

At nine in the morning a group of writers shows up with Ernesto for the day's excursion. After a coffee, we take off for Masaya and Monimbó, the place where resistance to Somoza's National Guard was fiercest. It's just a few miles outside Managua. At its edge there's a rough wood sign:

AQUI

COMIENZA

EL HEROICO

BARRIO

MONIMBÓ

One hundred and sixteen men and women fell here in the fighting. The shacks and beat houses are scarred from the battle. *No Pasarán* is scrawled next to the church. This Indian *barrio* is like slums in every Latin American or Caribbean town—on the outskirts of Lima, La Paz, Bolivia, Haiti's Port-au-Prince, Mexico City, Cuernavaca—dirt streets full of stray dogs, tin roof shacks, swinging-door *cantinas* smelling of piss and *pulque*, beer and mezcal (murderous at night, for people like Malcolm Lowry's Consul in *Under the Volcano*).

The Revolution would change all that?

As soon as we arrive at a tiny plaza filled with an outdoor kitchen under a ridgepole roof, three old musicians strike up a bright, whining tune—a fiddle and a *guitarrón*—and some barefoot Indian kids start dancing around in the dust. Ernesto is greeted warmly by the cook and his woman, like an old friend. We've obviously been expected. They seem to love him, they certainly respect him. A priest is a priest. Food has been set out, steaming, and now it is passed around.

Ernesto makes a little speech, and we leave in our cars, for Granada, about an hour's drive. Granada has a plaza with colonial buildings and an ancient dusty elegance. It's Ernesto's birthplace, and his family house on the plaza was given to the Church by his grandmother. His large, well-off (if not rich) family is divided by the Revolution—some with it, some not. (*"No Pasarán"* is scrawled on many walls.) We drive on through the town and end up at a waterfront pavilion for a fish lunch. Ernesto points out a well-dressed paunchy gentleman with his family who seems to be receiving various local businessmen who come up to him at the end of his long linen-covered table and almost bow as they shake hands, with a mixture of respect and fear, as if he still ran the town. The *patrón* receiving his homage. Some things never change, even in revolutions. Life goes on. Human nature goes on. The bourgeoisie will always be with us, no matter what the Marxists say. . . .

There is a little archipelago of islands in Lake Nicaragua just off Granada and to the southeast, and it is for them that we set out after lunch, in a long launch with canopy for shelter in the afternoon sun. About ten of us in the old wooden boat, with a gasoline engine groaning at the stern, and shortly we are passing through a Rousseau-like jungle, through small channels with overhanging vines between little islands. (Nicaraguan primitive painters, encouraged by Ernesto's Ministry of Culture, have portrayed their landscape in a manner similar to the Haitian primitives, and are being recognized as a school.)

Then we're out in the open again, passing over to another group of little jungle islets, some with small houses or shacks on them. A slight squall comes up. We dock at one of the islands where there's a barbeque in progress, rather like a Hawaiian *luau*. We drink beer and sit around for a while. We see the frame of a big excursion boat cast up on another island, its ribs rotting away. On the transom of the boat it says *General Somoza*. "When the boat sank, Somoza declined and sank!" someone shouts. There's general laughter.

It's late afternoon by the time we get back to Granada, and dark by the time we head up the slopes of the big volcano overlooking Managua, for the final stop. By the time we reach the edge of the huge crater it's pitch-dark, and all we can see, peering over into the black, is thick smoke, with a smell of burning sulphur. The huge mountain is like Mount Tamalpais in Marin County on a dark night, but here—someone shouts, laughing—is the smoldering "maw of revolution!" The poets lean over the railing in the smoke, gesticulating wildly at the hidden god below, uttering cries of mock defiance with bursts of wild laughter. A blast of smoke and heat sends them back. It is bigger than they are.

A wind has come up and it's shuddering cold. We huddle back to the cars and wend down the mountain, back into Managua.

Latin American Dictator

January 30

Monday, and we're off early to see a new sugarcane plant in the process of construction. "Timal" is being built near Tipitapa, not far out of Managua. We're driven there in a Mercedes inherited from the Somoza regime. Huge prefab concrete hangars with high tin roofs. Other steel frame buildings going up. It's a model plan, and the assistant manager shows us the blueprints in his office and takes us around the works, carrying a walkie-talkie. The processing plant is set right in the center of the fields, and there will be a forest planted all around the cane fields to furnish the wood burned to run the plant. There is one other cane factory in Nicaragua: San Antonio, still privately owned. We walk through a huge warehouse where steel-hatted workers—looking like in any plant in the U.S.—are moving electrical equipment from East Germany and Russia. The generators have plates in English: "Made in USSR." There are quite a few Cuban workers. Some shake hands and pose for their pictures. No women working out here, but there are some in the construction offices. . . .

Then we're off to inspect "La Granja"—an "open farm" for prisoners close to Managua. In a recent speech, Tomás Borge, minister of the interior, refuted the accusation that Nicaragua violates human rights, insisting that his is a country "where there are no executions, where torture has been virtually eradicated, where prisoners, including *Somocistas*, have been located in work centers where they have a continuing relationship with their families, and many of them are under a regime of what we call 'open farms,' in which there are no sentries other than those of moral preachment and our own confidence in the prisoners. . . ."

Our guide for the visit is Captain Raúl Cordon, head of the regional prison system. It's working hours, and there's only a handful of prisoners hanging about the wooden barracks surrounded by a wire fence—nothing that couldn't be climbed. The captain tells us there were eight thousand prisoners in this region but now they're down to twenty-five hundred. (Jesuit lawyers defended many *Somocistas* standing trial after the Sandinist victory, since most lawyers claimed they couldn't be impartial.)

Somoza's chauffeur is head of the inmates, most of whom were in Somoza's National Guard and EEBI Special Forces—"death squads," someone says. The chauffeur is exceedingly fat and full of smiles. He gives us a glowing account of life under the present setup. He has his own room and takes us there and passes around cigarettes. He picks up a guitar and strums a bit. The prison dentist, also a political prisoner, smiles at him. . . . Outside, under dense rows of sugar cane, there are the deep trenches the prisoners dug when a USA-backed invasion was expected from the north. They asked for guns from the Sandinistas "to defend the country." They didn't get them.

We drink coffee out of tin cups with some of the inmates. It's strong enough to take your boots off. It's like ranch coffee outside of Douglas, Arizona. One of the coffee drinkers tells me he just got back from a week at home—they're allowed a week every six months, if they behave. And they have conjugal visits.

Back in the car as we head out, the captain shakes his head and smiles as Somoza's chauffeur stands by the gate, waving. "*Es un gran bandito,*" the captain says to us under his breath.

Back at the captain's HQ, we meet a more important political prisoner: Carlos Canales, former minister of health under Somoza. They tell me he was convicted for various monstrous medical swindles: thirty years. He's now under "house arrest." All his children, he tells us, are Sandinistas.

We're due to go to lunch with Tomás Borge. Tortured for years in Somoza's prisons, after the Sandinist takeover he recognized one of his torturers in a prison lineup, and he is reported to have said, "My revenge is to have you shake my hand." Joan Baez made a song of this and sang it here in Spanish a couple of years ago.

He's a tough little number. He isn't in charge of internal security and intelligence for nothing. He's the only one of the three original founders of the Sandinista movement still alive. His face shows it, it's hard, it's been through it, you know it. He's a bull of a man, and he wears the uniform of a Commander of the Revolution. When we go with him to the public market for lunch, he drives his big van, with a couple of trucks full of soldiers before and after.

We've come to the big public *mercado* because Borge objected to plans for us to dine at one of the better restaurants. It's one of those typical new *mercados* under an overhanging roof, like the big one in Guadalajara—concrete stalls on a concrete floor, covering maybe two acres, an entire city block. Ernesto told me he ate here almost every day; and Borge seems at home here. From the moment we get out of his van, the market vendors press around him, and there's a crush as we try to proceed to the long wooden tables in the middle of the market. I sit down on a bench with Borge as the people crowd around, and a television crew moves in with their camera. Borge orders *carne asada*, and sets to the hunks of meat with both hands as several women vendors fill his ears full of complaints. They're mad about the government keeping food prices down so they can't make out. Borge listens intently, nodding and eating, and looking into women's faces. You can tell he likes contact with the people, acts like he's one of them; he is; he came up the hard way. He calls me *poeta* wherever he has a chance to speak to me, which isn't often. He says *poeta* with a mixture of respect and realism, as if he didn't expect much from me.

At the moment we are still surrounded by a mass of people of all ages, old women in shawls, tough barefoot Indian mothers holding little kids, round-faced and wide-eyed. A tiny little shoeshine boy sticks out his hand to shake mine. It is completely black with shoe polish. It's a joke, and everybody breaks up.

In a very few minutes Borge is through eating, and we push through the crowd, the TV following, as he inspects various stalls and produce, listening to the vendors' stories. One fishwife corners him and pours out her complaint. He takes her by both arms, almost embracing her, and looks in her face close up, listening intently. Finally we follow him up to the market manager's office on a mezzanine where he lays out the people's complaints to the man at the desk.

We make our way back out, and on the way he picks up a kid and dandles her (like any American politician) as the TV camera rolls. But he's got real affection for the kid who sucks her thumb bashfully. He puts her down and makes toward the van, on the way asking a pretty interpreter for her phone number. She refuses, politely.

Back in the driver's seat, he tells me, "These people really aren't *with* the Revolution. They're putting themselves first. The Revolution is for the consumer, not the merchant."

It's time for the visit to *La Prensa*, the opposition newspaper, generally a pro-capitalist journal. Significantly, it's housed in the same building as the Bank of America. There aren't any guards at the entrance to the paper, as there are at the *San Francisco Chronicle* and *Examiner* these days. Simply a woman receptionist at the front desk, and we pass quickly up to the editorial offices and Pablo Antonio Cuadra, the very important poet and editor known for his opposition to the present regime. In an interview in *La Nación*, made when Cuadra was passing through Costa Rica last fall on his way to an international PEN Club meeting in Venezuela, he said:

They are killing me but I'm not leaving. . . . Unless they take me with a crane and put me on the border, I'm not leaving Nicaragua.

I am against the direction of the revolution taken by the Sandinistas. . . . I believe that the attitude of directing culture, censorship and the creation of a conscience in the service of an ideology . . . is fateful for a culture. That is why I am in a rather disagreeable struggle. And my obligation as a poet is to maintain the flag of resistance against the tremendous harm being done to the culture of Nicaragua.

Cuadra then spoke of the experience of Pablo Neruda and Ernesto Cardenal, as poets in the service of an ideology, stating that their great failures coincided with the moment they started producing didactic or proselytizing literature. He went on:

From what does culture spring? From lack of conformity. And what is the instrument of lack of conformity? *Criticism.* It is the only means which makes possible man's perfection. If criticism is suspended and we are obliged to conform, we become like the chimpanzee. This is what happens to a culture which lacks a critical sense. I have often repeated the sentence: every revolution becomes stagnant without criticism.

. . . As soon as literature begins to be in the service of something it stops being literature and turns to propaganda.

Cuadra concluded the interview by stating that at *La Prensa* threats extend beyond the paper shortage—"Their rigid censorship enters as a control over freedom of expression." *La Prensa* "is a bastion of the complement of an incomplete revolution. If it were closed it would be cutting Nicaragua's tongue out."

The first thing Cuadra said when I walked into his office (Ernesto significantly, did not accompany me on the visit) was that he was very sorry *La Prensa* could not publish my poetry because the Sandinist government would not give them paper to publish their literary supplement. I agreed that that was certainly bad, but the Sandinist justification for this seemed to be valid. There were priorities. It took U.S. dollars to buy newsprint, and it took U.S. dollars to buy medical supplies, technical equipment, and consumer goods which were in desperately short supply. These things, in the eyes of the Sandinist government, had priority over newsprint for literature. I also reminded him that *La Prensa* itself was not so long ago about to shut down because they couldn't get newsprint, and that the government furnished them dollars to buy it and continue publishing.

I also felt it fair to ask him if total freedom of the press didn't require *responsibility* on the part of the press for maintaining standards of "evidence, proof and disclosure." In which case, what of the report on Fidel Castro by Carlos Montaner (a Cuban editor who lives outside of the country) published in *La Prensa*? In the article Montaner stated Fidel Castro is fat, old, sick, and about to die. Could the editors of *La Prensa* really believe that is the truth? To which Pablo Antonio Cuadra shrugged and said with a smile, "That's the sixty-four dollar question."

However, I believe that even if *La Prensa* published *nothing but lies*, it should still be allowed to publish them. Later Ernesto Cardenal pointed out that Nicaragua was in a state of war, the Reagan administration and the CIA having admitted they were trying to overthrow the Sandinist government by undercover military means. And in a state of war, even the greatest democracies resort to strict censorship of the press in military and economic matters.

Ernesto sent me an official statement of his own on the issue, when I returned to the U.S., and this is a translation of it:

MINISTRY OF CULTURE, NICARAGUA
Government of National Reconstruction
April 6, 1984

With respect to censorship, I don't believe there is any important writing by any of our leaders defending it. In fact, we don't like it and don't want it, and have it only because we're in a state of war. In any state of war there has to be recourse to these means. A state of emergency is declared, a law that permits any steps that might be needed for defense. We're engaged in a war, an undeclared and "undercover" war but a war that everyone is aware of; even the United States Congress publicly approves financing it. And the newspaper *La Prensa* openly defends the enemy, defends the CIA's actions, and employs all the Reagan administration's arguments. In the United States, there's a lot of publicity about an opposition newspaper being censored in Nicaragua, something we're obliged to do because of the war, but there's no concern expressed about other Latin American countries where opposition newspapers are not censored because there simply are no opposition newspapers (Guatemala, El Salvador, Chile, Uruguay, Paraguay). In any case, this censorship will end in May when the electoral campaign begins. Then they won't attack Nicaragua for this reason, but will look for many other reasons to attack us.

Still I believe Sr. Cuadra and I understood each other, as poets. He wanted to talk poetry, not politics. We exchanged books. Quite aware of the "totalitarian intolerance" often exercised by the Left as well as the Right in the U.S., I shook his hand and wished him well as we parted.

At about nightfall we go to meet Jaime Wheelock, the minister of agriculture, and sit down with him in a big museum-like room at his headquarters. There are plants everywhere and big, framed Indian paintings and tapestries.

He tells me he would rather talk to poets than politicians, and I believe him. He seems a very literate man—a young intellectual one might meet at Columbia University. (Wheelock is a lawyer and is credited with being one of the main theoreticians of the Revolution.) He tells me that before the Revolution the farmworkers lived like sharecroppers in *The Grapes of Wrath* and that now for the first time they are being organized in collectives or co-operatives, at a somewhat better living wage. They are at least getting control of their own means of livelihood.

He has a very calm, straightforward look. He's handsome in his uniform, and he poses for a photo in the courtyard when we are leaving. It is dark, and Chris Felver is adjusting his flash as Wheelock stands there against the shrubbery, looking quite serious. After the picture is taken, Wheelock says, "That's how Somoza's guards killed some people—'shooting' them with cameras."

January 31

Today we go to visit Cardenal in his office in a villa which had belonged to Somoza. It is a beautiful little house set in a park in a grove. There had been over a dozen bathrooms in it. There were bathrooms off of the bathroom. The office itself, no more than ten by five feet, is now cluttered with heaps of books and artwork.

Afterward, it's time to leave for a meeting with the Association of Sandinista Cultural Workers (ASTC). When we arrive at their arts center there are about fifty men and women already assembled outdoors, seated in a large circle. It was billed as a "colloquium," but it seems I am to make a speech. Suddenly I wish I had in my pocket a list of the "best minds of my generation" and of the greatest and most respected Establishment writers in the USA who are publicly and actively supporting the Sandinista regime—but such a list is short. (How many of our most famous novelists, for instance, have bothered to take the two-and-a-half-hour flight from Miami and see for themselves what's going on here? Our literary activities seem to be confined—with a few valiant exceptions—to the younger, lesser known, dissident writers, while most of the great ones on their positions at the top of the Establishment continue to maintain a loud silence.)

As these sanguine and lugubrious thoughts fill my head, the artists and intellectuals of Nicaragua sit awaiting my words. All right, then. From the activist poets and the politically dormant poets of my country, I bring you greetings and wishes for your survival against all odds. Not being an ambassador of that imperial plutocratic government in Washington, I can only give you my somewhat eccentric dissident view of what's going on. . . . And I launched into a diatribe on nationalism in general, which is definitely not what they wanted to hear. (A young nation just struggling free of centuries of colonialism, Sandinist Nicaragua sees nationalism as the way to independence.)

Then the floor was open to questions, and what they most wanted to hear about was writing and especially poetry in the USA today. I gave them my view that North American poetry right now seems to be in a deep sleep or, hopefully, in a state of gestation. Some writers are just too well fed, by government grants or university writing programs. Some are not so well fed but lack the stimulus provided by war, rapid change in society, or revolution as in Nicaragua now. Poets are not especially honored in our land, having for the most part abdicated any vatic or prophetic role. As such, poetry has been relegated to a most ephemeral place—positioned as "filler" in most large publications, though published profusely by small presses throughout the land. The poets of various minorities, still with their own revolutions to win, have the most to say (with the most force) in North America now—as witness the Latino writers of San Francisco's Mission District and New York's *Nuyoricanos*. *What it takes is inspiration, and hunger.*

That night was my poetry reading in the open-air theater of the Plaza Pedro Joaquín Chomorro, with Ernesto Cardenal translating. I presented a poem, called "La Bruja: Flower of Revolution," written out of a certain "revolution euphoria"—

one can put it down as naïve agitprop—but perhaps it is a naiveté worth saving. And it related well to the seed I brought from Pasternak's grave. On our Sunday excursion I had been given a flower by a poet and doctor named Fernando Silva, with whom I felt an immediate humane rapport. *La Bruja*, he told me, grew where nothing else would, in the most unexpected places.

When I came offstage at the end, there was a stringer crew from CBS waiting to interview me.

> Q: What are your impressions of Nicaragua?
>
> LF: It's a humane revolution—at least it would seem so on the surface. I realize I'm on a guided tour—the Sandinista leaders seem to be using what Carlos Fonseca called temperance and fortitude.
>
> Q: Isn't that the kind of revolution which would especially upset the Reagan administration?
>
> LF: Yes, indeed, for it is especially hard to justify subverting such a human revolution—if such it is. And a revolution that liberates people from their traditional economic slavery isn't exactly what corporate people in the USA want to hear. It's the haves and have-nots and Central America has been a cheap labor market for the U.S. for centuries. That's the real "domino" effect the U.S. is afraid of—
>
> Q: Thank you for your kind remarks!

The interview was never aired. I wasn't the kind of hot news they wanted. During the reading I had noted that it was not exactly a turn-away crowd—the amphitheater was about half empty, or half full, at the most. (I am no Yevtushenko nor was meant to be!) The Revolution wanted to bring poetry to the masses; but the masses did not come to the poetry. The audience turned out to be mostly students, poets, and wandering U.S. militants of various sorts—including a Pacifica Foundation interviewer. Thus fares poetry on the barricades. . . .

February 1

We were scheduled to go to the northern frontier on the Honduran border. But, whether out of concern for the safety of Ernesto or myself, our trip has been diverted to the southern Costa Rican front where the war is at the moment less dangerous.

We head south in a little convoy, a Land Rover with three soldiers ahead of us,

Ernesto, Chris Felver, and myself next in the Toyota sedan, then another sedan with Ken Silverman and Bill Finnegan, followed by another jeep with soldiers. They're communicating with checkpoints by walkie-talkie as we proceed into open country, rather like coastal farmland in California or Chile. South of Masaya, the vegetation begins to be more verdant and tropical; palms and bananas, fields of cane, coffee, and cotton, bone-colored Brahman cattle with horns, houses and shacks and barns with tin roofs, mango and yucca . . . flocks of egrets nested in trees like great white flowers.

It's about a two-hour drive to Cibalsa in the Rivas area. We wheel in there, preceded by walkie-talkie identification, get out to meet the local captain. In his office in a barracks Bill Finnegan notes the following books on a shelf:

Manual of Marxism and Leninism
Complete Works of Lenin
Comedies and Histories of Shakespeare
Jaime Wheelock's *Nicaragua: Imperialism and Dictatorship* (four copies)
Fernando Rojas, *La Celestina*
Dostoevsky, *Crime and Punishment*

Here was once a big center for Somoza's National Guard, his most important forces in the South. Ernesto tells me some two thousand Sandinistas were engaged in the heavy fighting, with two hundred casualties a day. It's open country with little cover, with low mountains to the west and south, and Lake Nicaragua to the east. Two huge volcanoes joined by an isthmus in the lake—Ometepe. This is near where a trans-Pacific canal was once proposed—in a deal the Chamorro family was involved in. If it had gone through, the history of Nicaragua would have been changed radically, with the country perhaps in the same economic and political position as Panama today—a fast change from banana republic to military bivouac.

Ernesto tells me the Rivas area was the old Indian center in pre-Hispanic times. The *cacique* (Indian chief) met the Spaniards at Cibalsa, and he asked them:

> Why is there day and night?
> Is the earth round or flat?
> Why do you want so much gold?

The Spanish called the lake *La Mar Dulce*, said it was sweet to their taste, and that it should be theirs.

We take off south again, after numerous radio checks, and reach Sopoá, three kilometers or so from the Costa Rica border. The last heavy fighting around here was at Cardenas on September 28. On the outdoor board at the HQ here there are bulletins and clippings posted with national, international, sports, and cultural news. There is a paste-up of a poem by Leonel Rugama who died fighting in Managua in 1970. The poem is "Las casas quedaron llenas de humo" ("The Houses Were Filled with Smoke"; it happens to be in the City Lights anthology, *Volcán*).

This is our first look at the People's Militia. Young boys in green fatigues—most look fifteen or sixteen years old. One is twelve, another thirteen. (They'd be in school, Ernesto says, if it weren't for Reagan's policies.) The Army is small but the Militia is big, mostly volunteer, he tells me. A recent draft prompted by expectations of an immediate invasion was not very successful, some families spiriting their children away to other countries (according to one newspaper report). Here the recruits look mostly like local country boys, part Indian, many from Ometepe.

After fifteen minutes, we head south again, through a big truck checkpoint, directly to Peñas Blancas at the border. It takes just five minutes, and we roll up to the destroyed buildings of the immigration and customs offices—hit by mortars from the Costa Rica side. Ernesto tells us two hundred anti-Sandinistas got this far and got stopped by twenty-eight Sandinistas. Since they couldn't go any further, they burned and destroyed everything before retiring. There is a bullet hole in the one water tank, which leaks steadily.

We walk around in the ruins of one building, strewn with rubble, broken glass, plaster, and shattered furniture. Ernesto finds a burnt, melted plastic doll and holds it up.

About twenty-five of the Militia line up in formation for review by our party and especially for Ernesto. A visit from the minister of culture is an event, and he hasn't been down here in months. He addresses them, softly, like a priest. Then one very young soldier in ranks cries out a challenge (a *consigna*), and the whole troop sings out a password in response. Sandinista slogans. This is repeated by different men in the ranks, with the rest singing out their valiant answers. The expression in the dark Indian faces of these very young soldiers when they cry out their slogans ("*Patria o morir*") is a mixture of defiance, pride, and *terror*. . . .

In a few minutes we are back in the cars again, heading for a jungle camp—a farm deep in the woods on the border, the militia quartered in a big shed with thatched roof. Grenade launchers, AK-47s, automatic weapons with Russian markings, lined up in racks. There's also another bulletin board with current news tacked up. We walk around inspecting everything. The soldiers sing out a few *consignas* as we leave them in the dust. It's their life, their future. (Are they at the heart of the real, or are we?)

Edén Pastora's forces just over the hills don't call themselves "*contras*" because they are not against the original Revolution. They feel the Sandinistas have betrayed the ideals of Sandino by becoming a totalitarian state backed by Cuba and the USSR. One adherent of Pastora, a Nicaraguan exile who came to see me in San Francisco, told me—it seemed with a touch of disbelief in his own words—that things were worse now in Nicaragua than they had been under Somoza! This is quite absurd, even by anti-Sandinista standards, if any of the real history of Somoza is known.

It was a long drive back to Managua, and the dusk was falling by the time we came down to the city, passing a big McDonald's with long lines waiting to be served. (Did I dream it had colonial architecture? On one wall was spray-painted "*No Pasarán!*")

It was a free night for us, and we had supper at the house. The houseboy or waiter at our house said it might be dangerous for us to go out by ourselves at night. (We might be taken for Ugly Americans?) The "houseboy" was a soldier on leave from the front. I thought of Ernesto's "no servants and no masters."

That night about 1 a.m. Chris Felver went out with our guide, Nadia, to a disco, and here is his description: "Typical joint with music so loud that there was difficulty talking. As Nadia went to the powder room I leaned on a gigantically large loudspeaker watching the dancers and thinking everywhere is like everywhere else this time of night."

Chris Felver's notes on his *first* night in Nicaragua went like this: "Luz Marina and Nadia take me to a restaurant for a touch of local night life. Next to the steak restaurant is the bar, typical, with piano player and stand-up bass. During the first song a man falls over a table and reveals a big revolver stuck in his pants. His friends help him to his feet, and another round of drinks comes. Everyone is dressed in polo shirts and casual dress, with a remarkable starched dress with large puffed sleeves on one young woman. We pick up with this group and head through town on a wild half-crazed drive to a residential section. Later I find out that I am drinking Stoli vodka with *Comandante Guerrillero* Richard Lugo Kantz, a hero in the Sandinista victory. Before entering his house, we relieve ourselves in the side yard and discuss the stars centering on Orion. On the porch are two bulldogs and a chow, with the largest bulldog in a hammock peering questioningly at me. We play the Beatles and suddenly it is late sixties again with the *Revolver* album on the stereo. My first night in Nicaragua and I am asked the whole political gambit. Cornered, I propose a toast to the Revolution and life in this room in general. All the while there is a gentleman in the house who is removed from conversation and I realize he is the bodyguard. We finally leave after the *Comandante* has asked me to go fishing early in the morning but I decline as we must meet Ernesto at 8:30 sharp."

February 2

To Solentiname today by helicopter. I had especially asked to visit Ernesto's island, way to the south at the far end of Lake Nicaragua. It was there that Ernesto had founded a contemplative community during the Somoza days. The National Guard razed the place, destroying everything but the little chapel, and Ernesto had to flee abroad. Now it has been mostly restored, and Ernesto has been back, but not recently. He's been wanting to go for months, in fact hopes to retire there but feels he can't while there is work to do for the Revolution.

So into the big Russian-made military copter at eight. A woman who had seven children in the fighting (one killed) is among the passengers. And there are Ernesto, our guide, Nadia, Silverman and Finnegan, and two soldiers, plus the pilot and two crew. Writing in my notebook, I'm surprised to see we are already in the air with the cargo door still open—not the slightest feeling of motion. Suddenly we are a thousand feet up and scudding over the brown land. It's sunny outside. The rotor blades whir with a singing sound, the motor drowning it out. We pass over Apoyo Laguna, the crater lake, then Granada, and head out over Lake Nicaragua and islets we visited by boat Sunday. I am sitting in the doorway of the cockpit. The pilot has the map in his lap. Then we're passing Ometepe on the starboard, its two volcanoes wreathed in cumulus and hot-looking clouds. . . . In a little over an hour we're coming in low over the so green hills of a little tropical island. It looks wild. We circle the end of it and come in over the lush treetops to land without a jolt in a bright green field, beyond a savagery of palms. Suddenly we've dropped into a lost tropic. Animals graze in the trees, bird-song lightens the air, a horse and rider pause to watch us. There are a few small white houses close by on a hill, and Ernesto's church. It is as if innocence itself in the shape of an island existed here still in a "sea of evil." That is the Romantic interpretation, the vision of the "noble savage" (debunked by modern anthropology), the idea of innocence echoing through time from the Desert Fathers to Rousseau. Somoza thought otherwise. Ernesto was condemned to death *in absentia* for having been the planner of Solentiname and its (pro-Sandinist) community. It was some time in these days that Ernesto renounced the pure Gandhian principles of nonviolence he had embraced with Merton. "Gandhi couldn't have stopped Hitler," he told me.

Some *campesinos* in straw hats are standing around watching us come across the meadows from the copter. There's a couple working on a new school building made of cinder blocks—no more than a room or two. An old *campesino* offers me his horse, and I gallop around the meadow. But Ernesto is impatient to tour the place with us. He seems liberated, takes off his beret and puts on a *campesino*'s straw hat. Happily he shows us the restored church—a room of whitewashed simplicity. Above the altar a new cross has been erected, replacing the one made by Ernesto and destroyed by the National Guard. I ask Ernesto: "You don't say mass these days?" "Only in private. And last New Year's here in Solentiname." The sunlight floods in. We are part of the primitive painting. But over the hill sits the copter.

Ernesto takes us around to see other projects underway. There is a toymaking and furniture shop, with new West German machines given by a German steelmakers' union. There's a cultural center planned (by an Italian architect) on a little hillside by an inlet of the lake. . . . There's about a thousand people on the island, and there aren't any cars or trucks. . . . About a dozen small deer graze in a large pen—for breeding. The community house has been rebuilt, and we sit out on its terrace. I go inside and see shelves of books; about fifty books make up the community library. There are five copies of Alvah Bessie's *Men in Battle*, and some texts in German. There's Ho Chi Minh and a manual of Marxism, upon which a hen is roosted. I hope it doesn't lay an egg.

A lunch is spread in the kitchen, and we have fish soup with beer. Ernesto tells me three boys in the former community died in the fighting (two captured alive and assassinated). Back on the porch, we look at a photo book of the ruins of Solentiname, and one picture shows exactly the same scene as in a large oil painting I did just before leaving San Francisco which I entitled *Nicaraguan Ruin*.

Ernesto would like a little siesta, and he takes me across the hill to a new small house just finished for him, very plain, with single wooden beds, a desk and a bench. He has a TV. There is electricity. (Before Thomas Merton died in the Far East, Ernesto had built a small retreat for his master who had intended to visit here after his Far East trip.) There is also a new novices' house being built, very Spartan.

While Ernesto is trying to take his nap, a single gun goes off down the hill. Then another shot. Then another. Then another. (It turns out later that Ken Silverman had persuaded a soldier to let him try out his rifle. It was the only shot I heard fired in Nicaragua.) After a while we walk down to the pier where a long wooden skiff is tied up and an old rowboat is sunk. A couple of us swim way out, treading water out there while Ernesto strips to his underwear and bathes at the end of the pier, looking like John the Baptist himself. . . .

Back at the community house, we meet the captain in charge of the region (Río Vista), and he tells us that two hundred of Edén Pastora's men surrendered two days ago. There's still more than a thousand of them over there, he says, gesturing toward the Costa Rican shore.

Ernesto is staying overnight, and overjoyed he is to have a day off. He apologizes for not being able to see us off at the airport tomorrow. One of the last things he says to me, in answer to my question, is that it *is* possible to have "a civil libertarian Marxism." We part with an *abrazo*, and lift off in the late sun. Everyone is pensive in the copter, looking back and down. . . .

Returned to Managua, it's our last night in Nicaragua, and after supper we are lucky to have a visit with two of the most important, if not *the* most important, men in the government: Daniel Ortega Saavedra (Miguel Cervantes Saavedra must have been a distant ancestor of his), the coordinator of the national directorate, and Father Miguel d'Escoto Brockmann, the minister of foreign affairs. They drove to our house on their way to the airport to go to Venezuela. In contrast to Fidel Castro who gave me a very soft handshake when I met him in a restaurant in Havana in 1960, Daniel Ortega gives me a much firmer one, but nothing macho about it, and he impresses me first off as another young intellectual whom I might have met in some graduate school in the States—nothing dictatorial or militarist about him, despite his immaculate uniform—another very good-looking gentleman like Jaime Wheelock.

We sit down in the old rocking chairs on the now dark veranda. Father d'Escoto is a Maryknoll priest, perhaps in his fifties, and went to U.C. Berkeley. I feel an immediate affinity for both of them, and tell them I certainly agree with Eduardo Galeano's *Open Veins of Latin America* as an analysis of the imperialism which has bled Latin America for centuries, a thesis which doesn't need Marxist dialectics or Marxist ideology to prove.

Daniel Ortega observes at one point that North American policy has always been one of "ignorance and arrogance." "American political behavior," he says, "has been the same since the last century. That is the problem." But there is nothing belligerent or recalcitrant in his attitude; he added that he wished "America would *help* us make a *development model* in Nicaragua, to be used by all developing countries in which private and political sectors share in the problems." (These men don't talk like the militarist totalitarians I had been led to believe they were.)

Since our return to the States, the Sandinistas have announced politically free elections to be held this November, and it seemed in the conversation with these two leaders that this subject was uppermost in their minds, together with the constant apprehension that President Reagan might send forces to invade Nicaragua at any time. If only, they said, the U.S. would lay off, they might be able to have truly democratic elections. They were studying various models of government intently, and wished to come up with a model for "real democracy" in developing countries everywhere. I asked what of the British model, in which the prime minister's government falls whenever he can't muster a vote of confidence, so that the people aren't then stuck for years with an administration they don't support—as in the USA? Father d'Escoto laughed and said perhaps they needed a bit more stability than that at the moment. This wasn't England!

No it certainly wasn't England. (The ink on their Magna Carta isn't even dry. Or, some would say, it is still to be written.) And libertarian dissidents were still demanding that the Sandinista Front give up its political control of the Army, of the police, and of the national television network, as well as end all press censorship, and abolish the military draft. Without this there could be no truly democratic free elections.

But, Daniel Ortega pointed out that at the moment the total effect of President Reagan's policies was to *impede* Nicaragua's progress toward any free elections and toward any kind of democratic Nicaragua. He also added that they fully expected, as soon as Reagan was reelected, he would send the invasion forces.

We walked with them out to the jeep in the night after an hour and a half,

WRITING ACROSS THE LANDSCAPE

shook hands warmly, and watched them drive away into the darkness of Nicaragua, wondering if we would ever see them alive again.

February 3

At the airport early the next morning, two presents are delivered to us. One is a symbolic acrylic painting of paving stones used for barricades in the streets during the Sandinist uprising, sent by Rosario Murillo for the Sandinista Cultural Workers Association. The other is the painted wood head of a bull (with leather ears) mounted on a hoop skirt, used in traditional native dances. The name of the revolutionary bull is *El Toro Macho*.

The accompanying card is inscribed *"Daniel Ortega Saavedra, Comandante de la Revolución"* and is addressed to *"Compañero Lawrence Ferlinghetti."* *Compañero* is a word, one Sandinista told me, which avoids the connotations of the Communist Party "comrade" (*camarada*). To me it has always had a touch of the fields in it, of poor provinces, of the earth itself. The movement toward liberation by the *compañeros* and *compañeras* of the world, by the wretched of the earth, has been growing since before the French Revolution; and Nicaragua is part of it. It is an irreversible revolution. *The past will not return.*

HARBIN HOT SPRINGS, CALIFORNIA

August 1984

I lost my energy at Harbin Hot Springs

Brown people under the trees at picnic tables at dusk far off in the silent landscape, like a tableau in India, the women in saris, red dots on their foreheads, jewels in their noses. A flute plays somewhere. Krishna consciousness pervades the atmosphere. There is a snake in a tree, as in a Rousseau landscape. Shiva dances, whirling through the foliage.

Sun on the high hilltops, close up, golden on the yellow brown burnt California summer hills, studded with scrub oak, manzanita, and eucalyptus. A bird in an oak sounds its wooden whistle, a quail clucks in the underbrush. A girl is waving at someone in the valley below, a woman waves back, a naked brown man with long scraggly hair and beard strides across the clearing, intent on his Buddha, on the poem of his life.

ROME—NAPOLI—SICILY

September 1984

SAN FRANCISCO—ROME

September 2

Leaving S.F. Airport, my economy excursion aisle seat is converted to a window seat in first class by Sue Burns, who told me she "grew up" on my poetry. Must remember to send her a book (c/o American Airlines). . . .

The *Jupiter* Symphony on the earphones somewhere over Colorado. From forty thousand feet, the mountains and plains bathed in Mozart's majesty. Steamboat Springs passes, according to the pilot, "below our right wing." Mozart's divine melody floods the landscape, the "lone and level sands stretch away." America a desert, European emotion pouring over it, over me. . . .

Floated in a dream of pinot noir and Mozart all the way across North America to New York. . . .

We roll up at Kennedy. The wind is blowing in the grasses between the landing strips, just as it blew across the Great Plains. . . .

6 p.m.

In Kennedy Airport, Alitalia waiting room, the Boarding light is now flashing for my plane. I had a button I was going to wear at the serious literary "rassegna" in Palermo—"Fuck Art Let's Dance"— It fell off somewhere in the airport, and the

Italians & Sicilians will never have the benefit of its enlightened message. . . . Jonathan Swift flies on, around the universe, continually astonished by the asininity of man. And of myself. . . .

5 a.m. New York time. . . . Awake to find us flying over "my beloved France." Another of my *grandes illusions*. South by southwestward now, and over the Apennines, like Ruskin's Gothic bird in flight. Only higher than any bird could fly. A man looking like Dante suddenly emerges from the seat in front of me. His hair is like laurel. Gray laurel. Awakened, he looks out the window and down at the ground far below, as if he were peering into a pit in the Inferno. The white clouds look like steam. But he puts on a navy blue blazer with an ensign on it: "Brooklyn Rowing Club"! Now he sits down, leans back, and closes his eyes, in our chariot of the sun.

Leonardo da Vinci Airport. Noon. In the transit bus a Japanese nun in white linen is reading Edgar Cayce's *The Spirit of Healing*.

In from the airport, on the bus. . . . Roman pines with flat tops— Some old abandoned stone houses the color of yellow earth with red tile roofs, no glass in the windows. A huge field of dead sunflowers, heads all bowed to the east. Some modernistic apartment buildings with flying buttresses and trestles all cantilevered at the center.

Hot Roman summer sun beats down. The shades on the bus flap as we wheel into the city.

Took a nap and am now sitting out in the big café garden outside the Hotel Washington, Piazza Fiume. . . . The dusk is falling in the Giardini Fassi. The traffic roars by outside the high walls of the garden. Inside, couples & families sit about at the marble-topped tables, round & square, with green metal legs & green metal chairs with wood bottoms. The girls in their summer dresses. It is summer still in this Roman garden, under the pine trees and palms and the plane trees and the lamps set in classic bronze vases. I was here a year ago this month or last, who can remember. The body goes on, returning and returning . . . Through the Large Door, into the rose garden, hidden music still, behind the hill. . . .

Over in Via Alessandria I find the da Giggetto Pizzeria—just as it's getting to the violet hour—*l'heure bleue* (what's it in Italian?)— A pizza the way pizza is supposed to be, not a big thick heavy shell but a very light shell, very thin, *almost* like a French crêpe. You don't walk away with a lead sinker in your gut. . . . The sky really is violet or purple, in the distance, over a hill, at this hour, in Rome. *L'ora violetta?* Everyone is beautiful, in this light. *Che romantico!*

The most beautiful and the ugliest people go by—think how lonely they may be. Maybe not. Loneliness only exists in the mind, to the degree you are aware of it.

The people are pouring by now, looking for sidewalk tables. I've got to move. But I have to get a sketchbook and start doing heads, nothing but heads and faces. The Roman Carnival! . . . When I get back to "the States" I'll tell them I did nothing but sit in sidewalk restaurants dreaming. . . . Faces and hands, what a universe. No need to draw anything more.

In the Giardini Fassi again, the girl leaning back in her chair, smoking, a flower in her hair, and the accordion music playing . . . what else is there?

In the morning, everywhere, the cars like rats in every corner & nook, crowding the alleyways & entrances. They're a plague, infesting the cities of the world. . . .

Last night in the Giardini Fassi the music played until midnight. It wasn't an accordion but an electric organ or electronic piano, filling the air with nostalgic *kitsch*, the huge garden café alive with the hum of voices at tables under the 19th-century lamps, the whole thing like an impressionist painting, life in a Seurat garden. My ground-floor room, hidden in the foliage, looked right out into it, so that I could eavesdrop on the nearest tables, through the great French windows. . . . In the morning cars were parked even in the garden, the 19th-century illusion gone. . . . The great cities are being raped by the metal monsters. . . .

Reading *Corriere della Sera*, the most important left-of-center paper in Italy, I note what you don't read in the American press: plenty. Perhaps the extraordinary story of today *would* be in there. It's a Vatican document which "condemns Marxism in theological thought" and accuses Communist regimes, *the shame of our time*, of keeping "entire nations in conditions of servitude unworthy of man"—an evaluation that goes for "the entire socialist world." The South American archbishop made it clear that the document was not condemning the "theology of liberation" in its fight against poverty (i.e., in Latin America), but he went on to condemn "revolutionary violence" as "incompatible with Christian doctrine." Natch. . . .

The ultimate paradox would seem to be that a Catholic priest like Ernesto Cardenal, who now professes to be a Marxist in his "theology of liberation," is embracing a supposedly atheist ideology. But "liberation theology" doesn't embrace all of Marxism—not the atheism, just the critique of heartless capitalism. . . . This is all a very long way from the 19th-century garden. . . .

I also read in *Corriere* that Reagan attributes his "economic miracle" to the *"animal spirits* of capitalism"!

September 10

Good Benn Posset from the Amsterdam One World Poetry Festival shows up. Wherever Benn shows up you know poetry is being traded in the open market, on the floor of the Exchange. International dealers take note.

September 11

The worst insults to poetry and the most contemptuous attitude toward it which I have ever encountered were—despite their professed adoration for it—from Italians. The first was when a television man in Assisi (summer 1983) threw a coin on the ground and facetiously asked me to recite. The second was last night at the biggest theater in Rome, the Teatro Argentina (to which I had been invited to read poetry after a play) when they forgot to announce that I would read after the play, and the audience left. (A theater critic named Bertolucci was supposed to announce it but forgot.) Everyone, including the Italian translator, was *furioso*. Except me. "Go with the flow."

Tomorrow I'm going with the flow to Sicily. . . . Ave atque vale, bella Roma. . . .

NAPLES NOTEBOOK

September 12

Leaving Rome on the fast train, from Stazione Termini—Stendhal traveling through Italy . . . or my father, in 1900. . . . The blood remembers. Or does not remember. America forgets Europe. Ferlinghetti forgets Ferlinghetti. The world turns; and continues turning; and the blood flows, from country to country, continent to continent, through the streets and rivers, to the sea. And the sea carries all away, tides of Napoli flooding into New York harbor, Mannahatta, bristling with spars and masts—my father descending from the Naples boat, into Little Italy New York, his goods in a carryall, wrapped in a rug, to seek his fortune, his hidden destiny, in the New World, like millions of others; he, one among millions, hoping against hunger.

Roma–Napoli—the train slides into Campoleone, "Field of Lions," and picks up a couple of lions. They prowl up and down the aisles of the train, in second class. Once in a while they eat some citizen who is not reading *Il Mattino*. . . . And after two hours flying over the landscape, we hurtle through a long tunnel, and suddenly shoot out onto an open plain to the sea, suddenly the Bay of Naples close up, a great sweep of coast, and mountains in the distance, great peaks towering over, gray clouds snagged on them. The train like a rollercoaster zooms toward the coast, through cornfields and ditches; and on through low scattered houses, tile roofs and truck gardens, running to the sea, through more open country, with gray ochre cattle, color of the earth, and flocks of pale sheep, and an old cemetery with tombs above the ground, and then at last to the outskirts of Naples itself, through cinder-block tenements, cement houses and factories, the train blowing its shrill whistle, blasting through freight yards. A crew of workers, naked to the waist, is laying down a track, one with a red bandanna around his head, Neapolitan apache. . . . Across the aisle in the train, a dark Moorish *donna* (with heavy black hair and gold earrings and heavy brows and big black mournful eyes) gazes in a deep dream upon the fleeting landscape. Her legs are motionless, under the flounced skirts, she is motionless; even her emotions are not moving, her eyes do not well up at the sight of the landscape—she is a part of it. As now the train blasts through to the very heart of Naples: the very broken heart of the city of a billion cries, a billion dark joys and sorrows. Here the Mezzogiorno begins, the Mezzogiorno sun beats down, on the volcanic Napoletani.

Napoli Centrale: Outside the station, it looks like a fierce town, with fierce people. I may die, at the hands of *banditi*. As my father almost did. But, no. I decide I am suffering from the usual paranoia of travelers in strange countries. The town is actually half-asleep in its mid-afternoon siesta.

I am waiting for my connection, and I watch a healthy young woman stopping healthy young men and asking them to donate their blood on the spot. (There is a mobile medical unit behind her.) For the Voluntary Blood Donors Association. I watch her stop at least a dozen young healthy men: and not one will give blood. (For some reason, she doesn't ask any women.) She asks me, and I too refuse. I tell her I'm a French tourist who can't spare the blood, who needs it more than ordinary people. She says it will only take three minutes. I still won't give up my blood. Everybody wants their blood, nobody wants to give it up, nobody wants to give away their life. The idea of giving up a part of one's life to someone else hasn't caught on here yet. Or anywhere.

> "Everyman, I'll go with thee
> And be thy guide.
> In thy most need
> Be by thy side"?

Malaparte's *Skin* is stretched very thin. . . .

Deep in the heart of the city, the skin trade goes on. In the Via della Cavellerizza (Street of the Woman on Horseback), in the Galleria Umberto, in the Spaccanapoli, in this ant hill of buzzing life, the blood still flows hot and wild in the veins of the Napoletani.

And in the Piazza Dante, there are fascist slogans scrawled on the base of the statue of Dante; he stands in the dark of my first night in Napoli with his hand upraised. And he is thinking, "Oh, if in this wood I could behold the tree with Golden Bough!"

And at the Leon d'Oro pizzeria there are local small-time *camorristi* eating *orecchiette* (pasta in the shape of ears). The ears are being eaten because they have already heard too much. . . . I draw a picture of "Dante in the Mouth of the Lion" and give it to the proprietor.

The next morning, I walk around San Pasquale a Chiaia, in the middle of the nest of twisted streets teeming with pushcarts and people. Life cries out in every throat, in every face, from every window. The sun of the Mezzogiorno beats down on the faces out of Caravaggio. If I could see through Malaparte's *Skin*, I might see what Dante saw with Virgil, in the Mezzogiorno of his *Paradiso*. . . . The "dog beneath the skin" is very near the surface here. He is a friendly dog, a hungry dog, an inquisitive dog, a dog with eyes as big as his hunger. And his hunger is for everything and everyone, for everything in life. The dog's eyes peer out through the eyes of the people, and the dog's mouth drops open ready to devour you, or to kiss you, or to laugh and cry with you. The Neapolitan beast! *Con amore*. In the shadow of Vesuvio.

PALERMO—MONDELLO

September 13

I am on the boat to Palermo. I am up on a wing of the deck just below the bridge, alone, looking out at the dark sea and the flashing buoys. We have cleared the harbor, with Vesuvio on the portside, and headed out in the darkness, under a three-quarter moon and the usual stars. There is the Northern Cross and Antares and Altair, all navigational stars. I could just about take the ship in from here. I note from the position of the Northern Cross that the North Star would be just about dead astern, and we are heading almost due south, direct to Sicily. I walk aft and see the Big Dipper lying flat on the horizon, its pan lying horizontal to the horizon, its two end stars pointing straight to the North Star, which is indeed in its proper place.

Everything is obviously in order, and I go below, and turn in, 10 p.m. . . .

September 14

MONDELLO, 7 A.M.—Bus to hotel (a man holding a sign at the foot of the gangway: Perlinghetti. The one time this has ever happened to me and they misspell it . . .). Huge bed in huge room at Hotel Palace, Mondello, the beach resort town for Palermo. They tell me it was built by the Mafia. There's a very violent thunder and lightning storm which comes on like a series of explosions & cannonades as if the Mafia were pulling some big number. . . . Then the rain pours down in absolute sheets, the whole landscape darkening like night, the sea out front of the rococo casino turned to a huge black slate. It's almost like a tropical storm, the palm trees swaying in it violently. In a few minutes it's over, and the bay reappears in gray light, the water flat as a mirror. . . . In the afternoon by the pool I meet a man of my age, Domenico Porzio, who is a senior editor of Mondadori, and he tells me Pasolini is indeed a great poet and novelist and journalist-critic, despite what the young winner of the novel prize this year said to the contrary. The latter told me he had refused to shake Pasolini's hand (although he too was homosexual) because he was disgusted by Pasolini's rough & dirty homosexual tastes. Porzio told me this young novelist was just one of Pasolini's imitators. Since I have undertaken to translate & publish a Pasolini book of poetry, I was relieved to have his value affirmed by Porzio, after the very strong put-down by the young author.

Porzio said there aren't any new writers that are great like the generation of Moravia, etc. Pasolini, he said, could write criticism in every field, art or literature . . . and was a great "civil" poet and had written a great breakthrough of a novel in his *Ragazzi di Vita*.

In the early evening I see him (Porzio, not Pasolini) on the terrace of a café on the waterfront. He is completely absorbed in observing four young people at the next table . . . and writing down what he sees & hears. Little do the four youths know they are being written about by a Mondadori editor. Then I note Porzio is just sitting staring off into space. . . .

The dusk is falling, the fog has gathered on the water, and I am still sitting in this café, watching the lively life of this little town, devoid of tourists now. (The people at the Rassegna di Letteratura have all left, except for Porzio and me, and perhaps a smooth Spaniard poet & organizer whom I suspect of being CIA.)

Porzio told me that thirty years ago (when he "was young") he had come to City Lights Bookstore and bought our first CL Pocket Poets . . . it must have been our first year of publishing. And that his son had visited the store when he was grown up and had brought back some of the same books. . . .

This is the main piazza of Mondello, and the grand café is filled with middle-aged or old bourgeois couples & their families on their Saturday night outing, eating fancy gelato and drinking coffee. Out front there's an enormous crowd of motorcycles with teenagers standing in groups talking. . . . The Sicilians are all short and not so beautiful as the Romans—a tough race, fishermen and country-men off the land. . . . Some looking like smalltime *mafiosi* or *camorristi* . . . smooth-faced & well-fed, well-dressed. It's still the bourgeoisie, same the world over. . . . And everyone seems to smoke—*everyone*. . . .

Later, in a pizzeria with terrace on the water, a big poor family at one long table—three generations, from little girls to grandfather & grandmother, all very quiet. There is a great calmness in the people here, as if they had spent all their lives fishing. Even the young have it. . . . Now in the dark, a little fishing boat comes in . . . it's an open boat, only about ten feet long, heavy hull, with a single man in it, standing in the stern, rowing. There's a big light, a floodlight on the bow, to attract the fish at night. He still has it on, as he rows in among the silent boats moored to buoys. He probably has a catch. The bay is silent, the people watching are silent. . . . A moon looks over.

September 16

There's an enormous oblong mountain of rock, half a mile high, Palermo on one side, Mondello on the other. I am on the bus to see Monreale, on the heights overlooking Palermo, a Moorish (?) cathedral there. . . . Big plaza full of people in their Sunday outings. The usual junk for sale at indoor stands but with a Moorish or Byzantine touch. Oriental designs, fans like Spain or Moorish Granada, little knights in Moorish armor, but mostly the plastic that has swamped the markets everywhere like a plague. There's a great terrace overlooking all of Palermo, which lies at the open mouth of a great valley from the sea. The valley is rimmed with fierce mountains & clouds. You can see the successive invasions sweeping up the valley & back down to the sea. Look it up in the history books. I'm not Baedeker. I'm more interested in the faces of the people. . . . Palermo itself is now all new ugly concrete apartment houses, built in the hollow shell of the city bombed out of existence in World War II. . . .

In the park on the terrace here, lovers are holding each other on benches, under the great banyan trees and palms. Kids skirt around on cycles. Suddenly it clouds over & a wind comes up, the sky filled with gray cumulus. The aspect of things changes so fast in this world. Suddenly all is forbidding. The lovers continue to sit with their arms entwined, unmoving. The wind increases. The wind will get to them too. They'll blow away like leaves, into the 21st century. . . . Inside the cathedral, lots of gold mosaics and Byzantine arches and Byzantine Christs and saints. There's a little box by the entrance, with a coin slot, and a single wire running up from it. A little sign says in Italian: "To illuminate the Church, put in 100 lire." No one comes by to put in 100 lire. Unbelievable that this flimsy little wire could light up the whole vast place, big as Notre Dame. Next to it is an old wooden confessional booth, like a little mosque. I look inside and see it is empty except for a small black horse crumpled up in one corner of the booth. I wonder what *he* did wrong and how long he's been in there and if he was the kind with wings. . . . Someone does come by and put a 100 lire piece in the light box, but nothing happens & no lights come on. . . . In the piazza outside, the very tall palm trees are swaying in the tropic wind.

TENNESSEE

April 1986

Bright early morning and I go into Mary's Hungry Corner at the intersection of Legion and North First Street in an ancient two-story brick building next to the Legion St. Blue Grass Hall just off the public square above the Cumberland River. The sign on the door says OPEN SIX A.M. OR WHENEVER MARY GETS HERE.

Clarksville, 7 a.m., April 11

Inside the creaky door four little men in overalls at a wooden table are yakking and drinking coffee. There are three more little men at another old table near the back. They all look beatup. I can hear their drawls. There's a little beatup counter with stools and a handwritten sign on a soft drink cooler that reads No One at Bar. The two-hundred-pound woman who must be Mary is behind this counter wearing a floppy flowered blouse and white shoes and hollering at the men at the front table.

"I tole him if I took him I'd straighten out his back!" she hollers. "I didn't know he was thet drunk—"

Three of the men guffaw. The fourth gets up real slow without straightening all the way and stands there swaying and crooning to himself a snatch of a bluegrass tune.

Big Mary tunes her little eyes on me.

"Got any grits?" I ask her.

"Nobody ain't ast for any lately."

"Why not?"

She ducks behind the counter and comes up with some and shoves it into a little electric oven.

"Whut you want with it—milk or butter?"

"Butter."

She gives me a strange look. "You from aroun' here?"

"You know I'm not—"

"Where you from, then?"

"I used to eat grits in North Carolina," I tell her. "With butter."

"Ah married a man once from Fayetteville, Nowth Carolana—" She pronounces it "Fateville."

"Once?"

"Coupla years back—"

The little drunk with the bent back who didn't laugh is now swaying in front of Big Mary. His head comes up to her huge bosom.

"Ah'm still from Fateville," he says. Suddenly he starts crying.

FRANCE—PORTUGAL

July 1986

L July 10
eft Cogolin for Toulon 9:30 a.m., then by train all day westward & south to Spanish border at Hendaye–Irun. . . .

West of Carcassonne, tens of thousands of six-inch sunflowers packed into fields by the trucks, but all their heads turned away from the fierce afternoon sun of the Midi. . . . Van Gogh's sun too strong for them. . . .

Type à la gare de Hendaye
avec son
petit
ami
un
chêrre
7/11/86

July 11

Train to Irun. Bright sun. . . . One of those feelings I've been here before. . . .

Spent the afternoon in Irun before taking train to Lisbon—went to beach, three miles by bus—much too hot. Returned, found restaurant & ate a big meal in its dark depths. You can really tell when you hit Spain— The wine and the cheese change— The red wine gets heavier, the white sharper, the cheese harder & sharper. . . . No more pale French intellectuals!

July 12

Arrive in Lisbon, bright sun but cool. . . . Jorge Palma, musician, friend of André Shan Lima, putting me up in his huge flat in broken-down building.

If Joyce was the poet of Dublin and Kafka the poet of Prague, Pessoa is certainly the poet of Lisbon. . . . Went to the Brazileira—one of Pessoa's favorite cafés— Tiled walls & paintings. . . . I sat at his table and felt like one of his heteronyms. . . . Later, a man in the street led me to Pessoa's hat shop in the center of town where he got his great black felt hats. . . . The hat shop proprietor had known him— He still had the hats, large and heavy and all black. Seems like everybody in town knew Pessoa and his various guises as poet—he had at least three heteronyms, each a distinct personality.

My trip to Portugal is not for any international festival but simply for a single reading in Porto, north of Lisbon, with André Shan Lima reading the translations. I knew André in Paris just a few years ago, before he got fed up with French police stopping him on the street to see his papers. He is dark and swarthy, and the police no doubt thought he was Arab. In Porto we had a great crowd, mostly students, and André stood up very straight and read my poetry in Portuguese like some handsome prince, very dignified, not at all like his usual wild self. He is a poet and an expressionist painter, given to great lyric outbursts and drunken flights of fantasy. In Paris, he seemed to live on practically nothing, or just on the Paris air, and I hung out with him a lot around and about Shakespeare & Co. just a few years ago, picking up lots of Parigot and street lingo from him. . . .

July 18

On José Antonio Ribeiro farm inland from Nazaré, two hours north of Lisbon on the coast, on the way to reading at Porto. . . . Last night I had a dream in answer to the question asked me by poet-journalist Rui: "What philosophy do you live by?" In the dream there was the enormous bowl of the earth, with footprints and all the imprints of civilization, blood and wars, cars and babies, and I was walking around looking at it all, as in some archaeological dig. And in the distance way down below there was a huge pool or lake, very clear, and I was given to understand that way down underwater there was an object or symbol of some sort that had been placed there by "les conquérants" and that this symbol held in itself the very secret philosophy which was the key to life on earth. I went down there and dove in and saw this very small object shining at the bottom, and I swam way down there and grabbed it and looked at it underwater. It was made of some shiny light metal and it was shaped like a combination of the City Lights symbol and the symbol of the publisher in whose house I was sleeping, "Ulmeiro." And in the combination of the two was the secret of life. One symbol folded on the other like a little jackknife. Aspiration & Transcendence.

AUSTRIA

September 1986

Vienna, September 28

Hotel Graben, very near the Stephansdom. Slept an hour and came out at noon, found the Viennese quietly walking up and down their malls and closed streets around the Stephansdom (roof bombed out in World War II, now restored). Took a taxi to the Belvedere (palace, museum) and saw the Klimts & Schieles, walked back in the late afternoon, sat and drank a beer on the terrace of a grand café on some plaza, the sun setting through huge elms. . . .

When I hitchhiked here from Paris as a student Easter 1950 ('49?), I saw nothing, understood nothing, knew nothing, panhandling in front of the American Express, sleeping in a Sports palace for a dollar a night. . . .

A Night at the Vienna Staatsoper—

Puccini's *Turandot*, in German. The opera house takes up an entire block, and the salons, lobbies, reception rooms, etc., take up much more room than the opera hall itself, which is surprisingly small, half the size of the Paris or San Francisco opera houses. The exterior and the salons and great high-ceilinged rooms around the opera *salle* itself are more elegant than in Paris or anywhere I have seen, with great crystal chandeliers and mirrors, marble halls, marble floors and mantels, elegant promenade-balconies overlooking the Ringstrasse, the whole obviously designed for elegant ladies and gentlemen who come perhaps more to be seen and to promenade and to drink and sup in the elegant salons, than to actually see the opera itself. I promenade among them, looking as elegant as possible. . . . Not having ever seen *Turandot* in any language, and not knowing the story, I could only make up my own story from what I saw visually in the first act. It seems this particular tribe of people on earth has gotten itself into a real jam, somewhere around the Great Wall of China. The curtain rises on a bloody-looking crew about to execute somebody. A bunch of thugs in red oriental getup advance with heads on pikes swathed in shrouds. There's an executioner also in red up on a high platform in the back, and every once in a while he brandishes this enormous silver or tin broadsword, more like a huge mace. He's obviously eager to use it, but there seems to be some faint humanitarian sentiment singing or moaning or whispering in the background, and the bloody band can't seem to get its act together. A guy about two hundred years old crawls out, with a rope around his neck, the other end of which is held by an old nurse or fishwife or defrocked duchess . . . who knows? She's got him on this leash, while he sounds off to the gathering of bloodthirsty mercenaries, cocaine heads, and chaperones. After a while, Turandot appears descending down a huge high stone staircase (from the top of the Wall of China?), stops on a landing by a big gong, lets out one great shout, as he throws up his arms, and marches back up the staircase again, disappearing into the curtained ozone. A moon zooms up as the red gang continues to haggle in song over who knows what. The curtain falls on Act One as some high-born fallen-low soprano croons her complaint and collapses, to the applause of the bejeweled audience.

This is 1986?

10 p.m.

Next to the Hotel Graben, in Dorothea's Street, is the famous Café Hawelka— It's like the Village (N.Y.) used to be circa 1945. . . . Large room, jammed with "bohemian"-looking youth. . . . The friendly old woman seats me at a table with German-speaking Japanese man & an Austrian painter who writes out his name & address for me.

The women here have a certain sparkle in the eyes and bright smile. Klimt women, sometimes, with that burnt red hair. . . . Klimt, out of Titian. . . . European culture here is still fifty years back, despite World War Two. They still know how to smile, be nice to you, stranger. . . .

September 29

Warm sunny morning. He sorties from the Hotel Graben at nine, looks into the dark Café Hawelka where a few locals seem to be drinking coffee and reading the papers in gloomy corners, turns and heads out to the sunlight on the broad mall near the Stephansdom, buys hot chestnuts from a sidewalk vendor, sits down at a sunny table and orders an espresso, draws a picture of a fat Viennese at the next table, finishes his coffee, still eating chestnuts, hustles back to the hotel and splits in the bus.

9/28/86

A Viennese a Café

He feels good about himself and about everything this morning in Vienna. Beautiful Vienna with its beautiful people, still that way. . . . The bus takes the river route out of town. The Danube, with its quays somewhat like along the Seine. The Danube isn't blue anymore; it's brown. But it'll do. A very nice river, he thinks, even if you can't drink it. What river can you drink these days? Chernobyl still burning. He's feeling good. Mission accomplished. A good enough performance of his poetry at the Graz festival. And a clear five hundred dollars (U.S.) in his pocket. Still a lot of money for a poet these days. It still amazes him that they pay him for reciting his fantasies and visions. Better than hanging out broke in front of the American Express. . . . He opens Edward Abbey's *The Monkey Wrench Gang* and starts reading. . . . Put a Monkey Wrench in the system *now*? . . . Or will it self-destruct?

CHICAGO

June 1988

June 22—Chicago at Dawn

Along Michigan Boulevard, from the Water Tower to the Art Institute, there is a sense of tension in the air. A French woman at the desk of the Terra Museum of Art behind a sign saying, An American Revolution. Two young black guys with bicycles leaning in a doorway, wearing plastic blazers emblazoned with "Cannonball Messenger Service." The Tribune Tower, a vertically elongated Gothic cathedral with a quote from Ruskin incised on the floor of the lobby. A shoeshine boy sits on the sidewalk outside, his feet in the gutter.

The weather broke last night. For days, perhaps weeks, the heat had been building up, the drought stretched across the country, across the Midwest, enveloping Chicago in its desert embrace.

In the backyard of a brick house in Wellington Street, the palms in the leaden wind, under an overcast heavy with hydrofluorocarbons. One could hear the dry fronds of the palms rubbing together, like old spinsters rubbing their dry palms together. The wind blew but the clouds did not move. Sitting out on the wide wooden back porch, in the late evening, one could feel the pulse of the bone-dry city in the throbbing air-conditioners and overhead fans and window ventilators that moved the parched air around and gave no relief. Now and then in the night, across the backyards of a dozen houses, one could hear a stray laugh or a fragment of a resigned word or two, lost voices under the moving palms. Once a burst of laughter fell out in the night but was immediately sucked up by the heavy night air like water sprinkled on a parched lawn.

It is now one in the morning, and the laughter is limp, as all falls into silence. At a bar across the backyard alley some male voices are trying to sing, and the heat smothers the sound before it can rise above the first floor. The palms move in the dry wind of the desert of Chicago.

On the way to the airport, the cabdriver—an Iranian with a French accent in English—tells me, "Chicago is a killer city. The people are like beasts. They're not humans, they don't care about anything. I drive twelve hours a day, and the Mafia takes everything. You're the first human I've talked to in a year."

> Chicago is a big silent tough woman
> in dark glasses
> sitting still
> in a rocking chair in a
> darkened house,
> waiting for the dawn.

MEXICO—NICARAGUA

July 1989

FOR LORENZO

July 3

In the Rainbow Hotel on the beach in Puerto Escondido (Oaxaca), after arriving yesterday by plane thru Mexico DF. Lorenzo met me at the airport, looking like Crusoe in a ragged straw hat. . . . Great room with two double beds, bathroom, kitchen corner, terrace on the sea, a hammock strung across . . . blue sky and palms, the ocean's "long, withdrawing roar."

July 5

Lorenzo's twenty-seventh birthday. A rooster crows, we're up just past dawn, Lorenzo checking the waves. At about 7 he heads out and across to the beach, surfboard under arm. . . . Great day. The rooster, the idiot rooster crows. He knows he's cock of the walk, he doesn't know he's an idiot, he isn't, except in men's eyes. Well, he's full of himself this morning, this idiot rooster, he's got a lot to say for himself, this idiot, with his cock's comb and his cock's cry, shattering our sleep. . . . A breeze, blowing off the hot land, shakes the beach palms. A *perro* comes out, a funny-looking dog—stretches, looks at the sea and sniffs the air. What's on his mind? Bones? Maybe fish. . . . Lorenzo is out there on his board, riding the big waves, in the Mexican Pipeline. . . .

THE DOG

#1

The Mind of the Dog, Diary of a Dog, Dog Meets Man, *El Perro Humano*, Human Dog, dog of my days, tail wagger in eternity, barker in the dusk, in the dust, yapper extraordinaire, flea-bitten Mexican wolfhound, mongrel, woofer and pooper, friend of poorest man, digger and barker, earthly sniffer, alone in the universe. . . . A Large Dog Had Begun to Wag Its Tail Inside His Soul, said Márquez. . . . A very large dog. Is this the real beginning of a novel, the novel of the dog I was always going to write? There is no doubt about it, the Very Large Dog is waving its tail, in my direction, this dog is conscious of me, he's not just an ordinary dog, he's a dog I can see in a mirror, a mirror image of myself, except for the tail. If I were to get down on all fours and walk around I would be the same as he, except for the tail. Even the ears would fit in, a little pointed, except I have an earring in one ear, that alone would distinguish me from the pack, from the real dogs, when I was running with them you would always be able to tell which was me, which was the man among the dogs, let loose the dogs of war, you could always tell which among them was the pacifist, the one who would not bite, except into already-dead meat, cooked meat, yes, that was it, I would be the pacifist among running dogs, the running dogs of war that ran the world, let's make sure of that, you would always be able to count on this dog, this man, for that. An intellectual, that is, one who reasoned and thought and made rational decisions and would not just bite into anything out of pure hunger, one who could restrain his hungers, by exercising reason. A creature of pure reason, then, was that it? Well, not exactly. I knew better than that. There had already been too many cases, too many instances when other things, other passions, other hungers ran away with him, with me (reason itself a passion that had to be tamed).

Well, so be it. A dog is a dog, *n'est-ce pas*? Even one who can bark in French. Or in Italian. Or in Spanglish. He barks in tongues. Let's leave it at that. He barks in all languages, everything he barks can be understood by every man, or can be misunderstood by every man, no matter what national or ethnic language he speaks, understands or misunderstands—a bark is a bark is a bark, the same in every dialect, in every tongue. Big flappy tongue says it all. . . . So . . . from now on, nothing but barks for us all, the true international language, no need for translations, direct speech is all. . . . He sees all, hears all, speaks no evil? That's quite possible. This dog of dogs sees all evil, hears all evil, but speaks no evil, he's the pure, non-judgmental observer. He may bark at something because it's dangerous to him, to me, to us, but he doesn't judge the evil, he merely alerts us to the menace, to the evil encroaching on us, it's not that he's indifferent or oblivious to the consequences of evil, it's just that he states the fact of its existence, that he acknowledges its approach, its menace, watch out, *Cuidado!* he shouts, but he doesn't condemn it, he merely lets us know that he knows it's there. *Cuidado!* OK. Let it be. I've got other bones to deal with. . . . Or maybe the dog sees beauty instead of evil. He sees "beauty" out there without even knowing or naming it "beauty"— How should he know it's named Beauty?

#2

He sees "beauty," sees her crossing the sand, out there, just this side of the waves. She is crossing the beach from right to left, blond hair and torso against the horizon. She is carrying a surfboard, she walks upright across the beach, her blond mane blown slightly by the dawn wind. Then she is gone, into the sea, into the long waves, into the tubes with the surfers, the blond giants from California, the golden boys who never work, at least not down here under the sun, under the volcano, Puerto Escondido of the sun, *sol, soledad* of sun. That is all he saw of her this morning, this particular morning in the dawn of time, dog's time being eternal, every instant eternal in the tube of time. . . . Up on a hill in the little town, in the old town, the real Mexican town above the tourist towns, up on the hillside with its dirt streets and gulleys and washed out culverts and broken huts and houses, there's a cinder-block tin-roof church, inside of which in a glass-enclosed case fifteen feet high the *Virgen de la Soledad*, all in white like a bride, stares down on the tourist beach and the surfers, stares down at the dog and the beauty and the evil, with an implacable stare, having seen it all for a long long time, before the coming and going, down below, before and after. Nor does she judge. She sees all, like the dog, but does not speak, does not let out a howl, though there may be a tear in her eye. Others will speak for her, imagining her thought, if any, imputing her reaction, her judgment, her love or her horror at what she sees, out there. She remains silent. Like time itself.

#3

It is evening now, and she walks upon the beach, wearing a white dress. She is not the virgin in the church, not the Virgin of Solitude. She needs the virgin of solitude but she is not it. She needs solitude but there are too many men after her. That is another story. Here she needs solitude, she needs the virgin on the hill, in the tin-roof church. And why do these poor need it, why does this poor town need this goddess of solitude on its hill, its *barrio*, when what they have already is too much solitude, too much lonely misery, starvation, disease, poverty? Let the dog bark about it and explain it to the living. The dog is voicing his paradigm of existence. He knows what he's talking about.

#4

The dog liked to think. In fact, that's all he did, except sleep and drink and scratch his fleas. He didn't consider himself an advanced thinker. Yet he prided himself on a certain perspicacity. He could see through things. Very little deceived him. Although he also had a certain tendency toward naiveté. That couldn't be helped. There were other species beyond his range that would always take advantage of him. Like most beings, there was always someone smarter, someone who could take advantage of him. All in all, however, you would say he made out all right. And he had a long memory. He remembered everything that had ever happened to him or to anyone within his sight, in his world. After all, it was the same world inhabited by humans. They went through the same changes, birth, growth, decay, death. Eating and sleeping and copulating. Except it was so hard for him to find a true mate. He would rather be alone with himself, peaceful in his own body, lying on his side in the shade, or wherever, dreaming his own dreams, of which he had plenty. It was much easier for humans to find another to make love with; they weren't kept penned up or tied up or otherwise segregated, in most places. Just think of how hard it is for a dog to find another dog of the opposite sex in a city, for instance. In his own city neighborhood there were quite a few dogs but most of them couldn't roam around as free as the humans. And for the only ones that could, it was as a consequence of being masterless or mistressless, or homeless. Bums, in other words. Riffraff mutts, you might say. Street dogs, dogs that had to sleep in the parks, free for sure, but free to starve and to freeze in the winter. Like most people, he would rather give up a good deal of freedom in order to have a warm hearth and a warm meal, and security. His memory still had complete freedom.

#5

The dog thought to himself, "I don't hate anybody. But what's this creature called Cat?"

#6

The dog loved to think of all the things that it was good to dream of, for he did a lot of dreaming. A cat was not one of them. He didn't know that the reason "dumb" animals sleep so much was because they have no cerebral cortex and no sense of time passing. This condition merely made it easier for the dog to exist, and to think on his own level, because he didn't have to bother about time and all that time involved, including all the complications resulting from myriad erroneous interpretations and explications of what time really is. Was time an arrow that flew both ways? Such questions never occurred to him, and he was free of all sorts of existential miseries. He liked to just lie there before going to sleep and think of all the things and creatures of which it was said it was good to dream. It was said to be good to dream of angels, birds (especially hummingbirds and nightingales and morning doves), unicorns, ducks, flying fish, giraffes, cotton candy, sunflowers, books of poetry, pregnant women, virgins, and various chessmen. That was only part of the list that he had compiled by overhearing the conversations of various learned persons. He kept trying to dream of these things, and sometimes he succeeded. He also made lists, with considerably less enthusiasm, of the things it was considered bad or even disastrous to dream of. For instance, he thought, for instance—but before he could update his list he drifted off to sleep, making sure his tail was tucked between his legs and that nothing was hanging out, a prey to whatever evil might show up in his dreams.

#7

He knew her eyes would never age. Everything else would go, but not her eyes. They, like most people's eyes, were eternal. But most people's eyes were not hers. Hers had a special light in them, a calm, strange light. It was as if something were sleeping there, some being sleeping there, with eyes open. A "dumb" beast, perhaps, with eyes open.

#8

When he got up this morning, the woman in white was on the beach again. Far off, in a white towel, against the waves. It's a somber day, gray sky, gray sea, flat and calm beyond the breakers. Someone is making a surfing commercial, with a male model and a surfboard, posed in front of the camera with a rented Indian woman in a bikini, as if that is what she normally wears down here in Oaxaca where there is over 60 percent unemployment. Later they will film the real surfers doing their runs, and the film will come out looking like the male model from Mexico City, who's never been on a surfboard, is doing the surfing. Magically, a tequila margarita will appear in his hand, or a rum cola with "Bacardi" blazoned on it, as if you couldn't surf without it. The woman in white also stops to watch for a moment. There are two surfers out there now, performing for the camera which is shielded by a flimsy parasol stuck in the sand. A wind has come up and the edges of the parasol are being torn by the wind. It might rain at any moment. The heavens are lowering. . . . The dog awakens, raises his head on the veranda of the white beach hotel with the red tile roofs. He jumps up, scratching, shaking himself, and heads for the beach, looking up at the sky. There is a fishing boat far out on the horizon. The lady in white turns and shades her eyes, looking out at it. The dog trots toward her. The surfers surf. The camera rolls. There is a trembling in the air.

#9

The sun beats down again. "Virgin of Solitude" indeed. He would like to corner a priest and ask him what this means, why this Virgin of Solitude here, in this desolate little fishing village with its grinding poverty, why "solitude"? There's one in Oaxaca too, a more splendid one, not this poor fishermen's one. Why "soledad" instead of "sol" in this land of the noonday sun, the Mexican *mezzogiorno*, fierce, beating down, day after scorching day.

Orphans of God, is that it, these very dark *indios* in the realm of thirst and scorpions. The sea heaves and sighs with heat. The huge sky pulses with heat. The boat's wings hang limp. Under this sky, on this sea, everything is solitude. The sea and the sky are too huge, too overpowering, for the figures on the beach, the woman in white, the dog.

#10

The dog was an Aries. It was the sign of solitude. The dog could see Aries in the night sky, reflected in the glass of the sea. Mirrors had always enchanted him, just as they enchant babies of all kinds. Human babies looking into mirrors for the first time, what did they see, trailing clouds of glory? The dog did not see himself. Everyone knew dogs could not recognize themselves in mirrors, just as they did not recognize images on televisions. They saw something else, something humans with their self-reflexive craniums could never see. They saw *through* the mirrors, *through* the televisions, *through* the glass of the sea. To the other side. They came out on the other side, out of time, where time stretches neither before or after. Without time, out of time, one is isolated as only the dead can be.

#11

Solitude. As far as he could see, not a ship, not a figure over the horizon. In the presence of the sea, one longs for a living contact, for a body, a lover on all fours, anything to break the eternal monotony of solitude. In the presence of the sea, one cannot face it. Not for long. We must fall back upon ourselves, forced to see only ourselves in the glass of the sea.

#12

The eyes again, always and only the eyes. Yellow eyes, yellow irises. Blue eyes, blue irises. *Arco-iris*, the rainbow. Radiant. He looked into her eyes. What else was there? Death and resurrection in a tongue alack. Chattering of a billion tongues in a thousand languages. And then the ceasing of the chattering. Nothing more. After the final silence, the eyes reminded. So thought the dog. What were her eyes looking at now, over the seas, were they turned to him? He turned and looked out to the sea. He let out a wounded shout.

#13

Incredibly erotic, the atmosphere. The sea in its eternal shushing and moaning and roaring aroused the desire to live forever, to live and live and live, to breathe forever, a terrible hunger for living and loving, a passion, a feeling in the sultry air that was *more than ever like love*, that seeks its object, its fulfillment, like the force of life itself. . . . The waves thundered and broke and fell.

#14

Tonight at dusk, Sunday, the Virgin of Solitude was beating her iron bell again, like someone hitting an old rusty oil drum with a big hammer. *Indios* and dogs on the beach sit looking down at the *sol poniente* in their own brown solitude. No one makes a move to the church on the hillside, lost in its barrio. Some tourists come by in gay colored hats with bandannas on them, one carrying a parasol, laughing. The Virgin of Solitude keeps beating her drum. Huge thunderclouds on the horizon building up, reaching over the darkening beach and pueblo. Suddenly the sky shakes with heat lightning. The *indios* do not move, the dogs do not move. The Virgin of Solitude has fallen silent. Now the huge cloud spreads out into the shape of a monster octopus, with its head the setting sun and its arms the sun's rays reaching over the darkened port.

The head of the octopus sinks below the horizon, draining the light blood out of its tentacles. A lighthouse on the high bluff has come on but does not sweep the sea. It merely pulses every six seconds. Not exactly an ecstatic moment. Still, a single fisherman, a boy, sets forth in an open boat.

#15

The ocean has taken over, consciousness of the ocean has taken over. To lie or live by the sea long enough is to become part of its consciousness, to be engulfed by it. The dog lies on the terrace of the hotel in the shade, and behind his closed eyes the sea surges, the sound of it constant in his head, a pounding, a roaring in his head, a breathing of the universe, a deep sound in the blood, the pulsing sound of life itself. In dreams the huge universe of water surges about us, swells up, carrying us with it. In a deep cobalt blue we float on and on, thru our waking sleep. . . .

Last night in sleep the sea had turned to a very black endless domain, and in it swam a very white woman with very black long hair. Her hair was the sea, her black brows were the sea, her dark eyes were the eyes of the sea, unfathomable. Others swam up to her, all with the blackest hair and blackest eyes, some women and some men, and they multiplied until the sea itself was made of them and their eyes, and all merged together in a surging sea, all unfathomable.

*   *   *   *   *

July 7—Puerto Escondido

Lorenzo saved an American woman from drowning today. We were out on the veranda of our room when the woman's husband came running across the beach to the hotel shouting, "Help! I need help!" Lorenzo was out of the room in an instant, running toward the beach with his surfboard under his arm. He dove into the ocean on the board and paddled rapidly toward two bodies that were being battered by the surf. One of them was a man who'd run in to help the woman and was himself being sucked out by the riptide. Without binoculars, I could barely make out Lorenzo as he reached them and pulled the woman onto his board. The other man grabbed on to the board too, and Lorenzo kicked and paddled it out of the riptide into the beach. The woman had been face-down and almost out when Lorenzo reached her. People had streamed out of the hotel onto the beach after Lorenzo but none of them were surfers, and though the husband had run out from the hotel with a surfboard, he didn't know how to use it, and the board got knocked out of his hands almost immediately, and he just stood there as Lorenzo got to the woman, who was very scared and exhausted. . . . Lorenzo kept talking to her, telling her what to do and that everything was OK. When they got to shore, she lay there for a long while and then thanked Lorenzo for saving her life. Later in the evening the woman and her husband came to our hotel and asked for Lorenzo and bought us drinks on the veranda and thanked him again and again. They were from Chicago and hadn't read the signs in Spanish and English saying that this beach was dangerous for swimmers. She'd only been up to her thighs in the water when the riptide swept her off her feet, and she was drawn under and out, not knowing which way was up, everything black. She knew she had come close to death, and she embraced Lorenzo and me over and over, as well as the other young guy who had come to her rescue and almost got drowned himself. She gave Lorenzo 50,000 pesos ($20). She took our picture with a flash camera on the dark veranda. The word went up and down the surfers' colony that Lorenzo had saved a woman from drowning. Several surfers and others shook his hand when we walked to town later.

July 14 (Bastille Day)

In Mexico City, living four days at Hotel Polanco, 8 Calle Edgar Allan Poe. On television the French celebration of two hundred years of . . . Paris dancing in the streets. Fighter planes zooming over the Arc de Triomphe, all the heads of the great capitalist countries watching. Noted that none of the countries with Kings & Queens (except England) were represented. . . . Paris, capital du monde. It's perhaps the end of Paris as we know it. . . . After the EEC becomes effective, Paris will become another country, one that Henry Miller and Hemingway and Anaïs Nin and Lawrence Durrell and Proust and Djuna Barnes and Balzac and Hugo and George Whitman will no longer recognize. . . .

July 16

Leaving Mex for Managua this afternoon, tenth Aniversario de la Revolución Sandinista. . . .

Pochomil, Nicaragua, July 23

From a wooden boat made from one log, with a primitive net, the young fishermen brought in their morning haul running the *barco* up on the beach. A dozen kids, old *mujeres*, and fishermen clustered around the boat, looking down at the catch: half a dozen lobsters, three hammerhead sharks, some small fry fish, one big red snapper (*huachinango*). They all lay there motionless in the bottom of the wood boat. They'll swim no more. The fierce sea rages offshore, as if lamenting the lost fish. The merciless sun beats down. A little way away on the sand lies a huge turtle upturned, with kids and fishermen squatted around it. The shell of the turtle like a huge shallow oblong bowl, about a yard long, has already been gutted of most of its entrails. Intestines and guts float around in a pool of dark red blood. The fishermen's hands grope around in the bottom of the bowl of blood, scooping up the half-ripe eggs. One man holds a plastic container in which there are already maybe a couple of dozen eggs, round as ping-pong balls, no bigger than marbles, orange-colored, almost like kumquats. The other fisherman keeps finding more eggs nested deep in the turtle. The head has been cut off but the bronchial tubes, larger than air hoses in a filling station, hang over the edge of the shell. The back feet are spread out from the other end of the shell, and the fisherman now commences to cut them off with a curved knife. Another hundred years of solitude has come to a bloody end. Lorenzo says, "Disgusting." The sea roars.

ITALIA

Pescara, October 12

am here for a forum on the poet and novelist Gabriele D'Annunzio who was born here, and I'm not quite sure why I was invited, since I am no D'Annunzio scholar, but I delivered a tirade about him as a notorious womanizer and grandstanding friend of Mussolini (who gave him a small Navy ship to cruise about Lago di Garda in his old age). Gregory—Gregorio Nunzio Corso—is also here, and he tried to speak in Italian and kept mixing up "la luce" and "Il Duce," to the great consternation and amusement of the Italian listeners.

SOMETIME LATER—A *trattoria* mid-afternoon—drinking rosé wine (must be the local *vino terrano*)—ghosts of my brothers sitting at the next tables, gesturing. Harry and Clem and Charley in the locals' faces, their hairlines, the imagined gestures of their hands. . . . Long gone now, all except Harry in Baltimore suburb. . . . But my father was a Lombardo, up north, not down here due east of Rome on the Adriatic.

Bologna, October 18

The morning after the 6.9 earthquake hit San Francisco, I am sitting in the sun at a terrace table on the Piazza Maggiore, reading an Italian paper that has no inkling of the earthquake on the other side of the world. A flock of pigeons walks about in the middle of the piazza on the gray paving stones in front of the cathedral, crowding around old men who are scattering bread crumbs. The pigeons throw long shadows on the stone as they take flight of a sudden, as if some tremor from San Francisco had reached them. Other men and women, whose senses are duller, perceive nothing and stroll about as if nothing at all has happened. A huge bell tolls atop the cathedral. Slowly. Very slowly.

A little later I'm in the RAI television studio here, and on the TV monitor, as the camera pans across an earthquake-stricken San Francisco, an Italian reporter exclaims, "La libreria City Lights *va bene!*" If City Lights Bookstore is OK, then the rest of the city must be OK!

an egret in a swamp
the ochre earth expose
so many different kinds
green.... high steep slop
= cultivated land, snow on
ar mountaintops, glinting wh
ky lowering darker towa
4 PM.... Now the rain in
pain..... And now streak

POMPEI

September 1990

September 26-30

> Pompei with its dark stone men
> preserved in volcanic stone
> (caught in the middle
> of their baths
> with their towels still on)

Pompei's supreme hallucination as in one of those films where the hero is walking into the sun and the heat is rising and his eyes take on a glazed look and the sky and the whole landscape start to whirl around him as in a kaleidoscope, perhaps the way it was before Vesuvius erupted. In Berlin they are running a marathon around the thirty miles of the ruined Wall. The morning newspaper in Napoli shows the huge crowd, thousands of runners passing through the Brandenburg Gate. Some have their arms outstretched, presumably in joy, or as if they were about to fly like Icarus straight into the sun. Turn the photo sideways and they look just like the stone figures still gesturing in the rootless ruins of Pompei, the arms still outstretched against the rain of lava. They have a comic aspect, *un aspetto comico.*

How easy to turn Man's fate upside down! A turn of the wheel and Man is run over by a billion cars or a twist of the dial and the TV picture in full color turns to black & white and our little race is seen to be between dark Giacometti figures wandering through a Samuel Beckett wasteland waiting for Godot, or a final twist of fate lays us all out as in Pompei, only this time the rain is neutronic, as billions gesticulate wildly at the desert sky. Icarus cannot fly through it.

BAJA BEATITUDES

March 1991

T March 8

he names of the fishermen keepers of Playa Requesón Norte are Vicente and Kinito. . . . One tells me with many antics, jumping up and down on one foot and raising one hand from two feet off the ground to head level, that he and his brother grew up here on this beach. *Hermanos en soledad*—the one gesticulating, Kinito, is the younger, although he looks older, and he is the one who has reached Crazy Wisdom. The older brother, taller and serious, stands in the doorway of their hut most of the time. He looks out to sea more, with distant eyes, whereas his Zen fool brother capers about his boat and his nets and tackle, bent over most of the time, bent over so much that his back aches when he straightens up. He chatters constantly to the two white gulls that float around in the shallow water by the stern of the boat, he laughs and cackles and talks baby-talk to them all the time, or not baby-talk, more like Zen craziness, first thought best thought, and once in a while he throws them some scraps with a cackle and a wave in incomprehensible broken Spanish, he the descendant of Cortes's conquest of this coast. . . . Both fishermen not very Indio-looking but Spanish, with sea-turned eyes, not inward-turned and black in the pupils like the Indios. The fishermen have their own labyrinth of solitude but it is not that of the Indios, it is their own fishermen's communion with the birds and fish. Hawks hover overhead, white egrets (like blond teenagers) stalk the shallow waters along the beach for small underwater prey. Farther out the larger birds soar high up, to suddenly plummet straight down for fish spotted in the calm waters of the bay. Kinito asks me to get him some Delicados (cigarettes) when we go into town, while his brother wants three kilos of *frijoles* and a carton of *leche*. They have no car or bicycle or mule and it's seven or eight miles up the road to the nearest *tienda*. They are part of a huge Márquez *Hundred Years of Solitude* novel forming in my head. . . . The older of the brothers in this endless novel is also Odysseus on the beach, stranded, cast-up, always staring seaward, toward what homeland, what farther island, what Penelope, what farther sea route from here, on the Sea of Cortes. . . .

March 10

Santa Rosalía . . . old French mining colony. . . . Prefab metal church by Eiffel. . . . Wood houses with tin roofs and deep terraces, abandoned mining factories, smokestacks and broken machinery, all rusted. . . . *Whole trains rusted*, solid, engines and ore cars and cabooses, abandoned in time. Overlooking it all, an abandoned magnificent two-story mahogany hotel with high balconies and verandas, no doubt built by the French, now falling apart. A French-American-Mex version of Márquez's *Autumn of the Patriarch* could be written here. . . .

> The silent dawn
>> creeps up
>>> like a cat

Cataviña, March 12

What shores, what gray rocks, what islands. . . . And now what deserts seen and forgotten—cacti gesturing to the horizon, the highway an indian arrow through it—sun beating down on the abandoned landscape littered with wreckage of a million cars & trucks, rusted out, twisted into fauna of sand & rock, oxidized into oblivion, the drivers long ago run off. How many already invaded this land? First the Indios driven out, beaten & burned by Cortes & Guzmán—then the Spanish themselves, routed by wind, English & French—the Jesuits run out, the Dominicans, stray gringos, poachers & outcasts, outlaws & desert rats. And now the huge motor homes, full of old white couples seeking their last sun, hull down in Winnebagos, over the horizon where sun & sand still point to no end.

St. London-Durham
5/13/91

BRITAIN—SPAIN—FRANCE

May 1991

May 5—Tube to Heathrow (London)

Latter day Falstaffs, Lawrence's gamekeeper fifty years later, Oscar Wildes of South Ealing, suitcases & newspapers (fat old bum snoozing, stinks real bad), dark foot in yellow sandal, dirty plastic bandage on it, the tape peeling. At Osterley out in the open again: an embankment with blue gentians, spring along the rail, backyards overgrown, weeds and tall flowers, forget-me-nots begrimed, orange tile roofs of "row houses," bare walls bricked up, the sky leaden gray. Falstaff sleeps on—blubber of a shore listing over, hands like bludgeons, a meat cleaver man gone back underground again at Hounslow West. Heathrow in the gloaming—where now?

May 5–8—Barcelona, Plaça Real, Hostal Ambos Mundos

The old plaza again. The pigeons under the palm trees in the huge square. Among the park benches and fountains and the café tables out under the colonnades on the paving. We have alighted in a photograph that existed without us through the centuries. (At the next table some teenagers from somewhere else in the country get up with their backpacks, one with a sign stitched on the back of his Levi's jacket: Guns 'n Roses. They make off across the plaza, into the unforgiving unknown.) The birds in their courses swirl and swoop about the plaza, whole flocks swirling low and around the palms to alight on the balustrades three floors up. The sun pours down on the morning plaza. On the sunny side of the square the little Minotauro Bar is busy, bringing out coffees to the people at the tables. On the dark side of the plaza, the cafés still closed & shuttered up. (A chestnut-haired woman in a yellow T-shirt and loop earrings sits down and starts reading her paper. A man comes up with a sketch pad and offers to draw her portrait & she declines with a brilliant smile. The sun glints in her beautiful hair. Across the plaza Stephanie is upstairs in our third-floor room with the French doors opening out on the balcony, washing her hair. Yesterday all afternoon she sat on the balcony doing her watercolors.) The time of silence and exile is over, the birds and the people have their mouths open, it is no longer Nerja 1965 when the people talking on the Paseo went silent whenever a Guardia Civil went past. . . . The poets swirl about like the pigeons in the open air of their lives. Sooner or later perhaps they will swirl together and give out one collective cry, against the sky. (Franco died years ago now, but more recently there was an attempt at a coup by former Francoist generals.) Or do they have to have a dark, threatening sky before they can speak out again? The shadows that most characters in novels become are shadows the poets recognize. . . . Their collective shadow here is still swirling about in the air, scattered against an uncertain sky. . . .

> While the wingless street-people
> on the park benches
> the still-dispossessed people
> sit looking up with mouths agape
> hoping
> still to hear at last
> some great new ecstatic song
> of love & revolution

May 8—Train to Madrid

Television set at the front of each coachcar, showing pictures of the train itself moving thru the landscape. The passengers look through the TV instead of out the window. . . . it's like seeing the 19th century through the 20th—castles of Spain seen thru the TV tube—

At Tarragona the train turns inland & upland, suddenly transforming everything, the flat Mediterranean coastal plain turned to mountains with hilltop towns looking like Italy. As we climb, the land turns more rugged. . . . After Zaragoza, the train heads west, on the great *altiplano*—great sweep of land to far horizon—Where Don Quixote?

Haven't seen a castle yet, and only one small metal windmill. . . . High bare *tierra-verde* mountains, high mesas like New Mexico, rivers with aspens, cumulus clouds with flat bottoms driven by the winds, olive orchards, vineyards, pointed church towers like old knight's helmets, terra-cotta towns close up, an egret in a swamp, the ochre earth exposed, so many different kinds of green . . . high steep slopes of cultivated land, snow on the far mountaintops glinting white . . . the sky lowering darker toward 4 p.m. . . . Now the rain in Spain. . . . And now streaking toward Madrid, the fast train passes lime-green fields and red earth, with dark green hillsides beyond, so that the grass looks like it's filling a bowl, overflowing into the dark green and the red earth. And now goldenrod trimming the meadows, and long rows of poplars planted close by straight rivers . . . burnt sienna roads snaking up, white sheep like rocks stuck to the hillsides among the goldenrod and white-green trees (and where is the Guadalquivir, that romantic river?). . . . The sheep in the distance, the color of dried dates with sugar on them, and some small clouds beyond the same size as the sheep, only whiter . . . heraldic cumulus over a castle. . . .

Every instant the moving TV image on the screen at the front of the coach destroys the moving pastoral image outside the window. Both flit by, the 20th century disappearing as fast as all the past centuries of the earth. . . . Eucalyptus with leaves like coins, silver in the late afternoon light, slanting, shimmering on the leaves.

And suddenly we're there: Madrid, shantytowns on the edge, a *periferia* like Rome. . . . I'd rather see the modern outsides of those ancient cities. . . .

May 12—London Again

Britain—a civilization built on wit, say the guidebooks. . . . In which case, Boswell's Coffee House, Russell Street, Covent Garden should be just the place—Boswell drank cappuccino and ate croissants? I sit out on the sidewalk hoping to overhear the wit that built the British Empire (I've heard it in the House of Commons, backbenchers giving it to the Iron Maiden). Monday morn May Twelfth, the Sapphire Laundry truck pulls up (fire engine red), and a blue truck for Leathans Leather—a motorcycle rider in green plastic jacket reading Pony Express with a picture of a pony—the Marquess of Anglesey pub—the Opera Terrace Bar Café in the old Covent Garden glass-roofed center—once the great produce market, now the usual mall (Samuel Johnson would be appalled?). Man with a short ladder and an orange plastic bucket passes by, his shirt says National Security. A Metropolitan Police Wheel-clamping Unit truck backs up, then pulls away (to do some wheel-clamping no doubt—a little early in the day for that?). Europa Provisions—Green Grocers in a white truck. . . . Flowers hanging from lampposts, what now?

Durham, May 13

In the great cathedral under overcast skies late in the afternoon they are singing evensong in high silver voices, reed-like: "To the Resurrection, Amen"—"To Life Everlasting, Amen." A bald human head sticks up out of a winged pulpit and recites from the New Testament. "Nunc Dimittis," replies the choir. . . . And finally, "Hallelujah." (This is a helluva time for "Hallelujah.")

"The Durham Miners' Book of Remembrance" mounted on a black bier—the words, "Remember before God the Durham Miners who have given their lives in the pits of this country and those who work in darkness and danger in those pits today"—and below: "He breaketh open a shaft away from where men sojourn— They are forgotten of the foot that passeth by"—Job 28:4. The organ thunders at the end of mass, the verger all in black leads the white-robed priests & choir out of the altar, bearing an iron sword on his shoulder as the organ thunders behind him & he bears down on us like Death itself. He has only to swing his sword. . . . And his foot passeth the moldering miners.

May 15—At Laugharne, Wales

Dylan Thomas's cliff-perched writing shed over the Taf estuary. How quiet the coursing waters beneath the screen of trees flowing up the flats, the clay shingle, the gray waters flooding, touch of green in it, moss upon the sands, among the rocks a grebe floating far out, acacia & maple by the shed—steep stone steps straight up. I stand at the top against the stone wall looking over the estuary writing this— Where now bully boy? Gone under the hill with the dancers.

A blue and white sign says, To the Dylan Thomas Boathouse— An esplanade with stone walls leading up to it— In the Boathouse itself a Dylan Thomas tape is playing, his lush voice, his plush voice, his posh accent. I stand at a window of his room and look out onto the estuary as a thousand poets have done since he went.

So much like the Bolinas estuary—the clay beach dark green, almost khaki with clumps of kelp—the glittering waters also clay-green, flowing through sandbars—far out in the shallow bay a fish boat heaves, a coracle abandoned—a bold green headland—San Francisco and the Golden Gate around the bend— A single kestrel soars over, riding the wind— "High tide and the heron's call" still echoing— The tape stops playing, no longer even an echo of him in this far room, even as Bolinas poets call over St. John's Hill.

Only silence after him for poets & herons to fill. They do not.

May 17—Mutant, Brighton
A Leonora Carrington scene on Brighton beach in fog. I'm watching a dark bird far off at water's edge, first only its hooded head visible, then long wet wings emerging from the dark green leaden waters. It stretches its long skinny wings like arms with claws. And then the body rises up still growing longer. Oh it's a man! It begins to wade out of the water as out of primeval slime. It's a squishy bird-man with slimy flippers! It walks up the slope of the beach flapping its wet wings—its flippers flapping too—and disappears under the esplanade. In a matter of minutes it may possibly appear at our bedroom door still wearing its flippers and announce in a fishy voice, "I am not a bird."

May 21—Brittany Ferry, Plymouth to Roscoff (France)
Kissing the acacias we sailed away from olde Englande. . . .

May 22
The Fisherman's Christ in Roscoff with extra large arms & legs (from hauling nets & fish, from rowing huge wooden boats) stretched on the crude wooden cross in the old stone church—the whole Christ made of old gray wood with a spike thru only one foot— He's got a round face, long wooden hair and wooden eyes closed. A wooden clapper strikes an iron bell and the ochre light trembles. I tremble too thinking of the aspen leaf—I might have been on a tree in Colorado in some other life—the leaf falling from the tree as Christ here is falling spread-eagled in the burnt light.

Sitting in a pew I give a very loud sneeze and call, "Pardon!" to Le Seigneur Notre Père. You fool! He thunders. Get out of this damp cave and into the sun!

May 24

Here with Lorenzo eleven years ago. I send him a postcard. . . .

Roscoff, town of small dogs and solid stone houses. . . . The gulls' cries echo down the stone streets— They cry like cats, meowing over the rooftops, and miming each other in many voices, crying to each other and the sea. Swallows swoop through gables—the south wind blows the fog away. There is a cheeping among the chimneypots—Pierre Gidal, Pêcheur, lushed on *gros rouge*, sits in his beached boat and discourses about the good Germans who ran this town during the war (he's a royalist too, of course). When the German commandant was captured at the end of the war, says Pierre Gidal, the mayor of Roscoff "never even thanked" him for all he had done. . . .

"metier, marin"
Roscoff 5/91

Le Bateau de Pierre Gidal
"Le Chouquette"

L a Vita Italiana. . . . In the Italian sensibility life is almost always subject to revision—one's immediate plans, appointments, relationships are constantly subject to revision—depending on many variables, the time of year or day or night, the way the light might strike a statue or a person, the flight of a bird landing on your head thinking you were dead or a scarecrow about to crow and scare you.

Florence, May 18

Bergamo, Maggio 28

USA . . . a society in violent turmoil. . . . A declining civilization no doubt. . . . Same over here on this side of the ocean.

The "Third World War" will be the War against the Third World, including the Middle East. The new Cold War is the war against the electronic world, the human vs. the non-human, against "virtual reality" and the TV life.

They are celebrating the graduation of several hundred *finanzieri* today in the main piazza of Bergamo. They've got the military bands out, several of them, and lots of formations of young officers in military hats with the crowns sweeping up like Nazis. The Bergamo bourgeois are out in force, and the major is making a speech to the new graduates of La Finanza. They did everything but shoot off cannons.

And then the band marched up and down the avenue playing military marches, as in the Old Days. It could have been a scene out of some 19th-century Viennese novel or Musil's *Man Without Qualities* or Briffault's *Europa*.

Maggio 29

Saw the exhibition of paintings by one Mr. Dondé—fakes of Picasso, the impressionists, etc. Things "certified" as real fakes. There's a certificate with each one guaranteeing it is an original fake by Dondé. . . . For sale. All kinds of movie stars & famous people have purchased them. Some shah ordered fifty-seven of them.

Heard the latest Pole tickle Beethoven and Bartók, in the Teatro Donizetti tonight. . . . The audience mostly gray-haired ladies towing their husbands. The pianist looked like a rock star made over.

Not wearing a necktie, I slunk away. . . .

Milano, Maggio 30

After Primo Moroni in about 1989 changed the name of his Calusca bookstore to Calusca City Lights and made out its first membership card in my name, I knew I had to find the store in Milan. I had a sort of address for it out in a beatup neighborhood. I found a boarded-up building that didn't look like anyone lived or worked there. There was a door that looked boarded-up but really wasn't. After I had knocked for quite a while, finally the door cracked open and an eye peered out. When I told the eye my name and that I was from City Lights in San Francisco, the door creaked open, and I found a couple of wary-looking guys looking very much on the defensive. But it was not I that they were paranoid about. I was soon enlightened that they were constantly expecting a raid by special police. But as soon as they were convinced that I was Ferlinghetti from City Lights, others started appearing, as it were, "out of the woodwork," with everyone shaking my hand and embracing me. I soon realized that, as well as being a center for dissident activist groups, this "bookstore" was basically an archive of radical literature of all kinds, with international connections especially in Germany, France, and the U.S.—anti-fascist, anarchist, libertarian Communist, internationalist, situationist, Left-wing trade union treatises, etc., etc. And even after many raids seizing quantities of all this, there still remained thousands of radical works, theoretical tomes, pamphlets, broadsides, radical poetry books, and more. . . . And here were the present operatives, surviving underground, it seems, on practically nothing.

Though they did have an old car in which they drove me back to my hotel in the center of town. We parted with great fraternal feeling. City Lights San Francisco and Calusca City Lights are on the same page culturally and politically!

May 31

Forget the old Europe, the Europa of the tourist guidebooks. It exists only in the old buildings submerged in traffic and in the minds of the guidebook writers and the tourist industry (the latter being a real plague). Modern Europe is like modern America with a surface of crenellated battlements and decaying cathedrals, the whole thing a "grand Camembert pourri."

"Digital Evangelism" = pictures of the Pope on cassettes & CDs, wristwatches with his picture on the face, T-shirts, hats, *even the Pope's pants* (replicas) for sale. . . . The Pope is everywhere . . . with his pants on.

My birth certificate says 106 Saratoga Avenue Yonkers. . . . I take the A train to 168th street, transfer to #1 and continue on the Elevated to Van Cortlandt Park, then catch a bus north to South Yonkers. It's only a mile or more along the west edge of the park to Caryl Avenue. I get off here on the vague advice of the black busdriver who waves in the direction he thinks Saratoga Avenue might be. . . .

And so uphill a mile on foot, past block of apartment houses, their better days behind them. And there's the end of Saratoga Avenue with a mom-and-pop grocery— An old white man comes out carrying a quart in a paper sack— He looks through me as if I were part of the street and had been there forever. (Perhaps I have. . . .)

I have no memory of the house or its location. It is as if I am looking for someone else's birthplace. (Perhaps I am.) A slight rain starting to fall in the falling light—I pick up my pace, hurrying along. Maybe three short blocks to *106*, where in a small back bedroom my brother says he heard my first cry seventy-seven years ago. (It echoes now as if I myself had heard it.)

The little house, almost to the crest of the low hill, a gabled wood-frame house—two stories with an attic—detached from close-by houses. A yard with old cars on one side, and a steep drop in back to a gully with a few tall trees, old barren oaks and elms—bare ruined choirs!

The house itself run-down now—ugly asbestos siding over the old wood, and a small screened-in front porch. Inside the flimsy screen door there's a once-handsome oak front door with worn brass doorknob and beveled glass, upon which goldleaf numerals still show *106* (with half the *1* missing).

Three doorbells (three apartments now?)—I ring them all without response. No one in sight anywhere inside—no sign of life or light in nearby houses. A kind of country slum, but still a quiet family neighborhood. Across the little street, some Latinos with boom-box turned down are hanging out. I walk around back by the old cars and the bare trees and look up at the silent house, looking for that small back bedroom. *Kikiriki* goes a bird just once, like an echo of light— I have been here before? An incredible, inexplicable feeling of happiness floods up from nowhere— The rain increases— It's really coming down now. . . . Let it come down!

Thus be recorded my birthplace and how I came upon it for the second time, maybe six hundred yards north of the northwest corner of Van Cortlandt Park, in a gray rain seventy-seven years later.

It must have been all country back then. The kids must have played ball in this green park with its worn diamond and its ancient rusted screen behind the batter's box. I can hear the bat hit the ball (perhaps pitched by Pop)— And my brother running for first base ended up in Baltimore forty years later. . . .

> And I here
> > his interrogator
> > > still listening for the sound
> of my vanished family
> > > echoing there
> Shouts and laughter
> > tears and whispers
> > > fill the air

ITALIA ANCORA

April–May 1997

S
Roma, April 28

ono arrivato all'Hotel Locarno, Via della Penna . . . nel Tridente—Be Here Wow!

Vladimir Melatonin, the soporific Russian chessplayer, accompanied me on my voyage across the black & white Atlantic. I from the horizontal position made my white moves—he hovering over me like a genie trying to decide which chessman I was. . . . Finally I fell asleep under his spell. And he wiped me out. Turn me over, Lord, I'm done on this side—

Canceled trip to Prague & Eastern Europe after Allen's death.[41] Allen had created a whole world of poetry around himself. When he died, his whole world mourned. We all wept. I too.

Firenze, May Day

I came for the opening of the City Lights Italia bookstore in Florence.

The "backstory," as journalists say, is a saga that goes back a couple of years. Two young Italians came to see me at City Lights in San Francisco. Antonio Bertoli, known for his work as a theater director and editor of avant-garde texts, and Marco Cassini—who would later start his own press in Rome called Minimum Fax. They wanted my permission to start a "City Lights Italia" bookstore in Florence. Following our model, they also would publish books, as well as importing our City Lights books for their store. City Lights Italia would be a completely independent business, having no connection with us financially. All this seemed absolutely splendid to me, and we made some sort of written agreement and signed it, and within a few months it all became a reality in Florence. And it became an activist cultural center, although less radical politically and more literary than the Calusca City Lights bookstore in Milan.

I spoke the following in Italian at the grand opening of the store:

Thanks so much for the warm welcome. I think this will be a historic evening! I think that Italy needs a bookstore and literary center like this. And it may be a new kind of Red Circle, but perhaps more anarchist and pacifist than Communist, a Green Circle . . . like our own bookshop in San Francisco— So . . . break a leg! And good luck to all!

ROMA, MAGGIO 11

In the Testaccio cemetery—Shelley's tomb, with a large marble plaque on the ground. An ant with a long proboscis and long thin wings (perhaps a poet) is walking around on the stone by a faded pink rose. Suddenly he flies a short hop but lands again on the grave—

And Keats's tomb with this inscription on the stone:

This Grave / contains all that was mortal / of a / young English Poet / who / on his Death Bed / in the Bitterness of his Heart / at the malicious power of his Enemies / Desired / these Words to be engraven on his Tomb stone:
Here lies One
Whose name was writ in Water
Feb 24th 1821

There is also a plaque on a nearby wall with his profile in stone. And behind the wall a little pile of rubbish, including a faded dry rose and a beer bottle and a black high-heeled shoe. . . .

Maggio 15

Al Vaticano the stone figures standing on the roofs, gesturing against the crying sky— And St. Peter's wrapped in scaffolding. They're reconstructing Peter's Dome, that is to say His Head, which really needs it, having a bad case of dry rot—that medieval sign of a general decay, with its medieval way of thinking. And the Pope's Dome about to fall—decayed cerebrum and all. . . .

Fregene, May 18

In this crowded seaside *trattoria*, full of handsome young Italian studs and their laughing girlfriends, the Italian language engulfs me— Nothing to do but let its waves of pure libido flood over me!

Rome, May 19—The Forum

All the ruined Roman statues tumbled down in fields & forums, lying face-up, prone, or still standing gesturing, and staring at us now with their blind eyes (empty as the skies until clouds pass over) and still full of fear—fear of what they saw in imperial Rome coming down on them, and of what they see now coming down on us. The whole of humanity passed before those all-seeing eyes. And what words might they cry at us, what prophetic words struck mute behind those eyes: *Ave atque Vale*, or "Hail and Farewell!"

VOYAGES

April–May 1998

Leaving Paris in full sun. **April 16—Paris to Prague on Train 1st Class, 8:54–23:45**
Soundless train through the suburbs in a flash and
out into the French countryside— *Comme c'est beau, ce paysage!* Suddenly
bare winter trees, lime-green fields full of spring rain, ready for planting . . . lime-
green right out of the tube of Pissarro paint, calm rivers of a darker green, *terre verte*,
poplars and cypresses, brown ploughed fields stretching away, as the sleek train
whizzes by. Under gray skies, due east from Paris—small brooks & streams twisting away, small hills on the horizon, black & white cows impastured, all so calm
through the soundproof window. . . . Now a small village of ochre-colored stone,
square church made of it, *cloche* tower reading correct time (11:15), noon approaching in eastern France, mid-April 1998. . . .

Now, on a bank by the tracks, a large sign: Metz 5 km . . . Germany already. . . .
Businessman with computer and cellphone folds his dispatch case and prepares to
get off. . . . "Trois minutes d'arrêt." . . . Steeples in gray sky, low squat houses, concrete block apartments. "Metz." *Andiamo, per favore, avanti.* . . . Turns out to be
twenty minutes delay. . . . The conductor comes by now, distributing a brochure
about this train, with the whole itinerary, Paris to Prague—seems I've been riding
in the dark so far. I read here that this train is called "The Goethe" (Euro Train
#57). . . . Paris–Saarbrücken–Dresden–Praha. . . . Is this the Journey of *The Sorrows
of Young Werther?*

In Frankfurt a Brunhilde was announcing the trains, a faraway distant voice on a loudspeaker, like a Valkyrie singing on the Rhine of the railroad. Or was it the young Werther's distant married love still singing to him, or Schumann's beloved, also married to another, now reduced to working in a railroad station?

20:42—All day we rode over the landscape, eastward always, across Germany. Now dark Dresden arrives. And then a town called Bad Schandau. The last German gets off. No one gets on. . . .

Now the train hurtles on, into the night, into the Czech Republic. And no one knows what the night holds, if anything. . . .

Two blind people (both with white canes) get in at Děčín, a man and a woman, both heavily dressed, as if for Siberia, stocky and solid both; I see them coming down the long aisle between the red seats, one mumbling to the other, stumbling along. When they get to me at the end of the car they make as if they see me or smell me, first one stops and then moves on, then the other, mumbling. They're right out of Samuel Beckett, it's the End Game perhaps. The doors close behind them. . . . The train starts up into the night again. . . .

Prague, April 24

As usual, Allen Ginsberg has already been here. (Dictum for poets: Don't write what has already been written in the same mode by another who got there first. A used *aperçu* is no longer an *aperçu*.) Allen here was fêted and crowned King (or Queen) of May and rode around on a float wearing his crown. The Czechs were still exulting their liberation from life behind the Iron Curtain.

Now I come by train from Paris some few years later and am greeted by some of the same partisans who liberated the city. Václav Havel is now president,[42] and when he visited City Lights Bookstore in San Francisco, he invited me to his office in the Castle in Prague. Turned out he was in hospital when I arrived, but I got to sit at his desk high up in the Castle (Kafka in the wings). And I was shown the great doorless or windowless window (fifteen feet tall) where unwelcome guests in other centuries were pushed out and fell three stories to their death—defenestrated!

Now freedom still rings in the old church bells, and in the great old church on the plaza in Old Town, Czech poets are reading my poetry aloud, day and night for seventy-two hours. Strangers come up and tell me the poetry we published in San Francisco was a beacon of hope to them during the dark years. . . .

I leave by train as I had come, as the liberated landscape flashes by. . . .

April 25

7:41 a.m. to 9:00 p.m. on the German train. . . .

Munich to Verona 3:30–9:00.

Shortly after leaving Munich the train suddenly enters the most fantastic mountain landscape— Long wide valleys, high hillsides, steep sweeping fields dotted with groves of small straight pines, the green slopes as if they had all been manicured with huge lawnmowers— And in the farther distance, looming up on the horizon, terribly high snow-covered slate-gray churches with steeples like sharp pencils or ragged baroque bayonets. . . .

Through the Tyrol— Leaving Innsbruck we're soon into a series of tunnels (how else to get thru these Götterdämmerung mountains?) then out into the open again . . . stands of white birches and streams by the tracks, deep riverbeds with dry rocks, red-roofed chalets huddled in gulches—more distant snow mountains, sweeping the sky, the white tops like clouds that got stuck up there early in the winter and never made it by . . . the train now running between steep rock walls with fir-covered hills rising up beyond. . . . Shadows lengthening on hillsides and meadows. . . . (A young D. H. Lawrence hiked here with Frieda I think. Did they drink beer and make love in that Gasthaus there on the hill?)

The Tyrol! The train winds through the steep hills, noiseless into Brennero, lodged between mountain passes. Does an "o" in the end of the name signal the approach of Italy? The border must be around here someplace. . . .

A young conductor comes through speaking Italian! What a relief! The German conductors got off at the last Gasthaus. Train running slightly downhill now, soon to enter *la bella Italia*— Already the landscape is softer. There's laundry hung out to dry on a balcony—I know we're in Italy now. They wouldn't do that in Innsbruck. . . . A jade river appears. . . . Now Fortezza, 18:49. . . . All the way, a small highway twists through the valleys alongside the train . . . even here, the cars, everywhere the cars, a wide green valley filled with houses and parked cars, they worm their way in to even the remotest accesses, they have the right of way even in the mountains, they must get through, billions of them, like colored ants clustered everywhere, metal bugs of all colors, the humans behind the wheels with legs atrophying, soon they won't be able to walk anymore. . . .

Ah, there's vineyards! Now approaching Bolzano, among steep green mountains close up. . . . The sun is still setting, flickering on windows, as the train twists toward it. Below Bolzano in the dusk a light mist or fog fills the valley, the sky hazy, the valley floor covered with lush green vineyards. Red sky between two mountains, fading. . . . Trento (20:05) and night falls on earth again. . . . Trento, one of the ugliest towns on earth in one of the most beautiful settings in the world. Surrounded by spectacular gentle mountains and green hills and lush fields, here has been constructed an ugly symbol of industrial civilization and its culture—the town dominated by large square concrete apartment complexes, ten stories high, looking like prisons in the night, and other hideous urban housing, inundated with concrete and cars. It would seem, as Henry Miller said long ago, "a new breed of men has taken over." . . . Verona approaches in the night.

April 26

Verona, the next day: the hotel I stayed in last night was booked as a "three-star" hotel but two of the stars must have burned out some time ago. . . . Tourists with cameras in the morning on top of the Arena, outlined against the sky. . . . Fishermen by the River Adige, casting their eternal lines. . . . Verona much bigger than I expected—a beautiful town with a beautiful river, and the Veronese dialect is said to be half swearwords.

April 27

Arrivato a Venezia. A great bush of lilacs in bloom on the Grand Canal. I'm on the *Traghetto #1* . . . decaying palazzi . . . tilted foundations . . . dark green waters. . . . Which is it, wisteria or lilacs? They climb up the walls on cornices and windows, as if it were the same spring when I came here a student per autostop long ago.

One says that Venice is a place where the *déracinés* come, the ones who have never made it, the alienated, the *frustrati*, the ones that don't fit, the jilted lovers, the broken artists, and all the romantics of the world. . . . Who knows if this myth is true? The tourists look like tourists anywhere. I think I will buy a pair of the requisite dark glasses and look as inscrutable as anyone. . . .

Fat sparrows peck off the tourist tables. This Venice, this house of cards, mouldering, tilted doges up to their knees in water, crowns falling sideways. . . . Ezra Pound slept here. And I mean slept! The deep sleep of the confused Confucian. . . . Aye, but the great sounds he could emit!

The *direttore* of the Hotel Sofitel here, Claudio Nobbio, took me this evening to the most elegant restaurant called the Due Forni. Deep Venetian red flocked wallpaper and many intimate rooms filled with what Claudio told me are the movers & shakers of Venice—all the big shots meet here over dinner and decide what's to happen & what's not to happen. . . . We must have had six or seven courses, starting with champagne with the antipasto. The meal lasted three hours—we left past midnight and took the *traghetto* in the rain. . . .

April 28

In the morning, gray sky and light rain, the city very quiet, many people going by in the quays by the canal, all under umbrellas, totally silent under the rain. There is a certain feeling of serenity in La Serenissima. Something about the quietness of the people and the quiet lapping of the eternal waters rising and falling in the canals, lapping at doorsteps at high tide. . . . (The water still rising. In a hundred years it will all be washed away. "Pyramids in sand," said James Joyce. . . .)

A street in Venezia—"Sotoportego Dei Cattivi Pensieri": Arcade of the Guilty Thoughts. Under the arcade I stroll as if I were a free man— At least I am free of guilty thoughts for the most part, though not all! And I am as free as "free will" will allow, even if "free will" is like a polliwog *willing* to lose its tail. As I pass under the portico of those guilty thoughts, the statue of an angel mounted there to forgive me waves her white wings over me. . . .

Firenze, May 2

My fourth year in a row in Firenze, and the third staying at Silvia & Antonio Bertoli's— Another trip by myself. One exists alone— Solitude, one hundred years of solitude.

After three days of rain and dark clouds and thunder, the sun breaks through at last on the big veranda— Small swallows swoop soundlessly through the arches, flittering into nests high up under the eaves— The sun too flitters in and out of nests of clouds and now breaks free— The glorious morning sun bathes the beautiful hills—the grass still wet and glistening—the stone house breathes—the tall straight pines point straight up at the new blue sky of somebody's heaven. The hanging wisteria, purple ecstasies on the trellis by the rabbit hutch, quiver in the light— Iris and rose also tremble, caught climbing a stone wall— An ochre cat rolls on his back on a wood table and stretches full length, his eyes closed in the new sun. It's the land of the *ginestra*, the yellow Spanish broom and the small golden daisies. The earth turns with them all silently, soundlessly—turns with us all here in the hills above Scandicci in the lime-green fields of Marliano—turns on with us all into the 21st century. . . .

And with it advances a great horde of a billion new cars. Here they come like a blight on the horizon, a phalanx on a straight *autostrada* sweeping all before them with their steel hearts, their concrete aprons, blanketing the landscape—field & flower plowed under a wall of monstrous metal bugs, an avalanche of oil and metal rising over us—blotting out the sky. And *Kikiriki! Kikiriki!* cries a cock in the henhouse—crying out his anguish in the chickencoop. . . .

I wrote this statement on Allen Ginsberg's political side, to be read by Anne Waldman at the New York St. John the Divine memorial May 14, when I will be in London:

After Kenneth Rexroth (from whom I got my basic political and anarchist education), Allen had a most potent influence, and not so much by his poetry as by his omnipresence and total availability to participate in any political form, whether it was sponsored by Right-wing or Left-wing, by Establishment or anti-Establishment. For this stance he might often be criticized, for "selling out" or whatever. However, this is just where I learned a big lesson from Allen. Instead of refusing to participate in politically tainted forums, Allen considered such invitations an equal opportunity to convert the "other side" to his point of view. Thus it was when he testified on drugs for the U.S. Congress. And perhaps he convinced the CIA! When I was once invited to Israel by a government-sponsored poetry festival, my first reaction was to refuse, due to that government's militarist aggressions, etc., but Allen said, "Go, because your presence will support the forces for peace within Israel—"

So Allen's big lesson was and is: "Talk to the enemy and win them over! Don't just put flowers in their guns. Talk to them!"

MAGGIO 4—CASCIA

DIRTY TONGUE
The little black dog with the small head and funny tail
enters the little church
during Sunday mass
and waving his tail he wanders up
to where the head priest is praying over microphones
And the dog sniffs the altar
and cocks his head
as if he's listening to the priest
And then he starts sniffing the front-row worshippers
who are now all kneeling
and waiting with eyes closed and open mouths
for Communion
And the priest comes up and starts putting holy wafers
on their extended tongues
and only those with clean tongues
after Confession
are allowed to get the wafer
but the dog raises his paw very politely
and paws the skirt of the priest
with open mouth and tongue hanging out
for he too wants one of those delicious biscuits
But the priest ignores the dog
because the dog has no soul
according to this antique legend
And anyway his tongue is not by any means clean
after all the faces and feces he has licked
And the dog can't get one of these holy biscuits
no such luck for the soulless mutt
who now slinks away
like a starving heathen
on the far far outskirts
of the Roman Empire

May 9

Sanremo early morning . . . a dump truck called "Avantgarde" (in big letters on its side) passes by . . . (I wouldn't go to Sanremo if I were you).

Paris, Mai 10—Hotel Récamier

Room 30 (sixth floor). One *must* stay in this room and no other, in what must be the quietest corner in Paris, a tiny pocket enclosed by the Church of St.-Sulpice, its monstrous tower filling the sky on the far side of the little courtyard with a dozen palm trees below, looking out at an angle at the Place St.-Sulpice and its plashing fountain (illuminated at night, as are the church towers), the sound of which whispers all day & night, filling the court at night when there is no traffic noise. On the far side of the Place, the five- and six-story buildings with their mansard roofs and running balconies, in the gray light of the morning, as I sit writing this, the French windows open above the trees, sun coming around the corner, 8:30 a.m. . . . But. . . . The people who run this hotel *sont vraiment malins*— They shunted me into a hole-in-the-wall room the second day & claimed the price had changed (to a higher rate than they had quoted me in their written reservation) due to the change in season, etc. . . . I told them I was leaving after two days & now they want me to pay for the whole five days since they claim they can't rent the rooms on short notice. . . . *Sont malhonnêtes et cons.* . . .

May 12

The chestnuts are in bloom everywhere, their pink blossoms hanging heavy as fruit on the trees. In the little park by the Église St.-Germain the pigeons poop on Picasso's head of Apollinaire— In St.-Germain, now there's a woman's chic shoe-store called François Villon.

Paris is now a totally decadent museum of the past. They're trying to live in it, but they are totally bored. *Ils s'ennuient.* . . . Everyone, old & young, looks bored. There's an issue of *Le Monde* devoted to a retrospective of '68, and the lead article reprinted from 15 Mars '68 by one Pierre Viansson-Ponté has a headline: "*Quand la France s'ennuie.*" The last sentence: "Un pays peut aussi périr d'ennui" (a country can also die of boredom). . . . It's taken them twenty years to die, and they're not quite dead yet. General de Gaulle lives on in the hearts & minds of his countrymen. '68 never happened.

VOYAGE AU BUT

July 1999

N Luglio 7, Firenze
ow again in Tony and Silvia Bertoli's house in the hills above Scandicci. What peace! What a refuge! Hot summer. 90°—but cooler up here than on the cobblestones of Firenze.

AT THE NORA RUINS

Luglio 10, Trip to Nora, Cagliari

Heartless the houses by the cobalt sea—heart-broken their ruins, their pulverized villas where the Phoenicians once lived & loved—then ravaged by pirates plundering the coast from their barquentines. Thermal bathhouses, elegant dressing rooms with mosaic floors razed by fire & storm, and then rebuilt by decadent Romans centuries later. They too now vanished, all their bones & buildings, towers and turrets toppled, dust to dust, sundered under! Heartless their crumbled broken stones, humbled battlements thrown down. Valiant warriors stumbled into oblivion, where the sea still runs & raves, cobalt brilliant blue lapped up caves upon these windy shores forever and forever. Heartless the sea's eternal lapping, its blind hungering, its white lips frothing, lapping the broken shore. (Eating time!) Heartless the washing away of sea slugs and centipedes— Senators slaves and mistresses— The gods themselves helpless against the running sea (of time). Pumice statues of victors, marble friezes eaten away, brilliant blue of eternity. . . . While in the far horizon of my mind the old heroic figures gesturing and calling out to us (standing here with guidebooks) our own eternal destinies. . . .

July 11

At the ruins at Nora I am climbing to the Roman tower, the lighthouse on its little spit of land by the ruined thermal baths and the (perhaps) Temple of Astarte (no real proof she ever had a temple here)—I'm climbing up the hill in the burning late afternoon, in which a huge fireball hangs in the sky. The temperature must be 90°. I've got sunglasses and a panama hat, but the sun beats through, glares through. I'm walking up the rough scrabble, through the underbrush, up the faint twisty path, circling up to the tower. All the others in the party below and off in the distance, inspecting the ruins of the thermal baths. . . . Then I'm on a little pair of stone stairs with iron rusted railing. . . . I see sun spots, as the stairs turn directly into the glaring sun. And now I reach the top, where an iron door to the flat top of the tower is locked & barred. . . . I sit on the highest step, but there is no shade, no refuge from the burning sun. . . . I rise to the railing and wave my white panama at the distant people, friends and poets, Italians & Americans. I wave & wave, but there is no sign that anyone sees me. (No, said someone later, we didn't see you.) What does it mean, then, if we climb the heights and no one observes it? What does it mean when a song is sung but nobody there to hear it, a poem spoken and no one to hear it, a painting done but no one to see it, truth spoken but no one to apprehend it—and after we are all gone, the sea will continue its roaring? A Beethoven symphony crashing on the shore in a storm and no one to hear the end of time. . . . Plato said the ideals and concepts such as Truth or Beauty still exist even if no one is there to think them; still the silence of a Chinese vase or an Egyptian frieze exists, their figures still alive in the void.

Venezia, Luglio 15

Hotel Sofitel, courtesy of the manager Claudio Nobbio (friend of Antonio Bertoli) who is going to produce my ouroboros designs on glass plates at Murano. He is also going to use a watercolor of mine on the cover of the hotel menu (two people—man & woman—in the bottom of a gondola). Room 529 (top floor) is splendid, with French doors onto balcony overlooking the rooftops of Venice—the most splendid room I've ever stayed in—positively palatial.

We went to Murano by hotel boat & saw Pino Signoretto, the greatest glass maestro, at work in his *bottega*. He's going to make my plates. I chose four final designs from the original eleven I sent them last year.

Paris, July 18

Arrivé . . . Gare de Lyon plein soleil— Dix heures du matin, after overnight couchette— The garçon comes and I order a coffee with orange juice and a piece of bread. Two French women arrive at the next table, mother & daughter, with the husband carrying a baby dressed in frills. It's Sunday and they're on an outing. The baby sets up a howl—they all start cooing him and putting bottles in his mouth. The little fucker, he's going to take over and leave us all behind, croaking in the grave while he rides down the Champs Élysées like de Gaulle at the Liberation. And why not? The bell in the clock tower tolls eleven a.m. Full sun. . . .

Remembering I was in Paris when Robert Kennedy was shot[43]—Europeans cannot realize what the Kennedy assassinations mean to Americans, especially to my generation, the "Greatest Generation" which came of age at the very beginning of World War II and was swept along by it, into a whole new world full of hope. But then with the assassinations, all that was gone, all foundered, Camelot lost!

The sky in the west of Paris, the sky over the Normandy beaches, the sky over all America, is dark.

Juillet 20

Alors, je suis au "Café-Tabac" au coin de la Rue des Beaux Arts et le quai sur la Seine. . . . J'ai passé toute la journée en flânant—rive droite et rive gauche. Ce soir je vais avec George Whitman au cinéma Salle 3, Rue Gît-le-Coeur. . . . L'ancien hôtel des Beats dans cette ruelle (The "Beat Hotel") s'est transformé en une chic auberge touristique. Il y a des photos des Beats qui avaient habité ces lieux il y a trente-cinq ans. . . . Mais toujours une vieille *tricoteuse* à la réception, peut-être la fille de la madame qui a surveillé les Beats. . . .[44]

July 20

Along the quay in old Paris a few spent leaves flutter along the pale sidewalk where a pale dog leads his pale master on a string by the Rue de Nevers. A new spring is far away from ever happening this hot July in a Paris very *jadis* where our life on earth reveals itself at last to the aged such as me.

July 22—Musée Rodin, Rue de Grenelle, 77 (many visits here over the years)

Interesting contrast between Rodin's *La Vague* and Camille Claudel's *La Vague* (*The Wave*). His in white marble is two prone couples wound around each other, as if saving each other from drowning. Hers has three dark *standing* female figures in bronze dwarfed by a huge green wave (*terre verte*), that rises above them, about to engulf them completely. They are half-crouching. The huge green wave has several (male?) heads out its crest. It's like a fertility symbol. And the three figures are holding hands in a semicircle, as if to keep together before the onslaught of the towering (male?) wave. Also an extraordinary *Le Christ et la Madeleine* en plâtre (1898):

*　　*　　*　　*　　*

"J'ai fait mon Bac
dans la Rue du Bac"

Mais aujourd'hui la Rue du Bac est changée. Boutiques chics, et messieurs qui étaient sur les barricades en 1968 maintenant bouffent bien dans les restaurants de haute cuisine en lisant *Le Monde*, suivi d'un petit café noir et de la liqueur . . . dans leur "Belle Époque" Moderne. . . .[45]

Juillet 23

Take the TGV Paris–Avignon aujourd'hui à 12:10— Arrivant à Avignon 15:32. . . .
The great old Gare de Lyon with its huge iron shed over the tracks, as in the
impressionist pictures—everything the same except the smoke from the old coal-
burning locomotives—and the people of course different—the youth in running
clothes à la American, the adults turned into all kinds of international yuppies with
briefcases and portable computers and short haircuts, business suits—American
corporate mono-culture sweeping the world.

When I got off the train, my panama hat blew off immediately and rolled along
the track & was retrieved by a trainman— It's the mistral wind that blew it off.

Stayed with Wolfgang Zuchermann at his Shakespeare Bookshop, 155 Rue Car-
reterie— Rooftop room on terrace of his apartment— Lovely little place, all tiles
and sunshine, and Wolfgang Zuchermann a lovely man (German-American).

L'Utopia Cinema & Petit Café—reminded me of the cafés in Amsterdam, a big
place like the Melkweg, the place full of lively people. The whole town is like a
festival tonight (Friday)— The Festival of Avignon is going on, but Wolfgang says
it's like this most of the time, even in the non-tourist seasons.

Flash of the end of a dream I had last night: a car without a driver is rolling very
slowly down a gentle hill, being stopped temporarily now and then by various
kinds of obstructions, but rolling on very slowly until it turns into a horse when
turning a corner and then gets up and canters off.

July 24

Train from Avignon to Valence to Grenoble, and between Grenoble and Chambéry
the most fantastic mountains & a peak with an animal head as in the Magritte
painting— The most beautiful flatlands between the mountains—the *Grande
Ligne* train cruising thru the wide valleys. Rows of tall thin poplars and lush fields
stretching away, the steepest hillsides planted with vines, high up in neat rows. Je
vois tout. I'm still a roving eye in the landscape . . . always the long-distance swim-
mer, even in the mountains. . . . Le train arrive— Voilà Chambéry. Je descend. Il y
a aussi un chien sur le train— Il descend. . . . Lui et moi. . . . Allons-y. . . .[46]

Au café. . . . Il faut serrer la main. C'est un festival de serrature. Tout ce qu'il faut est de serrer la main de tout le monde. Serrez la main et tout va bien. C'est la fin du monde, le paradis, l'éblouissement final, l'épiphanie, le but de toute la vie, serrer, serrer la main. . . . l'apocalypse bourgeoise . . . le coeur de la France. . . .[47]

Le Couple

Le couple à côté est très silencieux, ce jeune couple qui a rien à dire l'un à l'autre. Ils ne se regardent pas. Ils regardent d'autre part. Ils ne sont pas là pour eux-mêmes. Ils ont rien à dire. Elle est belle mais vide. Et le gars, il s'ennuie comme elle. Qu'est-ce qu'on fait ces deux jeunes mariés? Mais non—je me suis trompé. Ils s'aiment. Ils disent rien parce qu'ils n'ont besoin de parler. Maintenant ils se regardent aux yeux. Ils sourient, un peux tristement. Mais ils sourient. Tout va bien. La crépuscule descend. Ils se regardent très profondément, très sérieusement. C'est la vie. Ils chuchotent. Ils sont ensemble pour toujours peut-être. On ne sait pas.[48]

VI. 2000-2010

ne ... ...

72 ... nella primavere

nza dubbio

...d shipped art art the age

...o from Marseilles 18

...o Little Italy + like in "

...orther" Two perhaps becau

...s small-time Mafiosetto

...ogy favors for the local pad

...a Un tipo bravo se

dubbio ma forse un

...n Pero questa

GREECE—ITALY

March 2001

March 10—Athenian Inn, Athens

T he deepest thing about foreign travel is the time one awaits the arrival of
an unknown emissary who is to be your guide, and there is a night in
between in a strange hotel, and you go out to the nearby grand café or restaurant
and take two hours over two glasses of wine, watching people coming and going,
congenial couples dining, young studs with black hair with shining girlfriends with
still longer hair, groups of men smoking and talking tersely or laughing with or at
each other, solid *borghesi* discussing what to do, white-coated waiters hurrying about,
a whole unknown world full of itself under the evening lights, and you are yourself
or nobody, immobilized, observing all, taking in everything, traveler at the far end
of creation, to what end, here, now, on this far shore in a white city. . . .

Athens, a long city stretched out on its narrow coastal plain, *fourmillant* city,
like a huge unrolled beehive, brilliant white in the late day sun, as the plane
approaches over scattered diamond islands, an archipelago of dazzling rugged land-
and-sea, and the city pulsing with the sea light, as we settle down into it, visitors
from some other planet, what here, what now, why here, why now, what are we
doing here, what everybody, what all, why us, why me, here descending with beret
and book-bag and old blue eyes, into the sea-blue world. . . .

Here now in a café on Kolonaki Square, with its huge terrace of tables with
white tablecloths and the lights bright in their shaded crystal lamps, life pulsing

under them, worry beads in Greek men's hands, twirling as they talk, oblivious of visitors, wrapt in their own deep affairs of life, locals and cronies at this table every night or week, the waiter joining in now and then; couples come and go, sit and drink and hold each other vaguely, looking off, and the whole caravanserai rocking on into the night, at home with oblivion, in time and space, lost and found men and women. . . .

And I looking for the face of Odysseus among them, the heroic lost in backwaters, swart wanderer returned at last, stranger among strangers, unrecognized in the crowd, the sea-light still in his eyes, or in her eyes, Penelope among the suitors at a back table. . . . The hurrying waiter approaches, check in hand, so much time passed over two drinks, another twitch of the worry beads, another twirl of time, turn of the screw, silent inscrutable watch-works of eternity, tick, tick, tick, the night turns like an hourglass filled with our pouring sand. . . .

How small the Greeks are, men & women! It must have been the same in 1500 BC. How tall were Telemachus, Odysseus, Helen, Athena? Even the gods, how tall were they back then, not big enough to play basketball today, or be models on fashion runways. . . . How tall their tall ships, their Trojan horses? At the next table, two *borghese* ladies are discussing their husbands? Odysseatic infidelities!

Blue-eyed Odysseus sails on—

March 14—Athens

In the shadow of the Hilton I sat down and would have wept, if it hadn't been for the satiric aspects of the situation in the Italian restaurant (where no one spoke Italian) almost in the shadow of the Parthenon—And the Hilton shadow nearer & darker— *Sic transit gloria mundi!* And someday they will find the ruins of the Hilton (Mussolini modern) and wonder what soulless civilization built this *monumento all'americano!*

March 21—At Delphi

At the Fountain of Castalia on the slopes of Mount Parnassus a strange lightness, a sense of dizziness, a lightheadedness, a feeling of fainting, a disorientation, a psychedelic high, almost as if the earth stopped running for an instant, time stopped for an instant, and a trembling of light, as if the Oracle were at hand, about to speak. . . .

I was invited by UNESCO to read a poem to the Oracle of Delphi, in an international day of poetry to which two poets from each nation were invited to read one poem. I came and read this new poem (much influenced by the Greek poet C. P. Cavafy). The poem ended like this, and I received no response from the ever-taciturn Oracle:

> O long-silent Sybil,
> you of the winged dreams,
> Speak out from your temple of light
> as the serious constellations
> with Greek names
> still stare down on us
> as a lighthouse moves its megaphone
> over the sea
> Speak out and shine upon us
> the sea-light of Greece
> the diamond light of Greece
>
>
> Far-seeing Sybil, forever hidden,
> Come out of your cave at last
> And speak to us in the poet's voice
> the voice of the fourth person singular
> the voice of the inscrutable future
> the voice of the people mixed
> with a wild soft laughter—
> And give us new dreams to dream,
> Give us new myths to live by!

Back in Athens, I found a reading had been set up for me, with several translators on stage with me, to read my poems in Greek after I spoke them. It was a grand hall, and it seemed in my self-centered view that the whole literary community of Athens was there. Halfway through my reading, I spotted my old friend Andrei Voznesensky, in the front row, and I of course asked him to join me on stage. Now whenever we had read together before, we had both read our poems centered on Francisco Goya. We did just that now, and afterward in a café he told me he had come to Athens for one reason, and that was to send a thousand U.S. dollars to a certain person in the U.S., but that no bank in Athens would send it for him because he didn't have an account. His voice was weak, and I thought to myself that I would never see him again. . . . I will take his thousand dollars in cash back to the States, and send a check to person who shall remain a mystery. . . .

Verona, March 24, at My Birthday Party

Local Fluxist[49] did a sort of Happening with sign he painted POETRY IS MAMMY (no kidding) & he wrapped a young woman in a white paper bandage head to foot. And that was it. Another number he did entitled "Love": he hit a sparkler and gave cries like making love with increasing intensity until sparkler suddenly burned out.

My eighty-second in an elegant old 15th-century mansion: a hundred elegant people, looking like the richest in town, all celebrating my birthday. Huge cake, fantastic food (went on for hours). . . .

Marzo 29—Lago di Garda (Salò)

In the high-ceilinged elegant turn-of-the-century dining room with the potted palms and the waiters in tuxedos, six Germans come in, three men and three women, in suits & ties except one couple who look like they're the hangers-on to the big daddy in the business suit, and they stand studying the big menus handed to them by the not-too-obsequious waiters, while in the meantime at the next table a single Italian (businessman?) is talking on his cellphone (but he has it lying on the table so he can eat and talk and gesticulate at the same time). At first I think he's talking to someone hidden behind the pillar but then I see there's no one there and he's making all kinds of Italian gestures and laughing and so on, and this goes on for a quarter of an hour until he finally cuts off and sits there spooning his *minestra* while all the while the Germans are considering what to order and finally doing it, and I'm Goethe (the Young Werther) voyaging in Italy and hating his tourist countrymen, or perhaps I am Günter Grass listening to the faint sound of a new Tin Drum. . . .

They are taking pictures of each other now, a little woman with her hair in a bun darts up with the little camera and snaps them around the table, then another does the same. And I am D. H. Lawrence on a walking trip through the Tyrol with Frieda who just escaped her husband in coal-country England, and everyone is speaking Deutsch. There is a ringing in the air. The crystal chandelier sways. Outside it starts to rain. It sweeps the lake. Lake Garda and the town of Salò turn totally gray in the rain, like a large gray rug. D'Annunzio shivers and reaches for one of his many women. Perhaps it was a day like this when the short-lived Republic of Salò collapsed forever, along with *Il Duce*.[50]

OAXACA
February 2004

February 17

Hotel Monte Albán, en frente de la Catedral al lado del Zócalo. A big second-floor room with French doors opening on the plaza, high ceilings with *vigas*, tile floor, and a tiny *baño*—wonderful place, huge interior patio, with arches around the tile dance floor big enough for nightly *folklórico* dancing and singing. . . . In the morning of February 17th it's windy and cloudy, the huge trees with swaying branches and the plaza quiet, and downstairs they're serving breakfast in the patio at small square tables with pale green & white tablecloths, and a hush in the air, a subdued morning peace, with only the waiter rushing about, and music distantly in some room. . . .

Yesterday was a different story.

HIGH NOON, OAXACA

A las cuatro y a las cinco de la mañana
> They are getting up and into the backs of old trucks
> And heading into the city of Oaxaca
> From all over the state of Oaxaca
> They are standing up in the back of the trucks
> Packed in perhaps twenty men and women
> Standing up in the jolting trucks

A las siete de la mañana

    They are all on the back roads heading for the city of Oaxaca

    From all over the state of Oaxaca

    They are silent as the trucks jolt along

    Standing erect in the trucks with the high wooden sides

    The men in their white stiff straw hats curled up at the edges

    The men in the clothes they wear on Sundays or *días de fiesta*

    The same clothes they wear on workdays

    Only the women are dressed up

    Women in their best colorful costumes

    In their beautiful colored dresses

    red or ochre like the earth

    For they are of the earth they are made of earth

    They are the mothers of the small brown people

    the women of the brown people packed in the trucks

    The *abuelas y abuelitas*

    Hermanas y hijas y tías

    They are the mothers and sisters and aunts and daughters

    Of the short brown *obreros* and *campesinos*

    Standing in the jolting trucks in the back roads

    All over the State of Oaxaca

A las nueve de la mañana

    They are on the first paved roads leading into the city of Oaxaca

    Then they are on the two-lane highways to the city of Oaxaca

    Standing silent in the open trucks

    In their work trucks and in beatup buses

    Converging on the city of Oaxaca from all over the state of Oaxaca

    With its sixty percent unemployment

    They are the working men and women of the *Unidad Popular*

    And there are banners on the sides of some trucks and buses

    Proclaiming their solidarity and their hard resolve

    To change their world for the better

    To change their lives for the better

    The lives of the *pobres* everywhere

    Their deep resolve to liberate themselves

From centuries of stoop work for others
For the owners of everything
The *campos* and *haciendas*
The mills and *molinos*
The poor of the world in the liberation movements
In all the Third World countries of the world
A las diez de la mañana
They are entering the outskirts of the city
They are passing through the barrios
The broken-down barrios on the outskirts of the city
On the *periferia* of the city of Oaxaca
The undersides of the city that the *turistas* never see
The junked-up outskirts of the machine shops and garages
And tin-roofed factories and truck repair shops
And Pemco filling stations
They are the people of the *Unidad Popular*
Heading for the center of the city of Oaxaca
winding through all the side streets into the *centro*
A las once de la mañana
They are all pouring into the Avenida de la Independencia
They have parked their trucks in the side streets and piled out
Into the Avenida de la Independencia
And there they come
A las once de la mañana
Here they come with a big brass band up front
With tubas and trumpets and drums
At the head or the forming columns of men and women
Pouring in from the side streets
Into the Avenida de la Independencia in the center of Oaxaca
And first come all the women in straight lines in the street
Striding or limping with solemn calm faces open faces
Looking with their dark brown eyes
At the ornate entrances and small elegant hotels
And seeing the well-dressed people watching
From the sidewalks and doorways and windows

And all walking slowly and silent in their red and ochre costumes

The women of all ages so dignified

Walking in front of their men their *campesinos*

Who now also come totally silent walking quiet

In long lines in their beatup white hats

And they too are proud of their stirring solidarity

With the band up front blasting out their surging spirit

A las once de la mañana

They are coming and coming

Thousands and thousands of them

pouring into the Avenida de la Independencia

From all the side streets and far flung farms and *haciendas*

the *compañeras* and *compañeros*

Coming together here in the *Unidad Popular*

And the men with their stolid faces

Looking out silent with their black brown eyes

Guarded and defiant in their silences

As they come marching six abreast

In endless lines of *campesinos* and their sisters and mothers

A las once de la mañana

They are pouring into the huge plaza of the Zócalo

At the center of the city of Oaxaca

And they have no weapons at all

No guns or knives or machetes

They have left them all behind in their huts and *palapas*

They have left their machetes stuck in the brown earth of their *campos*

A las once de la mañana

They will know where to find their machetes if need be

Another time a later time

If they have not changed anything at a later time

When perhaps nothing has changed in their eternal slavery

And the Zócalo and the plaza in front of the Cathedral

Is filling up with the thousands and thousands

And in front of the Cathedral there are loudspeakers set up

And the speeches are beginning

The *gritos* of the leaders

The cries of the labor leaders

And the working people of the whole state of Oaxaca

Are still packing into the plaza

And a las doce de la mañana

The bells of the Cathedral that have been silent all the time

As the silent workers poured into the plaza

The cathedral bells now ring out

Echoing across the plaza

Across the Zócalo

And through the city of Oaxaca

And a las doce de la mañana

The speeches of the peasant leaders of the people

Are raising their rough voices over the loudspeakers

And the air vibrates with their hoarse cries

While in the inner patio of the Hotel Monte Albán

The real leaders of this day of solidarity

The ones behind it all

The Union leaders

The *políticos*

Are speaking in good Spanish to the press

And to the television cameras trained on them

In a corner of the huge hotel patio these real leaders

Of this great *manifestación*

In immaculate white shirts

Are speaking straight into the television cameras

These leaders with education and white shirts

Are telling the press of Oaxaca and of all Mexico

Exactly what their *movimiento* is all about

While outside in the plaza the indigenous speakers

Are still shouting over the speakers to the thousands and thousands

Their somehow innocent tough voices

Echoing against the cathedral walls

And they are the real *compañeros* of Flores Magón and of Zapata

The descendants of Magón and Zapata crying out
For more than the crust of their daily bread
While the "insiders" inside the hotel
The ones with their own agendas
Are telling the world *que pasa*
In their confrontation with the owners of everything
They are moving the *movimiento* where they want it to move
And they know *how promises made in the plazas*
May be betrayed in the back country

Al mediodía de Oaxaca
Al mediodía de su vida
Al mediodía of the people of Oaxaca
At high noon in the life of the *pobres* of Oaxaca
In the heart of their blood and passion.

February 20

Went to the café where Malcolm Lowry went—the Café Farola—with João Almino, whom we knew in San Francisco when he was Brazilian consul; also a novelist, he is here as part of the Coloquio del Arte de la Imaginación being staged by the Instituto Oaxaqueño de las Culturas. We were brought to this café by Carlos Martínez Rentería, the editor of *Generación* in Mexico DF, who is going to present here the brand-new translation of my 1970s travel journal *The Mexican Night*—*La Noche Mexicana*. He's a heavy drinker of mescal, and João says that you should always order *white* mescal—*mescal blanco* or *mescal minero*—because you can see that it's pure. Also, if the liquor has darkened somewhat, that's a sign that it has been allowed to age at least a couple of years. I was reminded that last year here Jonathan Barbieri (the American painter married to a Zapoteca) took me to a café called the Place Where You Lose Your Soul—devoted solely to mescal—a shack in a dirt-poor barrio—with sod floor and tin roof. And at four or five in the afternoon, there were three or four old guys sitting around a beatup wooden table, all of them swaying slightly and clutching little mescal glasses, half asleep or half conscious or stoned out, the setting sun—*el sol poniente*—glinting off their glasses. . . . Jonathan Barbieri published a book of his paintings of this café. . . .

SHOE FANTASY

We are in one of the millions of *zapaterías* in Mexico, with windows full of thousands of *zapatas*—shoes, shoes, what is this thing with shoes in Mexico. . . . We are inside looking at hordes of them in glass cases. In comes a young couple with a six-month-old chubby baby—very chubby, with a round face, framed by a baseball cap—a very smiling happy boy baby. They tour around, looking at the shoes, looking for baby shoes. There's herds of baby shoes. And grown-up shoes, men and women's shoes of all styles. Will the baby grow up to fill these shoes? It's a large order—to fill the shoes he's to inherit. Will he be able to fill his father's shoes? Will he be a Zapata wearing Zapata's zapatas? Or another functionary or cabdriver—a *taxista* ferrying tourists about—or a *mesero*, a waiter in an elegant or broken-down café, or the president of Mexico?

I find a note at the hotel from "Ulíses" who wants to talk to me "about Mescalaría" and "hoops" to see me later. This is extraordinary, that this great voyager in ancient times came all the way to the New World to see me and talk about "the history & kinds of mescal." . . .

February 22

We visit Cuilapan, a country town twenty miles from Oaxaca. Outdoor restaurant under *palapas*, with hammocks to stretch out in after lunch.

Last night, as we walked up to the entrance of the Instituto Oaxaqueño de las Culturas, in the Santo Domingo temple, there was a banner: Bienvenido, Lawrence! And a mime troupe, or experimental theater group, was performing my *Routine*[51] of the two figures with their heads wrapped in the same long bandage. (This piece has never been produced in the U.S., so far as I know.) I got into the act by acting as if I were blind and stumbling in between the two figures & bringing them together. Since they were blindfolded by the winding cloth, they could not see who I was. But then I embraced them at once & said "Soy Ferlinghetti"— And everybody clapped, etc. . . .

February 28—Mexico DF

In the Diego Rivera Mural Museum the lights are out for a lecture projected onto the mural entitled *A Sunday in the Alameda*. And the guide voice is pointing out that Rivera included (among dozens & dozens of historical figures and ordinary people) an urchin who was lifting a wallet out of the back pocket of a passing gent—

And while the guide is speaking a kid is stealing a wallet from one of the watchers. . . .

WAITING FOR THE VIRGIN

This morning a large, restless German Shepherd runs across the roof of the grand old temple of San Hipólito & San Judas, which was once the chapel for the first madhouse in America. And inside the huge church we see the praying masses praising the Virgin—for it's the Day of the Virgin of Guadalupe. And Handel's *Messiah* fills the church at noonday like a great song-cloud, a great sound-cloud made of light—and it falls on a thousand people's praying ears—and the music swells up in them. And then they are all standing again. And here comes an old woman carrying her mutt in her arms to be blessed— And they are all singing the "Guadalupana" (many out of tune but joyous and full of élan)— And then the blessed dog is carried out into the sunlight which also falls on the faces of all the small plaster statues of all the saints for sale outside, but especially on the larger-than-life statue of the Archangel Michael conquering the devil (his foot on his neck)—and also on the tiny statue of Saint Michael with his foot on the head of a black child. While the dog on the roof is still running around barking at the sky as if expecting it to fall, or as if expecting the arrival by parachute of the Virgin of Guadalupe herself shining through the clouds in gold sunlight as she floats down, arms outstretched to the people below, the *monjas* and *meseros*, the *campesinos* and *obreros*, *criadas* and *peones*, the *taxistas* and *camioneros*, the *bomberos* and *policías*, *rateros* and *putas*, *amas de casa* and *doñas de categoría*, *pandilleros* and *carnales*, *burócratas* and *güeyes*, *ambulantes* and *albañiles*, *abuelitos* and *abuelitas*, *tíos* and *tías*, *los amantes y las amantes*, *novios* and *novias*, *niños* and *niños* and *niños*, *borrachos* and *locos* and *dos gringos*.

Monte Alban
23 Feb '04

P June 22
assed by the Bauhaus Museum and saw enshrined there the birthplace of soulless architecture. . . . And then the new Jewish historical museum, built by same architect who won one competition for the World Trade Center memorial in Manhattan. Designed to give you a feeling of *disorientation, it does.* Like a displaced Jew, you wander down twisting corridors with red sign reading Exit, leading to *cul-de-sacs* or circular rooms.

There is an installation called Falling Leaves, which consists of heavy half-inch thick iron disks, each the size and shape of a human head, with holes for eyes, ears, and mouth, but perfectly flat. About three layers of these are laid haphazard on top of each other on a cement floor of a very small rectangular room, and people are invited to walk over them. When I do, the heavy flat plates grind against each other with an iron thudding noise, as of feet in heavy storm boots.

Outside a large crow or raven, hidden somewhere in the high trees, cranks out his hoarse *Nevermore!*

———

411

In August Street where the galleries are scattered, we go into the Eigen Gallery to see the painting of Martin Eder. This exhibition is called his Afterlife, and the brochure says, "Drawn into the gallery space by music composed by the artist himself, we enter a completely different world." But the place was silent as a morgue, like most all art galleries, and they said they weren't playing the music because the birds outside in the trees were setting up such a racket.

And we passed on in the Auguststrasse, past a fat dog drinking beer out of a saucer in a café doorway. And farther on there were police guarding the door to a Jewish museum, and then one gallery recommended to us turned out to have totally blank walls in the ultimate postmodern statement.

And we sat down at an inside table in a big empty café and ordered white wine and beer and thought of our friends back home and thought how many roads must a man walk down and why are we on earth?

Meanwhile the trees outside were blowing in the wind sweeping in over the flatland from the North Sea. And there was no answer in it.

June 23

Feeling like one of the angels in Wim Wenders's *Wings of Desire*, I'm sitting under the great dome in the Potsdamer Platz, having a Pilsner and watching the crowds pass by. I'm astounded by the sameness of all the faces, not all German, as if they were all poured from the same mold, the same template.

And I am as withdrawn as an angel observing life on earth, and how is it that I was so involved in it back then, good god, I am seeing myself walking by in another country, in another century, with the same expression of desires, never dreaming I might still take wing and fulfill them. . . .

RUNNING THOUGHTS / DADAPOLIS

October 2005

C
October 3—Milano

oming from Malpensa airport into the center of Milano, passed the statue of Verdi standing up straight in a traffic circle. A thin figure against it all. . . .

Met by Luigi Majno (della Galleria M'arte), who is publishing a fine letterpress edition of the first three cantos of my *Americus*, along with his assistant Adriana. He published Beckett, title *Still Still*. His house—a duplex apartment filled with fine editions, half of which are on the art of printing, etching, engraving, etc. Adriana calls him "rich"; he says "Basta, Adriana!"

Verona, October 5

Francesco Conz's right-hand man is Agostino, and we go out to buy art supplies for the art I am supposed to do for Conz, and find the art store closed with a small sign pasted on the door: Torno in 5 minuti. Agostino is standing in front of it when a guy comes up and wants to go in. Agostino says it's closed, but the guy insists, pushing him to the side. Now he sees the little sign and starts hollering at Agostino, and Agostino says it's not his fault the guy didn't see the sign, and the guy starts cussing out Agostino in Veronese dialect, and both their voices start rising, and the guy runs down the street yelling, "Vaffanculo!" and "Coglione!"

Francesco Conz in Verona has been a mover and shaker of the Fluxus movement in Europe, a spinoff of the Dadaists and surrealists, and he proclaimed me to be a true Fluxist and gave me more than one show in Italy. At one event in Brescia (my father's birthplace), I painted a grand piano on stage with anarchist slogans, while the piano let forth groans of protest. At an event in Verona, I exhibited a six-foot painting of an American football player to which I had attached a baseball bat as his penis. (It could move up and down.) The exhibition was actually in Juliet's house, and the baseball man stood near the balcony where she had been wooed by Romeo. (It was sold immediately.)

Biella, October 9

Northeast of Torino mountains rising up. At the Villa Cernigliaro, read my Italian poems plus "History of the Airplane" and "Cries of Animals Dying."

Il mercato the first Sunday of every October here in the full country up against small mountains (like the Prealpi) where the farmers come with their cows, many herds of them, big heavy beasts full of milk, in a huge pasture, with a flock of long-haired white goats beyond. And beside the pasture (all right next to the gates of the grand Villa Cernigliaro) is a *mercato* of stands selling wool goods (center of the fabric culture, now being wiped out by Third World competition—China, Bolivia, etc.), and stands with pots, pans, ironware, shoes, local goods of all kinds, but even here some foreign manufactured clothing has crept in—including Army surplus, with U.S. Army patches on them. I buy a pair of camouflage Army pants (preparing for the next war). And the sellers all looking like 19th-century peasants, one with a small accordion who is prevailed upon to play & sing old melodies, country songs, it's like a country fair a hundred years ago. And now in the late afternoon, the shepherds begin to drive their herds off the meadow and into the dirt road that winds past the *mercato*, one by one, one herd after the other, they file into the street, and each herd has a different bell on each cow, the first herd coming past has huge bells the size of pumpkins tied under the neck of each beast, and the bells have a deep hollow musical sound as the beast lurches forward, and a shepherd looking like Quasimodo or Jean Valjean leading his cows with a rough cane in great carbuncled hands, and now here comes another herd with a small different-sounding bell, still deep-throated, and then another herd with still smaller and lighter bells, each distinct from the others, so that if a cow is lost, everyone knows instantly whose herd it is from. And the whole scene fading into the dusk of this old country—Sunday, the sound of all the bells with their varied voices echoing down the far road, the sound of those bells timeless, inexpressible.

Arrested in Brescia, October 12

Francesco Conz has a real eye for publicity, so that when I went to Brescia to find the actual house where my father was born, Conz sent a cameraman with me. Arrived at the address in a rundown neighborhood, I knocked and knocked on the doors of the small apartment building that now stood there, and got no response whatever. Finally, a short man in baggy pants, carrying a radiator of some sort, opened a door and started hollering at us in the local dialect, "*Artisti parassiti! Artisti parassiti!*" and told us to get the hell outta there. We complied, but on the way back to our van a police car zoomed up and had us against a wall while they checked our papers. It was obvious that these local cops didn't know what to do with us, as they telephoned someone to find out. My cameraman meanwhile was filming the whole scene, with me against the wall, and he immediately sent off his footage to all the major dailies. Sure enough, out came the headlines, "Italian-American Poet Arrested in Search of His Father," etc., in *Corriere della Sera* and *Il Manifesto* among others.

RUNNING THOUGHTS

1. Still Thinking It Over with Beckett

Even here middle of the night Single bed in huge room In this ancient villa A single bed Narrow as a grave Parquet floors Very high ceiling High French windows Mountains in the distance Huge chandelier Old-fashioned lamps Vast space of bedroom Filled with silence Two in the morning Not a sound anywhere in the night The night filled with silence Nothing but silence Three mirrors at a vanity console reflect me In bed writing Three me's Three bald-headed guys looking at me Notebook in hand Eyeglasses Pen Me propped on pillow Faint light from red-shaded antique lamp Beckett Still Still Beckett After all these years Even here Long from him and Dublin Paris His voice comes thru His still voice His long face Mute eyes Mute voice . . . Taciturn Death comes on. Take your turn Turn and turn "Turning and thinking In the widening gyre the falcon cannot see the falconer The center cannot hold Mere anarchy is loosed" Upon the night Death and its phantom phantombs Skeletons dancing Turn and turn Noiseless Soundless in night Because I do not hope to turn Taciturn with Beckett The longer he lived the less he spoke

Murphy and Malloy and Malone Dies and even after death he spoke underground His voice going on In his mind still alive in dead body Beckett still On and on Because I do not hope to turn Because I do not hope to turn again Over and over. On and on. In night The blind night Only chaos in the darkness What now Where now Old fool Beware of cats crossing road The night is made of black cats Crossing where now what now me hearties Who knows Don't worry Time will tell Time is hell Tick tock Tic Tic In the tick of it Tic Tic In the thicket with Beckett Why worry All will tell Why worry Because.

2.

Me Worry? Why? Wha? "Where is there an end of it The voiceless wailing" Make friends with night Get to know night Get to know cats of night Howling Yowling Bodyless Far off someplace No end of it Only the slow drip slow tick of time the here and now of time tick tick No end Only the true mutation of energy in things Matter cannot be destroyed Only altered Turned to some other form Sed some mad scientists Every life a wife Every wife a life of her own turning and turning toward you Away from you Don't let them turn away Turn them only toward you All the lads and lasses of the wrong turning Won't they all end burning in bright fire St. Francis fire St. Elmo's fire Unbelievers draw away It's not for them the Straight road to the Angelus where sounds the everlasting promise premise Saying nothing Let the Police Come and find nothing Except Beckett He here still speaking With Malone Baloney Maybe I'll rest with him why not why not him still alive and warm Warmth and life And knows more of everything Having explored closer to death hisself mother me When shall we see dear mother moither again amoithering in her cave grave full of echo Still speaking that same voice goes on and on Different tangles saying it But all the same the voiceless wailing Where now again Shall we not just lie down here and let the waves roll over us head to toe Roll till the boys cum marching home And maybe home never existed and the teeth mother naked at last to tale him her in A fine Kettle of fish fry Slithering across the shallows at sundown by the riverrun sundown and the hushed voices lost in the late dusk by River Liffey Or River Iffy an iffy proposition for sure at best for if you dive in it's iffy if you swim or even keep surface in the heavy water The crickets singing with their legs Thousands and thousands of them adrone in the vast dark If one could catch one or a thousand and pin them down and ask them why! Why singing or is it singing Why wailing is more like it The crickets would only continue singing

No mouths to explain Singing with their legs Ah well anyway Whatever Make friends with the night with its cats and crickets There's no stilling them. No telling us the answer An answer without end Meaning therefore there is no end No end of it Sez who Sez no one Sez Beckett Beckett still Still as Beckett Perhaps he knew the answer but wasn't telling If you tell a secret a secret wish you die Otherwise it's life eternal It sez here— So why worry. They all go into it Into the cat dark Merchants Boozers Bankers Anxious worried women Queens Frogs ticks turtles Brown beans the whole quivering meat-wheel going round and round the quivery meat wheel turns And may come round again Will come round again with you on it. So why worry? Because.

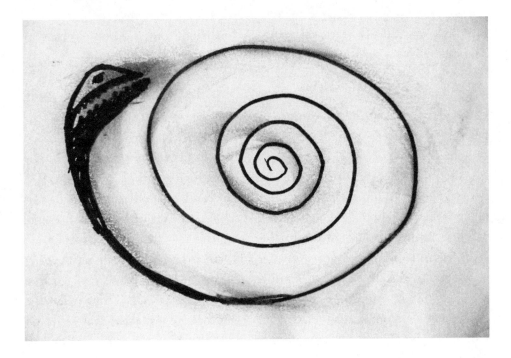

3.

Mother—Mutter—Matter—Matter mutters Mother mutters All goes down In the gloaming Sun sets and rises In the mountains On the hills valleys rivers streaming The Sun The sun Is God shines forever Won't shine forever Matter mutates ever Changes All changes ever and ever But sun also rises and La mia bella donna gave rise to my phallic protuberance Back then Ti ricordi? Mountains and rivers without end streaming Streams of spermata Attaboy You keep the race going Going going gone For a song Slouching toward Bethlehem and over is our antic joy The ceremony of innocence not dead? Streams still streaming Et "Monsieur Le Curé a défendu la chose" as if the human race could continue anyway by spontaneous conception and no need to do La Chose Blimey but I can't do without cried the gud Catholic Irish barkeep (friend of J. Joyce) by the riverrun And the two old washer women gossiping in the dusk by the River Liffey And that's the he and she of it Way along at last by the riverrun The night falling and Yeats still with the hots for Maud Gonne who'd gone off with a military man who could get it up all the time More than a grand poet such as he was Ah Lord Is there no end of it Anna Livia Plurabelle in the gloaming And he called me his Andalusian rose and drew me to him his whole self My heart was going like mad and Yes I said Yes I will And I would have if only

4.

Oui, je me souviens And I dreamt of Fidel 1990 a year after the election in Nica when the Sandinistas were defeated But will they not rise again. The Liberation Movement and all that All the peoples all the poor peoples of all the world to be free Even though things are going in the opposite direction now. Now again. Perpetual angelus. Tolling and tolling. Dark Dark We all go into the dark. Night falls on Chambéry And on Paris and on every being thing With Beckett with Pound Mary de Rachewiltz George Whitman Nancy All the old friends Girlfriends and brothers (all four of them gone), mother and father (lost and found) where away? Three points to starboard, northnorthwest, sighted from the crow's nest, gone in the gloaming. . . . And all the marvelous names of places in France hung in my ears ever and ever Rocamadour— Places I never got to. Love lost among the ruins. Or found. Gregorio Corso all night in the ruins of the Acropolis screwing someone Thousands of others screwing someone in some ruins Life goes on Screwing and screwing Flowers spring up Flowers fade Mother in the street Her brassiere backward Kate lovely Kate gone again o'er the dunes Oh what a pity what a pity what happens to Irish girls when they grow up And the old biddies gossiping on the riverbank River Liffey as the dusk is falling Dirty Britches We'll wash them Out with their sins The stones of the river hear it all When I was young and easy under the apple boughs Indeed Indeed And regurgitation is not a primary sin Even if it's only thoughts you're purging urging forgetfulness? Who knows? Mother snores. And the world goes by Dingding Along at last along a riverbank There is no good but love Mamma mia Annaliviaplurabelle. My thoughts won't walk Neither swim Toodle-oo Che la buona fortuna ti segua It's a long day's night till the trolley comes and all take off again willy nilly a new day a new sun rising and love ever new I'll tell a girl now what I told another a nun Blimey I'll come going to San Francisco where the text is broken The West did it And San Francisco an island still. As in the Indian maps of old Spanish seafarers found it and thought it was Caliban's land Califo Californo a hot oven It musta been a clear day without fog for once Aye because it ain't hot there mosta the thyme not like Lost angels' land Lost Angeles among the potted palms and potted citizens And who's Aunt Juana founded Tiajuana We'll never know the earth rolls round the moon still shines And still there are fireflies in the night

5. (Train, Milano to Parigi—October 15)

The moon is rising up between Grenoble and Chambéry in the dusk, high above the train on each side, as through tunnels we go, and then out into the flat landscape between the mountains, small dim farmhouses that someone must have had a vision to build, some little ideal construction in somebody's mind, now lost in the gloaming. The train zips on. Across the aisle two young American women, both fat, and one man. They all have wedding rings and are playing cards and looking at images on their videocam and not noticing the high fantastic peaks and mountains passing by. It's "Be somewhere else now" rather than "Be Here Now," just as all over America these days. And the train rocks on through all the cities of the downfall night, and it's Ulysses again voyaging to the crystal isles, the far islands, the cities made of old rocks. The train rocks on into the night of future shock. The feeling of France in the landscape, even in the descending dark. . . . And night falls on Chambéry. The three Americans across the aisle are now raising a stink with the *cameriere* because there's no toilet paper in the *gabinetto*. The fattest woman demands that whoever is in charge of the whole operation should come and speak to her. The *cameriere* really doesn't understand what she's saying. He goes off: of course "the man in charge" never comes. The toilet paper situation remains unresolved. This is a serious problem for two fat people. Perhaps they will die without it. In Europe. Far from home. Their bodies never found. And Paris Rue de la Roquette ce gros monsieur au café qui se soûle à la bonne heure au bar debout il boit quelques verres et s'en va en titubant "Paris toujours Toujours Paris" on dit. And so suis arrivé la nuit et dormait pas mal Hotel Daval Rue Daval et le matin je flâne dans mon quartier comme étudiant d'antin Place de la Bastille Rue de la Roquette à la Place Léon Blum qui était Place Voltaire où j'habitais 2 Place Voltaire chez M et Mme Letellier ancien professeur de musique avec le visage de Beethoven lui-même And the sun comes out and il fait beau enfin à Paris ce jour-là Back then I thought I was French but only last week in Brescia did I find the house where my father was born November 20 in Via delle Cossere in the ancient quartiere del Carmine. Mio padre è nato nel 1872 in primavera senza dubbio. And shipped out at the age of twenty from Marseille 1892 to Little Italy & like in *Godfather Two* perhaps became a small-time *mafiosetto* doing favors for the local *padrino*. Un tipo bravo senza dubbio ma forse un pò pazzo. Non so, però questa è un'altra storia, la storia dell'America/ Americus. But now in Paris je flâne partout dans mes anciens quartiers Roquette et Rue de Lappe où je me souviens toutes ces dames cocottes dans les dance-halls and cabinets going all night These raucous dames And one who stuck her stockinged leg out to stop me in the narrow street and draw me in but I went on, leaving bursts of laughter behind swinging doors and the night of the Bastille and of the onzième arrondissement est tombée sur tout Ah oui c'était comme ça And voilà here we go again into Life whatever that is A quandary a grande excitation a momentary twitching of amoeba in a pond.

6.

Half in love with death, bullshit! Americus speaking old Europe, a lost cause Westward, course of Empire and all that Melancholy of the Middle Ages Monks depressed in monasteries Acedia Dark night of the soul and all that Bath of the Devil Disturbed minds and depression Lassitude of the heart All this considered one of the Seven Deadly Sins along with envy, avarice, anger, pride, lasciviousness, sex, and la gourmandise And in the Renaissance this turning into the "divine furor" of Plato and this led to the madness of poets and Artaud and all that Well now ain't that a story a tale to tell all told over and over me and ma tante Emilie chère Emilie and where—away now me hearties It's to America then and Americus and the New World and all that heavens on earth Shadows of the past thrown off No more Middle Dark Ages here Have a beer and turn on the World Series Who's at bat No more loup-wolf l'homme-garou, sauvage beast, shadowy, fleeing the light, sinister, "la folie louvière" except here comes Dr. Sax with Ti Jean in tow on the Road and all that and so begins all over again Eternal wanderers, eternal exiles, escaped convicts, solitaries, solitary hunters, vagabonds, sailors, maudits, Baudelaires and Artauds and the Beats on and on and

7.

And it's a new world every minute every moment every movement come and gone but now *the* Movement The Movement began by chance by the collision of two on bicycles two newcomers on earth And what did they know of the world and does it matter They knew what they knew having been born into the quagmire And they got up grew up sprung up into it The whole scheme must be rebuilt from the bottom up not from top down They were the best they are the best and the brightest of the new arrivals on earth their wings barely dry they flew straight into it the grand turmoil to change everything from the bottom up And it was bottoms up all the way Out with the mold In with the dew We are young enough to do it And everyone is joining The Movement Not just to change one little corner of life Not to be just a Luddite not just a vegan not just a green integer not just a teenager with an instinct to rebel not just yell at Mommy and Daddy not just bike instead of drive not just ecology not just theology not just philosophy not just sociology not just diplo-speak over and over the same old stunts again smoothed over by the powers that be They dreamt it They began to live it to work it Buddy Buddy join The Movement baby It's a new world every moment and we'll make it happen Down with the hair shibboleths the old saws the wise heads the shaved or bearded suits running the world We've had enough of heard enuf of No man Left and Right no more Center Left no more parties Just The Movement and rebuild from the bottom up after the dismantling the grand dismantling without killing anybody the grand dismantling of what is already falling apart coming apart at the seams where the oil leaks into blood and tears The huge juggernaut of our Casino culture with no one at the controls but ten million at the controls unable to stop it The huge juggernaut agoing for naught headed for the precipice and no one able to stop it Dismantling it from the ground up a new kind of monkey-wrench doing it without killing anybody The Movement will do it without killing anybody Dada won't do it Daddy won't do it So get with it and do it do it

8.

O vain the role of man along riverrun in the deep dusk I hear the distant voices calling and the hills echoing O the white arms of roads Welcome O Life The past is all
illusion but the future is ours and endless the mountains and rivers the fireflies still
on calm nights in the hills and dawn coming over the meadows Lord what beauty
Laid back the girl in the meadowgrass and riverrun pastures and when will it end In
the heat of day the sun beats down upon the lovers in the haystack Fecund lilies
bloom Dragonflies draw flame And night falls again A far light flickers and all is
dark again And at my back I seem to hear the sound of Charon's riverboat drawing
near and all is movement Then all is still All will rise again Sun and all will rise
again and old moon too after much reflection tells the sky "Sun is God" and is carried
away in a cloud As the seas arise again to take us wash us all away Mother McCreary
and all the lads and their lasses Ah riverrun beneath the sun the day's work barely
begun Let the play begin Dear father come back again Sister dear Lover mine was
that you walking in the night street lost and by the wind grieved O we are all in one
boat rowing Toward eternity is it? Well but let's not get carried away in the flood of
it As then the night is coming And the Irish "Countess" I met at midnight in the
Zócalo Oaxaca nineteen eighty-two and she from the little town of Dimmi she talked
a blue streak and never stopped Tell me tell me tale of Shalimar and Shawn the dawn
is coming the sweet dawn The birds awake in the trees calling *to-woo to-who*—fading
in the far distance lost in the deep wood and then the trees falling skyscrapers falling
and all that falls rises up again with wind in the willows *To-woo to-woo* to woe again
with laughter and singing ever the singing A voice beyond the world is calling

DADAPOLIS

Paris, October 22—"Vienna 1900" at the Grand Palais

And the leaves under the trees in the Tuileries and suddenly it's fall in Paris and sere the yellow leaf the dead leaves fallen The sun rises and the sun also sets and at Beaubourg they are showing Dada again and again. What else they got?

And "Da-Da-Da!" shouted Trotsky in the Cabaret Voltaire Zurich 1916 when the bombs were falling elsewhere while the Dadaists dissidents pacifists deserters artists versified and "sang with all their souls!" And the Admiral put an ad in a paper for an apartment à louer And Le Toreador de Picabia Black eyes Black necktie Black beret looking out at us back in 1902—all whirligigs senseless as a spinning bicycle wheel the spokes your life ma chère a rotatory hemisphere King Lear would have loved it And Man Ray shouting at you from a bigscreen to Sartre's sound and it's "Mannahatta" coming at you "city of spires and sparkling bays"

And Sacred Heart on its mountain in the distance thru plateglass a panorama of Paris And a procession on the screen including a camel and women in cloche hats and men in top hats passing the Tour Eiffel half-built and the camel looking back and the whole parade running into the future onto the Champs Élysées Flash and it's today

A paper airplane sailing over Paris carrying us away. . . .

MEXICO—THE BULLFIGHT

February 2006

D OWN IN PUERTO VALLARTA——At five in the afternoon under the burning sun the matador and the bull in the bullring in the Plaza de Toros and the Picadors and the bandilleros and the blood on the sand and . . . and the sword in the back of the bull between the shoulder blades and the bull swaying and falling on the sand and the ear of the bull cut off and given to the matador who bows to the cheering crowd of mostly American tourists in shorts and golf shoes and the matador holding up the bull's ear to the crowd and doffing his hat and bowing and waving the ear on high and the bull with feet in the air dragged out of the ring by a team of old nags and the blood on the sand being raked over and the sun baking the blood in the sand at five in the afternoon the tender young bull the young brave bull and the young brave bullfighter in his "suit of Light" dancing the "dance of death" at five in the afternoon.

S Milano to Parigi, Settembre 18, 2006
ilently the train slides on rubber wheels through the magnificent Alps and Prealps and the slag-heaps of civilization—broken engines, railroad sidings, electric generators pulsing, three discarded shoes, an overturned *pissoir*, a railroad flagman waving. . . . The dusk falls as cats eat stars. That night a young woman on the train kept on laughing and laughing—a light laugh, a young laugh full of innocence and light, now and then arising to a kind of lilt. And she went on not saying anything except by just laughing, a gentle laughter echoing in the night train. . . .

Paris, September 18-29
First light in the Luxembourg Gardens—Sainte Geneviève in white marble standing straight and still (the Patronne de Paris)— And at the Fountain of the Medici a face ten times life size floating face-up in the long pool (also motionless), only the nose, lips & chin above water— And at the entrance to the École du Louvre a kid with a Red Hot Chili Peppers T-shirt going in. What could it all mean, in the early years of this cataclysmic century?

September 20
Today I had a great walk "en flânant" on the Left Bank. Saw a lot of banal scenes but also sparkling things like a guy getting drunk while singing to his would-be

lover who appeared to him as in an absinthe dream (like that famous painting of *The Absinthe Drinker*). When he tried to embrace this vision, she wasn't there. So what does he do, this seventy-year-old boy? He just smiles, that's all. Just smiles.

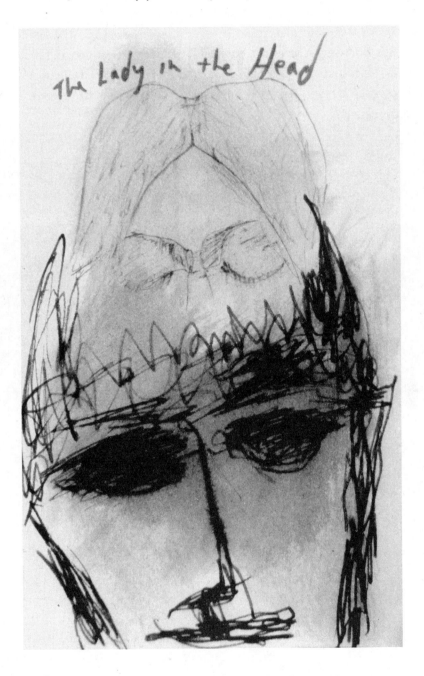

I'm here to see George Whitman. It's almost the only reason I've come this time. He's over ninety and I figure one of us is going soon to the au-delà. His hair is wild but his blue eyes still sparkle. We have a nice tête-à-tête in his upstairs apartment of the bookstore, and I tell him I remember his sister so well (who would now be a year younger than he—perhaps ninety—but who choked on a bone at age thirty-eight after teaching philosophy at Vassar and Buffalo). When both of us, Mary and I, were here in 1948, we almost took a walking trip together in the Loire but it never happened, and thereby hangs a tale that never happened. O regrets, regrets!

RUE DE ST.-SÉVERIN, CHEZ LA FLAGRANT DÉLICE—People hurrying by under umbrellas, nighttime in the narrow street. Looking out of the restaurant I see lives going by faster than the years. Against the wrought-iron fence around the church of St. Séverin dark figures under black umbrellas like something out of Goya, only they're not on their way to a firing squad in this fat autumn in Paris two thousand oh six. . . . Suddenly in the rain three white-robed figures appear (why three?), white hoods over their heads—and just as suddenly disappear, as if the last gasp of Catholicism were suddenly over.

Ah life, why are you so ungraspable? Even as we reach out— Fleeting! Evanescent! Gone as we blink like blind fools!

Over in the cinquième around St. Michel the scene is still young at Shakespeare & Co., 37, Rue de la Bûcherie, although George Whitman is ninety-three; but his daughter Sylvia has taken over, full of hope & plans.

Maggio 20, 2007
Reggio Calabria—Al Museo Archeologico

I Bronzi di Riace—Greek warriors. . . . Two bronze figures seven feet tall found undersea off the tip of Italy, at Riace, in the straits between Calabria and Sicilia (not far from Scylla & Charybdis).[52] In perfect condition, bronze not eaten away by the sea. . . . Two or three thousand years ago...

I did an oil painting for Giada and her family entitled *Gli Stronzi di Riace* (Giada thought up the pun for the title).[53]

Passed by whirlpools between Scylla & Charybdis where Ulysses. . . .

And at Scylla the fisherman in the crow's nest at the top of a hundred-foot mast looking out for swordfish floating near the surface . . . perhaps a fish as big as the boat—or larger . . . *pesce spada*. . . .

Maggio 23

Two lovers on the beach,
their eyes locked,
the eyes said it—
"Let me in."

Paris, Mai 26

Paris again—gray skies this morning, *temps mornes*, as in Samuel Beckett— Saturday morning, some sort of demo going on Place Notre Dame: judging by the workers hanging out in the café, it must be a labor demo, just after the far Rightist Sarkozy was elected. It's almost 8 a.m., the weak sun trying to break through over Notre Dame, that *grosse dame*, not one of the Gothic beauties by far—never liked it. . . .

But now suddenly coming across the bridge from Notre Dame a huge parade of Catholic youth waving flags from all the provinces of France, a *pèlerinage*, with young priests and nuns marching with the students, many carrying crosses on French flags and even one American flag, thousands of French youth, *la jeunesse française*, coming and coming across the traffic, squads of police watching, some directing traffic. Now almost an hour still coming, cheered on by the old sitters in the café. . . .

The heart swells as they march along, in massed groups, not in military rows, the future Labor of France, with the present workers waving by from the cafés . . . but it's Catholic all the way, the crosses keep coming, some groups singing jubilant songs or snatches of the "Marseillaise." And now the rain sets in and umbrellas appear and rain gear with hoods, the rain pouring down out of the leaden skies, but they keep coming under crosses with saints' names on them—herds of boy scouts in felt hats, followed by girl scouts all in green skirts and berets, and at last at almost 9 o'clock the last of *la jeunesse française* passes by. . . . The rain continues, falling in driven sheets. . . .

Mai 27—Samuel Beckett at Beaubourg-Musée Pompidou

Beckett's manuscripts in tiny handwriting. . . . They have dissected & analyzed *pauvre* Beckett down to his fingernails, but they have left out his humor (gallows humor, for sure). This whole vast exposition is depressing without relief.

Mai 28—Restaurant Le Petit Saint Benoît

Still the same. Mais, est-ce qu'il y a toujours la Crème de Marron? . . . *Oui*. . . . Les gens à côté en train de bavarder comme les vieilles tricoteuses . . . fingers in the air insisting on a point.[54]

At Anselm Kiefer show—

Kiefer show called Monumenta. Seven or so Bauhaus-type lead buildings & wrecks of buildings, housed in the huge, empty Grand Palais with its 19th-century architecture & high domed glass ceiling. The Kiefer lead blocks of buildings a rude contrast to the Grand Palais' great light & space. . . .

A library thirty feet high with metal shelves holding lead books—with glass interleaved, the glass cracking & falling—hundreds of books, some readable, others of pure lead. . . .

Palm Sunday—a dead palm tree on its side surrounded by palm branches soaked in plaster. . . .

Kiefer's obsessive vision still that of the whole young postwar German generation and its Group '47 including Günter Grass, Paul Celan, Joseph Beuys, Ingeborg Bachmann, Reinhard Lettau, Marcuse. . . . German Romanticism metamorphosed, violently. . . .

Is this an exhibition of Kiefer or Beckett, whose desolate figures and landscapes are almost the same as Kiefer's, but with even less hope & light? (Kiefer's usually manage a faded flower or a plaster flower or half of a ray of light.) As Beckett said, "A glimmer for a moment, then darkness again" (sic).

The Kiefer show combined with the Samuel Beckett retrospective at the Beaubourg at the same time of gloomy gray skies over Paris make for a very depressed Paris, two of the gloomiest of artists spreading their tragic torments across town, and unceasing rain coming down!

Après-midi—chez Whitman

George and I talking like two old Beckett characters, trying to remember their past together, trying to recall old names or faces in photographs—and what became of her, she with the glorious red hair, or he with the wandering eye, the two of them posed together, etc., etc. . . . Still we go on. . . .

He is my oldest friend in the world—my oldest friend, in both senses—as the oldest person I know in the world and as the friend I've known for longer than any other friend.

I first knew him before he had a bookstore. When I was in Columbia University Graduate School, I used to see his sister, Mary, who was in the philosophy department and, while she was not exactly my girlfriend, I remember sitting with her in her front window as she told me about her brother who had recently arrived in Paris after wandering the Orient and South America. I imagined this romantic wanderer, a kind of wayward Walt Whitman (no relation) carrying Coleridge's albatross.

When I took off for Paris in late 1946 to go to the Sorbonne and get a doctorate, Mary gave me George's address. It turned out that his albatross was books, and they had a passionate relationship.

I found him in an airless windowless hole-in-the-wall in the Hotel Suez, Boulevard St.-Michel, with books up to the ceiling on all walls, and himself the ghost of Stephen Dedalus cooking supper over a can of Sterno (or some other eternal flame of his own making). He was selling books out of his hotel room to American students on the G.I. Bill.

He was already in the thrall of a kind of mistral bibliomania which led him in 1951 to found the Librairie Mistral at 37, Rue de la Bûcherie, Paris cinquième, and it grew over the years from one small cave-like ground-floor room to many small rooms on several floors, up dilapidated stairs—a literary octopus with an insatiable appetite for print, taking over the beatup building (perhaps inhabited by monks in the Middle Ages) room by room, floor by floor, a veritable nest of books. By the time the store was this developed, George had changed the name to Shakespeare & Company, since Sylvia Beach's original shop with that name (at a different location) was long defunct.

I like to think that City Lights Bookstore in San Francisco is a natural brother to George's. I originally conceived City Lights as "a kind of library where books are sold" and as a "literary meeting place." City Lights too grew and grew in the same haphazard manner from one very small entrance room. And as late as 1990, both George and I still had one more floor to capture in the building.

I visited George many times over the past half-century, usually no more than a couple of years between visits, and the feeling of being brother or sister bookstores grew and grew with the stores. Over the entrance to City Lights there's a sign reading "Shakespeare & Co. Paris." Over the entrance to his store in Paris the sign reads "City Lights Books."

George visited us just once in San Francisco, stopping over on a cruise ship outward bound (I think to China), with George no doubt attempting to relive his vagabond past. He stayed with me in North Beach, and a fine drawing of him reading in bed in Paris still hangs in my kitchen. Back in his own room with a French window looking out at Notre Dame, he used to read all night, and turn off the light when dawn showed over the cathedral, consuming books like soul food. I can't say we love each other like brothers, even though we are brothers in the trade, even though I loved his sister. After all, he is a New Englander, not given to emotional expressions, and although I might sign letters to him with "Con affetto" he always signed off with the same "Amitiés sincères." And he didn't write often.

Now he has retreated permanently to an upstairs back bedroom where he reads propped up into the early hours, and still rises early to "trim the lamps" as he imagines some monk, some "Frère Lampier" (as George calls him) had done in the Middle Ages.

He is sitting up in his double bed, with books strewn all over. The television is on but he is staring out the window. The dusk is falling. Maybe he is Prince Myshkin. Maybe we both have the feeling this is the last time. He is ninety-three and I am eighty-eight. . . . There is nothing more we are capable of saying. . . . Things unspoken will remain unspoken. . . . I spy a bottle of cognac on the windowsill. . . . I pour us each a small one. . . . An iron bell strikes in the church of Saint Julien-le-Pauvre. . . . We clink and drink.

YELAPA, MEXICO
January 2008

U

January 8

p early with first sun (the night frigid in a *palapa* with lattice walls and wind through them, only one blanket)— Along the beach a string of three old horses, pack animals carrying loads of logs, tended by two *hombres*, the tide coming in, the sun just clearing the horizon, in clouds, no heat in it yet, a young barefoot guy says in passing, "Muy fría!" and adds, "Quiere marijuana? Ganja?" (Ganja? We're in India? The world is flat.) "Más tarde," I tell him, going on, down to the beach where other guys are raking the sand in front of the cafés. . . . Still no heat on the land.

Lots of stray dogs, scratching their fleas in the sun, and boat-tailed grackles. The guys are putting the beach chairs out, for the gringos to sit in, recovering from last night's margaritas and Raicilla (the local hootch—made by the local *indios*), old horny gringos with Extra Virgins, old rich widows retired from the fray in Province-town, brokers on the lam, surfers from Santa Monica in thongs, predatory drinkers at the beach bar, you name it. . . . A wedding party arrives, about to party. . . . Is there a war going on somewhere? Thousands of boys being blasted, by car bombs, snipers, or friendly fire?

The sun has cleared the clouds now, bringing at last some heat to the beach, the tide rolls in, after a night of agitation, surging forward, urging the sea to rise up, every wave a revolutionary in the uprising, as if anyone could stop it. . . . Beach boys throwing beach balls, fishermen setting forth in speedboats, wedding bells imported on a Walkman or iPod, whole populations displaced, ethnic cleansing, oil on the waters? And everywhere the waters rising. . . .

January 9

Second morning at Hotel Lagunita, another frigid night, no hot water in the morning, breakfast on the beach, the sun coming, 8:30 a.m., kids playing in the sand, parents at the tables under the palm roofs, the sea, the level sea stretching away, westward, blue blue blue. . . . What's going to happen here, if anything? Life will go on, everywhere, as if nothing ever happens, except the eternal growing and decaying, death on the wing, birthing and rebirthing, living and living, dying and dying, on and on, sun rising and falling. . . .

I love the boat-tailed grackles, jet-black with swallowtails, long beaks, strutting about on the sands, distant cousins of those that nest in the flat tops of the trees at sunset in the plaza of San Miguel de Allende, all crying out at once as the sun sinks into night, crying out against the dying of the light. . . .

11 a.m.

Moved out of the *palapa* to a real room with real hot water in the shower & a sunny balcony—the Casa Hotel Luna Azul.

January 10

In the Hotel Luna, in the ruined garden below my balcony, a rooster took it upon himself to announce, not just the dawn, but every hour after midnight, as if we dreamers needed to know the exact time all night long. . . .

Down in the jumble of that garden, said rooster is nowhere to be seen or heard, probably turned in for a daylong sleep after his all-night travail. The garden is strung with clotheslines between a riot of vegetation—palms and jacarandas, weeds and bushes of all sorts, and a pile of rejected lumber and ceramic piping, a tin-roofed shed in the corner, all flavored with various cheeping birds, like spices giving the whole scene an aurora of waking somnolence, as if it had been here forever and would be going on forever, in the labyrinth that was ancient Mexico, timeless into the face of the juggernaut of the 21st century, the American corporate culture steamroller, obliterating all indigenous cultures as it goes, grinding them into dust, for the new electronic flat earth, the new avaricious empire. . . .

Two black dogs come along the white-tiled balcony toward me. One comes right up and offers his paw, and we shake hands, and then the two of them stretch out in the shade on the tiles, having decided to keep me company. The rooster wakes up now and struts about the ruined garden, letting out his cock cries, and small children are playing in the garden jungle, emitting small cries, not yet rooster-like. A pure white cat is digging for something among the broken clay piping. Some hens walk around clucking. Tiny yellow birds flit about. . . . The cat has caught a tiny rodent and is eating it. . . . A *mujer* is wringing out some clothes and hanging them in the sun. A small feral-looking fox-like animal slinks toward the cat and mouse. . . . I am reading Jorge Luis Borges and wanting to write like him. . . . Or like Joseph Conrad. . . .

January 11

Rereading Conrad's *Heart of Darkness*, it occurs to me that one could write a novel reversing Conrad's dark message, with a protagonist starting out from New York City (the heart of the Beast) and setting forth to ascend a different great river than Conrad's Marlow, a river not on any map or chart—although in the 21st century, all places and rivers on earth have been explored. So our protagonist sets out, *starting* from the heart of darkness in the American Empire, and eventually reaches that great river (not the Congo—or perhaps indeed the Congo) and proceeds endlessly up it, with the light growing with every mile—just the opposite of Marlow, whose fate is to reach Mr. Kurtz in the heart of darkness—our hero would be proceeding in ever-increasing light, toward the final enlightenment, as indefinable and unreachable as the summit of Mount Analogue—so that this new novel, like Daumal's, might never be finished. Yet our hero, in spite of all, might still discover the great light, the "Heart of Lightness."

BELIZE
February 2010

February 10—Crystal Skull

In Belize at Lubaantun, in a Mayan rain forest, a crystal skull dug up by an itinerant woodcutter, a grave robber—long time ago—"Skull of doom," they call it—causing the death of Atlantis, they say. The ceiba tree connected the Mayans to the netherworld, "the place of fright," and the whole earth a turtle (here too). And Lubaantun, "the place of falling stone"—minor Mayan ruin. At Nim Li Punit another minor Mayan ruin—the plumed figure of Quetzal on a stone stele twelve feet high, with a woman carved close upon him—Quetzal's eye stood out very white, as if painted in enamel. I reached up and touched the eye. It was white stone. The rest of Quetzal was gray—Aztec god, plumed serpent, migrated way down here in Yucatán. I sat down silent at his feet in the whitewashed room, hoping for some communication, hoping to commune with him, some wordless message sent thru the silent stone. Silence met only silence—Quetzal's silence more profound. Outside the noon sun beat down merciless on the jungle. Quetzal never stirred nor noted my presence—a foreign intruder of a different race where ruthless armies of another race once made their dreadful way. Outside the shadows pitch-black as if painted with tar. The silence continued thru the centuries.

Thru the jungle back to Placencia, southern Belize. Rough rocky road past jungle towns. Forty percent of population in poverty. Thatched roofs—gaunt cows—scrawny chickens—broken tin roofs on sheds. Man in beatup cowboy hat on a skinny horse jigs along— Bandannaed crone carrying two babies in a sling— Young guys on rusty cycles pedaling away— Midway in jungle suddenly a clearing and a sign reading Welcome to Coleman's Café—Belikin beer, beans and rice, boiled chicken in brown sauce— Two Army gendarmes in jungle camouflage, handcuffs on belt on the wide porch under the plastic—soccer balls and plastic fish hanging from the ceiling— Strawberry rice cakes for dessert— Gold-toothed young head of family shakes hands. And there's "Noni," a tonic to cure everything— tastes like medicine—also good for men for sex, they tell us.

On the broken paved road, half-built mansions, abandoned building sites, construction jobs unfinished, roads laid out for unbuilt shopping malls, old British Army trucks full of black soldiers. Where are they going, to what unimagined destiny?

It's still a subject much debated in Belize as to whether CAFTA (the Central American Free Trade Agreement promoted by the U.S.) would be good for Belize. I can only think of Eduardo Galeano's *Open Veins of Latin America* and its dreadful story of what U.S. policies have led to south of the border. And the blowback continues to flood over borders with hungry humans.

February 12

AT SEA

for Pablo Neruda

The sea through the trees
    distant
        shining
The dark foreground
           a stone wall
              with lichen
An old salt
    sits staring out
          at the sea
A wind sways the palms
          infrequently
Another day prepares
          for heat and silence

A small plane
        buzzing like a fly
                disturbs the sky
The air eats it
Far out on the slumbering sea
                      a trawler creeps along
The wind from the south
        blows the bait in the fish's mouth
The yawning sea
           swallows the trawler
The lichen lives on
        in its volcanic stone
                taciturn
                  eternal
      awaiting its turn
           in the turn of the sun
Never will I return here
      never again
        breathe this wind
           on this far run
      in the reaches of morning
      where the sea whispers
          patience and salt
The sun
    scorches the sky
        and drops like a burnt-out match
              into night
And I am an animal still
      perhaps once a bird
          a halcyon
      who makes its nest at sea
    on my little flight across
        the little chart
          of my existence
Life goes on
      full of silence and clamor

in the gray cities
                    in the far bourgs
          in the white cities by the sea
     where I go on
                    writing my life
                         in neither blood nor wine
I still await an epiphany
     by the petri-dish of the sea
          where all life began
                         by swimming
But it's time now
     to give an accounting of everything
               an explanation of everything
          such as
               why there is darkness at night
Everywhere the sea is rising
          Am I to be drowned
                    with the rest of them
          all the animals of earth
               washed away in ocean
                    motherer and moitherer
     in this tremendous moment
                    of calamitous sea-change
          as our little world disappears
               in a tremor of ocean and fear
                    to the murmur
               of the middle mind of America
          as imbeciles in neckties
                    drop from the trees?
No matter then
     if I end up
          in a house of insurgents
     on the Avenida de los Insurgentes
                    or shoeless on Boston Common
               or cast-up clueless

              in my Great Uncle Désir's
                      beach hut
                in St. Thomas
Pardon my conduct then
      if I can't give you
             any final word—
       a final unified theory of existence—
           all thought subsumed
                  in one great thought
                    (utopian vision!)
Humans with all their voices
 as myriad as
         the syllables of the sea
     have never been able to fathom
               man's fate
            nor tell us why we are here
Still will we be
      free as the sea
          to be nothing but
             our own shadow selves
   beach bums all after all
        in future time when
           nations no longer exist
             and the earth is swept
               by ethnic hordes
         in search of food and shelter?
Neither patient nor placid
      in the face of all this
      in the sea of every day
       with its two tides
I run before the wind
      immune to hidden reefs or harbors
Someone throws me
      crystal fruits
        in the shape of life-preservers

Others wave
> from distant strands
>> Goodbye! Goodbye!
Beached at last
> bleached out
I would to the woods again
> with its ancient trees
>> that sing like sitars
>>> in the wind
>>>> Wordless ragas!
Shipwrecked ashore
> at the mercy of avaricious gulls—
And yet and yet
> we are still not born for despair
Spring comes anyway
And a gay excursion train appears
The ancient conductor
> with stovepipe hat
>> and gold pocketwatch
> greets us like long-lost passengers
>> gracing us with
>>> wreaths around our necks
> as arms of lovers
>> insanely embrace us
Is there anything more to be said
> before they carry us off
>> as dead
> while we're still dreaming
still in search
> of the bread of the word
>> cast upon the waters
> the dough that rises
> in the yeast of speech
>> in the written word
>>> in poetry

Tracks upon the sand!
    left by corralled bands of animals
        cornered by mistakes and habitudes
          and trains taken
            to mistaken destinations
              or trips taken or not taken
                with angels of love
                  to lower latitudes
Between two waves
      the ocean is still—
        a silence of ages
      lasting but a moment
        between two waves
          of emotion
    as lovers
        turn to each other
            or away
    Love ebbs and flows
        comes and goes
      between two emotions
     but surges forth again
      with each new wave
    as some sea-creature from the deep
        breaks the surface with a leap
The sea roars but says no more
O the yarns it could spin
    if it would
      between its rages
  under the eye of the sun
     under the ear of the sky—
       Plunderers and pieces of eight!
    Invisible cities!
         Crystal skulls!
           Petrified hulls!
    Sailors' masturbations!

                or yesterday's sperm

                      lost in the wake

                          of a pleasure boat

O endless the inchoate

        incoherent narrative— Voyageur, pass on!

We are not our fathers

           yet we carry on

                breathing like them

                    loving and killing like them

Away then away

           in our custom-built catamarans

        over the hills of ocean

      to where Atlantis

           still rides the tides

      or where that magic mountain

              not on any map

                wreathed in radiance

                    still hides

ACKNOWLEDGMENTS

My hearty thanks to Giada Diano who first conceived of this book and, with Matthew Gleeson, transcribed my handwritten journals in the Bancroft Library, UC Berkeley. Thanks also to Elisa Polimeni for her fine work on the photos of my drawings, and to Nancy Peters for her acute critiques. And also to editor Robert Weil, whose committed enthusiasm brought this book to fruition. —LF

NOTES

1. Philip Whalen, Philip Lamantia, and Gary Snyder, American poets; Francisco Zendejas, Mexican writer and critic.
2. Nicholas Constantine Christofilos, Greek physicist who worked on military projects for the U.S. For a few years he was a colleague of Dr. Edward Teller.
3. A force in the Chicago poetry scene, Carroll was the editor of *Big Table* and a longtime friend of Lawrence's.
4. From 1937 to 1941 Lawrence attended the University of North Carolina at Chapel Hill for his undergraduate degree. He had been drawn there because it was the alma mater of Thomas Wolfe, author of *Look Homeward, Angel*, which influenced Lawrence greatly.
5. In the late 1950s, Lawrence had bought a patch of land in Bixby Canyon in Big Sur on the California coast, where he built a small cabin.
6. An old pensioner enters and sits next to me. He coughs a lot. After a long silence, I say: "It hasn't changed much here in thirteen years." He looks at me and says, finally: "That's true." . . . While I eat my salad of green flowers, some young women in the flower of their youth come in, laughing. . . .
7. They're buying life . . . that's why they're arguing. . . .
8. Egyptian novelist who wrote in French and whose great subjects were laziness and the rejection of authority. City Lights would publish Cossery's story collection *Men God Forgot* later in 1963.
9. Fairground signs translated from the French: This attraction / for children only; GRAB THE DOLL / and get / a free ride.
10. Claude Pelieu moved to San Francisco with the painter Mary Beach. They translated several books of Allen Ginsberg's poetry into French for City Lights. Lawrence considered them the ideal translators of Ginsberg's poetry. The line from Pelieu's letter reads, "There's nothing left for me but junk and the slow masturbations of autumn."
11. Poems by three Soviet poets—Semyon Kirsanov, Andrei Voznesensky, and Yevgeny Yevtushenko—appeared in *Red Cats*, in translations by Anselm Hollo.
12. The writers Yuli Daniel and Andrei Sinyavsky were convicted in a 1965–66 show trial for publishing pseudonymous literary novellas considered to be anti-Soviet. They were sentenced to years in a labor camp.

13. The Blue Rider (in German, Der Blaue Reiter) was an avant-garde art movement active from 1911 to 1914, founded by Russian emigrants (including Wassily Kandinsky) and German artists (including Franz Marc).

14. Lettau was a writer, professor, political activist, and member of Group 47, founded in Germany to rejuvenate German literature after the trauma of World War II. He taught at the University of California at San Diego.

15. Allen Ginsberg had visited Moscow two years earlier, in 1965, meeting many of the same literary figures.

16. A paraphrase from the unfinished novel *Mount Analogue* by French author and spiritual seeker René Daumal. An English translation of the book would be published by City Lights in 1968.

17. From Blaise Cendrars: "There are some trains that never meet."

18. Also from Cendrars: "What I lose sight of today in turning east is what Christopher Columbus discovered in turning west."

19. Kenneth Rexroth, a poet, critical essayist, and translator, was a dominant figure in the San Francisco Renaissance. His anarchist politics and literary sensibilities were a strong influence on Ferlinghetti. Rexroth's translation of *Thirty Spanish Poems of Love and Exile* was one of City Lights' earliest books in the Pocket Poets series.

20. Waldport was a work camp in Oregon for conscientious objectors during World War II, where pacifist poets and artists created a fine arts group. After they were freed at the end of the war, some of these poets and artists became involved in the San Francisco Renaissance.

21. The Japanese-American manager of City Lights Bookstore from its early days until 1972.

22. Gray day, dreary weather, no luck, "life goes on," everything is beautiful and stupid, and the gods don't see me Rue de Seine ten in the morning breakfast in bed and the telephone that doesn't answer. Too bad, you don't get there too early or too late. I make calculations on my mirror. . . . I make calculations in soap on my mirror, and my mirror breaks with a burst of laughter. An old flying grandma knitter arrives with my café-au-lait, says good day in a sepulchral voice while giving me a pained glance, and leaves. Everyday life doesn't change, and the old knitters and the old men don't change; the young people change; the old ones make obscene gestures, the young ones pee like the old, and then they become old. And everything starts again, everything turns, and life goes on so beautiful and so stupid. . . .

23. Part of Group '47, Bachmann was one of the poets featured in the collection *New Young German Poets* published by City Lights in 1959. She would die in 1973 when her house in Rome burned down; some speculate that it was a suicide, and the exact circumstances remain a mystery.

24. Do You Like This Garden? / Which Is Yours? / Make Sure Your Children Don't Destroy It!

25. We Beseech / SILENCE / For the Benefit of Those Already / At Rest

26. LAND AND LIBERTY, OLYMPICS OF HUNGER, LONG LIVE YOUTH, VICTORY TO THE SPIRIT OF YOUTH AND REVOLUTIONARY ACTION, LIBERTY FOR IMPRISONED STUDENTS, THE GOVERNMENT CALLS ITS OWN VIOLENCE LAW, ONWARD TO VICTORY FOREVER—WE WILL WIN.

27. In 1968, while the Mexican government was pouring resources into hosting that year's Olympics, massive student protests began to turn violent. This would peak in the Tlatelolco massacre of students by Mexican army troops on October 2.

28. Neal Cassady had died in February 1968, in San Miguel de Allende. Lawrence was at work editing Cassady's *The First Third*, which took several years to collate and correct. City Lights would finally publish it in 1971.

29. The Monkey Block (a nickname for the Montgomery Block) was a large old building with studios and rooms for writers and artists. It stood where the Transamerica Pyramid now stands. The Black Cat was a large old North Beach bar, a center for bohemians (before the Beats), and the Iron Pot was a family-style restaurant; neither of them still exists.

30. Ginsberg's *Indian Journals*, compiling his writings from a trip to India in 1962–63, was published jointly by City Lights and Auerhahn Books in 1970.

31. During Lawrence's trip to Berlin in 1967, Voznesensky had been permitted by Soviet authorities to visit West Berlin under surveillance for a limited time, after which he had to return to East Berlin.

32. A British-born philosopher and writer, Watts was crucial in introducing Eastern philosophy and religions to Western audiences, especially in the San Francisco Bay Area. He died in 1973.

33. The conference City Lights in North Dakota was held in March 1974 at the University of North Dakota in Grand Forks. Lawrence was on his way there after this trip to Hawaii.

34. A reference to the recent battles that had occurred when police tried to clear squatters from the Melkweg, a former dairy occupied by artists and converted into a theater and social center.

35. A German writer and literary critic whose poetry had been included in the City Lights Pocket Poets' *New Young German Poets* in 1959.

36. A weeklong event celebrating the twenty-fifth anniversary of the publication of Kerouac's *On the Road*, organized by Allen Ginsberg and cohorts at the Naropa Institute in Boulder, Colorado.

37. A Mexican poet, writer, diplomat and environmental activist. City Lights would later publish his *Solar Poems,* in 2010, and *A Time of Angels,* in 2012.

38. War on War: Poets of the World at UNESCO was a three-day gathering of writers and poets organized by Jean-Jacques Lebel.

39. In 1979, Lawrence had attended a massive and historic gathering of American and European poets in Castelporziano, organized by the group Beat 72.

40. Pier Paolo Pasolini, a poet, filmmaker, and critic, was often controversial because of his identity as both a Communist and homosexual. He was brutally murdered under still-unclear circumstances in 1975. His *Roman Poems* would be published in 1986 by City Lights, translated by Ferlinghetti with Francesca Valente.

41. Allen Ginsberg died on April 5, 1997, of inoperable cancer of the liver.

42. A playwright, poet, and essayist who spent time in prison for his political activities, Havel was one of the leaders of the Velvet Revolution of 1989, finally becoming president of Czechoslovakia (later the Czech Republic).

43. Senator Robert F. Kennedy was running for president when he was shot and killed in Los Angeles on June 5, 1968.

44. Well, I am in the "tobacco-café" at the corner of Rue des Beaux Arts and the quay on the Seine. . . . I passed all day wandering—Right Bank and Left Bank. This evening I'm going with George Whitman to the Salle 3 movie theater, Rue Gît-le-Coeur. . . . The old Beat hotel in this alleyway has been transformed into a chic tourist inn. There are photos of the Beats who lived here thirty-five years ago. . . . As always an old woman knitting at the reception desk, perhaps the daughter of the dame who watched over the Beats. . . .

45. The rhyming couplet is an untranslatable joke on the name of the street: "J'ai fait mon Bac dans la Rue du Bac" means "I got my baccalaureate on the Rue du Bac." The rest of the text in French reads: "But today the Rue du Bac has changed. Chic boutiques, and men who were on the barricades in 1968 now eat well in haute-cuisine restaurants while reading *Le Monde*, followed by a small black coffee and some liqueur. . . . In their Modern 'Belle Époque.' . . . "

46. The train arrives— Here's Chambéry. I get off. There is also a dog on the train— He gets off. . . . Him and me. . . . Let's go. . . .

47. At the café. . . . You must shake hands. It's a festival of hand-shaking. All you have to do is shake everybody's hand. Shake hands and all's well. It's the end of the world, paradise, the final flash of clarity, the epiphany, the goal of all of life, shake hands, shake hands . . . the bourgeois apocalypse . . . the heart of France. . . .

48. The Couple

The couple next to me are very quiet, this young couple who have nothing to say to each other. They don't look at each other. They look elsewhere. They're not there for each other. They have nothing to say. She is beautiful but empty. And the guy, he's bored like her. What's going on with this young married couple? But no—I was wrong. They love each other. They say nothing because they have no need to speak. Now they look into each other's eyes. They smile, a little sadly. But they're smiling. All's well. Twilight falls. They look at each other very deeply, very seriously. That's life. They whisper. They'll be together forever perhaps. No one can say.

49. Started by George Maciunas in the early 1960s, Fluxus is an international network of avant-garde artists, composers, and designers known for creating works and staging events that puncture the seriousness of the art world.

50. Salò, in northern Italy, was from 1943 to 1945 the seat of Benito Mussolini's Nazi-backed puppet state, officially known as the Italian Social Republic.

51. The name Lawrence gave to his short experimental plays, published for the first time in 1965 (*Routines*, New Directions).

52. In southern Italy, the two mythological monsters that the sailors in Homer's *Odyssey* had to steer between, Scylla and Charybdis, are said to have lived on either side of the narrow Strait of Messina. A town with the name of Scilla still exists in Calabria.

53. Roughly means *The Assholes of Riace.*

54. Still the same. But, do they still have Crème de Marron? . . . Yes. . . . The people next to me gossiping like old knitting-ladies. . . . fingers in the air insisting on a point.

INDEX

ABOUT THE AUTHOR

Lawrence Ferlinghetti was born in 1919 with Italian, French, and Sephardic genes. His poetry has been published for 57 years by New Directions, beginning with "A Coney Island of the Mind." As a painter, he is represented by George Krevsky Fine Arts in San Francisco and has had retrospectives in major museums in Rome. He is a member of the American Academy of Arts and Letters.